Just Off the Motorway

Nothing in his early career marked John Slater to be the likely author of a guide book. Having failed to fulfil what little promise his youthful years displayed and having achieved an almost excellent third at Oxford he retired to the brazen world of television – there to inflict his ordinary prejudices on other people. After five years on *World In Action* he was set loose, as Editor, on Granada's nightly magazine programme. Presently John Slater is a freelance television producer/director and is looking for a job.

Slater's Motorists' Manual

JUST MOTOR

text illustrations by Peter Clark and Jim Kane **Pan Original** Pan Books London and Sydney

OFF THE WAY

First published 1978 by Pan Books Ltd,
Cavaye Place, London SW10 9PG
3rd printing 1979

ISBN 0 330 25574 6
Printed and bound in Great Britain by
Richard Clay (The Chaucer Press) Ltd, Bungay, Suffolk

Contents

Introduction by Russell Harty

Preface

Guide to map symbols

M1

M3

M4

M5

M6

M18

M32

M50

M56

M61

M62

M69

Introduction

I have never believed that it is better to travel hopefully than to arrive. Eve, clutching the expelled Adam's hand, must have had some destination in mind. Marco Polo didn't set out to Cathay from boredom. Columbus spent much of his time with his hand shading his eyes, looking for a new-found land. Neil Armstrong has, with lunatic disregard for man's comfort, taken the journey out of our gravitational pull, and almost, out of our interest. All these journeys were epics. Here, then, is John Slater's domestic foray, combining the explorer's intrepidity with the needs of what are soon to be the eighties.

Those of us who spend hours locked into the network of motorways, fearful of losing their hypnotic line and rhythm, marking a vicious progress by the recognition of a bell tower, shunning the plastic convenience of the laughingly called 'service station', and arriving in a deadened lump, are hereby offered some small but significant salvation.

Like any good book about travel (and there are as many shades and degrees as there are journeymen) it is a lazily attractive book to read without stirring from the chair. The accuracy of its information and the slant of the observer's eye can be checked by referring at once to your own nearest concrete ribbon and paddling about in that area to sample the local delights.

Allow me, anyway, to recommend the angle of this observer's particular eye. It can be beady. It is always practical, but, even better, it has a pleasing aesthetic glance. If he doesn't like the popularity or, more precisely, the populousness of a place, he will tell you. Home-brewed beer and homemade bread are both indicated and approved. Blood-red beef excites his nostrils. A building of warm stone is *vaut le détour*. These miniatures are a signal of his larger approach.

Cars and children are both unpredictable, noisy, liable to empty themselves capriciously and in constant need of refilling. Children and cars hold closing times and weekends in high contempt. They tend to malfunction at times of greatest inconvenience. There is plenty of information here which will help the traveller, after common closing times, to fill up one and empty the other, or vice-versa.

Twenty-five years ago, our family's Sunday afternoon outing was invariably taken, by brand new car, from Blackburn to the sparkling new service station at Charnock Richard on the novel highway called the M6. We partook of weak tea and drove back again, marvelling at this new constructional wonder.

An earnest of the changed times is mirrored in this book. Stop the world, we want to get off. If it does nothing else, it will cut down, quite drastically, the accident rate, the fraying of our corporate nerves and the consumption of hot buttered librium. Anything that can do all those things in one flick of the page, can't be all that bad.

Russell Harty 1978

Acknowledgements: To the planners, creators, builders and owners of Britain's motorway service areas, without whom this book would not have been necessary.

And to Gail and Chris and Chris and Steve and Jules and Bob and Jane and Peter and Jonathan and Sandy and Donald and David and Russell and Pat and Colin and Annie and Aggie and Louise and Rick and Michael and Carol and Mary and Eric and David, who talked to me sometimes.

To those at Fiat who helped me with car problems.

And to Clare and Ken and Peter and Jim, who got the book together.

And for Gillie and Imogen and Emma and Adam and Thelma and Hil and Ronnie.

Preface

Few travellers, if any, use our motorway service areas as a matter of rational choice. It is grim necessity that forces one to pull off for petrol, food or toilets. Nor were the service areas built to provide any real joy or interest for the eye, stomach and brain. They are little more than transit camps for captive travellers speeding between distant points. Because they have a monopoly the price of petrol, for instance, is very high – often as much as 10 or 15p a gallon more than off the motorway. Because they have no competition the food they offer, in general, has little to recommend it at any price.

The greatest benefit of the motorway system is that it offers quick and predictable travel times. A monotonous journey maybe – but somehow safe. However, particularly in summer, one can often waste an awful lot of precious time queueing for a tray of very standard food.

This guide book gives you a whole range of new choices and, with a little bit of planning, could lead you to many pleasurable places. Just off the motorway at most junctions it is possible to find cheap and convenient petrol, a café or restaurant, a pub which sells snacks, or any number of other things – picnic spots, parks, ruined castles or museums. You can make your own choice in terms of what you need and how much time you have to spare. Not surprisingly some junctions are very much better than others – these are the places to plan for. A few junctions offer very little – so the advice given is not to turn off.

You will note that I have not included in this guide all the motorways in Britain – there are in fact about forty of them. For obvious (I hope) reasons, this guide covers only the motorways that take longer than half an hour to drive along at average speed.

There are some people who now plan motorway journeys as if they were leaving for an expedition to the Andes – hampers and cutlery, flasks and bottles, flannels and footballs. Anything to avoid the service areas. Other people are terrified of turning off a motorway. What, if anything, will they find? How far will it be? How much time will be wasted? Will they, God forbid, get lost? At best, this guide should remove the need for expeditionary planning and assuage some of the fears of turning off into the unknown.

So first and foremost this guide book provides safety and predictability. The maps, symbols and list tell you what is available, when it's available, where it is and, roughly, what kind of journey you will have to make in order to find it. Real choices can be made. How far one is prepared to journey off the motorway is up to the individual. The limit in this guide is set at about three miles – given decent roads and an obvious route. In country areas it is usually simple to travel three miles. Not so in urban areas – so here the three-mile limit is reduced.

But this guide is also about pleasure – finding those special places that are worth visiting in their own right. There are not too many such places, so use them when you can. The text facing the map tells you about the places I liked or disliked. Obviously I didn't break down in every garage, eat in every restaurant, drink in every pub or stay in every hotel. The list is to tell you what is available – the text to give details of some of these places.

Many tastes are catered for in this guide. It is for those who need cheap petrol – and fast. For those who have children agitating with boredom. For those with no faith in things mechanical. For those who want a decent meal. And it is also for those who like to seek out interesting and strange places. But throughout I have been largely catering for my own taste. I thought it would be easier for others to judge the book if the likes and dislikes (some would say prejudices) of the author were apparent.

No one needs to be told that everything changes. Inflation will make a mockery of all prices listed. A guide book is out of date before it ever meets its printer. And, no doubt, some of these changes will prove annoying. A garage will no longer be cheap. The cook has departed with his white hat and skill. The unspoilt pub has been modernized. There will also be mistakes of omission and opinion. There will have been some places missed. I might have visited a restaurant on a bad night. And, no doubt, there will be some mistakes of fact. For these, I apologize.

So this guide should only be a starting point. If it is to improve it needs you travellers to comment upon the places included and to recommend other places for inclusion. Most people seem to have a favoured stopping place just off the motorway. Guide books, if they work, can also exert some pressure on the quality of the goods and services by encouraging or denying custom. So please let me have your comments, criticisms and suggestions.

suggestions welcome

If you have any comments, corrections,
or up-to-date information that you have discovered,
please write to:

John Slater
c/o Pan Books Ltd
Cavaye Place
London
SW10 9PG

so that they can be incorporated in future editions of this guide.

GUIDE TO MAP SYMBOLS

 PETROL

 GARAGE AND BREAKDOWN

 PUB

 POST OFFICE

 TELEPHONE

 SHOP

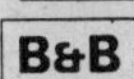

BED AND BREAKFAST

 HOTEL

 PICNIC SPOT

 FISH AND CHIPS

PARKING

RAC

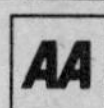

AA

MUSEUM

 RESTAURANT

HOSPITAL

 WINE BAR

 POLICE STATION

 POTTERY

 SWIMMING POOL

M1

Certain junctions are not included: they are either intersections with other motorways, don't exist, or offer no real alternative services. They are listed below.

J1

J2

J3

J4

J7

J10

J17

J32

J33

J42

J43

petrol

The only good thing about this junction is the availability of fairly cheap petrol at all hours. Although the Heron Self Service **2** is a couple of miles from the junction it is very easy to rejoin at **J6** if you are travelling northwards. At more normal hours the Elton Way Service Station **1** is closer; they also do breakdowns and repairs during pump hours.

Letchmore Heath is a very pretty village with a green and pond. A good place to have a quick stop on a warm day. *The Three Horseshoes* **4** is an attractive pub right on the edge of the green. Of the other pubs on the junction *The Three Compasses* **3** is an old but plain building; it offers a range of fried foods. *The Crown* **6** sells draught bitter and has a restaurant attached.

Both the hotels are quite expensive but far cheaper than most places in London. *The Beehive* **8**, although more expensive for a single person, would work out cheaper if you had a couple of children with you. The restaurant is closed on a Sunday evening and will serve children's portions. *The Spiders Web* **9** has a heated swimming-pool and a heated paddling pool but children are charged at the rate of £5 a head and there are only children's prices in the restaurant at Sunday lunchtime. But they could always eat à la carte.

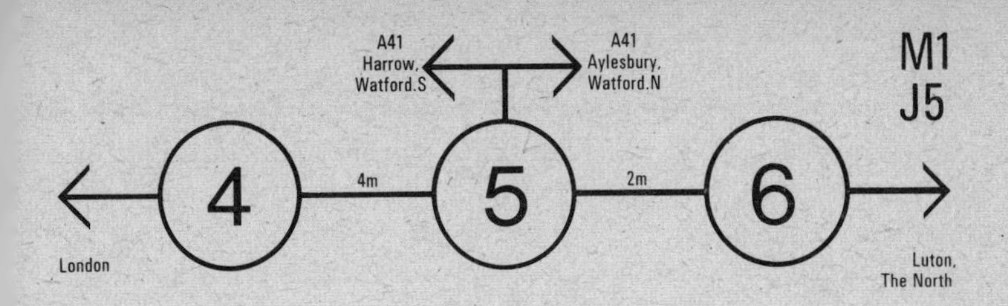

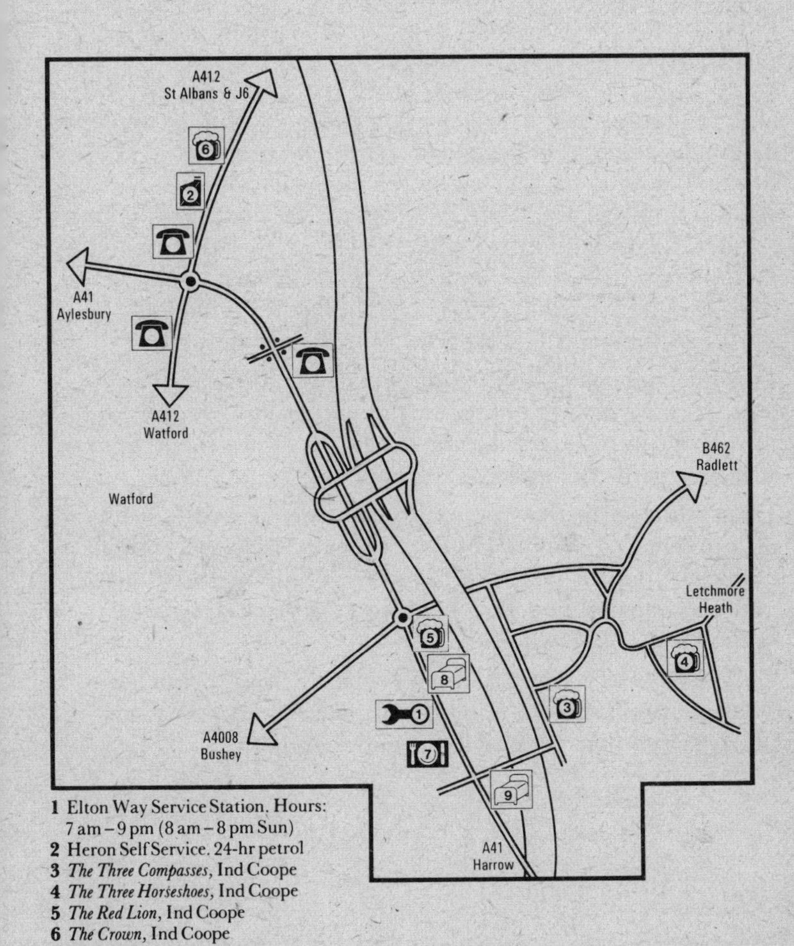

1 Elton Way Service Station. Hours: 7 am – 9 pm (8 am – 8 pm Sun)
2 Heron Self Service. 24-hr petrol
3 *The Three Compasses,* Ind Coope
4 *The Three Horseshoes,* Ind Coope
5 *The Red Lion,* Ind Coope
6 *The Crown,* Ind Coope
7 *Wallys New Café*
8 *The Beehive Hotel and Restaurant* (Watford 35881)
9 *The Spiders Web Hotel* (01 950 6211)

petrol/pubs/transport cafés

Petrol is cheap, convenient, and always available on this junction, although that description doesn't fit any one garage. The cheapest petrol is at the Classic **2**, which isn't closest to the junction and keeps the shortest hours. The Chequers **1** is the most convenient and is only slightly more expensive. 24-hour petrol at the Heron **4** which is over a mile away, but if you were travelling towards London you would continue on this road and rejoin at **J5**.

Buried deep in Bricket Woods, much of which is common land, is a small pub on a road going nowhere. It is a lovely location for *The Old Fox* **8** which sells draught beer. The road to Bricket Wood is actually off the motorway link on the south-bound side. After nearly a mile you pass under a railway bridge and turn sharp right, signposted to Old Bricket Wood; now, just follow this windy and narrow lane. The pub down here used to be called *The Fox with its Teeth Drawn*. It was closed down by Lord Knutsford who found his labourers in it once too often. That was last century. The brewery then bought up two cottages and converted them into the existing pub. The Painted House is also worth looking at and there are good walks through the wood.

Two other pubs have decent gardens, and both also serve draught beer. *The Black Boy* **5** is very close to the junction and has a garden surrounded by rose trees; it serves snacks. *The Fox and Hounds* **6** has an enormous garden for the kids to play in.

There are two plain transport cafés on the junction, both of which serve decent food. *The Dell* **12** has a large messy parking lot in front of it which is normally very full of large lorries. *The Horseshoe* **13**, being right on a junction, presents something of a parking problem for lorries and is therefore quieter.

The Noke Hotel **14** is quite an attractive place. Fairly expensive but children under fourteen are free if they share their parents' room. Children's portions are available in the restaurant.

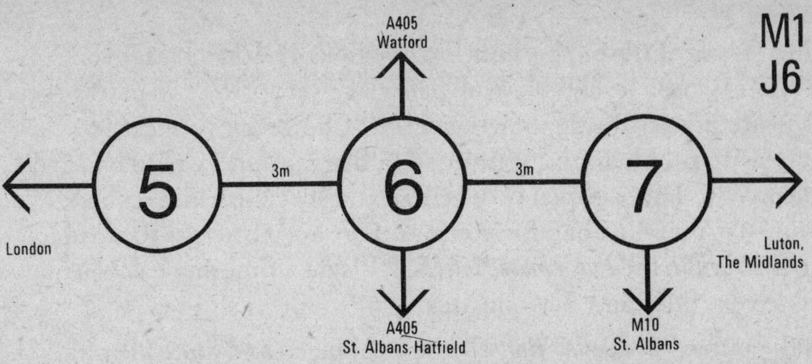

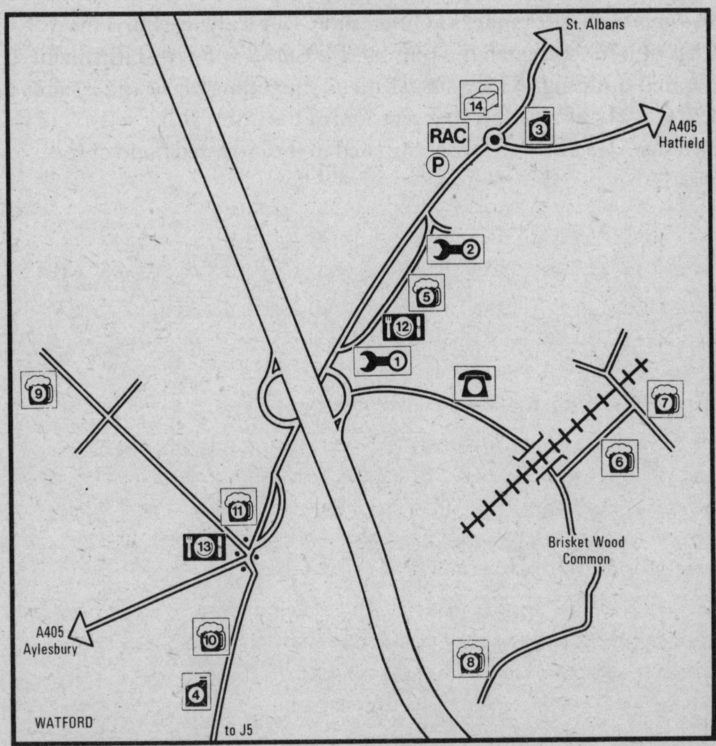

1 Chequers Service Station. Hours: 7 am – 10.30 pm (8 am – 8 pm Sun). Workshop
2 Classic Service Station. Hours: 8 am – 6.30 pm (closed Sun). Workshop
3 Humming Bird Garage. Hours: 8 am – 9 pm (10 am – 6 pm Sun)
4 Heron Self Service. 24-hr petrol
5 *The Black Boy*, Ind Coope
6 *The Fox and Hounds*, Ind Coope
7 *The Gate*, Ind Coope
8 *The Old Fox*, Ind Coope
9 *The Swan*, Greene King
10 *The Crown*, Ind Coope
11 *The Three Horseshoes*, Ind Coope
12 *The Dell Transport Café*. Hours: 6.15 am – 4 pm (closes 8.30 am Sat, all day Sun)
13 *The Horseshoe Café*. Hours: 6.30 am – 4 pm (closes 2 pm Sat, all day Sun)
14 *The Noke Hotel* (St Albans 54252)

petrol

There is very little on this built-up junction. The only reason for stopping would be to buy cheap petrol at either of the two places – on opposite sides of the dual carriageway. If, however, your car was giving you problems the Spur Road Filling Station **1** would be a good place to go. They seemed very helpful and specialize in tyres and exhausts. You can abandon your car there and go across the road to the Buttery in the *Post House Hotel* **6**. If it's mealtime anyway you may waste very little time by doing this.

Of the pubs, *The Leather Bottle* **3** is low ceilinged and quite pleasant; they have a range of snacks at lunchtime. But it always hurts me in such a pub to see dead hand pumps. *The Crab Tree* **5** is an old, much extended building. A long snacks menu, including pizza and lasagne and a Cavalier Steak Bar. Nice garden at the front, and it sells Benskins Ale, which in fact is clutched in the large red hand of Ind Coope.

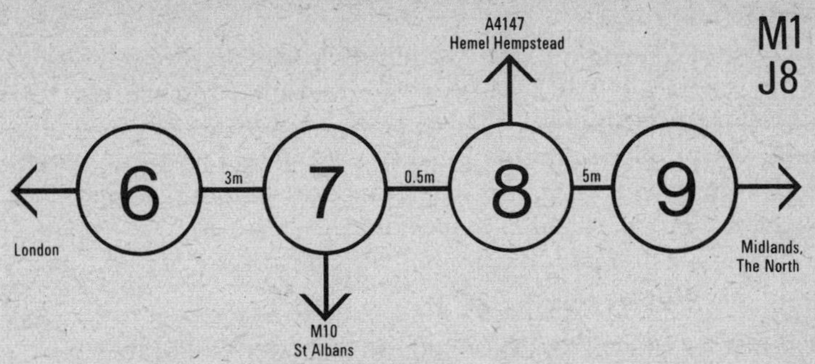

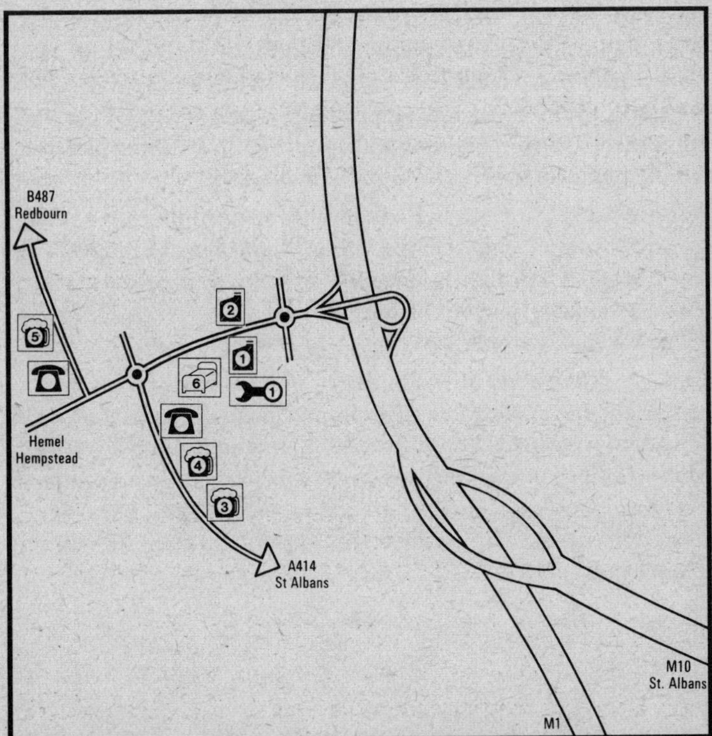

1 Spur Road Filling Station. Hours: 7 am – 10 pm (opens 8 am Sun). Breakdown during opening hours (Hemel Hempstead 42504)

2 City Petroleum. Hours: 7 am – 11 pm (8 am – 10 pm Sun)

3 *The Leather Bottle*, Ind Coope

4 *The White Horse*, Whitbread

5 *The Crab Tree*, Benskins

6 *Post House Hotel*. Buttery open 7.30 am – 10.30 pm. (Hemel Hempstead 51122)

petrol/food/pubs

A very useful junction. Cheap petrol at Bylands **1** and even cheaper petrol at the Packhorse **3**, which is over three miles from the junction, but is included because there is 24-hour attendant service – if heading north continue on the A5 to Dunstable and turn right to rejoin at **J11**. The Watling Street Filling Station **4** is not nearly as cheap but it is very close.

Redbourn, particularly the very large green, is a nice village. To enjoy the green go to *The Cricketers* **5** – draught beer and food – or to *The Holly Bush* **6** at the far end, very close to the squat-towered St Mary's Church **16**. The church is worth a visit to see its ancient rood screen, dated to 1448; parts of the nave, with the heavy round columns, are visibly Norman. *The Holly Bush* boasts, and rightly so, of using no frozen food; the menu includes homemade steak and kidney pie and cottage pie. It's an old building with quite a few interesting pictures. For a plainer meal try *The Bull* **7** on the main road.

There are two restaurants in Redbourn. Most lunchtimes you would have no difficulty in choosing since only *The Old Forge* **12** is open. *The Country House* **11** has slightly longer hours in the evening and is also open on Mondays; but you will have to make your own choice from the window menus.

For snacks, *The Watling Street Transport Café* **13**, with its very long hours, or the *Little Chef* **14**, with its normal menu. Quite useful for kids when not too crowded. You will probably not think of staying at *The Executive Hotel* **15** unless you so describe yourself and have a company expense account – it's a new, smart and expensive hotel. The only consolation is a small B&B called *The Chequers*, just at the first turning to Flamstead.

1 Bylands Service Station. Hours: 7 am – 9.30 pm (open 8 am Sat, 9 am Sun)
2 Fordmark Garage. 24-hr breakdown (Redbourn 2320)
3 Packhorse Garage. 24-hr petrol
4 Watling Street Filling Station
5 *The Cricketers*, Ind Coope

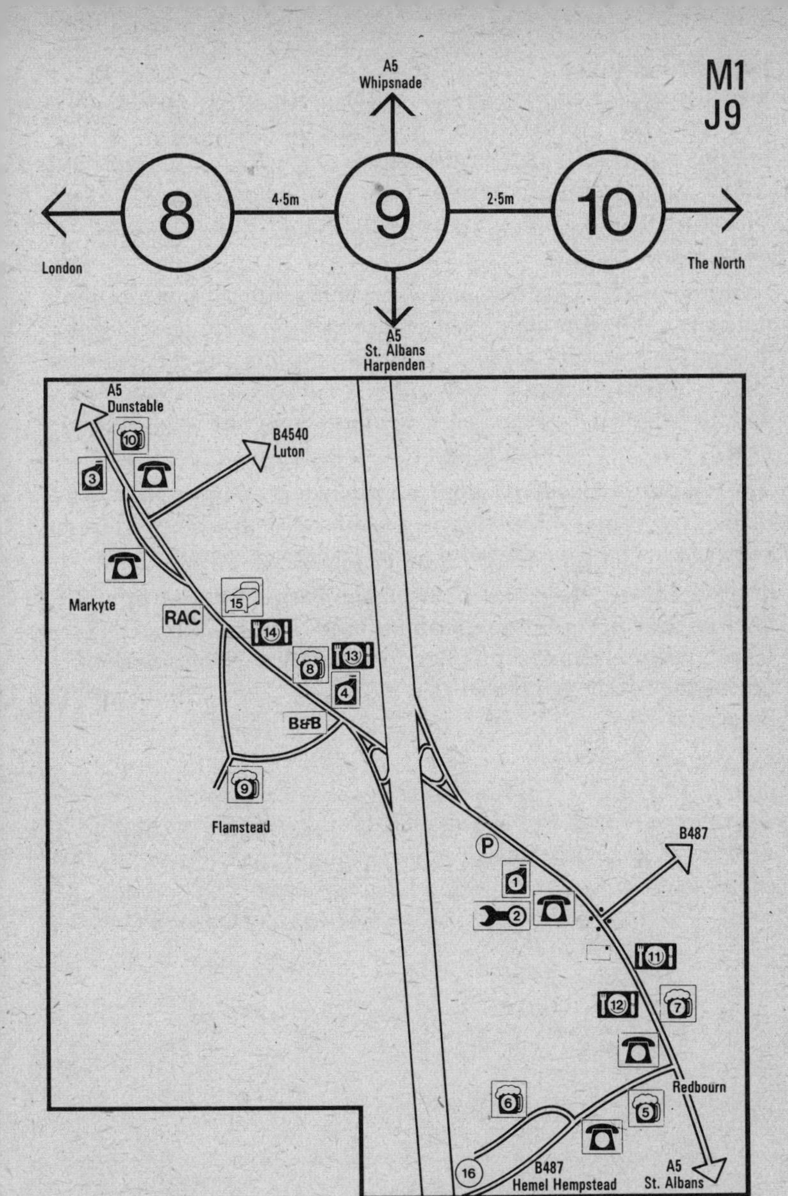

6 *The Holly Bush,* Ind Coope
7 *The Bull,* McMullen
8 *The Coach and Horses,* Whitbread
9 *The Three Blackbirds,* Watney
10 *The Horse and Jockey,* Free house
11 *The Country House Restaurant.* Dinner, Mon – Sat, 7 – 10.30 pm. (Redbourn 2756)
12 *The Old Forge Restaurant.* Lunch, Tue – Fri. Dinner, Tue – Sat. (Redbourn 3419)
13 *The Watling Street Transport Café.* 5 am – 10.30 pm (closed Sat)
14 *Little Chef*
15 *The Executive Hotel* (Luton 840823)
16 St Mary's Church

petrol

The three junctions close to Luton are all pretty awful – put the best of what they have to offer on one junction and there is only just about reason to stop. The single good reason to drop off here is the Jet petrol station called 645 Dunstable Road **1** – it's on a small slip road off the A505 towards Luton. You will save at least 10p a gallon on normal motorway prices.

Next door is the Luton *Crest Motel* **2** – within spitting distance of the motorway and all its nightly noise. It will set you back about £13 for staying there, but at least you might be able to mix with the football stars. It is thought by some that Luton is half-way between London and the Midlands so they come to the *Crest* for the final, highly secret, deal.

The two pubs are both roadhouses and have very little to recommend them.

If it's late at night and you are heading south, and you need petrol desperately, take the A505 for Dunstable. Turn left in the centre of town on the A5. You are now heading for **J9** – so take a look at that map. There is a very cheap 24-hour petrol station within a couple of miles – the Packhorse Garage.

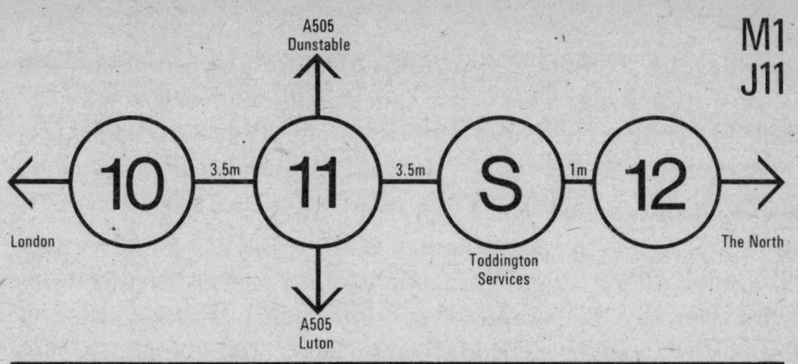

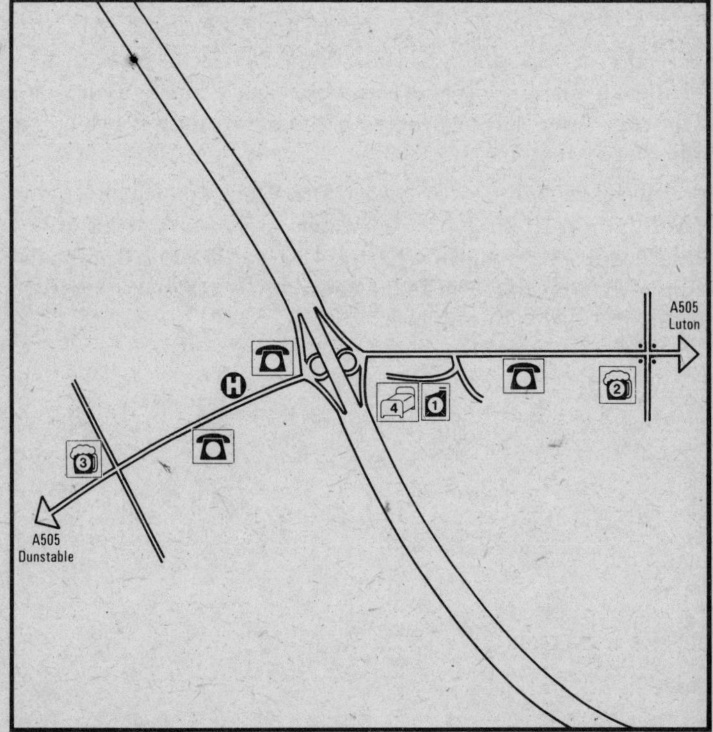

1 645 Dunstable Road. Hours: 7 am – 11 pm (8 am – 10 pm Sun)
2 *The Leicester Arms,* Bass Charrington
3 *The Halfway House,* Whitbread
4 *Crest Motel* (Luton 55955)

pubs

The village of Toddington, on the A5120 towards Dunstable, consists of a very attractive green, a lovely church, some antique shops and a whole lot of pubs. There are also three garages, only the cheapest of which is mentioned for unlikely use, and a licensed dealer in game.

Of the pubs *The Sow and Pigs* **4** is by far the nicest. A warm atmosphere, good but rather limited food, excellent beer and a variety of pub games – but beginners should beware the locals, they looked to have a keen edge. It also appears to be the haunt of the local prize carrot grower and the less said about such objects the better.

For kids, and quite close to the motorway, try *The Fancott Arms* **9**. In the direction of Dunstable again take the first left off the main road. After about a mile and just after turning left at a T-junction you will find the pub. A very large garden with a miniature railway to take the minding out of stopping.

Back in Toddington, go to *The Bedford Arms* **8** for food – which is right at the other end of town. It has a comprehensive menu starting with sandwiches at 30p through to a full meal for £3. *The Griffin* **3** normally has some accommodation available. Finally, *The Oddfellows Arms* **6**, for those who like Watney's plush.

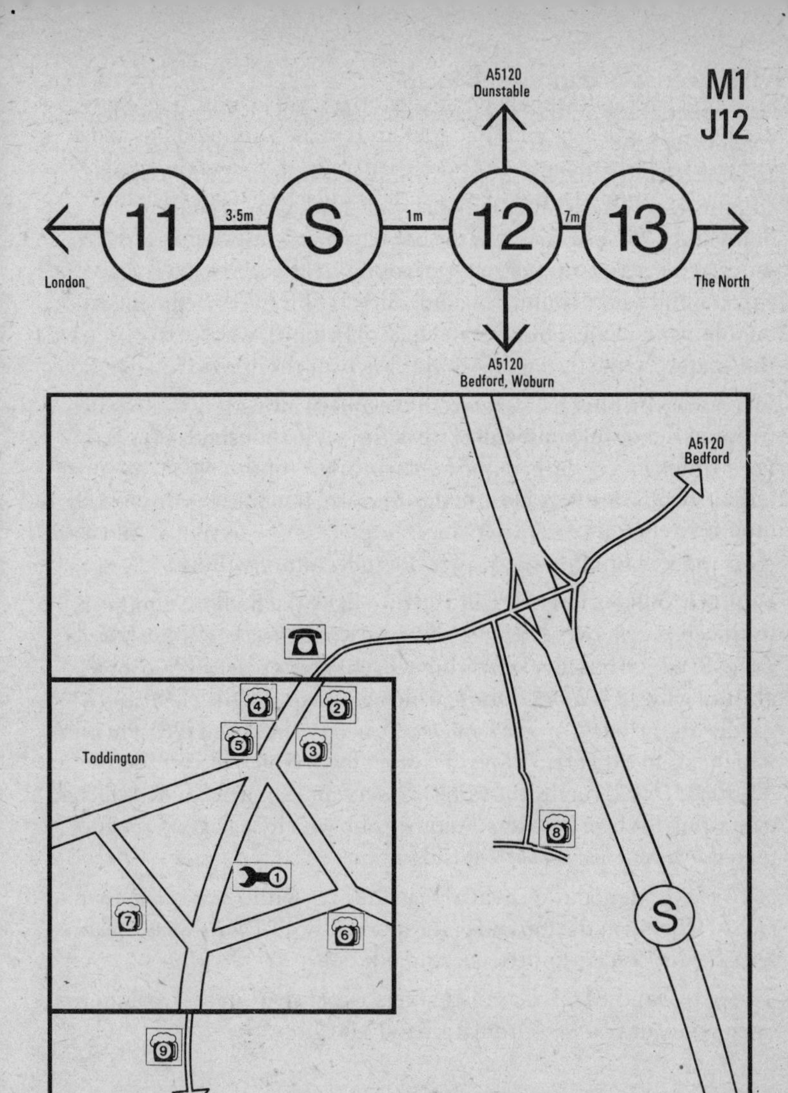

1 The Old Forge Garage
2 *The Nags Head*, Wells
3 *The Griffin*, Greene King
4 *The Sow and Pigs*, Greene King
5 *The Bell*, Whitbread
6 *The Oddfellows Arms*, Watney
7 *The Red Lion*, Whitbread
8 *The Bedford Arms*, Wells
9 *The Fancott Arms*, Whitbread

visit/accommodation/pub food

The aristocracy, or parts of it, continually seem to come up with ideas for survival. At the turn of the century it was American heiresses. But the law dictates that heiresses can only come one at a time, whereas tourists can come in their millions, each with a few pounds to contribute. Since nearly half the population of this country already work in the service industries, serious thought ought to be given to turning the whole country over to tourism – for the enrichment, if not enoblement, of all. The present Duke of Bedford, whose father started the 'stately home business', would clearly be the man to run the show.

Of course you have a head start in the tourist industry if you happen to own a beautiful house full of treasures set in thousands of acres of land which can be turned into a safari park. Woburn Abbey **14**, or at least its walls, are very close to the junction, but once inside you still have great distances to drive since the place is so enormous. And it all costs money, but there is an awful lot to see – time willing.

Woburn Village, largely built and owned by the Bedford family, is itself very attractive. Places to eat there would be *The Woburn Wine Lodge* **9**, which has nice salads but will charge you nearly 50p for a glass of wine, *The Black Horse* **4**, which has plain English food and a garden at the back, or *The Royal Oak* **3**, a very small and pleasant pub which has five different pâtés and other food. Not to be confused with *The Royal Oak* **2**, run by the same brewery, in Woburn Sands, which is a nice pub for beer drinkers. Another pub which has a good range of food is *The Rose and Crown* **8** in Ridgmont.

A lot of accommodation available in the area with *The Bedford Arms Hotel* **10** being at the top end of the market. Both *The Rose and Crown* and *The Bell* **7** have limited accommodation.

The petrol at the Halt Garage **1** is very expensive but the workshop is open seven days a week from 8 am to 10.30 pm.

M1 J13

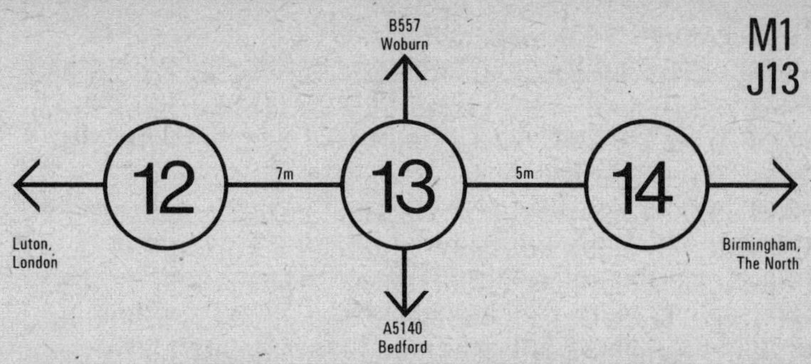

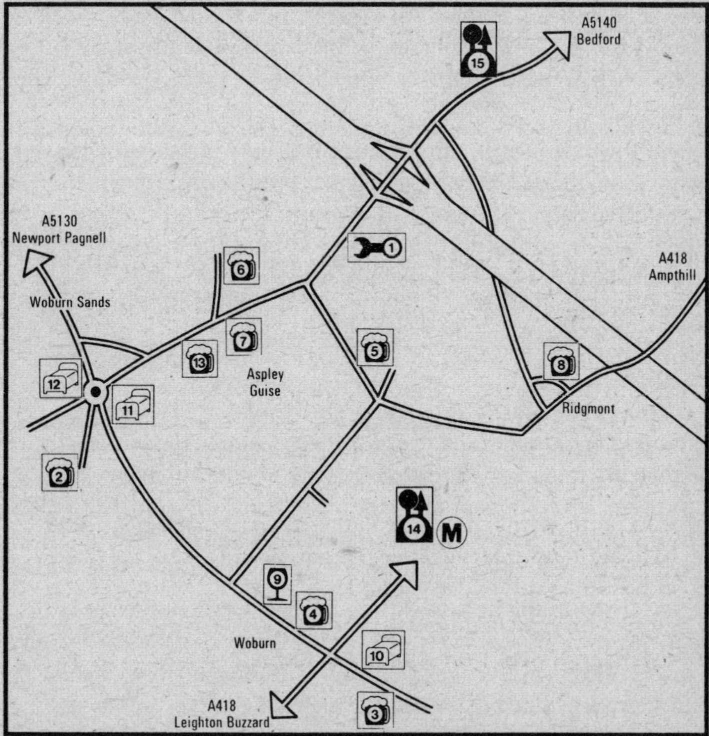

1 Halt Garage. 24-hr breakdown (day, Woburn Sands 583247, night, Milton Keynes 678162)
2 *The Royal Oak,* Greene King
3 *The Royal Oak,* Greene King
4 *The Black Horse,* Free house
5 *The White Horse,* Whitbread
6 *The Anchor,* Wells
7 *The Bell,* Ind Coope
8 *The Rose and Crown,* Wells
9 *The Woburn Wine Lodge*
10 *The Bedford Arms Hotel* (Woburn 441)
11 *The Fir Tree Hotel,* Wells. (Woburn Sands 582127)
12 *The Swan Hotel* (Woburn Sands 583204)
13 *The Holt Hotel*
14 Woburn Abbey and Wild Animal Kingdom
15 Brogborough Hill picnic site

Milton Keynes

Building a new town is rather like freezing history – suddenly a style is imposed and fixed on the landscape – for good or bad. Everything down to the last tree is planted, planned, and marked down on charts. Milton Keynes is better than this because it is based on villages, new and old; and the new villages have different architects. Take a look at Fishermead **14**, and Springfield **13**. Everywhere roads which go nowhere, a plethora of signs like MK9 or MK15 or V8, regimented young saplings, and everything unfinished. It's all very exciting but one still worries about the baleful hand of overplanning when one looks at Fishermead. If you want to take time off and have a serious look at Milton Keynes, go first to the Information Centre at the Wavendon Tower **10**. There is an unofficial Architects Guide which is very useful.

The new town derives its name from the village which in turn derived its name from the de Keynes family, one of whom was rector of the Church of All Saints **12** in the 14th century. There are many old churches and buildings dotted around, the most spectacular being the church of St Mary **11** at Willen which now stands on a hill overlooking a new lake. Built in 1680 and designed by Robert Hooke – his only complete work still standing – a man of great and varied brilliance.

The Cross Keyes **3**, *The Old Swan* **4** and *The Swan* **5** are all listed buildings. *The Cross Keyes* has recently been restored but has been furnished in a dull way. *The Old Swan* is just about to undergo changes and expansion; one hopes the brewery won't make too much of a mess of a lovely old building. Food is available there and children can be catered for. Lovely walks nearby to the village green and canal.

The petrol on the junction, in Newport Pagnell, is none too cheap. Also in the town *The Swan Revived* **9**, which hardly deserves that name. It's pricey. Having stayed there, I would recommend that you find somewhere else – like *The Cannon* **7**, which has a number of rooms.

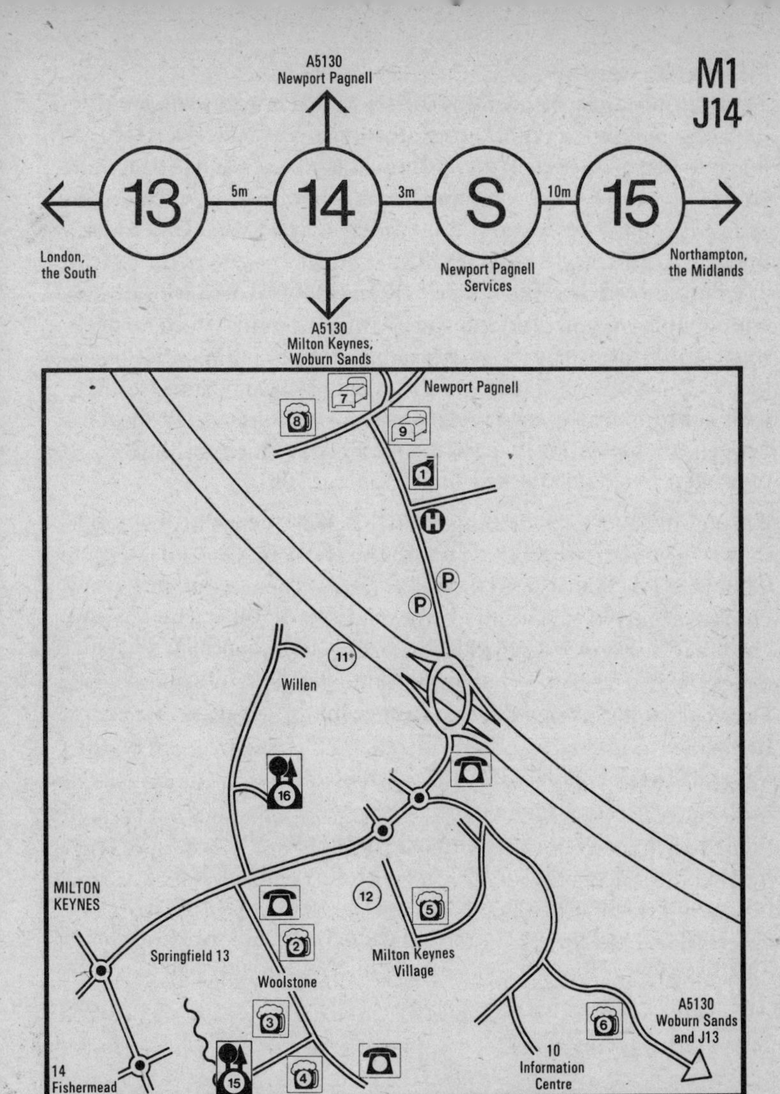

1 Cannon Service Station. Hours: 7.45 am – 10.15 pm. Audi and VW agent
2 *The Barge Inn,* Bass Charrington
3 *The Cross Keyes,* Wells
4 *The Old Swan,* Watney
5 *The Swan,* Whitbread
6 *The Leathern Bottle,* Wells
7 *The Cannon,* Allied Breweries
8 *The Dolphin,* Wells
9 *The Swan Revived Hotel* (Newport Pagnell 610565)
10 Wavendon Tower – information centre
11 St Mary Magdalene Church
12 Church of All Saints
13 Springfield
14 Fishermead
15 Woughton Green and Grand Union Canal
16 Willen Lake picnic spot

pub/ food/ visit/petrol

There is only one sensible thing to do and that is to go to Stoke Bruerne. Follow the A508 in the direction of Milton Keynes for about three miles and turn right at the appropriate sign. Alongside the Grand Union Canal you will find the Waterways Museum **13**, a pub called *The Boat* **3**, and a restaurant called *The Butty Boat* **10**. In its own right Stoke Bruerne is a lovely village well known to canal enthusiasts. The canal arrived here in about 1800 and stopped because it took another five years to complete the Blisworth Tunnel which is only a short distance north of the village. At 3075 yards it is now the longest tunnel in use on the waterway system. The Museum, once a grain warehouse, gives the history of the canals, the boats and the boat people. An interesting place with a very good guide book. Large numbers of boats are parked outside – all private.

By the Museum is *The Butty Boat* which is a tea room until 6 pm and then reopens at 7.30 in the evening as an Italian restaurant. It would seem to be a very nice place to have a meal on a fine summer evening, but you will need to book at the weekend. On the other side of the canal is *The Boat,* a fine old pub which sells draught beer and has good snacks. It also has a tea room which is open in the summer.

Very cheap petrol is available at Collingtree **1**, and the petrol at Burbridges **2** is also reasonably priced. Of the other places *The Queen Victoria* **4** in Gayton sells draught Ruddles and has a restaurant as well as bar snacks. *The Yeomen of England* **9** serves lunches and suppers, and *The George* **8** has a fair range of snacks. *The Blisworth Hotel* **12** is reasonably priced and you will pay half or less for children. Its restaurant specializes in game and there are children's portions. *The Old Manor Hotel* **11** is expensive and children are not really welcome; 'businessmen you see', I was told. A plush and private place.

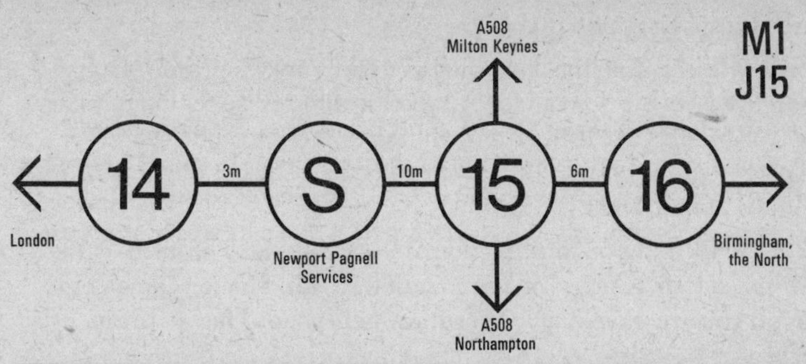

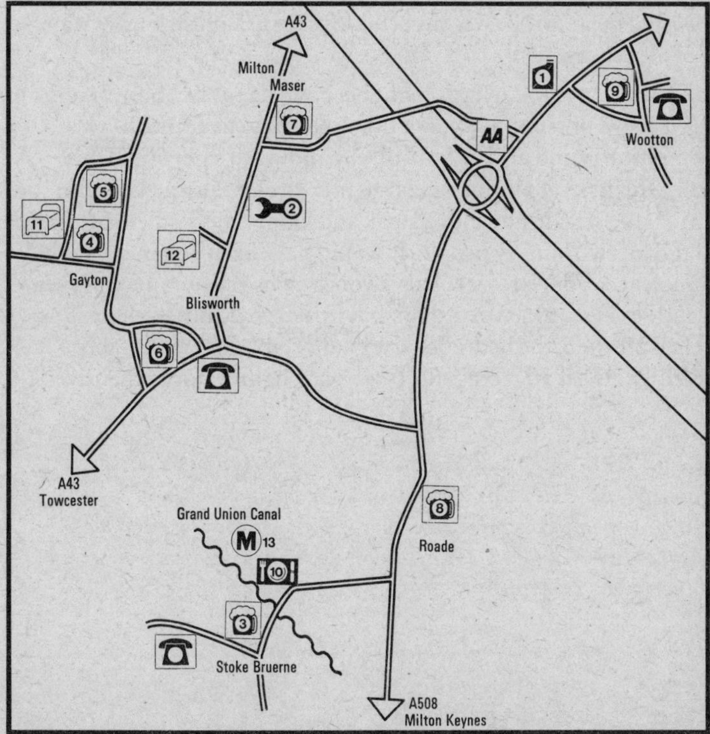

1 Collingtree Turn Self Service. Hours: 7.30 am – 10.30 pm (opens 9 am Sun)
2 Burbridge's Garage. Hours: 7.30 am – 7.30 pm (9 am – 7 pm Sun). Workshop
3 *The Boat*, Free house
4 *Queen Victoria Inn*, Free house
5 *The Eykyn Arms*, Wells
6 *The Royal Oak*, Watney
7 *The Greyhound*, Watney
8 *The George*, Watney
9 *The Yeomen of England*, Watney
10 *The Butty Boat*. Closed Sun evening and Mon. (Roade 863654)
11 *The Old Manor Farm Hotel* (Northampton 858425)
12 *The Blisworth Hotel* (Northampton 858246)
13 Waterways Museum. Closed Mon

accommodation/breakdown/food

It would seem that the only thing you can conveniently do on this junction is break down. Only Clarke Brothers **3** sell reasonably cheap petrol and it is hardly worth travelling to Weedon and beyond for that. So wait for **J15** or **J20** for cheap petrol. The price at Greens **3** is almost at motorway level.

None of the pubs on this junction are very special. The nicest is *The Narrow Boat* **6**, which is on the edge of the Grand Union Canal, but again you are travelling to Weedon and beyond. They sell draught beer and a good range of food including curries. *The White Hart* **4** sells pressured beers but it is a comfortable place in a plush kind of way; coffee and snacks.

The Crossroads Hotel **9** sells draught beer and has a sizeable restaurant. It is clearly a popular place, not that it seems to have much competition round about. It is still expanding to cater for all this trade, which is not always a good sign. A straightforward English menu in the restaurant with a steak and kidney pie, homemade, large enough for two hungry people. It would have been better to have half as much at a reduced price. I also wonder why restaurants can't serve vegetables in season rather than dull frozen peas. But the hotel was nicely furnished; the bedroom was comfortable and reasonably priced. *The Globe* **10**, across the road, was slightly more expensive.

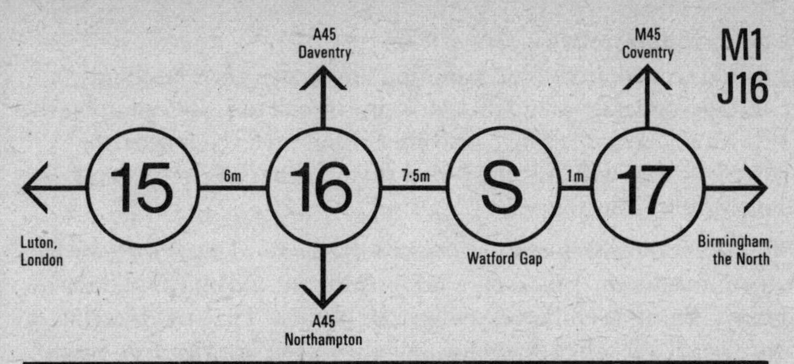

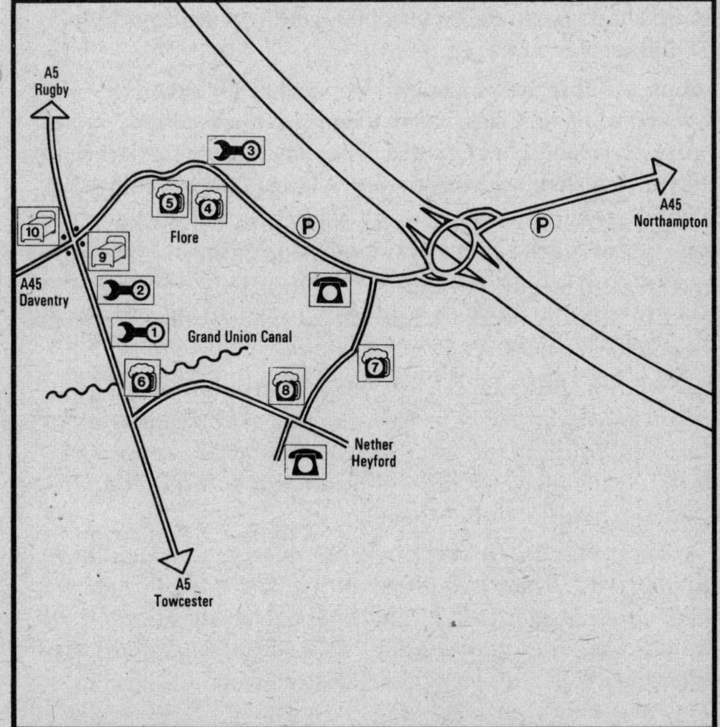

1 Clarke Brothers. Hours: 8 am – 8 pm. 24-hr breakdown (Weedon, day 40369, night 40426)

2 Freeways Garage. 24-hr breakdown (Weedon 40344)

3 P. J. Green. 24-hr breakdown (Weedon, day 40287, night 40446)

4 *The White Hart*, Watney

5 *The Royal Oak*, Watney

6 *The Narrow Boat*, Wells

7 *The Old Sun*, Watney

8 *The Forresters*, Watneys

9 *The Crossroads Hotel*, Free house (Weedon 40354)

10 *The Globe Hotel* (Weedon 40336)

pub food and pubs

The stretch of the A5 close to this junction is notorious for its lack of cheap petrol stations and the shortage of their hours. The petrol at the Halfway Garage **1** is as expensive as the motorway: it is listed for emergency use only. It has a petrol machine that takes 50p pieces. You should really buy your petrol at **J15** or **J20**.

This junction possesses three pubs called the Red Lion, all owned by the same brewery – another example of the wit and imagination that guides Watney's marketing policy. *The Red Lion* **7** in Crick is certainly the most attractive of this genus. A light luncheon menu and things like steak and trout in the evenings – but not Wednesday or Sunday; nor children or coaches.

A couple of pubs sell nice food and can cater for children. *The Wheatsheaf* **6**, also in Crick, is very friendly. It has a number of rooms, a dining-room and a large garden. The food ranges from pork chops to pizzas and omelettes. There are games, but no food on a Sunday.

The Halfway House **2** has a lunchtime dining area and a garden. The landlady says that they usually have homemade bread, home-grown vegetables and home-cooked meats. Her husband – a butcher – agreed, but I'd already eaten that evening. The pub doesn't open till 7 pm and there is no food on a Sunday.

Those who love beautiful English villages and those who like good beer will find it worthwhile to drive the one and a half miles to Ashby St Ledgers. You head southwards on the A5 and take a dangerous turn off it in the village of Kilsby – onto the A361. *The Coach and Horses* **11** is off this road but the sign hangs on it.

Never forget that *Post Houses* **12** have butteries that are open from 6 am to 10 pm and have a children's menu, but for accommodation *The Hillmorton Manor Hotel* **13** would be about half the price. *The Old Royal Oak* **3** has a very nice location on the edge of the Oxford Canal, a garden and a children's playroom. It also sells food at all times.

M1 J18

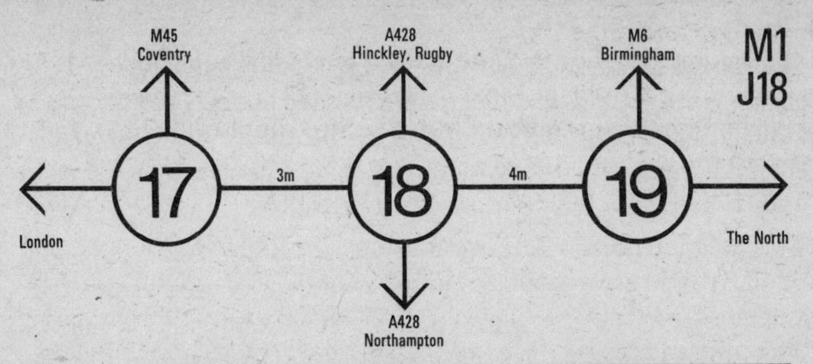

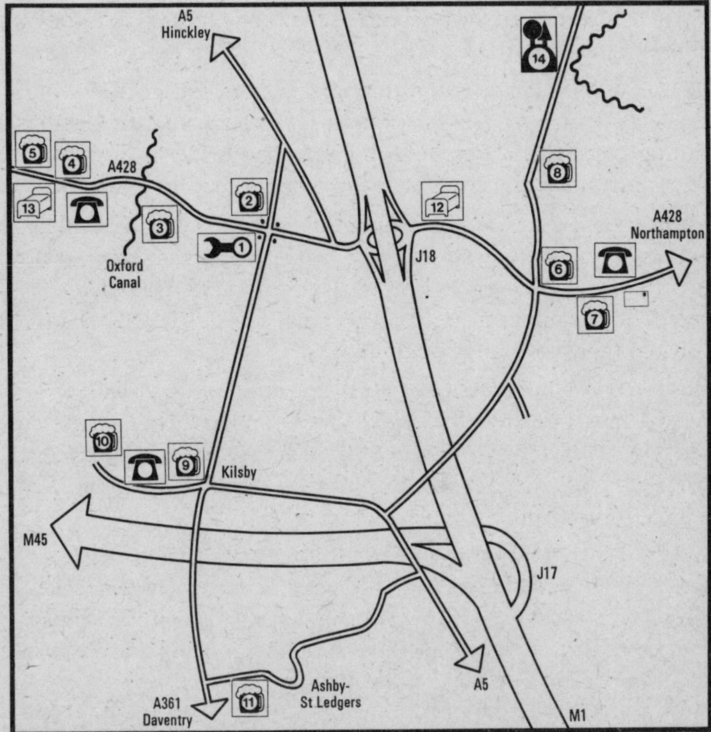

1 Halfway Garage. Hours: 9 am – 6 pm (half-day Sat, closed Sun). Petrol machine. Fiat agent
2 *The Halfway House*, Watney
3 *The Old Royal Oak*, Free house
4 *The Bell*, Mitchells and Butlers
5 *The Red Lion*, Watney
6 *The Wheatsheaf*, Watney
7 *The Red Lion*, Watney
8 *The Royal Oak*, Watney
9 *The George Hotel*, Mitchells and Butlers
10 *The Red Lion*, Watney
11 *The Coach and Horses*, Ruddle
12 *Post House Hotel* (Rugby 822101)
13 *The Hillmorton Manor Hotel* (Rugby 76512)
14 The Grand Union Canal walk

J19

Intersection with the M6. Note that it is impossible to get to the M1 travelling north from the M6. Likewise it is not possible when travelling south to get onto the M6. The M69 supplies this link – and cuts the corner.

GUIDE TO MAP SYMBOLS

 PETROL

 GARAGE AND BREAKDOWN

 PUB

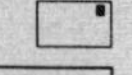 POST OFFICE

 TELEPHONE

 SHOP

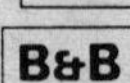

BED AND BREAKFAST

 HOTEL

 PICNIC SPOT

 FISH AND CHIPS

PARKING

RAC

AA

MUSEUM

 RESTAURANT

HOSPITAL

 WINE BAR

 POLICE STATION

 POTTERY

 SWIMMING POOL

petrol/pubs/hotels

Not an interesting junction because the only town of any size, Lutterworth, is not particularly interesting. There is cheap petrol in town and it is worth going there for that since it is so close to the junction. The Lutterworth Garage **1** has the cheapest petrol – just – but it also keeps the shortest hours.

Coming into town you will find two hotels both fairly reasonable in their prices. First *The Denbigh Arms Hotel* **14**, which has a restaurant heavily overwritten in French. I am sure that writing 'choix d'omelettes' doesn't make the eggs taste any better. A short distance up the road is the smaller and cheaper *Hind Hotel* **13**. The new management have plans for change but there is a lot to do. Lunchtime food in the dining area.

A large number of brewers have pubs dotted round this junction. In the very attractive village of Bitteswell there are two Davenports pubs – it is a mile north of Lutterworth on the B577. *The Man at Arms* **8** is a large place which has the distinction of being recommended by both the Campaign for Real Ale and the Country Gentlefolks Association. If you want to avoid such an unlikely mixture of people go to *The Royal Oak* **7**, which is rather an odd pub with jazz evenings.

Just outside Lutterworth on the A427 to Coventry is *The Flying Saucer* **9**, a large modern pub. It doesn't really look like a flying saucer from the outside: inside, anything would be better than its padded nouveau-plush. There is a dining area and luckily the smell of deep-fried food only hits the car park.

On the other side of the Motorway *The Tavern* **11** has food at almost all times – both plate meals and snacks. It is probably the best bet for a quick stop. It also has a small garden overlooking the cabbage patch. A couple of miles further along the road is the rather sparse *White Lion* **12** in North Kilworth – but the beer is good.

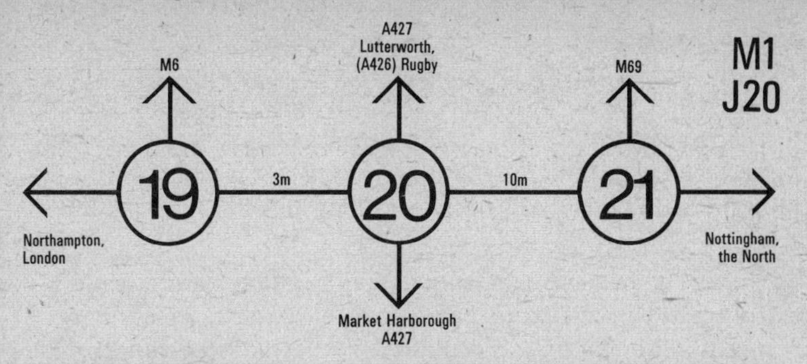

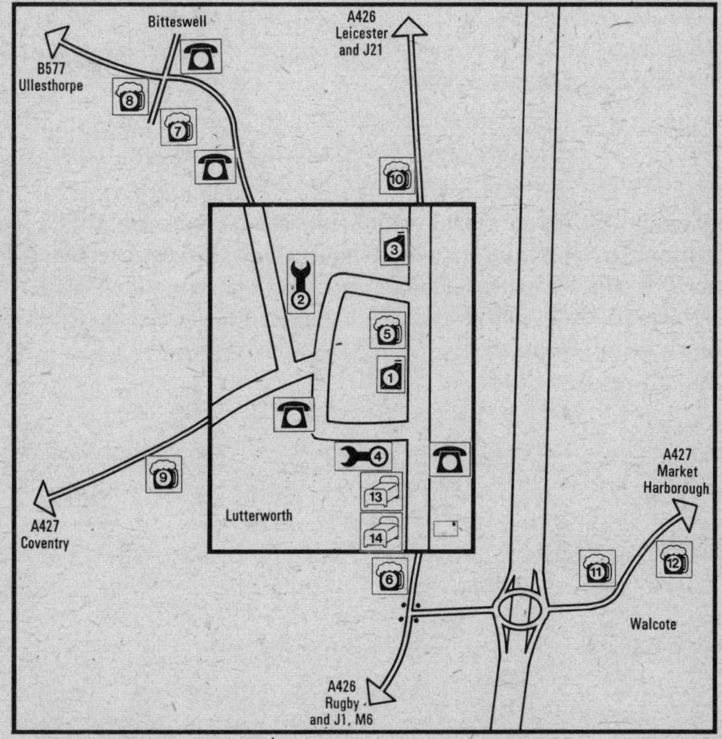

1 Lutterworth Garage. Hours: 8 am – 6.30 pm (closes 5.30 pm Sat, all day Sun)
2 Wycliffe Garage. Hours: 8 am – 7 pm (closes 6 pm Sat, half-day Sun)
3 St Mary's Filling Station. Hours: 7.30 am – 8 pm
4 Burtons Garage. 24-hr breakdown (Lutterworth 2363)
5 *The Cavalier,* Mitchells and Butlers
6 *The Fox,* Whitbread
7 *The Royal Oak,* Davenports
8 *The Man-at-Arms,* Davenports
9 *The Flying Saucer,* Home
10 *The Sir Frank Whittle,* Everards
11 *The Tavern,* Free house
12 *The White Lion,* Marston
13 *The Hind Hotel* (Lutterworth 2341)
14 *The Denbigh Arms Hotel* (Lutterworth 3537)

petrol/hotels

This junction has become a motorway intersection with the opening of the M69 for Coventry. On the other side there is a half-mile spur of M-road onto the A46 and then a long stretch of dual carriageway into Leicester – the kind of road that makes you feel that the car is a recognized disease since there are very high mesh barriers on either side.

So nothing is convenient on this junction. But there is very cheap petrol after you drive a couple of miles at the Rowley Fields Service Station **1** just on the first set of traffic lights. At the second intersection the very large *Braunstone* **5** is on the left and the small *Bianco Lodge Hotel and Restaurant* **12** is on the right. *The Braunstone* has normal pub food at all times except Sunday evening.

Turning left at the first junction on the A46 you will eventually find the nicest pub on the junction, *The Shakespeare* **4**. A long, large, white, thatched building with a large field at the back.

Taking the A46 in the other direction, towards Narborough, there is a garage and a pub on the first roundabout. Mack's **2** keeps irregular hours but sells cheap petrol. *The Foxhunter* **6** is a large roadhouse which has food and snacks available at most times. Passing under the motorway and taking the road into Narborough you find the reasonably priced *Charnwood Hotel* **11**.

M1
J21

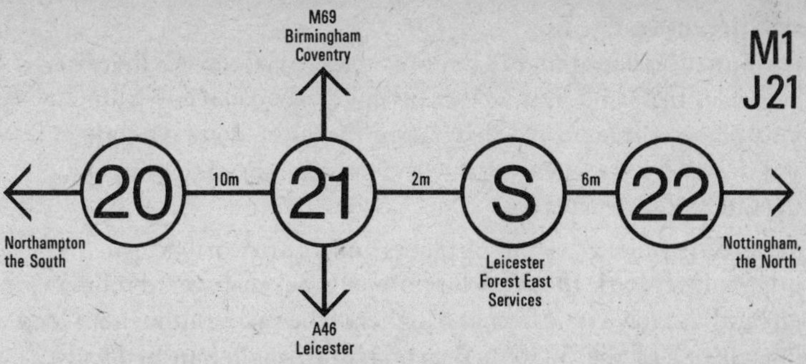

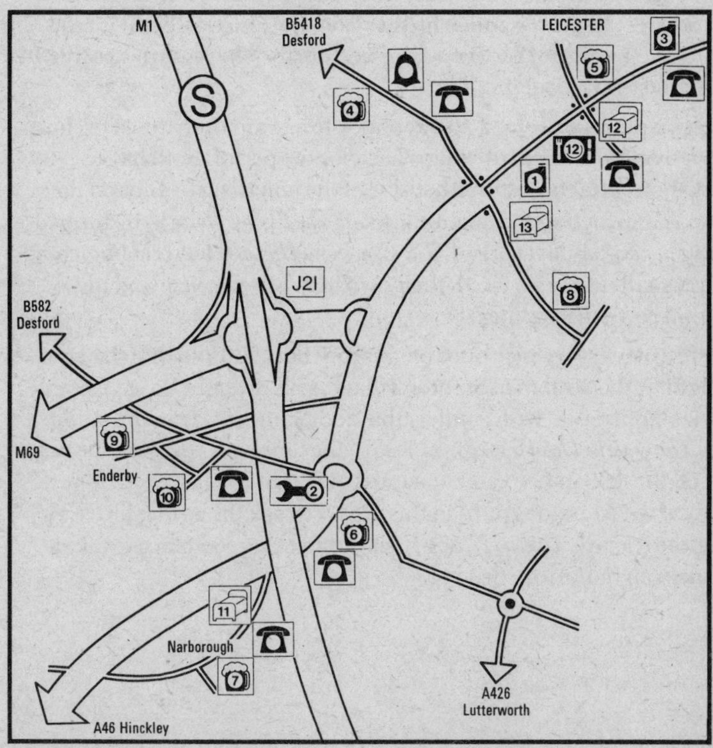

1 Rowley Fields Service Station. Hours: 8 am – 10 pm
2 Mack's Garage. Hours: usually 8.30 am – 6 pm
3 Forum Service Station. Hours: 7 am – 10 pm
4 *The Shakespeare*, Everards
5 *The Braunstone*, Everards
6 *The Foxhunter*, Mitchells and Butlers
7 *The Bell*, Ansells
8 *The Union Inn*, Marston
9 *The New Inn*, Everards
10 *The Nags Head*, Ansells
11 *The Charnwood Hotel* (Leicester 862218)
12 *The Bianco Lodge Hotel* (Leicester 825982)
13 *Post House Hotel* (Leicester 896688)

visits/petrol and pubs

The countryside around this junction, particularly on the Leicester side, is very beautiful. But, not surprisingly, most of it is private. Round every corner, as you drive along the lanes, there is another secret driveway disappearing into the silver birches and more notices with statements of privacy.

But there are quite a few public places and all are worth a visit. Bradgate Deer Park **13** is very large, with bracken-covered rolling open land. Lovely views from the higher of the two monuments. Good for a walk or a picnic. So too is Beacon Hill **15**, eight hundred and a few odd feet high. It is much further from the junction but it is easy enough to rejoin at **J23** if you are going north. The Nature Reserve **14** is smaller and wooded.

The two petrol stations **1** and **2**, opposite one another, are very cheap – so it would be worth turning off just for the petrol. Both have workshops attached. On either side of the junction are pubs on the main A50 which serve lunchtime food. *The Flying Horse* **9**, by the two garages, has a buffet spread. *The Coach and Horses* **8** has real homemade soup usually, they say, with their own home-grown veg, and the normal run of fried things.

There are two very nice pubs on this junction. The old thatched *Crown* **6**, right at the bottom of Stanton village, sells draught Bass. A simple old-fashioned pub with comfortable and plain seating in the public bar. *The Queens Head* **5** is quite close to the junction. Just take the first exit off the A50 to Leicester and cross over that road on the bridge. Most of the Marstons pubs in this area only sell the strong bitter, as does the friendly *Queens Head* which would be a good place to take a break from motorway driving.

M1 J22

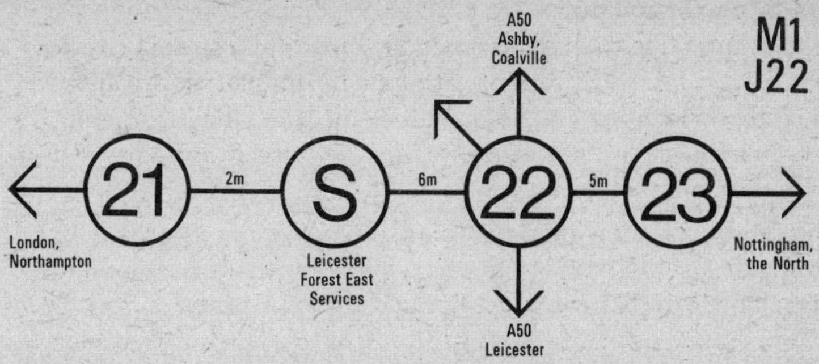

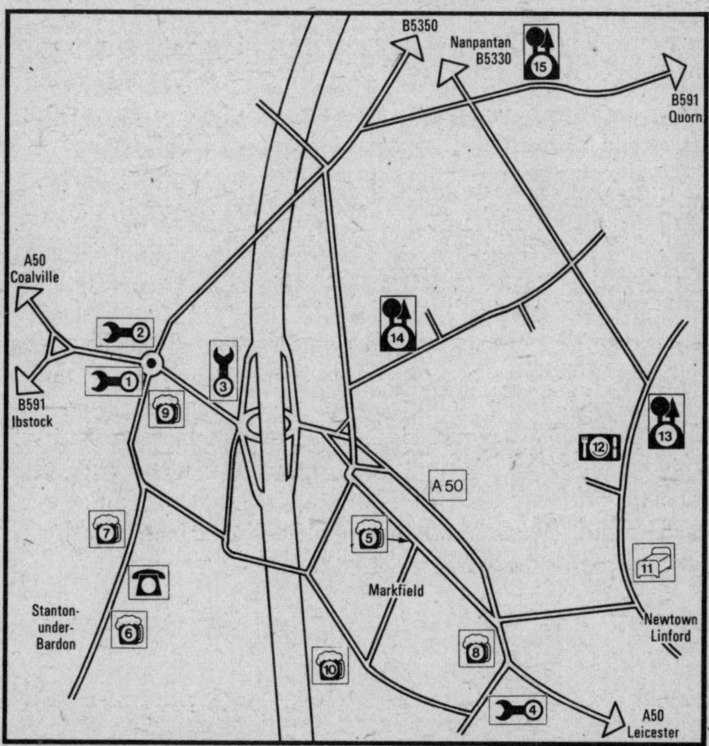

1 Sunray Garage. Hours: 7 am – 9 pm (later opening Sat, Sun)
2 Browns Blue Garage. Hours: 7 am – 7.30 pm (opens 2 pm Sun)
3 Deuce Recovery. 24-hr breakdown (Markfield 2256)
4 Bob Jones. Tyres and batteries
5 *The Queens Head,* Marston
6 *The Crown,* Mitchells and Butlers
7 *The Plough Inn,* Marston
8 *The Coach and Horses,* Everards
9 *The Flying Horse,* Ansells
10 *The Bulls Head,* Marston
11 *The Johnscliffe Hotel* (Markfield 3281)
12 *The Grey Lady Restaurant*
13 Bradgate Deer Park
14 Nature Reserve
15 Beacon Hill

walks/picnics/pubs

There aren't too many good reasons for stopping off at this junction. There are petrol stations within a mile in either direction on the A512. But they are not particularly cheap; nor do they keep very long hours.

If you are travelling south the best option for this junction is to use the countryside and rejoin at **J22** – the two maps overlap so you shouldn't get lost. Out Woods **10** would be a good place to cut loose, and perhaps lose, the children. Beacon Hill **11**, as the name suggests, is a high and windy place. Good views and a nice place to have a walk.

No-one in *The Priory* **3** could tell me where the name Nanpantan came from – nothing to do with Panyan or Nappysan apparently. Someone suggested a Frenchman of the Norman variety. *The Priory* lacks such age – it is a large 'thirties' pub which was once called *The 19th Hole*. The coloured friezes on the wall depict the comic hazards of golf. Quite an interesting place with cheap beer, a garden and snacks.

Over three miles from the junction on the A512 to Ashby is *The Bulls Head* **7**. At night it lights up the whole horizon. Food on weekday lunchtimes and snacks always available. A garden or dining-room for children eating. There is also one and only one family room for an overnight stop – and at a reasonable price. Ring Coalville 222389.

There are many pubs in the unattractive and awkward little town of Shepshed – though as a village it must once have been attractive. *The Charnwood Forest Railway Inn* **5** is the place for those interested in pubs. At the other end of town is a Spanish restaurant, *La Casita* **8**. Quite pleasant but not cheap.

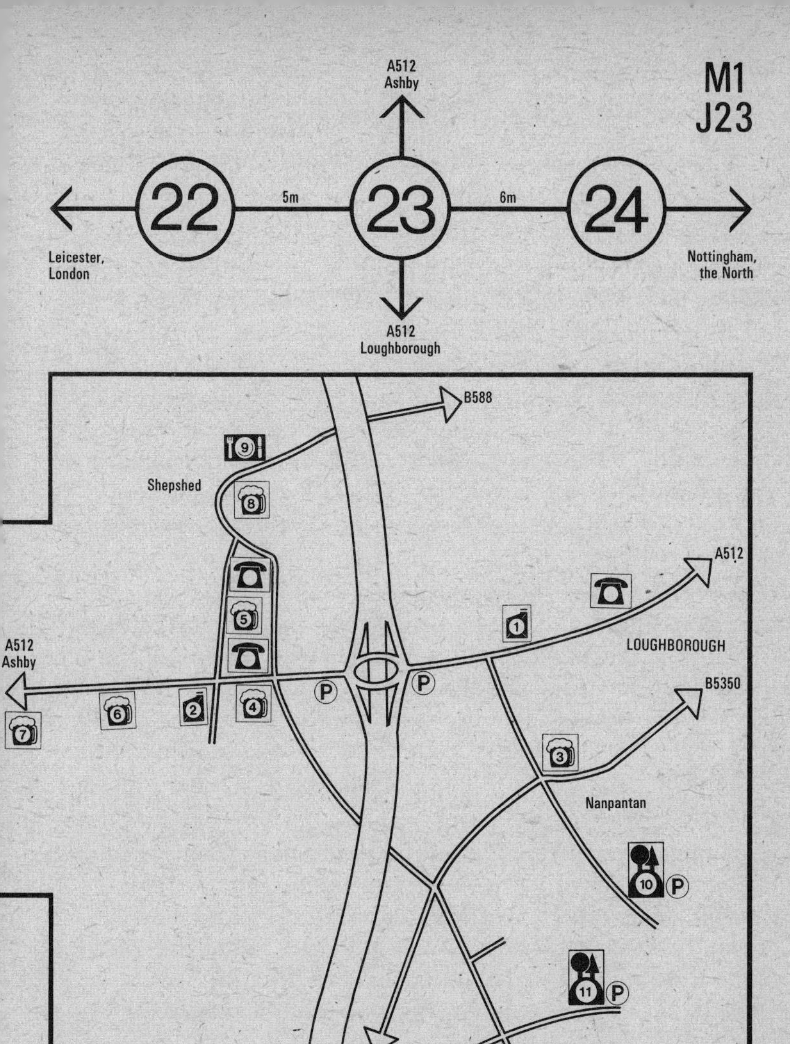

1 Temple Filling Station. Hours: 7.15 am – 8.30 pm (9 am – 7.30 pm Sun)
2 Abbey Filling Station. Hours: 8.15 am – 9 pm (closes 6 pm Sun)
3 *The Priory*, Home
4 *The De Lisle Arms*, Shipstone
5 *The Charnwood Forest Railway Inn*, Mitchells and Butlers
6 *The White Horse*, Marston
7 *The Bulls Head*, Shipstone
8 *The Crown Hotel*, Everards
9 *La Casita Restaurant* (Shepshed 2843)
10 Out Woods
11 Beacon Hill

pubs/food/visit

A very good junction which one could with pleasure visit a number of times – there are certainly too many places too spread out for any one visit. There is also a lot of water around – the Rivers Trent and Soar, and the Trent and Mersey Canal.

The petrol is mostly cheap – the three stations mentioned certainly are – saving about 10p on motorway prices. The Cavendish Bridge **2** seems to provide most garage services you could want, as well as a cheap overnight camping spot.

Shardlow, on the A6 to Derby, seems to be full of pubs owned by different brewers. Taking the small right turning signposted to Great Wilne one eventually crosses the canal and finds a couple of pubs on the bankside – one is *The Malt Shovel* **12**. Most of the pubs roundabout seemed quite interesting. I liked my brief visit to *The Dog and Duck* **9** for the long and detailed discussion on the varieties of black pudding and how you cook it.

Both *The Anchor* **6**, on the edge of the Soar, and *The Donnington Arms* **11** have food at lunchtime and can cater for children. But there are a variety of cafés and restaurants spread over the junction – all English in the kind of food they offer. The nicest pub by far, for my taste, is the tiny *Cap and Stocking* **5** in the back streets of Kegworth. Beer from an enamel jug, two small rooms, plain wooden seating and walls covered with stuffed fish and birds. I hope no foolish person decides to make changes to the place.

Visit the Motor Museum **17** if you have the time and money – adults £1, kids and grannies 50p. You enter down an avenue of old petrol pumps to find a collection of racing cars (a lot of BRMs) and of Leyland cars – and soon they all may be there. Café and bar. *The Castle Manor Hotel* **16**, in the attractive village/town of Castle Donnington, was a nice place to stay and served one of the best English breakfasts I had.

1 Sawley Cross Roads Service Station. Hours: 8 am – 9 pm (closes 8 pm Sat, open 9 am – 7 pm Sun)

2 Cavendish Bridge Filling Station. Hours: 6.30 am – 9 pm. Breakdown service in normal working hours (Derby 792209). Workshop

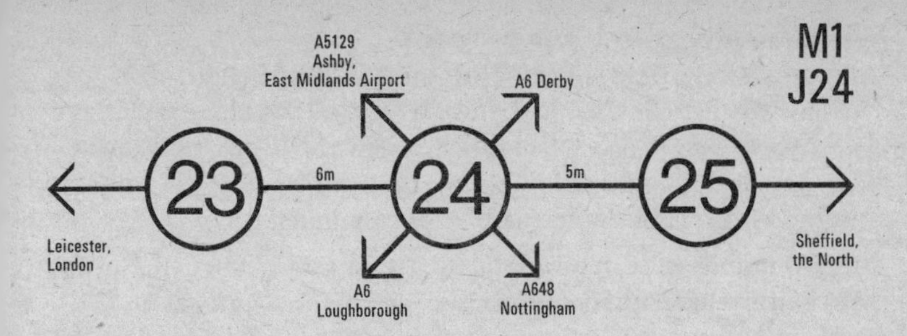

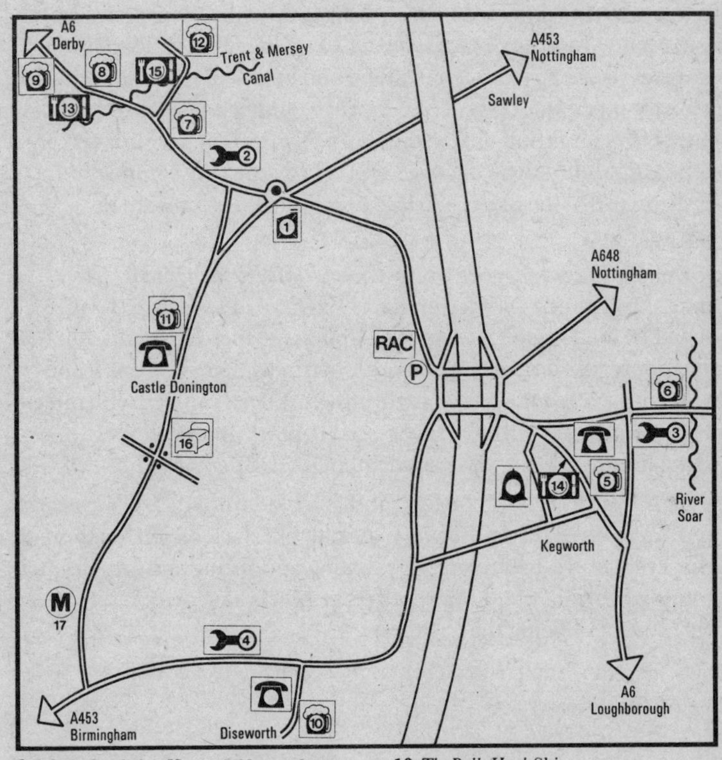

3 John's Car Sales. Hours: 7.30 am – 6 pm (shorter at weekends). Workshop. Fiat agent
4 Smiths of Diceworth. 24-hr breakdown (Derby 810467)
5 *The Cap and Stocking*, Bass Worthington
6 *The Anchor Inn*, Bass Worthington
7 *The Navigation Inn*, Davenports
8 *The Skakespeare Inn*, Home
9 *The Dog and Duck*, Marston
10 *The Bulls Head*, Shipstone
11 *The Donnington Arms*, Ansells
12 *The Malt Shovel*, Marston
13 *The Highway Grill Café*
14 *The Trent House Café*
15 *The Lady in Grey Restaurant* (Derby 792331)
16 *The Donnington Manor Hotel* (Derby 810253)
17 Donnington Motor Museum. Hours: 10 am – 6 pm every day

restaurants/petrol/visit/pubs/hotels

At first sight a terrible junction. Just the A52 blasting its dual carriageway between Nottingham and Derby. Half-blocked the day I was there because a coach had careered down an 80-ft embankment. The same night there was a public meeting to discuss the spending of another £4½ million on the road. More of nothing.

But, in another sense, it turned out to be a smashing junction. Cheap petrol all around with some of the cheapest in the country at Burden and Cox **3**. Too far to drive to save a few more pence a gallon – but if you were driving a Jag with empty tanks you could almost buy the price of a meal at *The Stable Restaurant* **11** on the saving. Not that the restaurant is cheap – but it has a long and interesting menu. The other reason for going this distance for petrol would be a visit to Elvaston Castle **16**. A large and unspectacular house, but the grounds are lovely. Capability Brown, however, turned down the commission with the words: 'the place is so flat, and there is such a want of capability in it.'

Pride of place, for me, goes to *The Grange Farm Restaurant* **10**. A five-course supper and coffee for under £4. Nor could I finish all I was given. The food wasn't that special – plain northern English – but the atmosphere was terrific: just before Christmas there was tinsel and glitter with everyone dressed to the nines. A posh canteen with fifteen or more waitresses, all smartly dressed in black and white, rushing and dashing. Ladies with stoles drinking Asti Spumante!

The Bulls Head **5** serves good food and has a kids' room. *The Navigation* **6** and *Steamboat* **7** are neither very special, but the location, on the edge of the Trent and allied rivers, is. Walking and sitting and lots of water for children to fall into. Finally, all three hotels have reasonable rates, with *The Firs* **11** being the cheapest.

1 Risley Garage. Hours: 8 am – 8 pm (opens 9 am Sun). 24-hr breakdown (Nottingham 398472)
2 Burnetts. Hours: 7 am – 10.30 pm. Workshop
3 Burden and Cox. Hours: 8 am – 10 pm (opens 9 am Sat, closes 6 pm Sun)

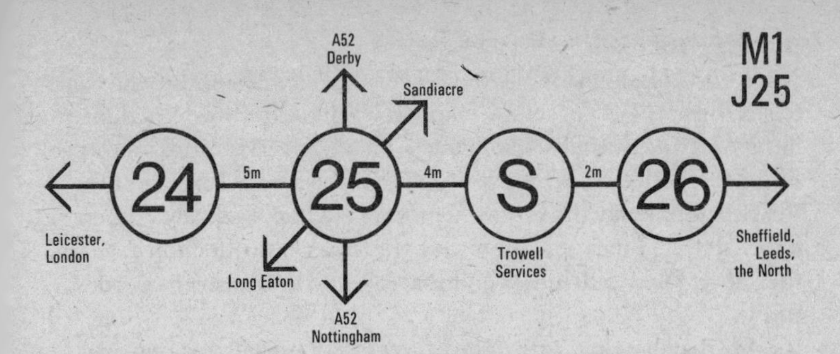

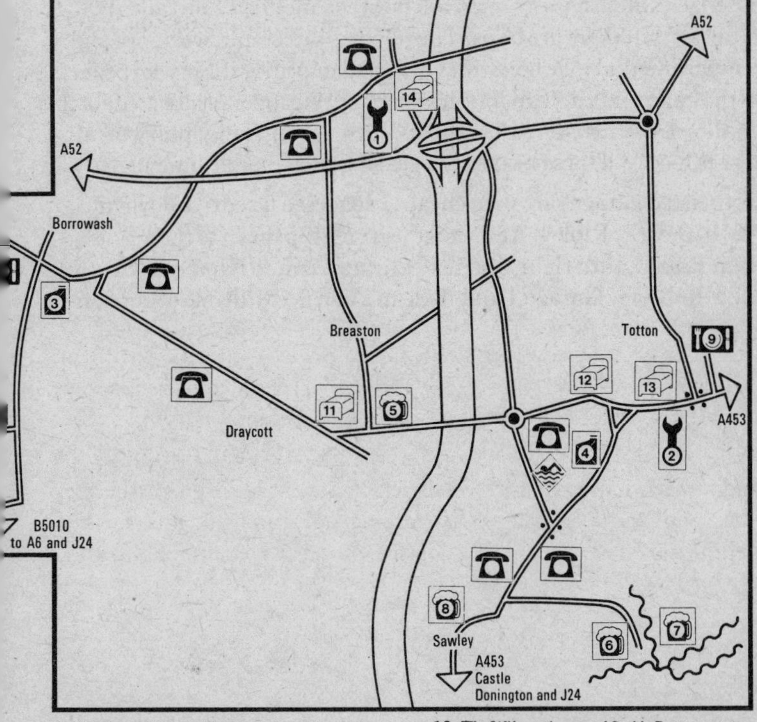

4 Lindleys Garage. Hours: 8 am – 7 pm (closes 5 pm Sat, closed Sun)
5 *The Bull's Head*, Marston
6 *The Trent Navigation Inn*, Home
7 *The Steamboat Inn*, Free house
8 *The Harrington Arms*, Hardys and Hansons
9 *The Grange Farm Restaurant* (Long Eaton 69426)
10 *The Wilmot Arms and Stable Restaurant* (Derby 672222)
11 *The Firs Hotel* (Draycott 2535)
12 *The Europa Hotel* (Long Eaton 68481)
13 *The Camden Hotel* (Long Eaton 62901)
14 *Nottingham Post House*. Buttery hours: 6 am – 10 pm. (Nottingham 397800)
15 Elvaston Castle Country Park

pubs/petrol

Not a good junction for all-round offerings – only for those who want to see the home of the yellow raspberry – that extraordinary thing that hangs outside the pubs belonging to Hardys and Hansons, makers of Kimberley Ales. So the place to go is Kimberley – where they brew the stuff. Some say the yellow raspberry is a hop. Unlikely. Others say a mis-shapen pineapple the wrong way up. Very little choice, therefore, for beer drinkers in this area – and that's never a good thing.

The Nelson and Railway **3**, right next to the brewery, is a nice pub. I failed to establish the connection between the good Lord and the railroad, but there are baps. The pub has a decrepit, worn-out and temperamental juke box with very good music for those who peaked in the early sixties. If anyone has a spare Wurlitzer please contact the landlord. *The Lord Clyde* **6** is also in town. Another nice pub which serves food. All these brave men gracing such establishments!

Both listed garages are very cheap. I suggest a fast drive down the A610 towards Ripley. At the first turn-off, dip down to the roundabout, turn right, and take the first right to Kimberley. Petrol at the Kimberley Garage **1** and then an audience with one of our heroes.

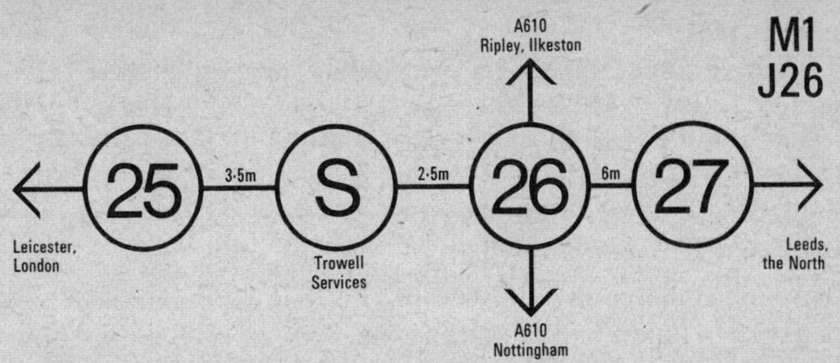

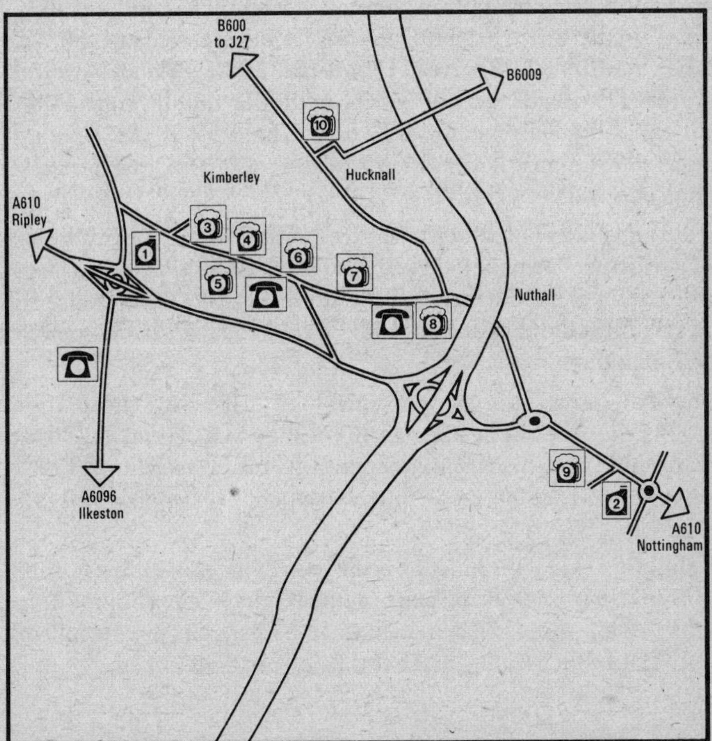

1 Kimberley Garage. Hours: 7.30 am – 9 pm (9 am – 8 pm Sun)
2 St Mary's Filling Station. Hours: 7 am – 10 pm (8.30 am – 8.30 pm Sun)
3 *The Nelson and Railway*, Hardys and Hansons
4 *The Cricketers Rest*, Hardys and Hansons
5 *The Queens Head*, Hardys and Hansons
6 *The Lord Clyde*, Hardys and Hansons
7 *The Stag Inn*, Shipstone
8 *The Three Ponds*, Hardys and Hansons
9 *The Broxtowe Arms*, Home
10 *The Queens Head*, Home

pubs/petrol

If you drive around this junction you find coal tips, old and new, terraced housing, estates of the small box variety and a general drabness. But visiting Bagthorpe you find it difficult to imagine that you are in an industrial area. A lovely valley following a stream with small cottages on either side. And two marvellous pubs – *The Dixies Arms* **5** and *The Travellers Rest* **6**.

To get to Bagthorpe take the A608 towards Derby and Eastwood and then the first right after a mile; then it's signposted left. But Bagthorpe too was once an industrial area – for outworkers. The landlord at *The Dixies* said there used to be 191 stocking frames in the village. The pub got its name from the Reverend Dixie who was a large landowner in the area. There had been a discussion in the pub the other night, the landlord said: some regulars said it used to be called *The Red Hand*; but, he said, he knew it was called *The Dixies* in 1700 at least, because he had checked the records!

An old and lovely pub. But if it's a nice day and you've got kids with you, go further down the valley to *The Travellers Rest* which has a large garden at the front. Further on, in Selston, *The Crown* **7** has a kids' playground at the back and an adults' games room upstairs – some food but nothing special.

None of the garages are very convenient but all listed are cheap. If you go to Bagthorpe while heading north you may as well head for **J28** via Selston and Pinxton, getting your petrol at Sheaf Petroleum **1**. The roads are small but there is an interesting pub, *The Horse and Jockey* **13** on the way.

On the other side of the junction is the pretty village of Linby. A drink at *The Horse and Groom* **8** and petrol at the Wighay Filling Station **3**. It seems possible to me to have a picnic in the woods on the wide split on the A611 **14**. But parking might be difficult on this fast road.

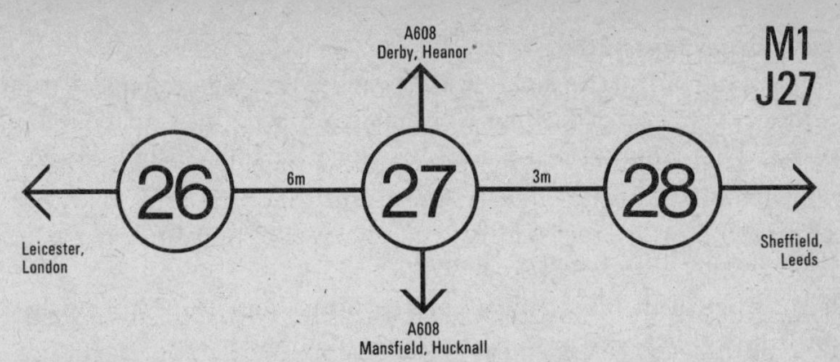

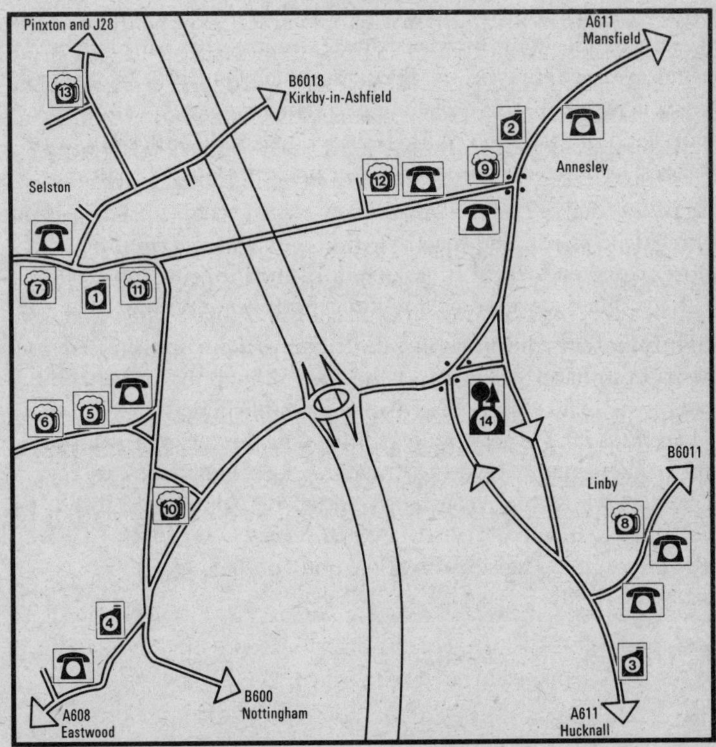

1 Sheaf Fuel Services. Hours: 7.45 am – 10 pm
2 Derby Road Garage. Hours: 7 am – 9 pm
3 Wighay Filling Station. Hours: 8.30 am – 7.00 pm (closes 6 pm Sat, open 10 am – 4 pm Sun)
4 Brinsley Service Station
5 *The Dixies Arms,* Home
6 *The Travellers Rest,* Home
7 *The Crown,* Hardys and Hansons
8 *The Horse and Groom,* Home
9 *The Badger Box,* Hardys and Hansons
10 *The Sandhills,* Home
11 *The White Lion,* Shipstone
12 *The Forest Tavern,* Mansfield
13 *The Horse and Jockey,* Free house
14 Picnic spot (?)

petrol/garages/pubs

The main road on this junction is now called the A38 – but not all the time or even most of the time. The majority of signs insist that it is the A615. This confused me because I had followed the A38 for the length of the M5 from Exeter to Birmingham and there it was a good provider of useful places. Now the A38 has apparently reached Mansfield with a change of character.

All the petrol on this junction is pretty cheap – the cheapest being the furthest at Sheaf Petroleum **2**. Coleman's Garage **1** is very convenient, being only a short distance off the A38 towards Mansfield. The hours listed are the minimum – they can often be longer, irregular maybe, but the garage seemed helpful. Close by is Wards **5** where there is a 24-hour petrol machine. AA spanners flourish on this junction. Wards Autopoint **3** and Kettles **4**, related garages, both have a lot – so this is the place to stop for repairs.

The Duke of Sussex **7** seemed an unlikely place to chalk up a first – a pub selling deep-fried squid rings. Not that the locals, apparently, appreciate their luck. Scallops, haddock and the usual run of pub grub too. Food at weekday lunchtimes and every evening.

Slightly closer to the junction is the friendly *Kilcote Arms* **6** where you can try your hand at skittles. Of the many other pubs that litter the area most are little more than drinking establishments. Thus *The Workpeople's Inn* **11**, beautifully painted outside, very sparse inside, and fitting its name. If you are travelling south take a look at **J27** because it is possible to continue your journey southwards if you wanted to visit, and it's worth it, *The Horse and Jockey* **13**. But if it's dark and you've got no sense of direction, don't bother.

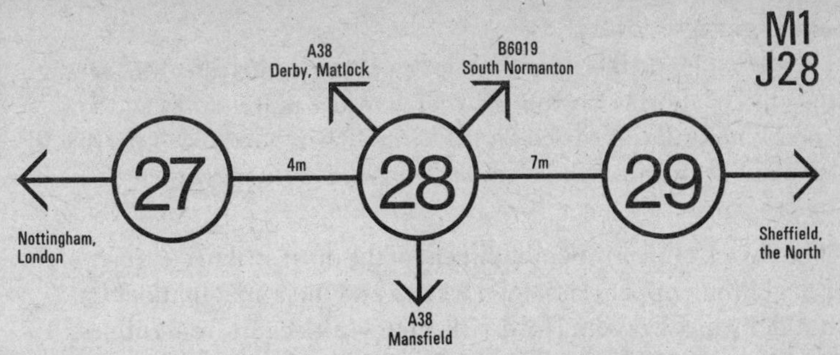

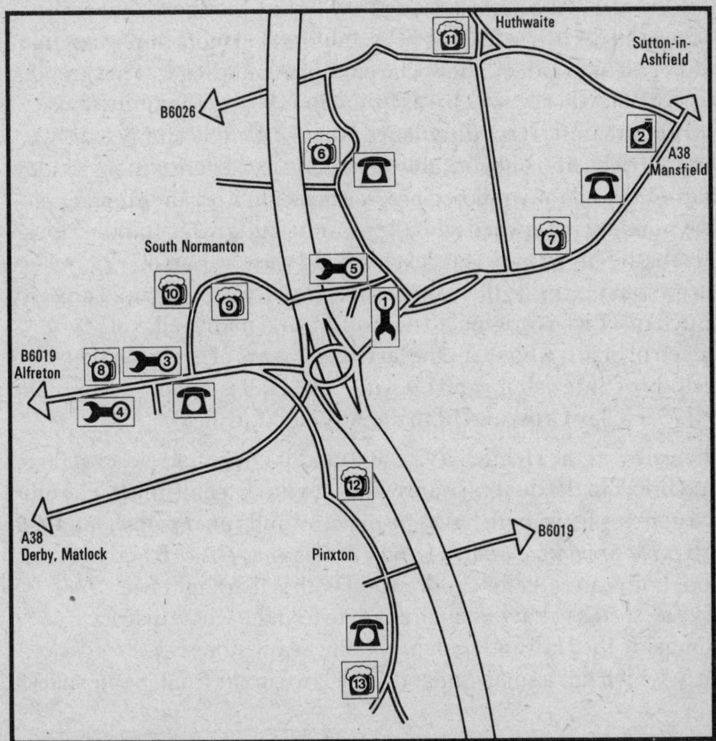

1 Coleman's Garage. Hours: 8 am – 6.30 pm (closes 5 pm Sat, 1 pm Sun). 24-hr breakdown (Ripley 811542)
2 Sheaf Petroleum. Hours: 6.30 am – 10.30 pm (8 am – 8 pm Sun)
3 Autopoint. Hours: 8 am – 7 pm. Saab and Honda agent
4 Arthur Kettle and Son. Hours: 8 am – 8 pm. 24-hr breakdown (Ripley 811251). Ford and Skoda agents
5 Syd Ward. 24-hr petrol machine. General repairs
6 *The Kilcote Arms*, Hardys and Hansons
7 *The Duke of Sussex*, Hardys and Hansons
8 *The Hawthorns*, Shipstone
9 *The Miners Arms*, Tetley
10 *The Angel Inn*, Hardys and Hansons
11 *The Workpeople's Inn*, Home
12 *The Greyhound*, Mansfield
13 *The Horse and Jockey*, Free house

visit

Hardwick Hall **10** is the reason for stopping at this junction. Set high on a hill in enormous grounds, there are also many walks and a picnic spot. The Hall was closed for the winter when I arrived, so Dr David Starkey, who knows the place well, has penned a piece to persuade you to pause.

'Hardwick Hall is the embodiment of the most striking features of the Elizabethan upper class: their wealth and their imagination. Its builder was Elizabeth Hardwick. Her wealth came from ruthless exploitation of the marriage market. She saw four husbands to the grave, and each died leaving her wealthier and more important than before. Next to money and social climbing, building was her grand passion. Hardwick, which was begun in 1590, was her third house and her greatest. It is a disciplined fantasy: compact, impeccably symmetrical, and unbelievably light and airy. There is more window than wall, and the windows increase in height from the ground up. The building is crowned with the gigantic initials ES, standing for Elizabeth Shrewsbury (her last husband was the Earl of Shrewsbury). Inside there is notable plaster-work; splendid tapestry (much of which is original to the house); and many relics of Mary, Queen of Scots, who spent the last fifteen years of her life in the custody of Shrewsbury and his wife.' The Hall is signposted from the A6175 to Clay Cross and from the A617 to Mansfield.

The petrol at the Heath Service Station **1** is cheap and close *but* there is no break in the dual carriageway for two and a half miles. The other two garages listed both have cheap petrol and run repair shops. Of the pubs, *The Shoulder of Mutton* **4** and *The Horse and Groom* **6** both serve food, both can cater for children and both sell draught beer. *The Shoulder* seems to have enough space to feed the whole district. Alongside the Hall and built in equally heavy stone is *The Hardwick Inn* **5**, which has a small bar and large lawn in the front. Some snacks.

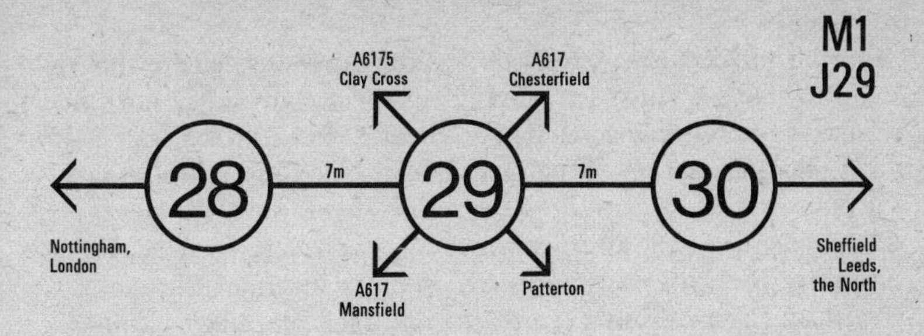

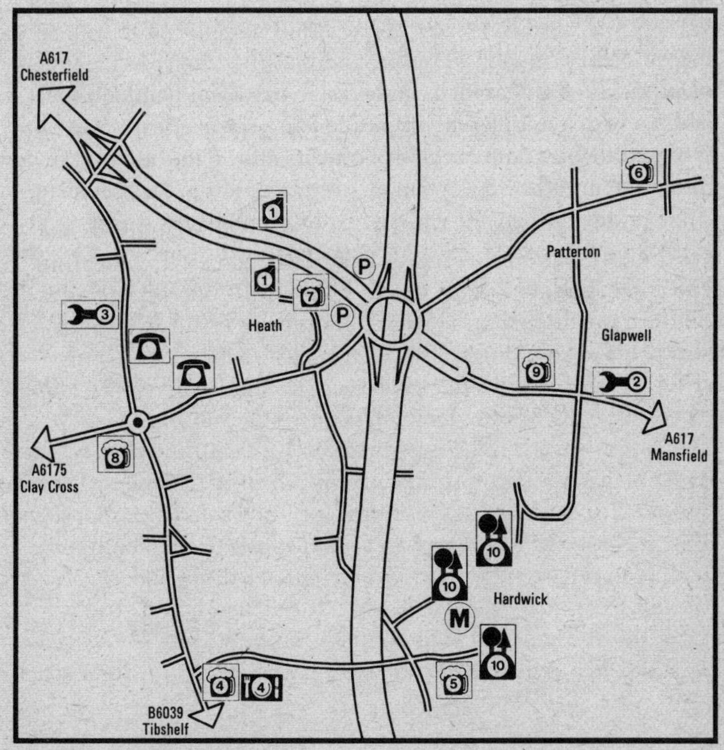

1 Heath Service Stations. Hours: 7 am – 8 pm (9 am – 8 pm Sun)
2 Stayleys Garage. Hours: 7.30 am – 9 pm (9 am – 9 pm Sun)
3 Temple Normanton Garage. Hours: 8 am – 6.30 pm (closes 1.30 pm Sun)
4 *The Shoulder of Mutton*, Free house. Restaurant (Chesterfield 850276)
5 *The Hardwick Inn*, Free house
6 *The Horse and Groom*, Home
7 *The Elm Tree*, Mansfield
8 *The Williamthorpe Hotel*, Hardys and Hansons
9 *The Young Vanish Inn*, Whitbread
10 Hardwick Hall (National Trust)

pub food

A boring and not very useful junction. The petrol is expensive and the two garages have only been listed for emergency buying – although the garage closest to the junction, the Bridge House **1** has a workshop and breakdown service. None of the pubs are very special, but two of the pubs in Barlborough offer a very wide range of food. *The Rose and Crown* **4** has a chippie attached which is open on Tuesday, Friday and Saturday. It also has bar snacks at most times, including fish and steaks, and a restaurant where one can get a solid evening meal for about £3. There is space for children to eat at all times. Just down the road is *The Royal Oak* **5**, which has an up-market restaurant menu and very good sandwiches for snacks.

The Dusty Miller **6** is a large, recently converted, open-plan pub. Plushish – with four different lagers and four pressure beers. *The Angel* **8**, in Spinkhill, has a similar kind of conversion and the best beer close to the junction.

Further afield is *The Sitwell Arms* **10** – named after the family – which serves draught Bass and a range of food. Two rooms with a lot of bits and pieces to look at – but not touch. The pub also offers B&B but I found the room more than a bit cold for the price I paid. *The Park Hotel* **11** strikes me as very pricey for what it appears to be – £12.50 plus VAT for a single person – but it has a nice location. Not really for kids but there are reduced rates for them in the restaurant.

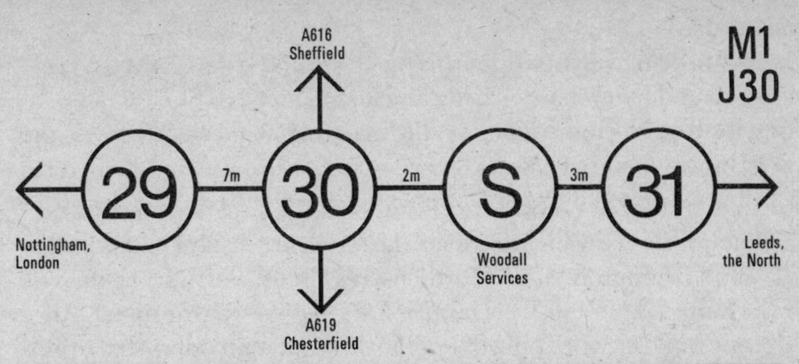

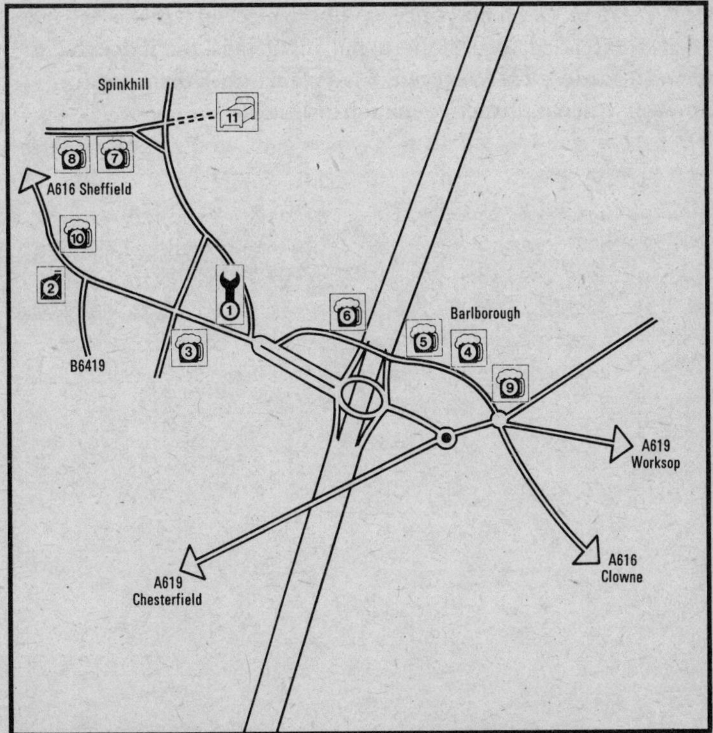

1 Bridge House Garage. Workshop. 24-hr breakdown (Chesterfield 810677)
2 Renishaw Service Station
3 *The Blacksmiths Arms,* Bass Charrington
4 *The Rose and Crown,* Bass Charrington
5 *The Royal Oak,* Bass Charrington
6 *The Dusty Miller,* Free house
7 *The Bootmakers Arms,* Courage
8 *The Angel Hotel,* Tetley
9 *The de Rodes Arms,* Bass Charrington
10 *The Sitwell Arms,* Bass Charrington. B&B (Eckington 2086)
11 *The Park Hall Hotel and Restaurant* (Eckington 3285)

visit/petrol

There is little reason to stop at this junction, unless you want to visit the small and lovely church dedicated to St Peter and St Paul in Todwick **8**. A Norman doorway, 14th-century chancel, box pews, and an old bible dated 1611.

Cheap petrol at the Aston Service Station **1**. None of the pubs close to the junction are very nice and even those in more distant villages like Ulley and Brampton-en-le-Morthen – it's almost worth going there for the name – aren't too special. *The Robin Hood* **4** was the nicest. An old stone building with only one of the three rooms modernized to any extent. *The Royal Oak* **5** may once have been nice but it seems to have been over-extended, all in stone, to pull in the Jags. But it does have food and a garden. *The Rising Deer* **6** is a plain pub in the village of Brampton which is attractive enough to visit.

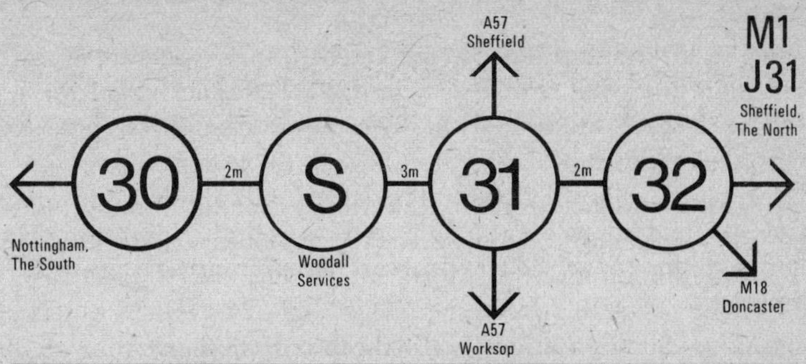

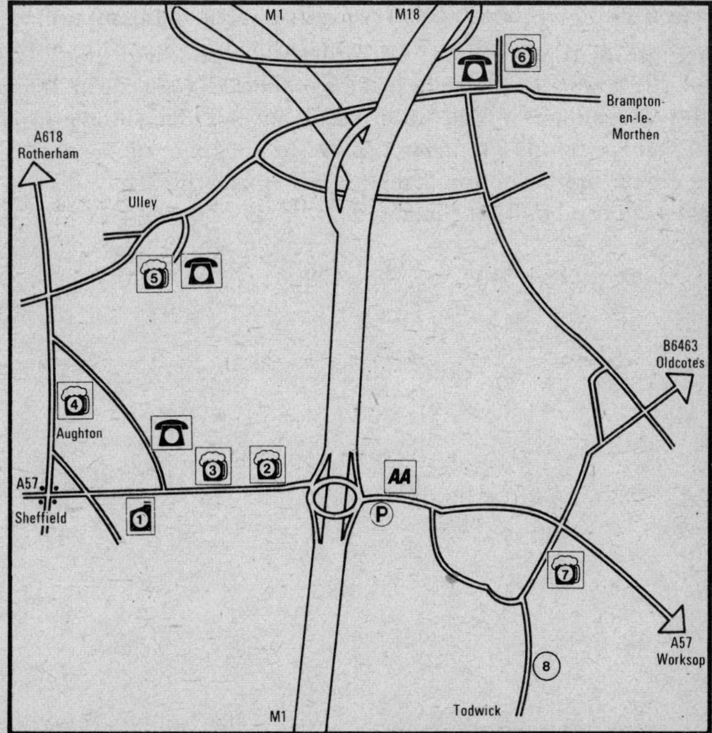

1 Aston Service Station. Hours: 7 am – 9.45 pm (closes 10.45 pm Sat)
2 *The Yellow Lion,* Whitbread
3 *The Blue Bell,* Bass Charrington
4 *The Robin Hood,* Bass Charrington
5 *The Royal Oak,* Samuel Smith
6 *The Rising Deer,* Stones
7 *The Red Lion,* Whitbread
8 Todwick Church

petrol
If you lack the spirit of adventure do not attempt to navigate this junction. There is only one good reason for doing so in any case and that is to buy very cheap petrol at the Vulcan Service Station **1**.

This complex junction ought to be known as the spider – sitting with its eight legs on top of a highly industrialized and half-destroyed area. The entry and exit points of the junction are separated by a distance of half a mile and connected by a dual carriageway running beneath the motorway.

The Murco Service Station **2** is also cheap and is next door to a modern pub, *The Pike and Heron* **4**, which has a restaurant upstairs.

There are many pubs on the A630 to Sheffield starting with the modern *Plumpers* **3** right on the junction – or rather, one of them. It has little to recommend it. You can also take your pick from the others you find. But apparently *The Carbrook Hall Hotel* **5** was once famous as the home of the Bright family and there is still a room with fine plasterwork and wall panelling.

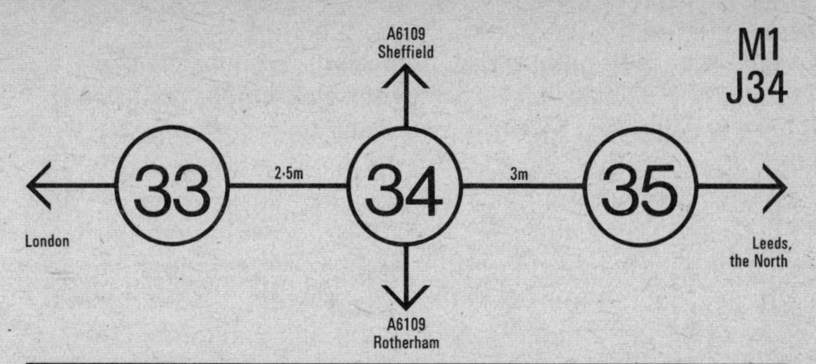

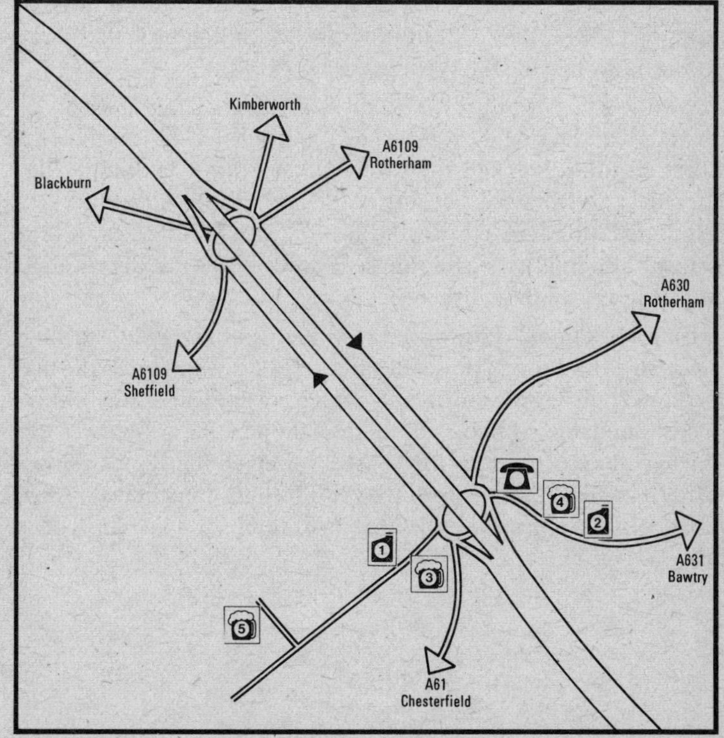

1 Vulcan Service Station. Hours: 7 am – 11 pm (9 am – 11 pm Sat, 10 am – 6 pm Sun)

2 Murco. Hours: 7 am – 11 pm (8 am – 10 pm Sat, Sun)

3 *The Plumpers*, Bass Charrington

4 *The Pike and Heron*, Mansfield

5 *The Carbrook Hall Hotel*, Bass Charrington

visit/pub food

Wentworth is the place to visit, particularly if you are travelling towards Leeds, since it is very simple to rejoin at **J36** via Hoyland Nether. Wentworth Woodhouse **12** is a massive structure built for the 1st Marquis of Rockingham. It is the largest house in England – its principal frontage being 600ft – Buckingham Palace being only 352ft. Looking at it you assume they would have needed to go round the house by bicycle or skateboard. It is now a college of education and so not open, but there are public footpaths. Close by is Hoober Stand Tower **13** which some guide books say commemorates the Treaty of Aix-la-Chapelle (1748); others say it was the crushing of the Stuart rebellion (1745). Also in Wentworth are two churches **14**, the older having many relics of the Wentworth family.

In Wentworth, two pubs: *The Rockingham Arms* **8** is a free house and very popular. During the week it has a cold buffet and a variety of hot dishes including homemade steak and kidney pies. Children can be catered for and they sell Theakstons. There is also reasonably priced accommodation across the road (Barnsley 742198). *The George and Dragon* **7** also calls itself a free house but seems to be tied to pressure beer. It serves solid English food.

Getting away from Wentworth there are two pubs very close to the motorway – on a road dead-ended by it. *The Travellers Rest* **3** is an over-decorated pub with a plain menu, but it has a garden and there are woods roundabout. On the other side of the junction is *The Ball* **4** which has food of the deep-fried basket variety. But nicer than either is *The Horse and Tiger* **5** – an ordinary local selling draught beer. After a distance of two miles along the A629 to Rotherham, some very cheap garages spring up.

M1
J35

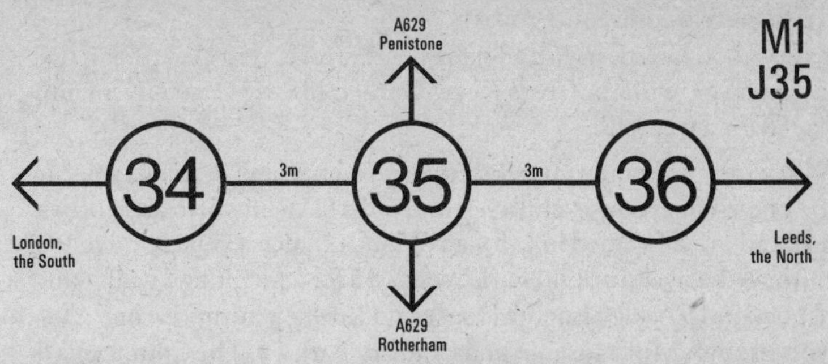

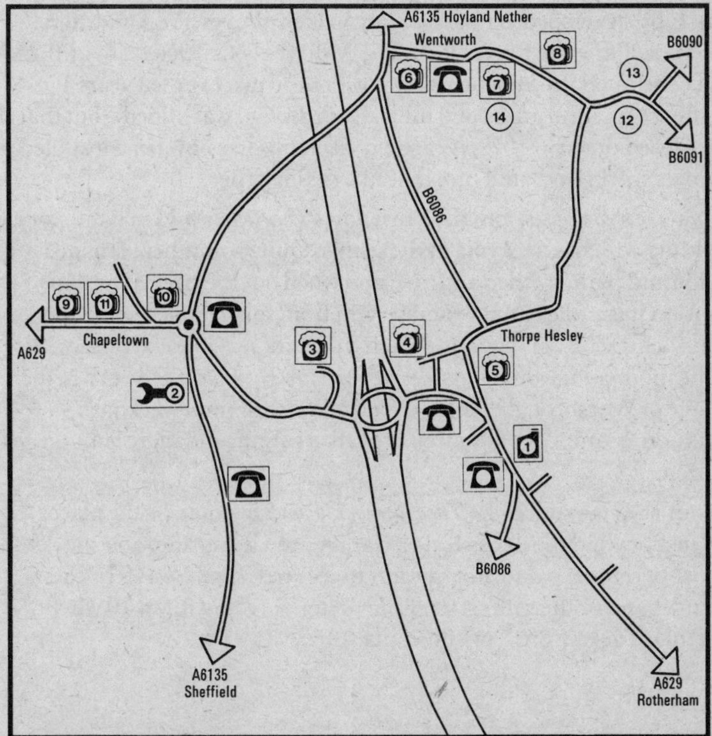

1 Scholes Service Station. Hours: 8.30 am – 7 pm (closes 5 pm Sat, Sun)
2 Chapeltown Garage
3 *The Travellers Rest*, Bass Charrington
4 *The Ball*, Tetley
5 *The Horse and Tiger*, Tetley
6 *The Horseshoe Inn*, John Smith
7 *The George and Dragon*, Free house
8 *The Rockingham Arms*, Free house
9 *The Prince of Wales*, Ward
10 *The Waggon and Horses*, Tetley
11 *The Carousel*, John Smith
12 Wentworth Woodhouse
13 Hoober Stand Tower
14 Wentworth churches

visits/petrol/pub food/pubs

A very good junction with a lot to offer. Petrol is very cheap at all the listed places, with the Cross Keyes Garage **1** being very conveniently placed for a quick fill.

With a little time on your hands there are a number of things you can do. The village, house, churches and pubs of Wentworth are worth a visit and are described in **J35** – an obvious choice if you are travelling south. Otherwise the Old Park Woods **15** for a picnic and walk – and just beyond Rockley Engine House and Rockley Furnace – or Worsbrough Mill Museum and Country Park **14**. The Country Park isn't fully developed yet but one can walk by the reservoir and, across the road, along the River Dove. The Mill was constructed about 1625 and continued working on water power until just over ten years ago. In the 19th century a second mill, steam driven, was added – but that was closed down in 1922. A rare old oil engine has now been installed to do its work. Both mills are now in working order.

Just across the road from the Museum is *The Red Lion* **11**, a large stone building which is decaying at the seams. Quite a number of rooms inside and plain snacks; a garden and wood out the back. Given its location it is a place that would benefit from some money being spent on it – a little bit of imagination and a piece of sensible conversion. So at the moment it would be wiser to head for *The Edmunds Arms* **6** in the village of Worsbrough. There is food at lunchtime on weekdays – gammon, scampi etc. Children are OK if eating, and there is a garden.

If your stop is a quick one *The Hare and Hounds* **5** would be the place. It's just beyond the Cross Keyes Garage, and it has soup and snacks. Those of refined palate might want to seek out *The Furnace* **9** by the village pond or the rather imposing (exterior) *Royal Albert* **10** where you might get a word from the mina.

1 Cross Keyes Garage. Hours: 8 am – 9 pm (9 am – 9 pm Sun). 24-hr breakdown (Barnsley, day 743331, night 743117)
2 Fairfield Filling Station. Hours: 8 am – 9 pm (shorter at weekends)
3 Hilltop Service Station. Hours: 7.45 am – 9 pm (9 am – 5 pm Sun)

M1 J36

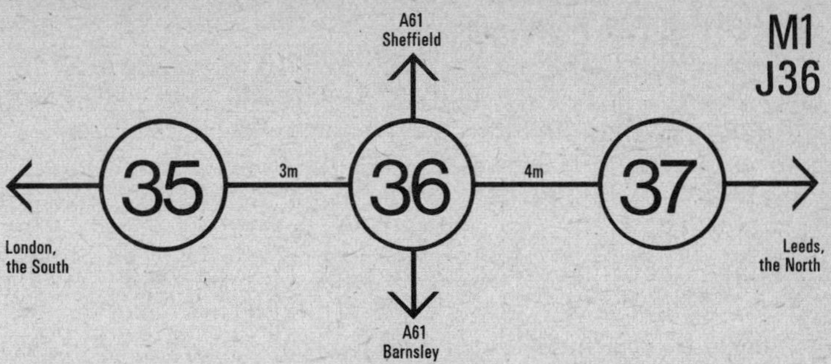

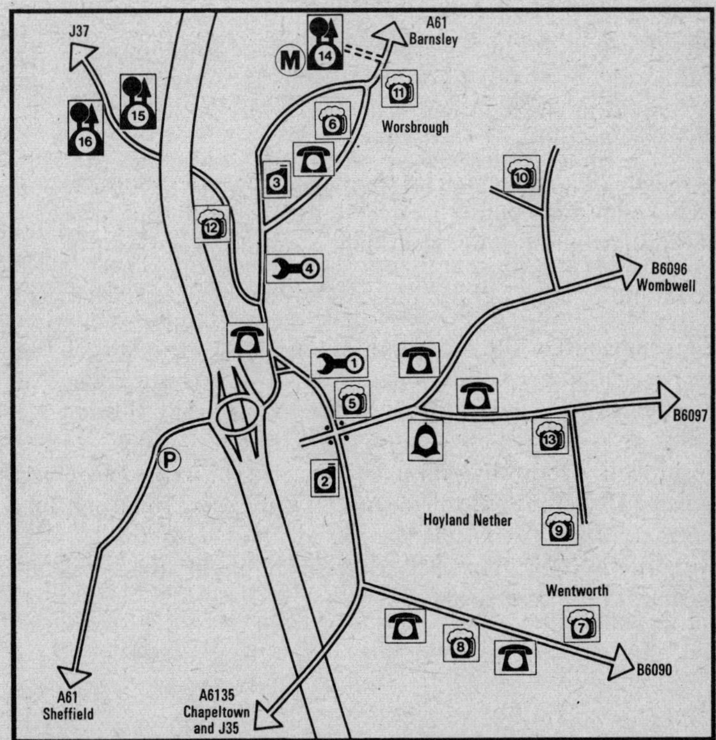

4 Central Garage. 24-hr breakdown (Barnsley 754643)
5 *The Hare and Hounds*, John Smith
6 *The Edmunds Arms*, Sam Smith
7 *The Rockingham Arms*, Free house
8 *The George and Dragon*, Free house
9 *The Furnace*, Ward
10 *The Royal Albert*, Ward
11 *The Red Lion*, John Smith
12 *The Cock*, Bass Charrington
13 *Olivers Ale House*, Websters
14 Worsbrough Mill Museum and Country Park. Open 10 am – 6 pm (or dusk). Museum closed Mon and Tues
15 Old Park Woods, Don Forest
16 Greensprings Holiday Park. Caravans and tents

petrol/food

Folk from Barnsley appear to be the butt end of Yorkshire humour – they're supposed to be a bit simple and a bit tight fisted. The Barnsley chop – nothing to do with the northern branch of the martial arts – disproves this view. Up there they've found the solution for all those who feel cheated by chops – two mouthfulls and that's your lot. Not so in Barnsley. The true Barnsley chop – and never accept a pale imitation – is ten of them living back to back. This you will find at *Brooklands Restaurant* **14**. A gigantic arch of meat set in front of you. It's not as big as it looks but it's a real meal. You pay real prices too in this restaurant but it's well worth a visit. Short menu with everything as fresh as it can be. It's highly popular – standing room only on a Saturday night. It's also full of loud Yorkshire businessmen – the kind who eat prawns and steak twice a day and loudly. Nice ladies serve you in a good plain way.

Petrol at the Service Garage **1** is cheap but its hours are quite short. Into Barnsley, Petropolis **2** has much longer hours, but you have to dodge round the one-way system in the centre of town to get to it.

The most interesting of the pubs is *The Strafford Arms* **7**. You have to go through Dodworth, cut back down to the motorway, and take the right turning just before you cross it. It's the nicest one-room pub I've seen. An old building backing on to the Wentworth Castle Estate. An old fashioned grate and lots of old pictures. Sandwiches. Heading southwards it is quite easy to return to **J36** by going through Worsbrough. At the other end of the junction if you went to *The Crown and Anchor* **10** you go to **J38** on the A637. *The Crown* is a small pub full of brass and copper. Homemade soup and pies at lunch. In Cawthorne *The Spencer Arms* **9** has dishes of the day like braised oxtail or carbonade de boeuf for about £1.

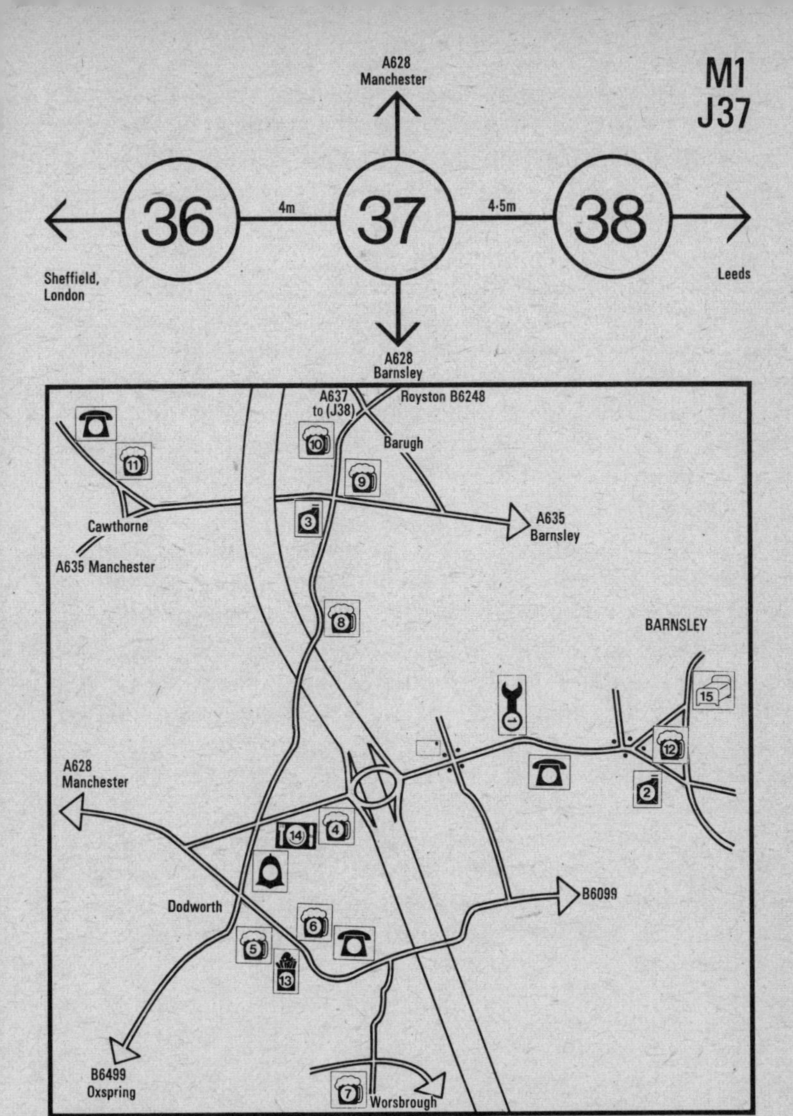

1 Service Garage. Hours: 8 am – 8 pm (closes 6 pm Sat, 10 am – 5 pm Sun). Workshop. Ford agent
2 Petropolis. Hours: 7 am – 11 pm (8 am – 10 pm Sun)
3 Mosley's Garage. Hours: 8.30 am – 6.30 pm (a few hours on Sun)
4 *The Gate Inn*, John Smith
5 *The Horse and Jockey*, Tetley
6 *The Thorneley Arms*, John Smith
7 *The Strafford Arms*, John Smith
8 *The Hermit Inn*, Free house
9 *The Spencer Arms*, John Smith
10 *The Crown and Anchor*, Tetley
11 *The Spencer Arms*, Whitbread
12 *The Three Travellers*, John Smith
13 *High St Fisheries*. Closed Wed and Sun
14 *Brooklands Restaurant* (Barnsley 6364)
15 *The Royal Hotel* (Barnsley 5895)

J38 don't

But if you were heading southwards you might find it time-saving if you were going to use **J37** to come off here and take the A637 towards Barnsley. Having gone through Darton turn right on the B6428 to Barugh.

GUIDE TO MAP SYMBOLS

 PETROL

 GARAGE AND BREAKDOWN

 PUB

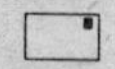 POST OFFICE

 TELEPHONE

 SHOP

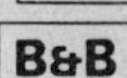

BED AND BREAKFAST

 HOTEL

 PICNIC SPOT

 FISH AND CHIPS

PARKING

RAC

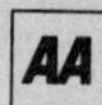

AA

MUSEUM

 RESTAURANT

HOSPITAL

 WINE BAR

 POLICE STATION

 POTTERY

 SWIMMING POOL

petrol/food/walk

On a half decent day Newmillerdam **14** would be the place to go. Easy parking opposite *The Fox and Hounds* **9**, an expanse of water and nice woods to walk through. Nearby you have a wide choice of pubs, their beers and their food. Actually slightly less choice than you would guess since the 'converters' have had their hands on them – and the results are remarkably similar. *The Fox and Hounds* has gone in for heavy Regency plush and it's bad news. *The Dam* **8** is a stone and wood job fully equipped with an interior drawbridge – but at least that goes to a dining-room with a fish and steak menu. *The Pledwick* **7** has large stone fireplaces filled with well-lit plants! Probably has a claim to fame in selling Camerons this far south. It does B&B (Wakefield 255088) but is usually fully booked. *The Star Inn* **6** is one large room, but the bareness of the open space is saved by a lot of brass and knick-knacks including a show-case of police hats. Hot lunches and snacks at other times. *The Walnut Tree* **11** is a modern pub. Only *The Three Houses* **10** hasn't recently been hit by the dull pickaxe of modernization. A dining-room and a jovial landlord.

Don't make too much of a detour to see Sandal Castle **15** because there isn't too much to see. This area round Newmillerdam has the garage with the cheapest petrol and the longest hours – the Walnut Filling Station **3**. To get to this area take the first right off the A636 to Wakefield. Then bear immediately left and follow the signs for Crofton on the B6378. Close to the junction are two places selling cheap petrol, a Tyre and Exhaust Centre **4** with useful hours – they claim to have an exhaust for just about any model in stock – and a fish and chip restaurant/take-away **13** which keeps late hours and is locally popular.

The Navigation **12** is a small old-fashioned pub on the Aire and Calder Navigation. Even here modernization in the form of that sixties craze for Fablon has hit every possible surface. But it's a fine pub with well kept beer.

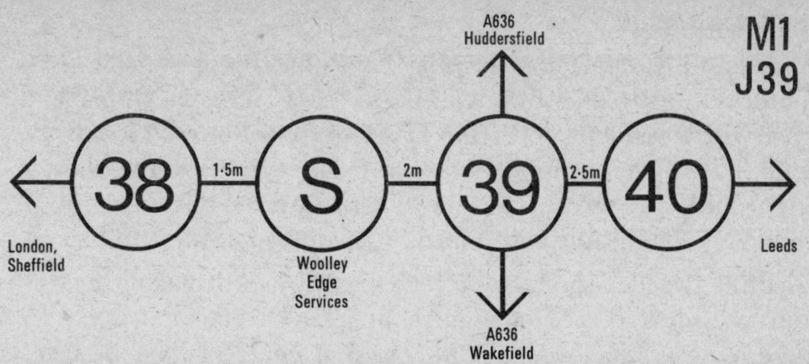

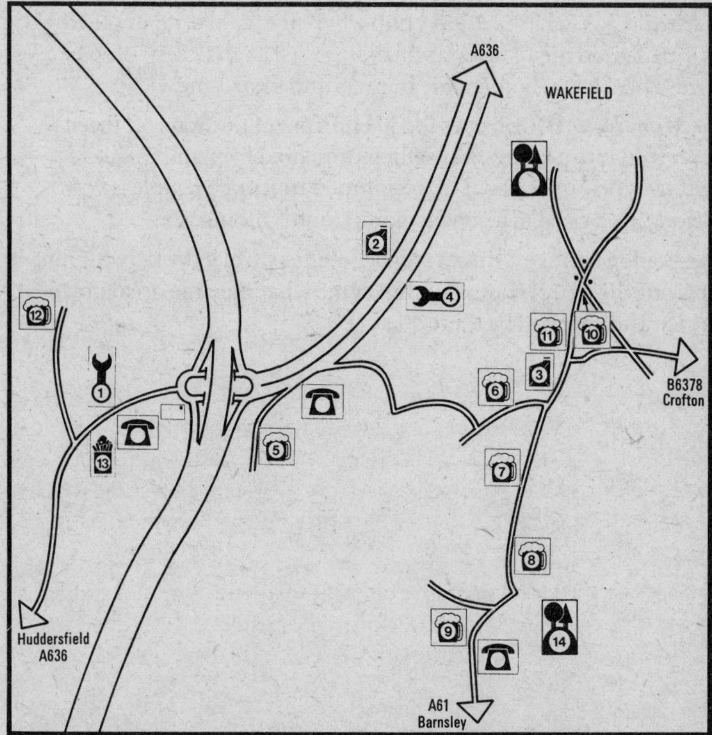

1 Grove Service Station. Hours: 7 am – 7 pm (closes 5 pm Sat, open 9 am – 4 pm Sun) Workshop
2 Grange Service Station. Hours: 8 am – 7.45 pm (closes 6 pm Sat, opens 10 am – 5 pm Sun)
3 Walnut Filling Station. Hours: 7.30 am – 10 pm (opens 9 am Sun)
4 Tyre and Exhaust Centre. Hours: 9 am – 6 pm (10 am – 4 pm Sun)
5 *The New Inn,* Tetley
6 *The Star Inn,* John Smith
7 *The Pledwick Well Inn,* Camerons
8 *The Dam,* Bass Charrington. Restaurant closed Sun and Mon evening
9 *The Fox and Hounds,* Whitbread
10 *The Three Houses,* John Smith. Restaurant
11 *The Walnut Tree,* Tetley
12 *The Navigation,* Tetley
13 *Fish and Chip Café.* Open 8 – 12.15 am
14 Newmillerdam
15 Sandal Castle

petrol/food

A func junc – useful but unexciting. For a quick break from the motorway save money by buying petrol at the Heron **1** – permanently open with a cashier. Food in the THF *Post House* Buttery **11**, open from seven in the morning till eleven at night every day. This short trip would take you no more time than a stop in a service area – it would also be cheaper and, hopefully, slightly more pleasurable.

Gledhill's **2** sells very cheap petrol but hardly worth making the journey unless you needed some shopping in Ossett or unless you were going to have food in *The Red Lion* **5**. A smart (of the stone, fake beam and gas log fire variety) pub where the local up-market crowd go. But a good menu of food which is served at all times – chip butties, corned beef hash, homemade burgers and steak sandwiches.

The Mews Hotel **10** also does food. The front of the hotel has been converted into a lounge bar selling pressured beer and pizzas of various types and sizes. The accommodation for a couple is very reasonably priced in a good looking stone building.

The Bridge Garage **3** might still be selling petrol if the lady running it sorts out the petrol company. But come what may the breakdown service and café will be there.

M1
J40

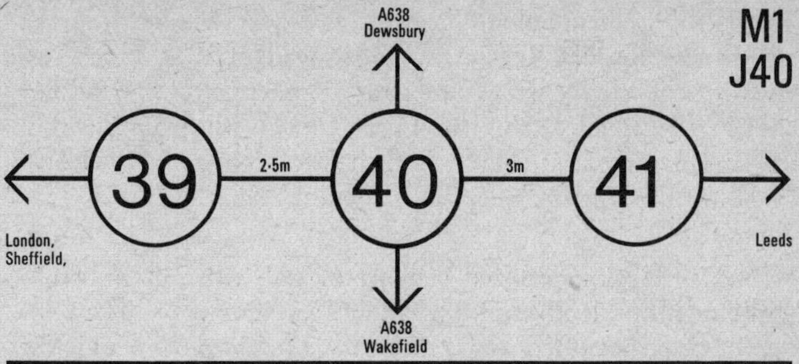

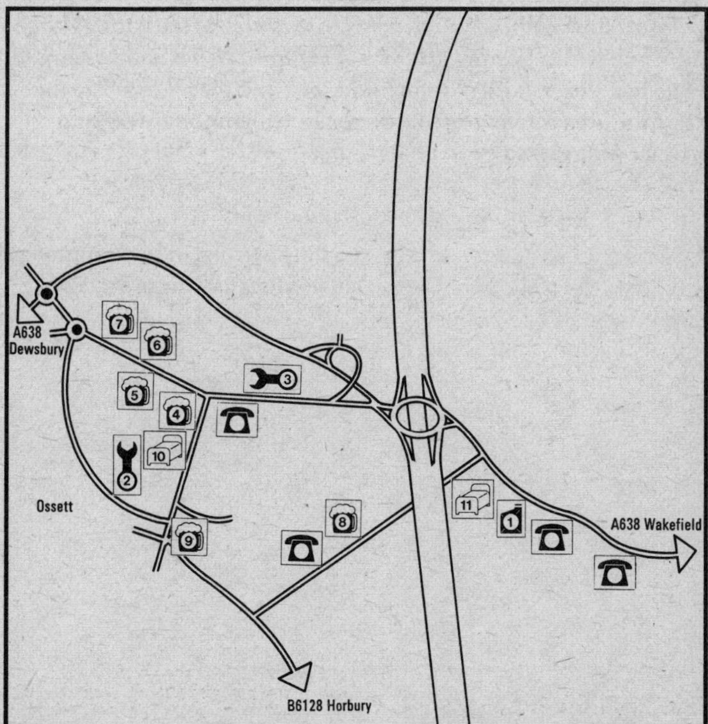

1 Heron Self Service. 24-hr petrol
2 Gledhill's Garage. Hours: 8 am – 7 pm (closes 5 pm Sat, open 9 am – 5 pm Sun). Workshop. Leyland agent
3 Bridge Garage. 24-hr breakdown (Ossett 273368). Transport café open 8 am – 5.30 pm weekdays
4 *The Commercial*, Bass Charrington
5 *The Red Lion*, Watney
6 *The Flying Horse*, Bass Charrington
7 *The Hammer and Stithy*, John Smith
8 *The Two Brewers*, Bass Charrington
9 *The Tawny Owl*, Websters
10 *The Mews Hotel* (Ossett 273982)
11 *Wakefield Post House* (Wakefield 276388)

Not a good or useful junction. The petrol at Glovers **1** is cheap but the hours are none too long. If you are going to head towards Manchester on the M62 consult **J28** if that motorway for other petrol stations. For the M1 south wait for **J40**. Otherwise use Glovers who would also be useful for minor repairs. There are other petrol stations on the A650 but they are all surprisingly expensive – one more so than the motorway.

The Wheel Inn **3** is a modernized, comfortable pub with quite a good range of lunchtime food – scampi, haddock, beefburgers – all for well under £1. Good beer there and good beer at *The Malt Shovel* **4** which is very close to the motorway and has a large garden at the back. A large friendly pub with a leaning to horses. *The Bay Horse* **5** is another large pub and has a beer garden. Lunchtime food and the place where the youth of the area converge in the evening – clutching a corner and each other with glazed eyes.

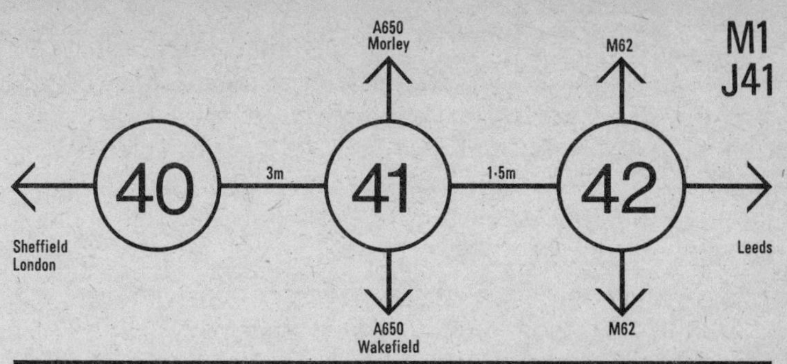

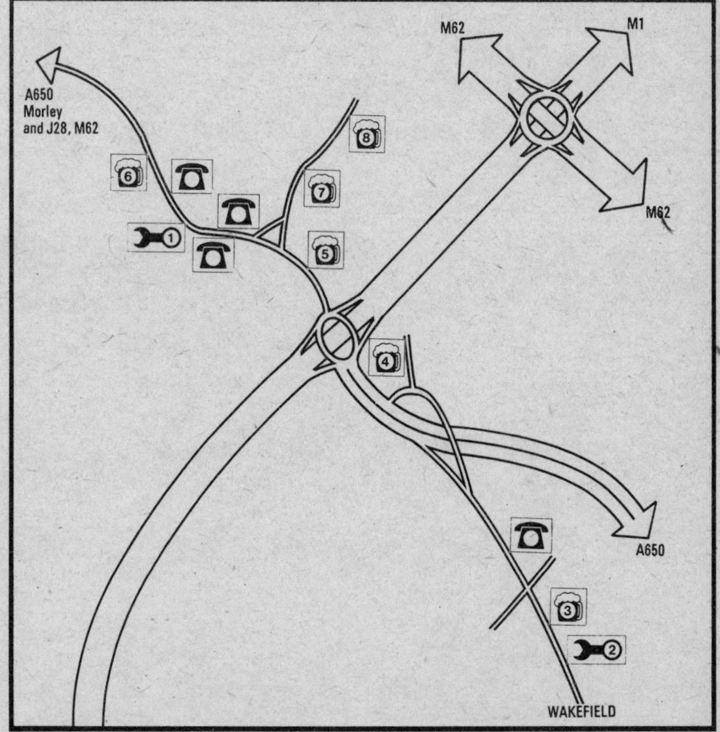

1 Glovers Garage. Hours: 8 am – 7.30 pm (closes 6 pm Sat, open 9 am – 1 pm Sun). Workshop in same hours
2 Special Tyre Services
3 *The Wheel Inn*, Sam Smith
4 *The Malt Shovel*, Bass Charrington
5 *The Bay Horse*, Tetley
6 *The Bulls Head*, Tetley
7 *The Bedford Arms*, John Smith
8 *The White Horse*, Whitbread

M3

Certain junctions are not included: they are either intersections with other motorways, don't exist, or offer no real alternative services. They are listed below.

J1

J2

petrol

Not a particularly inspiring junction but it would be possible to get most things here. First a choice between Lightwater and Bagshot – Lightwater being closer to the junction but Bagshot being the larger place.

All four garages have cheap petrol so if it is just a question of a full tank and a quick break from the motorway, go to the Brandon Service Station **1** and then to *The Red Lion* **8** – or let the kids loose in the small country park **15**. Otherwise take your pick from what Bagshot has to offer.

For those in an elegant frame of mind *The Fox* **6** at Bisley would provide morning coffee; it also has a good lounge bar.

For those of a horticultural frame of mind, it's the trip through Bagshot to Waterer's Garden Centre **16** – acres of plants, a plethora of shrubs and garden goodies galore.

And for those drowning in a sea of Courage repair to *The Half Moon* **9** in the delightful village of Windlesham. Food and snacks on weekday lunchtimes and Badger beer.

1 Brandon Service Station. Hours: 7.30 am – 10 pm. 24-hr breakdown (Bagshot 73060 and 72721)
2 Woodville Motors
3 West End Garage. Hours: 8 am – 9 pm (9 am – 6 pm Sun)

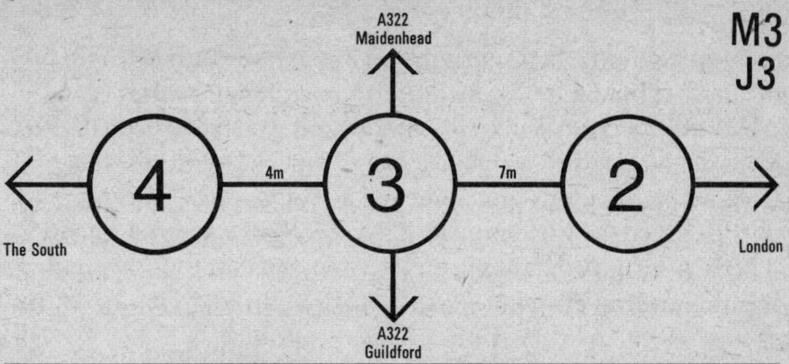

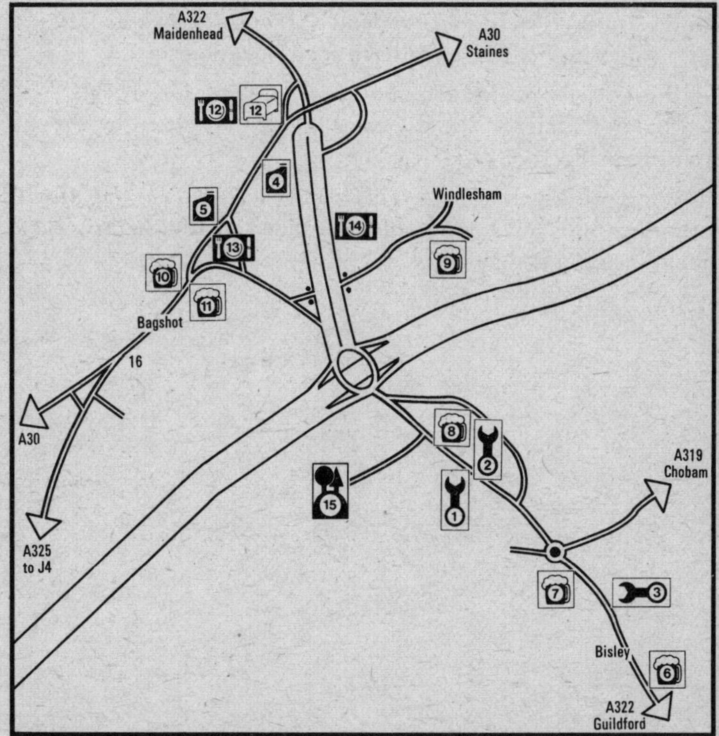

4 Heron. Hours 7 am – 11 pm (8 am – 10 pm Sun)
5 Red Flash Garage. Hours: 8 am – 8 pm (closed Sun)
6 *The Fox Inn*, Courage
7 *The Wheatsheaf*, Courage
8 *The Red Lion*, Courage
9 *The Half Moon*, Free house
10 *The Hero*, Courage
11 *The Fighting Cocks*, Bass Charrington
12 *The Cricketers Inn*. Restaurant (Bagshot 73196)
13 *Bert's Gone Mad*. Transport café and B&B (Bagshot 79193)
14 Tea stalls
15 Country Park
16 Waterer's Garden Centre

petrol

If humans, like cars, lived on petrol all would be well at this desolate spot. Sadly it's not the case. So the recommendation here is cheap petrol at Whites **1** or the Marn Garage **2** and straight back on the motorway. Should you want food and/or a drink in an interesting pub, move on to the next junction. Or you could spin a coin and choose between the various pubs listed. *The Royal Standard* **4** should win because of its proximity to the junction, but for little other reason. Nor is this even an attractive junction to drive around. Camberley is Surrey's answer to urban sprawl, with a vengeance.

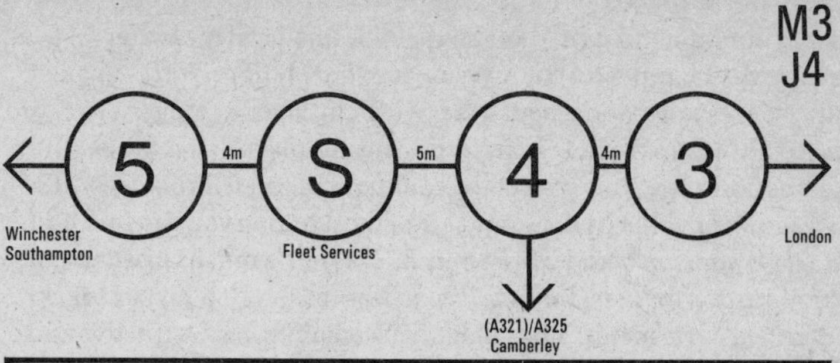

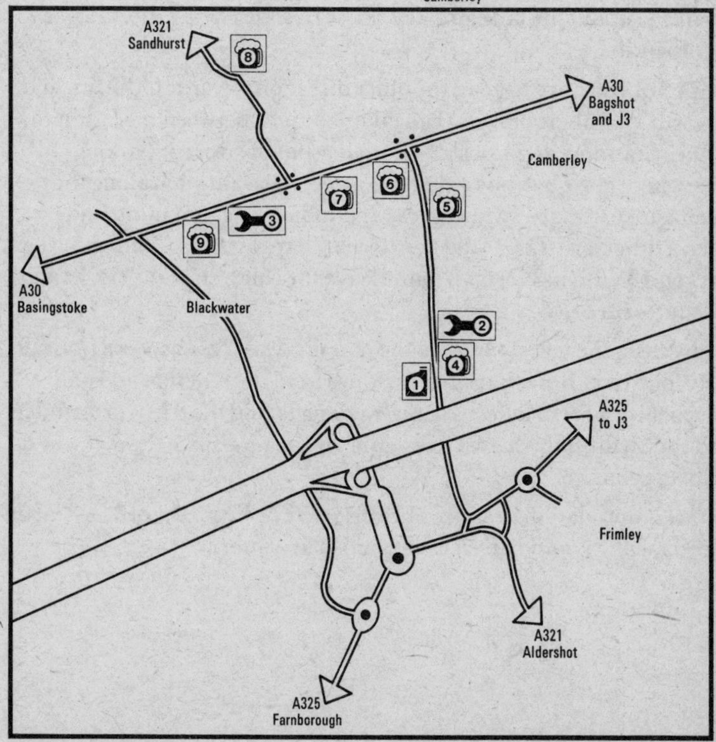

1 Whites Garage. Hours: 7 am – 10 pm (9 am – 9 pm Sun)
2 Marn Garage. Hours: 8 am – 10.30 pm
3 Three Post Boys Garage. Hours: 8 am – 10 pm (8 am – 8 pm Sat, 9 am – 6 pm Sun)
4 *The Royal Standard*, Morland
5 *The William IV*, Courage
6 *The Grand Old Duke of York*, Courage
7 *The Kings Arms*, Courage
8 *The Jolly Farmer*, Courage
9 *The Lamb*, Morland

petrol/pubs/places

A good junction this one – best on the M3 – made all the better because the Hampshire countryside is so fine. If time is on your side and you are exploration-bent, start with a little something in *The Country Style Café* **11**. Bert King, who runs the place, is a mine of information about this part of the country and can tell you more than this page ever will. On the same side of the junction you can find both *The Old White Hart* **6** and *The Phoenix* **8**. *The Hart* is much closer and has a large garden for kids, but *The Phoenix* has the food – both bar snacks and an à la carte menu. The village of Newham is very attractive and worth a visit but the landlord at *The Old House at Home* **7** didn't seem over friendly.

For petrol you have to go in the other direction towards Odiham, and in North Warnborough you can take your pick between the Odiham Service Station **1** and Locks **2** – both reasonably priced. Parking somewhere close by you could have a very pleasant walk along the Basingstoke Canal – swans, geese and rolling English countryside. Then a quickie at *The Anchor* **4**. Alternatively, a visit to Odiham Church **13** with its Norman font. Leave the children in the stocks and drop into *The Bell* **3**.

To my taste the nicest place on the junction was *The Coach and Horses* **9** in Rotherwick. But it is quite a distance from the junction and only gourmets or beer drinkers are really going to find the trip worthwhile. And they will enjoy themselves again and again – since the menu and the beers change.

For accommodation in a nice old inn go to *The Kings Arms* **10**. A hearty breakfast always and an electric blanket in winter.

M3 J5

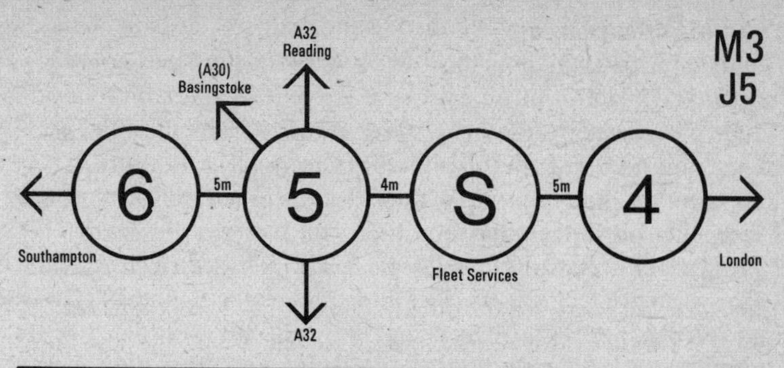

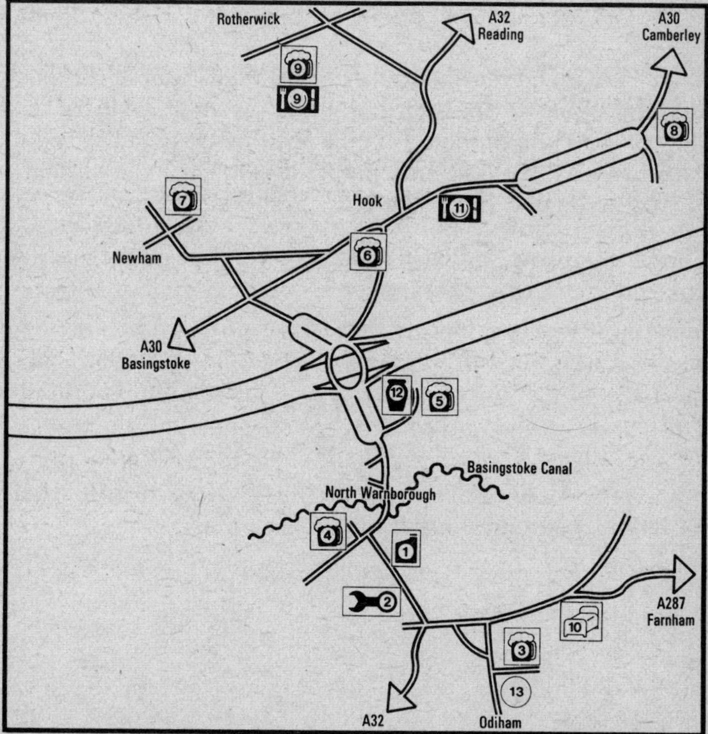

1 Odiham Service Station. Hours: 8 am – 8 pm (opens 9 am Sun)
2 Locks Garage. Hours: 7.30 am – 9 pm (closes 8 pm Sat, open 9 am – 8 pm Sun)
3 *The Bell*, Courage
4 *The Anchor*, Courage
5 *The Lord Derby*, Free house
6 *The Old White Hart*, Morland
7 *The Old House at Home*, Courage
8 *The Phoenix Inn*, Ind Coope
9 *The Coach and Horses*, Free house. Restaurant (Hook 2542)
10 *The Kings Arms*, Watney. (Odiham 2559)
11 *The Country Style Café*
12 Bartley Heath Pottery
13 Odiham church

Neither **J5** nor **J7** are very far distant and both provide better places for eating and drinking. One should also use the junctions towards London for cheap petrol.

There's Basingstoke and Old Basing. The former has a complicated one-way system and serried ranks of geometrically arranged estates. The latter is a pretty but wee town with lanes called Milking Pen and Churn. During the summer months it would certainly be worth having a look at Basing House **5** which is grandly described as a ruin.

Little to choose between the pubs in Old Basing. The local jet set lunch at *The Bolton Arms* **2**. *The Crown* **1** seemed to have the better beer and a decent garden for summer use. *The Hatch* **3** is really only for pub games.

If it's a fine day and you feel like a drive into rural Hampshire then you will not mind driving the five or so miles to *The Swan* **4** in the village of Sherborne St John. Take the A340 towards Reading and then turn left when you see an appropriate sign. There you will find quite a pleasant thatched village pub.

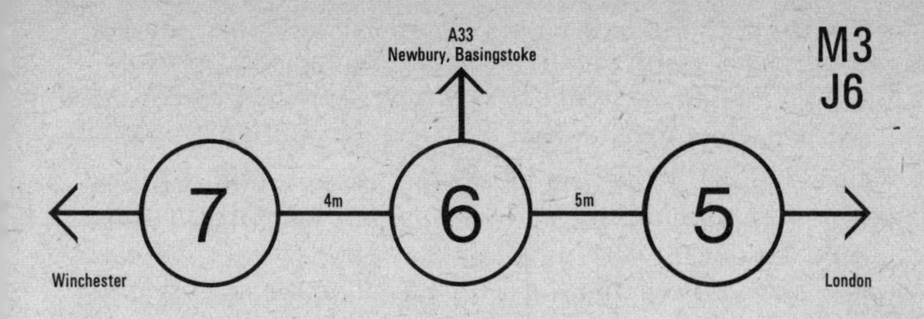

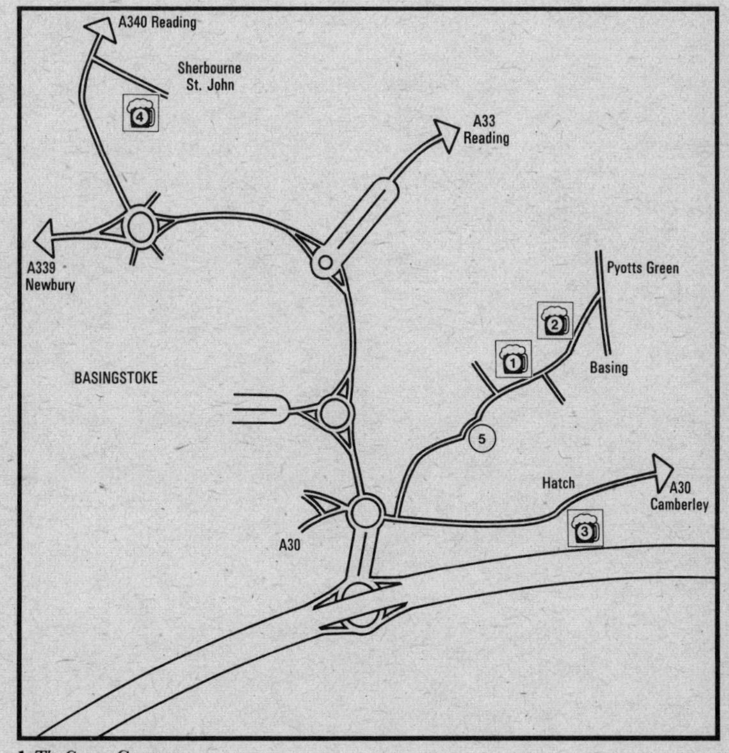

1 *The Crown,* Courage
2 *The Bolton Arms,* Courage
3 *The Hatch,* Courage
4 *The Swan,* Whitbread
5 Basing House. Open March – Sept

pub food

Although only a short distance from the growing sprawl of Basingstoke, the area around this junction is very sparsely populated – which to some extent explains the sparse nature of the offerings . . .

Either *The Fox* **1** or *The Queen* **4** for a drink and some food, *The Queen* having the advantage of being very close to the junction in the small village of Dummer. It has the longer menu, food at lunch and in the evening, and a decent range of beers. Both the other pubs listed also serve food.

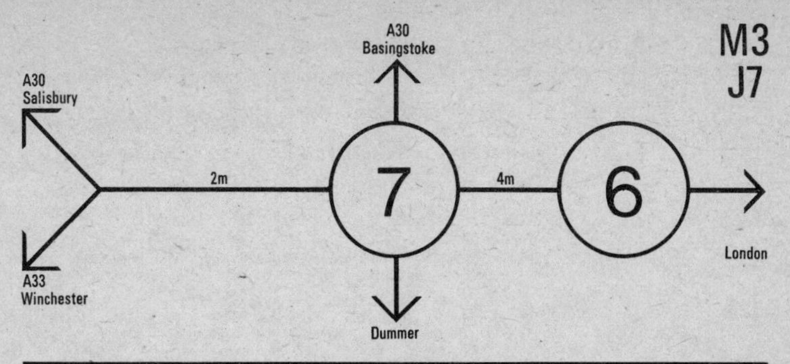

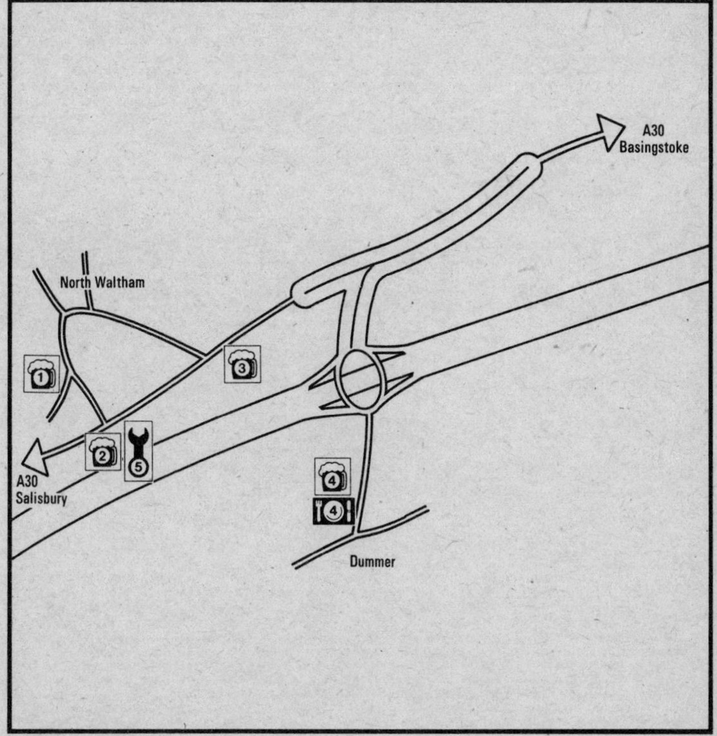

1 *The Fox,* Courage
2 *The Wheatsheaf,* Ind Coope
3 *The Sun,* Courage
4 *The Queen,* Free house. Restaurant (Dummer 367)
5 The Wheatsheaf Garage. Breakdown (Dummer 234)

M4

Certain junctions are not included: they are either intersections with other motorways, don't exist, or they offer no real alternative services. They are listed below.

J10

J19

J20

J23

J1/2
Both these junctions are on the overhead section of the motorway which only has two lanes. Even a minor breakdown on this section causes instant tailback.

So in either direction use the A4 as an alternative; travelling west you can rejoin the motorway at **J3**, **J4** or **J5**; travelling into town, if the traffic is tailbacking to **J3** there is a four-mile jam ahead of you, so get off.

J2 provides an alternative route into London along the Chiswick High Road to Hammersmith. There are a number of cheap garages and decent pubs along this road.

GUIDE TO MAP SYMBOLS

 PETROL

 GARAGE AND BREAKDOWN

 PUB

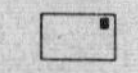 POST OFFICE

 TELEPHONE

 SHOP

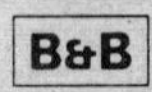

BED AND BREAKFAST

 HOTEL

 PICNIC SPOT

 FISH AND CHIPS

PARKING

RAC

AA

MUSEUM

 RESTAURANT

HOSPITAL

 WINE BAR

 POLICE STATION

 POTTERY

 SWIMMING POOL

petrol

These two junctions are included purely for the purpose of buying petrol and saving money.

If you are heading for London you come off at **J4** and take the A408 towards Uxbridge. At the roundabout which occurs within a hundred yards you take the last turning off which runs parallel to the motorway. On your right is Heathrow Service Station **4**, open 24 hours a day; it will give you a saving of about 8p.

Leaving London and having passed Heston Services, you will have been warned that the next service station is 56 miles. Worse, the M4 is very bad for cheap, convenient petrol, so it would be wise to fill up here. Turn off at **J3**, and take the Hayes road, the A312. At the mini-roundabout turn right. You have a choice of two garages. If you arrive within the right hours go to Keenor Service Station **2**, saving you 12p a gallon. For all hours, the Murco station **1**, and a smaller saving.

It is also quite possible, as the map shows, to leave at one junction and rejoin at the other. The North Hyde Service Station **3** has cheap petrol and carries two AA spanners for its workshop.

Only one of the pubs is at all interesting, and it's the furthest away. *The Queen's Head* **10** serves good beer and homemade food at lunchtimes from Monday to Friday. There is dining space for children, but the pub does tend to get crowded. If you are travelling towards London, or the M4 looks very crowded, or you hear on the radio that a vehicle has broken down on the overhead section, use the A4.

The Crane **7** and *The Victoria* **8** both serve food but the location of *The Grand Junction* **5** and *The Olde Oak Tree* **6**, alongside the Grand Union Canal, is preferable. All the hotels in this area are expensive, but *The Arlington* **11** is cheaper than most. If only they wouldn't write things like: 'After a leisurely drink at the friendly bar, the delights of the restaurant await you.'

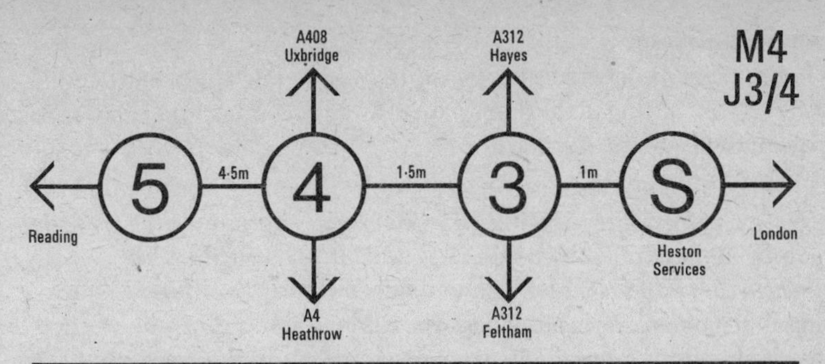

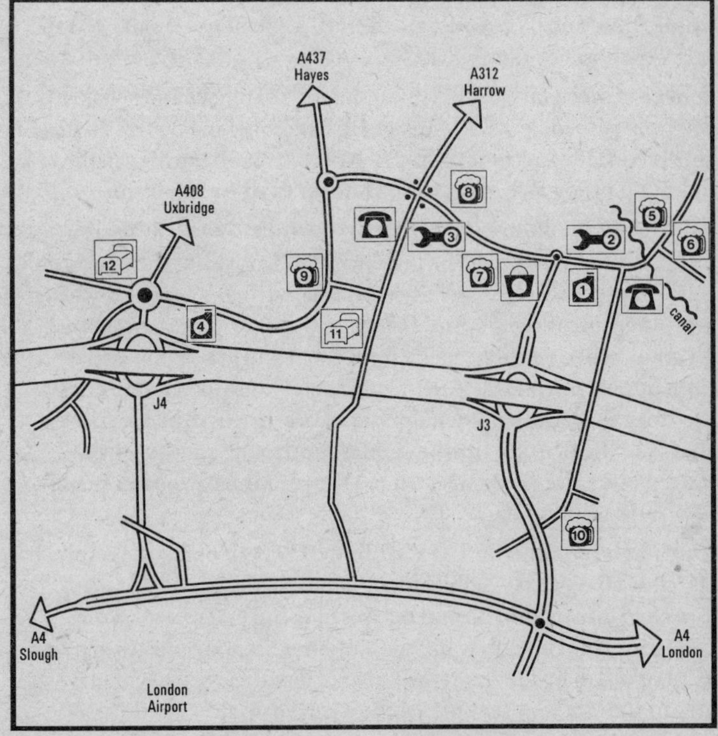

1 Murco Service Station. 24-hr petrol
2 Keenor Service Station. Hours: 7 am – 9 pm (8.30 am – 8.15 pm Sun). Workshop on 5½-day week
3 North Hyde Service Station. Hours: 7 am – 11 pm (8 am – 10 pm Sun). Workshop on 5½-day week. Amex & Diners
4 Heathrow Service Station. 24-hr petrol
5 *Grand Junction*, Watney
6 *The Olde Oak Tree*, Courage
7 *The Crane*, Courage
8 *The Victoria*, Courage
9 *The Great Western*, Ind Coope
10 *The Queens Head*, Fuller
11 *The Arlington Hotel and Restaurant* (01 573 6162)
12 *Holiday Inn* (West Drayton 45555)

petrol/pub food

I have at last discovered a use for piped music – muzak – whatever it is. If you are sitting in the flight path of aircraft coming into Heathrow any diverting noise is good.

Cheap petrol is available at all times at the Heron Service Station **1** after you have doubled round an awkward junction where the road for Colnbrook separates from the A4. Behind the Heron hides *The Ambassador Hotel* **13**, which is functional and pricey for the trade that flies in. In two paragraphs it describes its own restaurant with words like tremendous, unrivalled, devoted, eminently, unique, interesting, intimate, inviting, courteous, wonderful. I hope I never have to eat words like those.

Datchet is a nice place to go. It's on the edge of the Thames, has a reasonably priced hotel, *The Manor* **12**, a nice looking bistro, *La Bougie* **11** and a couple of acceptable pubs. Not the easiest journey in the world but it is possible to get from Datchet to **J6** via Windsor.

The Ostrich **4** in Colnbrook claims to be the third oldest pub in the land. I've come across that particular claim before but the one thing it does allow you to do is overcharge. For instance, the Directors Bitter is 6p a pint more there than at *The Crown* **6**. The menu at *The Ostrich* looks good, with items like fish flake, prawn and grape pie. If that doesn't appeal to your taste then you can have a straight steak and kidney for £1.70. Both homemade, as are the prices. Still you'll probably all flock to see the third oldest pub in the country. I shall probably be at *The Crown* which has a simple range of food, a small garden, and muzak.

One would have thought that a 'clubhouse' overlooking the reservoir at Datchet **16** would be a good idea. A massive expanse of water, planes careering overhead and masses of sheep (therefore no dogs). But there is little room to walk, the clubhouse is none too attractive – open plan plush inside – and the bar staff lose their cool if you dare to point out that they've served you the wrong drink.

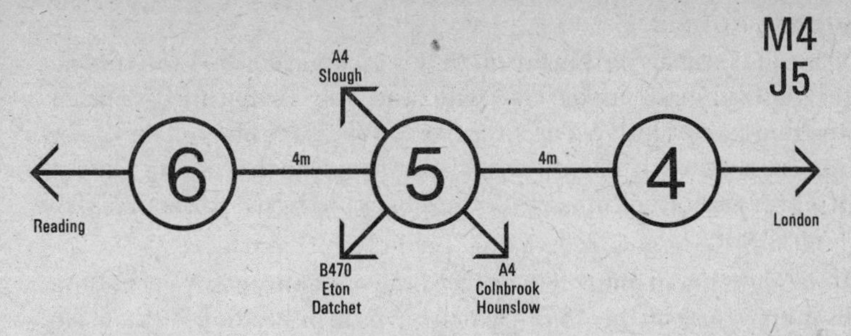

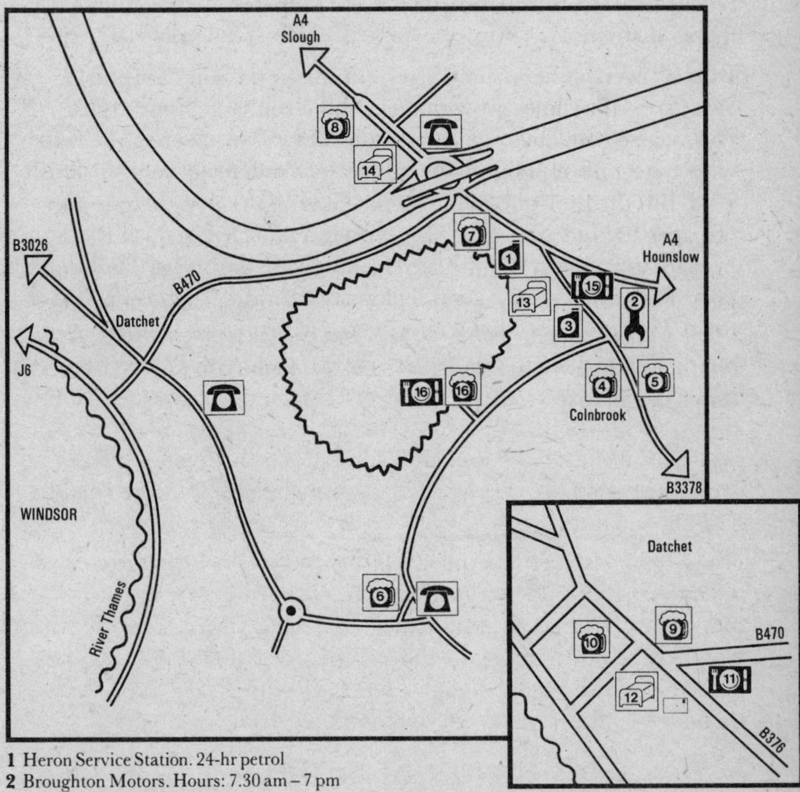

1 Heron Service Station. 24-hr petrol
2 Broughton Motors. Hours: 7.30 am – 7 pm (closes 5 pm Sat, no Sun)
3 Golden Cross Service Station
4 *The Ostrich*, Free house
5 *Ye Olde George*, Courage
6 *The Crown*, Courage
7 *The Plough*, Courage
8 *The Montague Arms*, Courage
9 *The Morning Star*, Courage
10 *The Royal Stag*, Ind Coope
11 *La Bougie Bistro*. Closed Mon (Slough 45428)
12 *The Manor Hotel* (Slough 43442). Restaurant
13 *The Ambassador Hotel* (Colnbrook 4001)
14 *Holiday Inn* (Slough 44244)
15 *Jock's Transport Café*
16 *The Queen Mother Reservoir*. Bar and restaurant

visit

The only reasonable thing to do on this junction is go to Eton, and not just to see the stiff-necked boys with tailcoats. It's an attractive place and one can walk across a footbridge to Windsor – home of the Queen and the public school industry – the only town in the country I know of where restaurants seem to outnumber pubs by five to one. This is Tourist City.

You might find it difficult to believe but you cannot easily get to Eton by going south on the A355 – which seems to be heading for Eton. No, go towards Slough and turn off right at the first roundabout; then follow the signs.

I shan't even bother to list the restaurants or pubs in Eton and Windsor – the choice is enormous – and if you've got time to go there you've also got time to wander around before you choose. The two wine bars, one each side of the bridge, have interesting and cheapish food. But the Eton one gets crowded fast and the Windsor one does not open at lunchtime – at least, the winter lunchtime I was there. Most of the pubs in Windsor sell Courage. By the bridge *The William IV* has bar snacks and a good-looking restaurant. At the other end of town *The Two Brewers* has walls covered with polo and ship life.

Neither of the two garages listed is really cheap – they are marked down just in case.

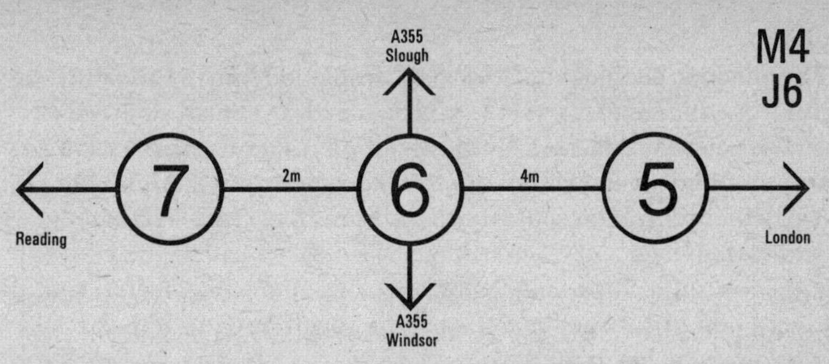

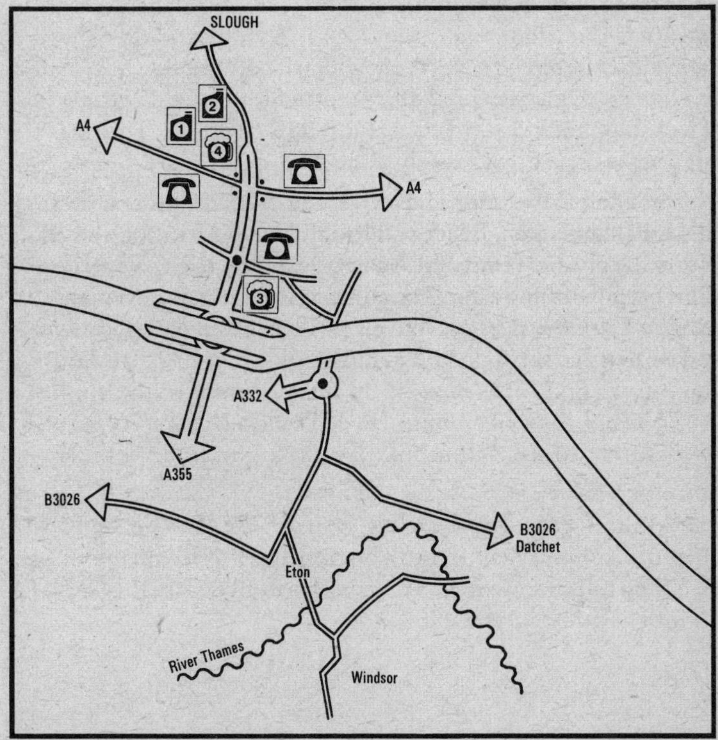

1 Chilton Self Service. Hours: 7 am – 11 pm (8 am – 10 pm Sun)
2 Mamos, Slough Ltd. Hours: 7 am – 11 pm (9 am – 6 pm Sun)
3 *The Flags*, Courage
4 *The Three Tuns*, Courage

visits

This junction should only be used by people with time to waste or children to exercise. Even then, apart from the weather, you need to choose your day. Wednesday is the only day in the week when you can get into the grounds and house at Cliveden **8** – adults 80p, children 40p. While there, you could lunch at *The Feathers* **7** which has draught beer, decent food and some attractive food dishes with invented names – Huntsman's, Coachman's, Cornishman's and, worst of all, Liver Pudd. An attractive setting with a rough garden out the back and some benches at the front.

Cliveden is about four miles away. Closer to the junction and the other side of the motorway is the common land **11** running down to the Thames at Boveney Lock **10**. It is possible to drive down towards the lock, but the land at the end of the road is all private. Park before you turn the corner. It's a lovely place to have a walk.

St James Church **9** is small and interesting. A small part of the church is thought to be Saxon. Inside you'll find a late Norman font, a 17th-century gallery and pews, and some wall paintings. To get there, take the first small turning right, March Lane, after crossing over the motorway. *The Pineapple* **2** is convenient for either of these locations. It has a garden and serves food. But further along the B3026 towards Eton you will find *The Greyhound* **5** up a small turning on the left. Just past *The Grapes* **4** – which claimed to be a 'drinker's paradise' when I was there (cheap beer at lunchtime!) – *The Greyhound* serves bitter from the barrel.

Another Courage pub which sells good beer is *The Oak and Saw* **6** in the village of Taplow. It has a garden but hardly needs it with the village green right outside. Signs for Taplow seem to give out, so just head for the church with the green spire.

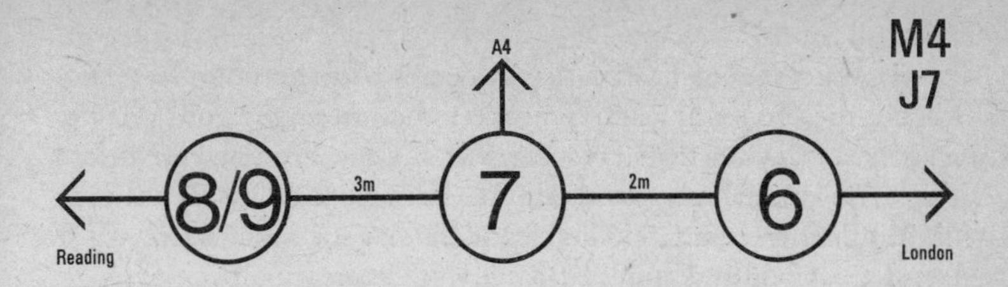

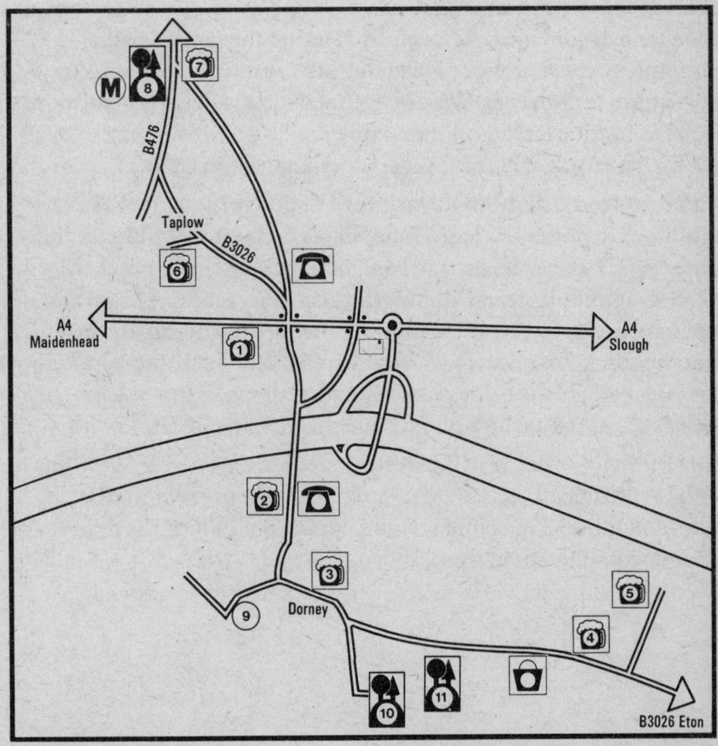

1 *The Horse and Groom,* Courage
2 *The Pineapple,* Ind Coope
3 *The Palmers Arms,* Courage
4 *The Grapes,* Ind Coope
5 *The Greyhound,* Courage
6 *The Oak and Saw,* Courage
7 *The Feathers,* Ind Coope
8 Clivedon. Grounds: Mar – Nov, 11 am – 6.30 pm Wed – Sun. House: Apr – Oct, 2.30 – 5.30 pm Wed, Sat, Sun
9 St James Church
10 Boveney Lock
11 Common Land

pubs/pub food

A great variety of good beer on this junction – proof that those selling to the middle classes, at least, know when they are on to a good thing – and some are cashing in by overcharging. But then the village of Bray is a brazenly opulent place and must have almost the most expensive restaurant in the country, outside London. The cheese board alone will cost you £2.50 as you sit and watch the Thames flow by.

The nicest pub on the junction is *The Belgian Arms* **3** just off the attractive village green in Holyport. It was once called *The Eagle* and had a suitable sign hanging outside. During World War I German POWs greatly annoyed the locals by saluting the symbol of the fatherland every time they passed the pub. So it was renamed after a fierce area of fighting. *The Belgian Arms* sells good beer and good food. There is a garden for kids in the summer.

The Crown **8** in Bray also sells real ale (Theakstons from the barrel) and decent food – slightly expensive with cottage pie at one pound. Quite a nice conversion with a number of seating areas and a dining area as well. Further down the road, another modernized pub, *The Ringers* **9**, with Fullers and Courage on draught. A fire, open on two sides, looks good but seems to provide little heat. And still further down the road, *The Hinds Head Hotel* **10**, which has a restaurant. The most attractive of the three pubs and the most expensive – their Theakstons is at least 5p a pint too much. No bar food.

While the price of petrol at Sawfords **1** seemed reasonable and while it is right at the end of the A308(M) spur you have to drive another half a mile along the A308 before you can double back along the dual carriageway. Pity about that.

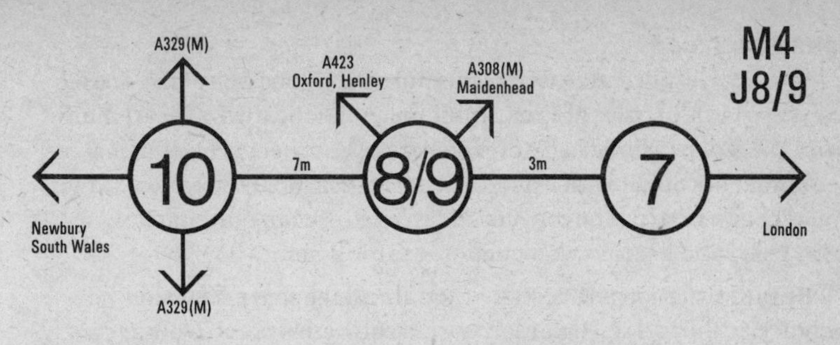

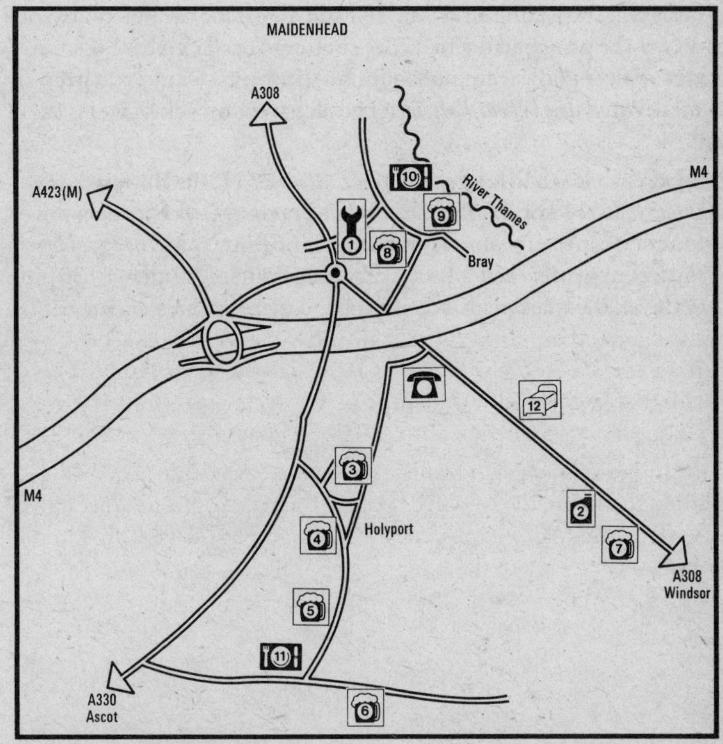

1 Sawfords. Hours: 8.30 am – 6 pm (8.30 am – 1 pm Sat, closed Sun). 24-hr breakdown (Maidenhead, day 20724, night 27762)

2 Queens Head Filling Station. Hours: 7.30 am – 9 pm (8 am – 6 pm Sat, opens 9 am Sun)

3 *The Belgian Arms*, Brakspear

4 *The George*, Courage

5 *The White Hart*, Morland

6 *The Rising Sun*, Morland

7 *The Queens Head*, Ind Coope

8 *The Crown*, Courage

9 *The Ringers*, Free house

10 *The Hind's Head Hotel Restaurant* (Maidenhead 26151)

11 *The Wheel of Fortune Restaurant*

12 *The Clericus Hotel* (Maidenhead 20004)

petrol

The City Garage **1** is extremely useful on this long petrol-dry stretch of the M4. A quarter of a mile from the junction; always open for any quantity of petrol; a cashier ready to take you money; no messing about at midnight with a note acceptor which doesn't really want to; and cheap petrol. The other garages listed are not quite as cheap as the City, and keep nowhere near the same hours.

The pub situation is different – they are all the same. You have no choice as they all sell Courage, and to rub in this point, Courage are building a giant new beer factory **10** right alongside the junction. Nor are any of the pubs particularly nice. Better to use **J12** where there is greater variety and decent pub food. But if you just want a rest from the motorway, *The Wheatsheaf* **7**, very much a country pub, seems the best.

For food you can choose between the *Little Chef* **11**, the Buttery in *The Post House Hotel* **14** or *The Black and White Transport Café* **12**, depending on your tastes. All are fairly convenient. The Buttery at *The Post House* is the most expensive but it keeps very long hours, 7.30 am – 10.30 pm, every day of the week. The food is OK and there is a kids' menu.

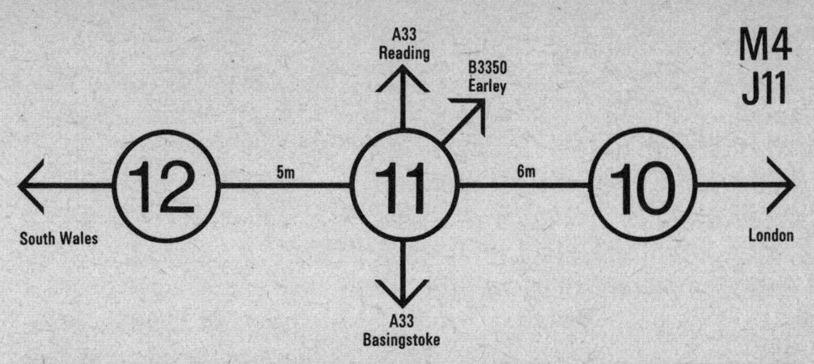

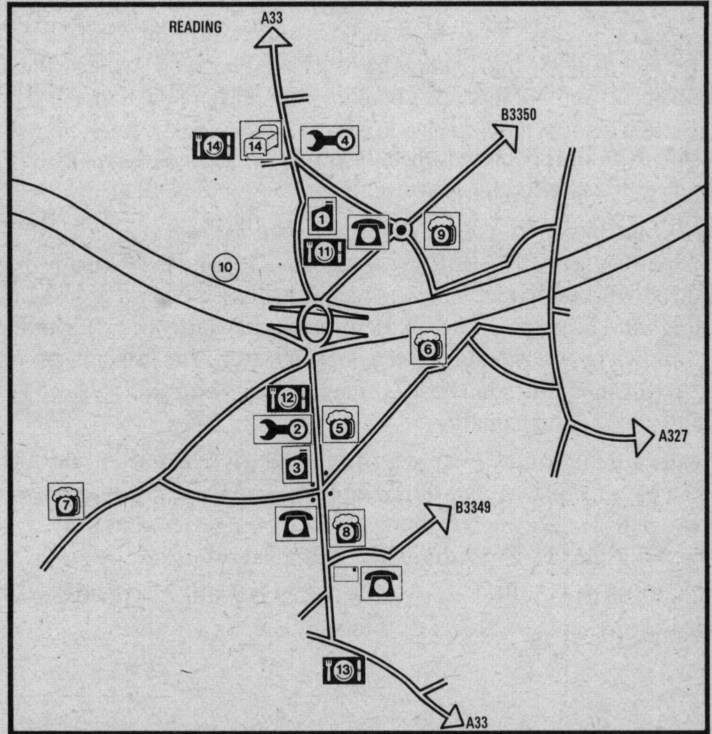

1 City Garage. 24-hr petrol with cashier
2 Hearn Brothers. Hours: 7.30 am – 8 pm (9 am – 8 pm Sun). Workshop on 5½-day week
3 Roman Road Service Station. Hours: 7 am – 10 pm (8 am – 9 pm Sun). 24-hr petrol machine
4 Whitley Wood Garage
5 *The Swan*, Courage
6 *The Six Bells*, Courage
7 *The Wheatsheaf*, Courage
8 *The Farriers Arms*, Courage
9 *The Engineers Arms*, Courage
10 *The Berkshire Brewery*, Courage
11 *Little Chef*
12 *Black and White Transport Café*
13 *Millhouse Restaurant*
14 *The Post House Hotel* (Reading 85485)

food/pub food/petrol

It has to be some variation of Sod's Law that more often than not the good places are furthest from the junction. In this case, the cheapest petrol, at Southcote Service Station **2**, the nicest pub location, *The Cunning Man* **6**, and the most interesting pub food, at *The Hatchgate Inn* **7** are all distant and take you on a longish journey – first on the **A4** towards Reading and then through the village of Burghfield, rejoining the motorway through the town of Theale.

The Cunning Man, with its very large garden, sits on the edge of the Kennet and Avon Canal. It serves above average pub food at all times – soup, sandwiches and salads – and there is a restaurant selling steaks and fish. *The Hatchgate Inn* also has a restaurant which, like the inn itself, is small. It only takes bookings but the bar food is more than acceptable – soup, pâté, steak and trout. Get there early. Real Ale hopheads would no doubt retire to *The Six Bells* **8** across the road – a simple pub which has basket food.

The Fox and Hounds **9** advertises itself as having a dozen great English and Scottish beers. The word great is not one I would use for many of the products but that's a matter of taste and at least they have draught Youngs and Marstons. The bar menu is long and fairly fried. Some of the sandwiches, reasonably priced, looked tasty – tuna fish or liver pâté with onion. But somehow *The Fox* seemed to be trying to offer quantity rather than quality.

Theale, although it is very close to the junction is by-passed by the A4 so you have to follow a slightly circuitous route to hit the town centre. Cheap petrol at *The Merlin* **3** and quite a range of restaurants and pubs. *The Falcon* **11** serves draught beer and large lunches.

One spin off from Sod's Law is that not everyone will take time off to go to the nicest places: therefore they won't get too crowded.

1 Penta Motors. Hours: 7.30 am – 7 pm (shorter at weekend)
2 Southcote Service Station. 24-hr petrol, cashier service. 24-hr breakdown (Reading 586425)
3 Merlin Service Station. Hours: 8 am – 8.30 pm (shorter at weekend)

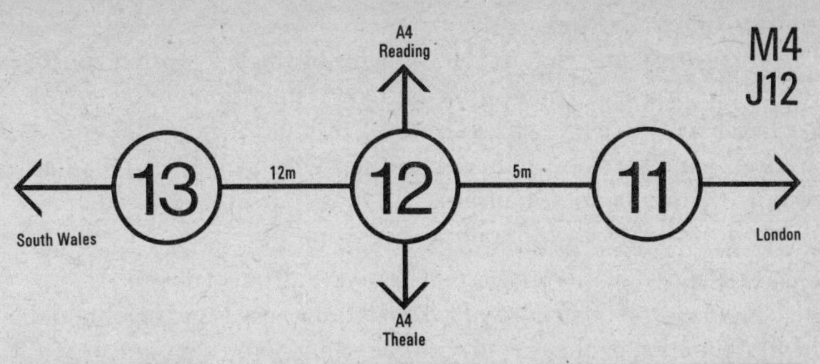

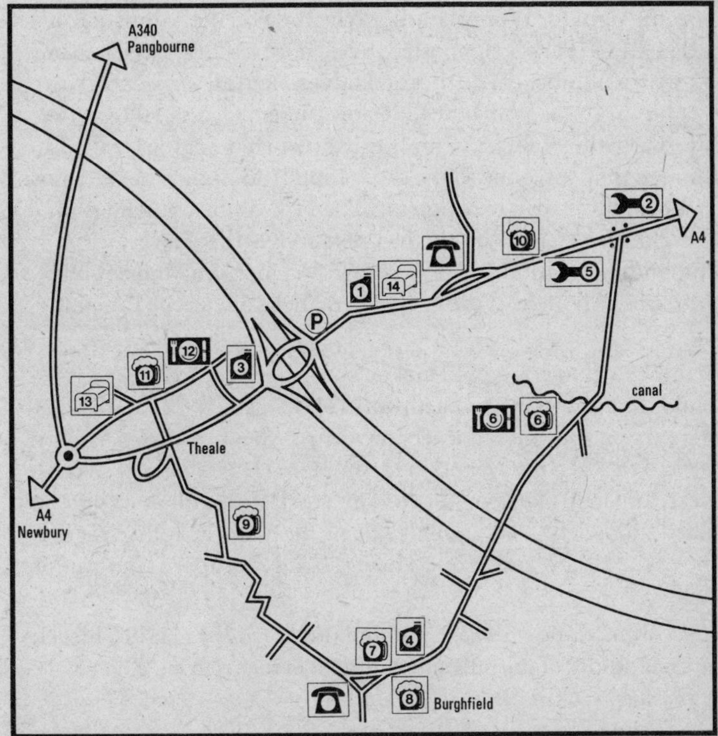

4 Hatchgate Service Garage. Hours: 8 am–6 pm (closed Sun)
5 Horncastle Garage. 24-hr breakdown (Reading 412021)
6 *The Cunning Man*, Courage. Restaurant
7 *The Hatchgate Inn*, Courage (Burghfield Common 2059)
8 *The Six Bells*, Courage
9 *The Fox and Hounds*, Free house. Restaurant
10 *The Travellers Friend*, Ind Coope
11 *The Falcon*, Courage
12 *The Wheel of Fortune Restaurant* (Reading 302756)
13 *The Old Lamb Motel and Restaurant*. Evenings only (Reading 302357)
14 *The Calcot Hotel and Restaurant*. Restaurant closed Sun (Reading 27297)

picnic/visit/pub food

The villages of Chieveley and Hermitage both have a Morland pub and a Free House. All four pubs have food at most times but only *The Red Lion* **5** in Chieveley, which also has a restaurant, can cater for children – and then only if they are eating. The town of Newbury has, of course, a number of restaurants and snack bars. It also has the usual one-way system and traffic congestion.

The three nicest places on this junction were all out of doors. Snelsmore Common Country Park **10** is quite easy to get to, although the first junction off the A34 towards Newbury looks complex. Just follow the signs for Winterbourne. When you hit the T-junction on the B4494, the Park is signposted. Snelsmore is a large, well laid out park with a number of benches and tables – and all surrounded by silver birch. It was from here that Government forces in the Civil War made one of their many attempts to capture Donnington Castle **11**. Although they surrounded the castle from 1643–6 and knocked most of it down, they failed to capture it. The 14th-century gatehouse and some of the best Civil War earthworks survive. It has a very commanding position and is worth a visit. Open at all times, and guides can be bought at the Post Office when you turn off the main road.

It is unlikely that you would make a special journey to the woods around the almost hidden earthworks of Grimsbury Castle **12**. The woods are private but it is a very nice spot if you were taking a bite at *The Fox* **4** or *The White Horse* **3** in Hermitage. *The Fox* has a wide range of beer, and food like homemade game soup, ham with pineapple and toasted sandwiches. For a small village, the petrol at both garages is quite cheap, Black and White **3** being slightly cheaper at the time of visit.

For accommodation first ask the landlord of *The Red Lion* in Chieveley. The ex-landlord of the pub has a number of rooms to let. Then try *The Donnington Castle* **9**.

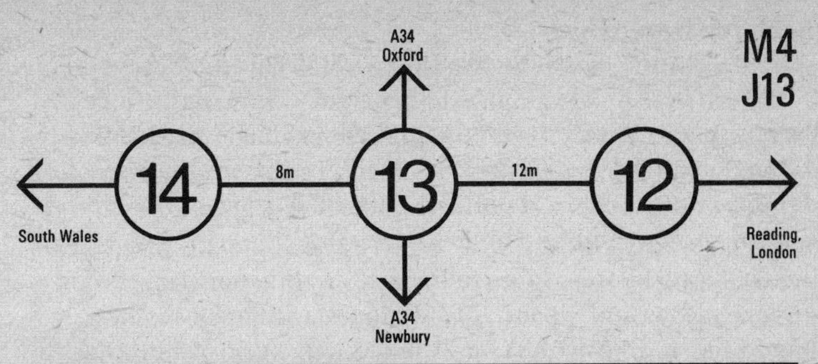

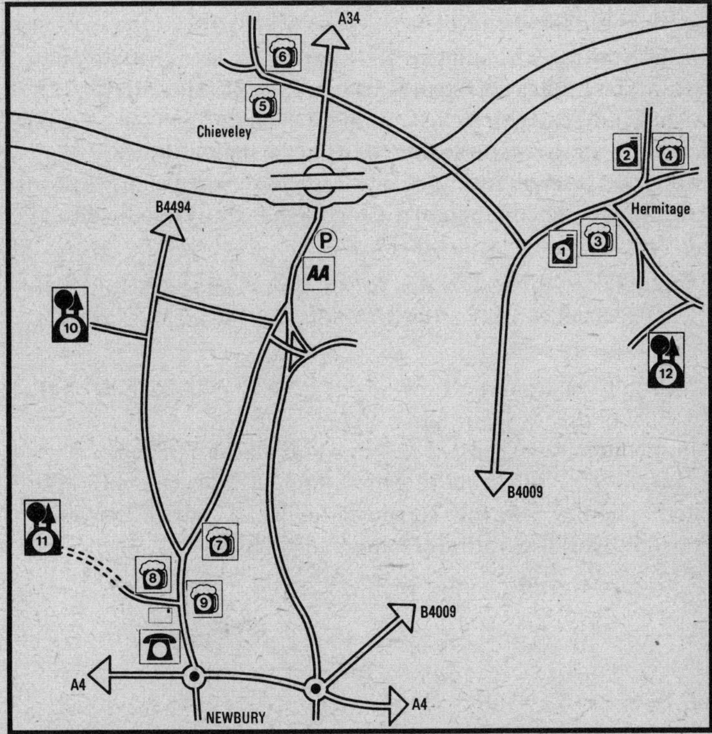

1 A and B Motors. Hours: 7.30 am – 6 pm (closes 4 pm Sat, 1 pm Sun)
2 Black and White Garages. Hours 8 am – 7 pm (closes 5 pm Sat, no Sun)
3 *The White Horse,* Morland
4 *The Fox,* Free house
5 *Ye Olde Red Lion,* Free house. Restaurant closed Sun
6 *The Wheatsheaf,* Morland
7 *The Fox and Hounds,* Courage
8 *The Three Horseshoes,* Watney
9 *The Donnington Castle,* Whitbread. B&B
10 Snelsmore Common Country Park
11 Donnington Castle
12 Grimsbury Castle Woods

pub food/pubs

Oh Carol, I know you wanted me to find you a cheap garage on this junction. There isn't one – in fact, they seem to be in competition to keep prices up. But then everything on this junction is expensive. Hungerford appears to me to be the Mecca for Americans in search of antiques. But you know about the local wealth anyway.

And a further apology to you, a drinker *manquée*, the only places I can find on this junction are pubs selling real ale. But they also sell food – interesting food and expensive food. Almost within sight of the junction is *The Pheasant* **1**. A small dining area, a dish of the day and a place for kids. Both beer and food a bit pricey.

Two miles north of the junction in the opposite direction to the one you want is the village of Great Shefford. *The Swan* **2** is a nicely furnished pub selling draught Courage, including Directors. A good snack menu and a restaurant overlooking the shallow River Lambourne. It serves fresh lobster – fresh from the cellar anyway – at prices an American might find reasonable. You can take me there any time.

In Wickham you can try *The Five Bells* **4**. Game soup with chili sherry followed by Kennet trout or boeuf Wellington. I wonder if anyone takes chili sherry neat?

On the route you want, to Hungerford, is *The Tally Ho* **3** where, and this is further useless information for you, children can be accommodated to eat the more normal pub snacks. But you must visit *The Bear Hotel* **5**. Not too many of these kinds of old-fashioned hotels left in the country. Someone somewhere will have plans to convert it into an olde worlde paradise of some golden age.

PS Get your petrol at **J11**, any time.

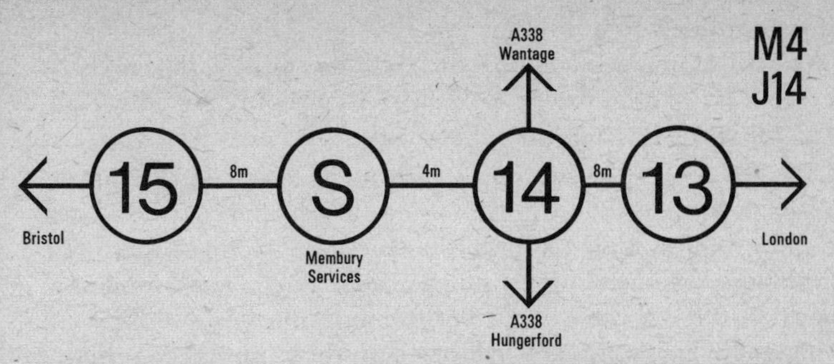

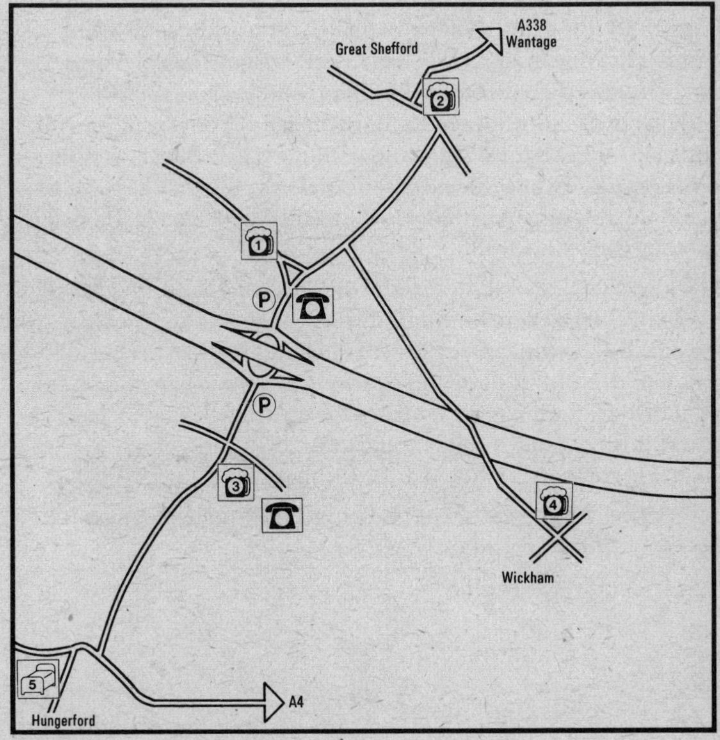

1 *The Pheasant*, Arkells
2 *The Swan*, Courage. Restaurant (Great Shefford 271)
3 *The Tally Ho*, Wadworth
4 *The Five Bells*, Ushers
5 *The Bear Hotel*, Free house

picnic spots/pubs

Not too good a junction. If you are heading for Bristol wait for **J16**; if towards London, and depending on what you want, wait for alternatives.

Barbury Castle **13** is worth a visit on a fine day but it is five miles away. An ancient earthwork with good views of the surrounding land. A more recently man-made spot for a break is Coate Water **12**. It's just about two miles from the junction in the direction of Swindon and you pass the only cheapish garage hereabouts on the way – the Coate Garage **1** which seems to provide most services.

Almost your first sight of Coate Water is a tattered Union Jack fluttering bravely from a finely shaped, all-concrete, thirties diving board. As you climb the embankment around the lake you realize that the diving boards are not connected to dry land. Your suspicions are confirmed by a notice saying that swimming is forbidden. All rather strange, as is the work of some poseur who has dotted the landscape with boulders – some with holes through them. Still you might find it a nice place to have a walk.

There are a lot of pubs dotted round the area but none are convenient or special. However on the B4507 through Wanborough there are two pubs which serve lunches during the week and draught beer at all times. Children are allowed to eat at *The Black Horse* **3** and there is a garden. Down the hill is the thatched *Plough* **4** which has omelettes, soused herrings, stuffed peppers and a dish of the day, all at reasonable prices. You should drink the Bass here.

Another *Plough* **7** serves draught bitter and is close enough to the junction to allow one a quick break.

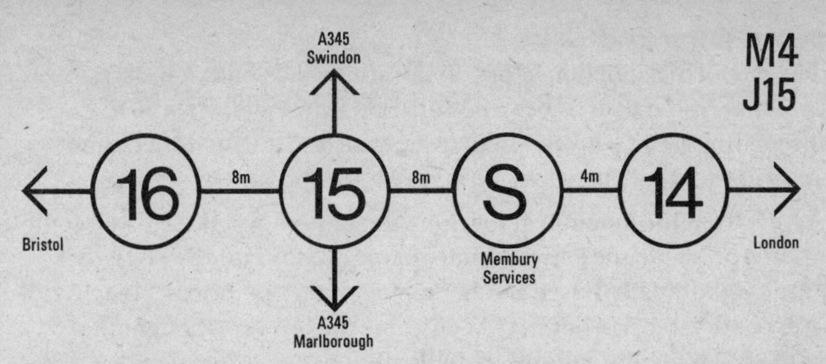

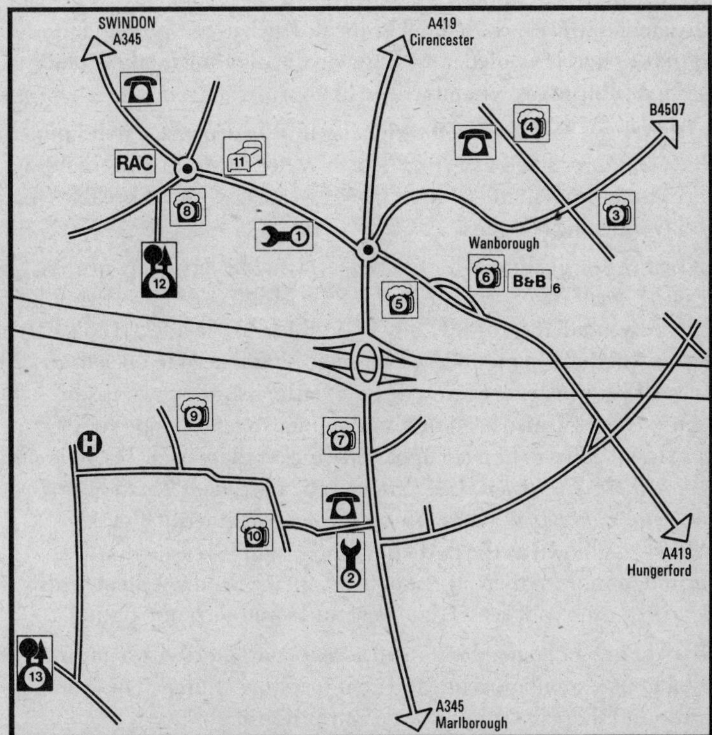

1 Coate Garage. Hours: 8 am – 8 pm (9 am – 8 pm Sun, open till 12 pm Sat and all summer). 24-hr breakdown (Swindon, day 25783, night 27733)
2 Chiseldon Service Station. Hours: 7 am – 9 pm (opens later Sat, Sun)
3 *The Black Horse*, Arkells
4 *The Plough*, Whitbread
5 *The Sun*, Courage
6 *The Bell Inn*, Whitbread. B&B
7 *The Plough*, Arkells
8 *The Sun Inn*, Arkells
9 *The Calley Arms*, Wadworth
10 *The Patriots Arms*, Courage
11 *The Post House* (Swindon 24601)
12 Coate Water
13 Barbury Castle Country Park

petrol/pubs/food/visit

The fate of this junction hangs on the ability of Wootton Bassett to provide. And it does – cheap petrol, 24 hour breakdown, cafés, interesting pubs, a lovely small restaurant and adequate overnight accommodation but, sorry, no luxury hotels or motels.

A mile from the junction in the direction of Wootton Bassett you come upon a pub with the extraordinary name of *Sally Pussy* **3**. The lady's name was actually Pusey and her picture hangs in the bar – black dress and Victorian bonnet. At one time the brewery thought the name wasn't really suitable so, with great imagination, they rechristened it *The Wheatsheaf*. The locals stuck to the 'proper' name and that's what it's called now. Extensive rebuilding is taking place so it is impossible to say what it will be like.

You then pass *The Churchill* **9** which has nine bedrooms, a swimming pool, a restaurant and a parrot. A lot crowded into one small building but reasonable enough – although it was a struggle to get breakfast on Sunday morning.

Just before you get into Wootton Bassett you are very likely to miss *The Loaves and Fishes* **8** – it's just before the Mobil petrol station on the left. A very small restaurant, only four tables, in a lovely old house. It also has the shortest menu I've ever seen. You'll need to book in any case, so if your tastes are limited you'd better ask about what's cooking. You will also need time and money to really enjoy yourself. But in town you will find cheaper and quicker places like *The Magnolia Restaurant* **10**, *The Crown Hotel Restaurant* **6**, *The Chilton Tea Room* or *The Bamboo Inn*. *The Borough Arms* **4** is certainly worth a visit. Try the public bar – known as the potty bar for the simple reason that a hundred or more of them are hanging from the beams. You may also care to examine your seat. Good beer and some accommodation.

Lydiard Park **12** is smashing – 140 acres of parkland with a nature trail, a house, small museum and an interesting church. The grounds are free and there is a small charge for the house.

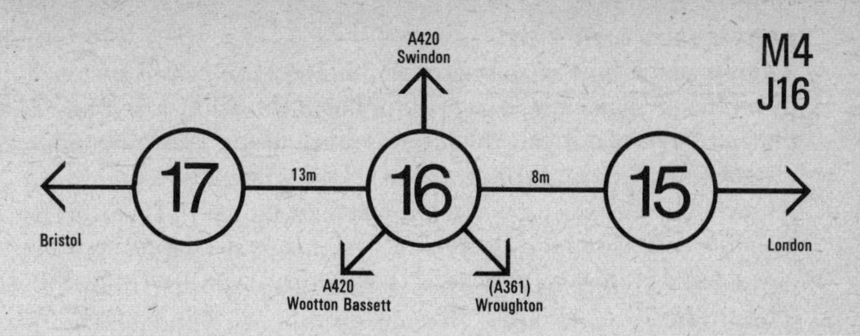

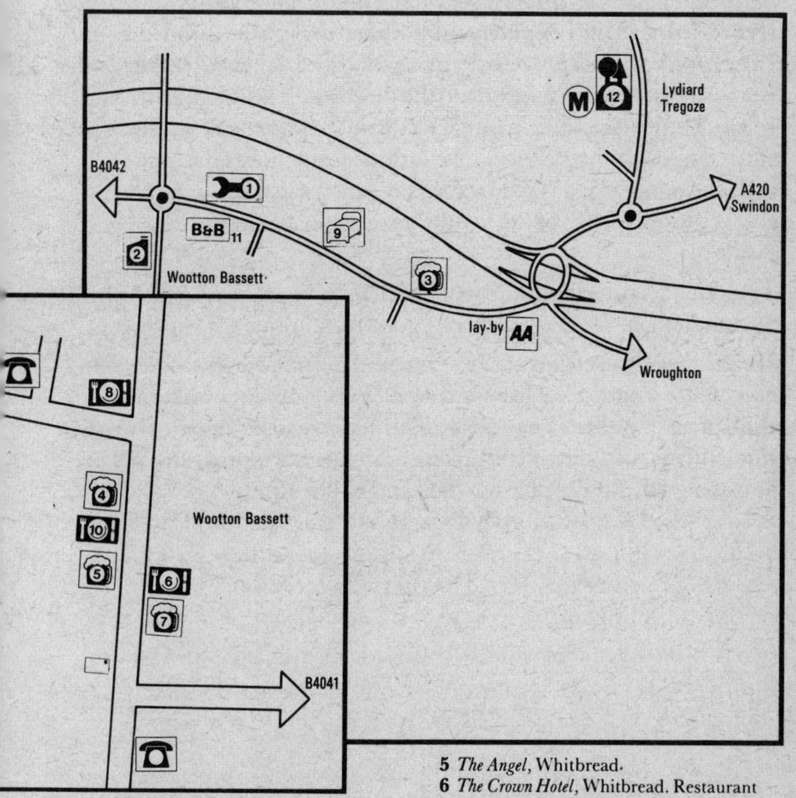

1 Coped Hall Service Station. Hours: 7 am – 9 pm. 24-hr breakdown (day Wootton Bassett 2755, night Swindon 29175). Café hours: 7.30 am – 4.30 pm (closed Sun)
2 Showmeades Service Station. Hours: 7 am – 11 pm (8 am – 10 pm Sun)
3 *The Sally Pussy,* Arkells
4 *The Borough Arms,* Arkells. B&B (Wootton Bassett 2252)
5 *The Angel,* Whitbread.
6 *The Crown Hotel,* Whitbread. Restaurant
7 *The Cross Keys,* Whitbread
8 *The Loaves and Fishes Restaurant.* Dinner Tues – Sat, Sun lunch (Wootton Bassett 3597)
9 *The Churchill Guest House and Restaurant* (Wootton Bassett 2867)
10 *The Magnolia Restaurant*
11 *Fairview.* B&B
12 Lydiard Park. House: 10 am – 1 pm, 2 pm – 5.30 pm (Sun afternoon only)

pubs

This is an awkward, strung-out junction and can only be recommended for a break from the motorway for a quick half-pint and a snack. None of the convenient garages are cheap. The Corston **1** gives some saving and appears to be helpful with minor running repairs. The Wiltshire **2** on the Chippenham by-pass is cheap but over four miles from the junction. Other garages in Chippenham are cheap but it is only worth making that journey if you need other things from the town.

Sutton Benger is an interesting small village. The two pubs there, *The Wellesley Arms* **3** and *The Vintage* **4** both sell draught Wadworths. Everything about *The Wellesley* looks solid and dependable – from the shape and size of the building to the pub sign. It sells light snacks. It was at *The Vintage,* long before it was a pub, that the Fry family first started making their chocolates. A stone upstairs has the date 1729 with the name Fry. Harveys of Bristol later used the building as a sherry store and two of the 'vaults' are now in use for the pub. Food is available.

The small, comfortable and expensive *Bell House Hotel* **7** is also in Sutton Benger. It is said to have a good restaurant.

The Jolly Huntsman **6** has the best range of pub food and would make a good place to stop for a light lunch; they sell draught Ushers and Whitbread PA. *The Plough* **5** is a plain country pub. Close to it are two small picnic areas either side of the main road. The forest walk **9** at Stanton Park is quite nice but parking is difficult.

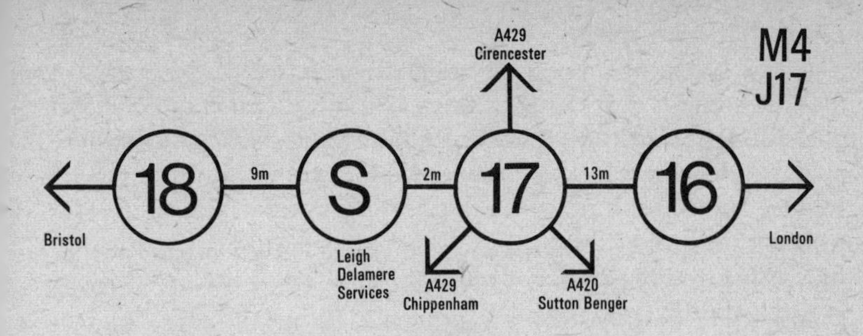

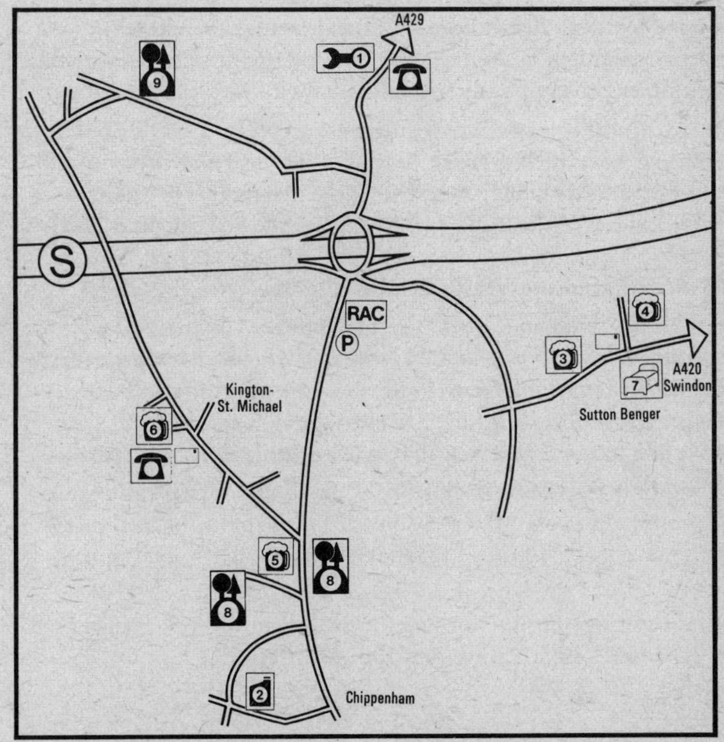

1 Corston Garage. Hours: 8 am – 7.30 pm (closes 7 pm Sun). Workshop in normal hours. Ford dealer
2 Wiltshire Garage. 24-hr petrol machine. Toyota agent
3 *The Wellesley Arms*, Wadworth
4 *The Vintage*, Wadworth
5 *The Plough*, Ushers
6 *The Jolly Huntsman*, Free house
7 *The Bell House Hotel* (Seagry 720401)
8 Picnic areas with toilets
9 Stanton Park Forest Walk

food/visits/overnight

A good junction for almost everything except petrol, but you will have to travel some distance for most things. Strictly the junction belongs to Wadworths for the beer and Boots for the land – their pension fund owns much to the south, and who would believe that looking at the rolling countryside?

Both garages listed give you a fair saving on motorway prices and the Blue Star can arrange a breakdown service. For convenient pub food choose either *The Compass* **5** or *The Crown* **3**. The menu at *The Compass* is longer and more varied but its beer is more expensive. *The Crown* serves homemade steak and kidney or cottage pie for under a pound. Both can cater for children; *The Compass*, with a nice garden, would be the summer choice and it's also a nice place to stay.

The prize for the longest bar-menu goes to *The Dog* **6** in Old Sodbury. Snails in garlic, chicken curry, paella . . . The beer is on pressure and time will be needed, but it could be a deserved treat. There is a restaurant as well with kids' prices. Also in Old Sodbury and a bit difficult to find is *Dornden House* B&B **10** – a fine old house which would be a decent and reasonable place to stay.

On a fine day Dyreham Deer Park **11** should be visited – 220 acres of beautiful National Trust land. There is a charge for that and an extra charge to visit the house with its lovely period furniture. It's worth going just to see the smashing driveway. And there's a church with interesting tombs, brasses, wall plaques and tiles.

Dodington Park **12** is very close to the junction. You will need time and money, and possibly a good day, to fully explore the possibilities of this place. Over 700 acres of land once handled by Capability Brown.

My favourite on the junction was the homemade chocolate cake from *The Tollgate Café* **9**. Erratic hours but worth a try.

1 Blue Star Garage. Hours: 8 am – 6 pm (closed Sun, in summer open till 9 pm including Sun). Breakdown service (Chipping Sodbury 312044)
2 Jones Brothers. Hours: 8 am – 6 pm (half-day Sat, closed Sun). Peugeot agents

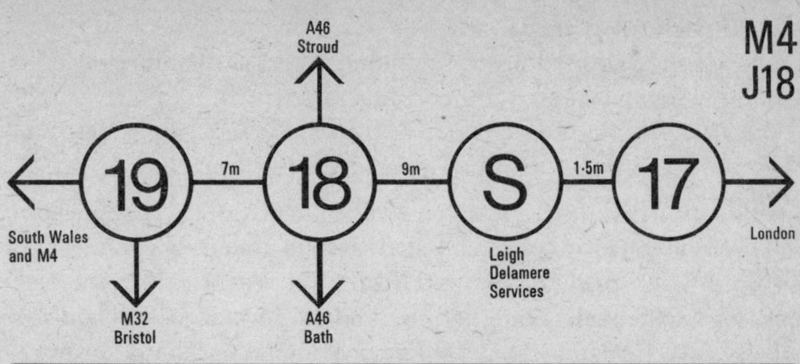

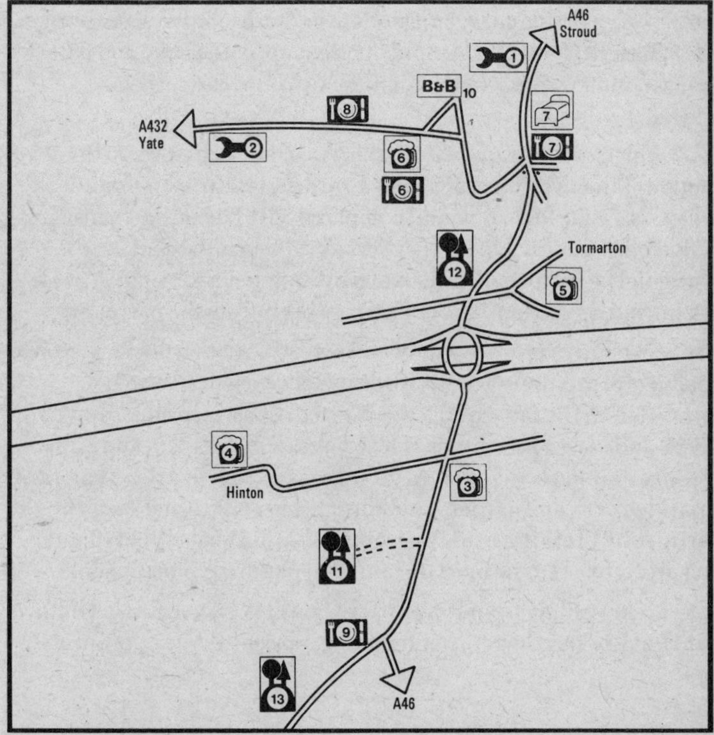

3 *The Crown*, Wadworth
4 *The Bull*, Wadworth
5 *The Compass Inn*, Free house. B&B (Badminton 242)
6 *The Dog Inn and Restaurant* (Chipping Sodbury 312006)
7 *The Crosshands Hotel and Restaurant* (Chipping Sodbury 313000)
8 *La Capanna Restaurant* (Chipping Sodbury 318604)
9 *The Tollgate Café*
10 *Dornden House*. B&B (Chipping Sodbury 313325)
11 Dyrham Park. Park: May – Sep, 11 am – 6 pm. House: June – Sep, 2 – 6 pm (also in Apr – May except Mon, Tues)
12 Dodington Park. Hours: 11 am – 6.30 pm
13 Picnic spot

petrol/breakdown/pub food

You have a very clear choice at this junction – you either turn off for Aust Services or you make other arrangements.

On petrol you can save 8p a gallon by going to the Forge **1**, or Pilning Garage **3**. But Pilning is three miles away and it would not be worth travelling that distance unless there were other offerings. The garage itself provides all forms of mechanical services, toilets, telephone, tea ('as required'), a general store and B&B. Across the road is *The Cross Hands Inn* **6** which sells draught bitter and the normal choice of pub grub. Slightly further away is *The Plough* **5** but it is worth the journey. Before you get to the garage turn left over the disused railway bridge and then right. It has cheap homemade soup, cottage pie and pâté amongst other things. Neither of these two pubs can cater for children.

A pub which can, *The Boar's Head* **4** in Aust, is much closer to the junction. It has a dining room and a garden. It also offers you a seafood pancake for one pound compared with bacon, egg, sausage and baked beans for 99p at Aust Services. I found the choice surprisingly easy to make. Then there was homemade soup, herring with mustard sauce and so on. Courage beers from the barrel.

Aust Service area is drab, windy and spread out but it does give you a good view of the ailing Severn Bridge. Good views can also be obtained from the three picnic spots listed. Once boats ran from the Old **10** and New **11** Passages. The bridge replaced them and both areas are now fairly derelict. At New Passage there is a dead hotel and its parking area and garden can be used. There is a firing range nearby – the times are listed on a noticeboard. Whale Wharf **9** is the most attractive but the most distant, and parking is a bit difficult.

If you are travelling from Wales to the South West you can get onto the M5 at **J17** by going through Pilning. So consult the appropriate page.

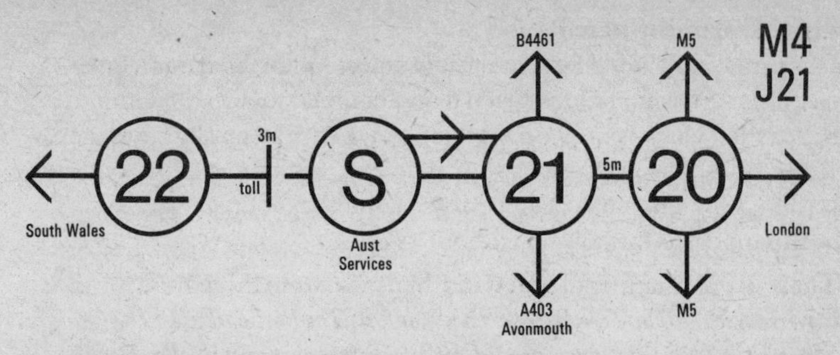

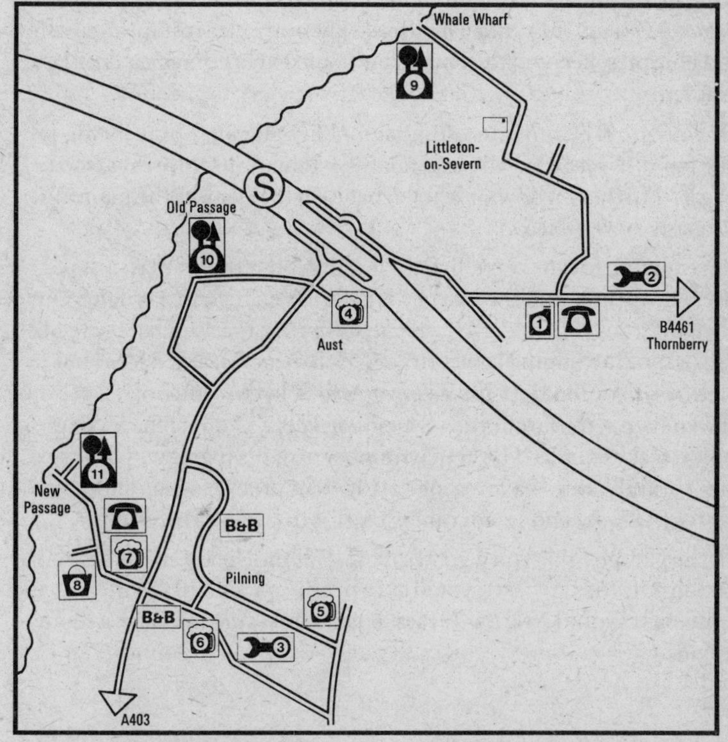

1 Forge Service Station. Hours: 8.30 am – 6.30 pm (until 12 noon Sun). Tyre service
2 Tockington Service and Repair Station. 24-hr breakdown (Thornberry, day 414670, night 414812)
3 Pilning Garage. Hours: 8 am – 8 pm. 24-hr breakdown (day Pilning 2909, night Thornberry 412402)
4 *The Boars Head*, Courage
5 *The Plough*, Wadworth
6 *The Cross Hands Inn*, Courage
7 *The Kings Arms*, Courage
8 Redwick Stores
9 Whale Wharf
10 Old Passage
11 New Passage

visit/overnight/petrol

Chepstow is a walled city, much of it still standing, and has a fine castle **1**. A Norman lord started it and his great tower still dominates the castle, which is built on a narrow ridge with steep cliffs into the River Wye. The reason why the castle survives in such good condition is that, although it has been besieged a number of times, the occupants usually gave up without a fight.

There are all manner of hotels in Chepstow, from three stars downwards – *The Two Rivers, The Beaufort, The Portwall* and *The George* **10**, which I found reasonable. Cheaper places would be *The Castle Guest House* and *The Castle View Hotel*. There are also restaurants, cafés and chippies, keeping the hours you would expect. Parking is little problem.

The Five Alls **6** has an interesting sign: 'I fight for all, I pray for all, I rule for all, I plead for all', and finally, a John Bull figure says, 'I pay for all.' Further on down the town beneath the castle is the plain and pleasant *Three Tuns* **5**.

Shirenewton means travelling for five miles but there are two interesting pubs and the journey is pleasant enough in daylight. On the B4325 you will find *The Carpenters Arms* **9**, a nicely decorated pub with a separate dining room, draught Wadworths, and decent but slightly pricey food. At *The Tredegar Arms* **8**, in the centre of Shirenewton, the landlord, a Scotsman, keeps 54 out of the 55 single malt whiskys made. The actual number of malts is greater because some brand names have a range of different proofs and ages. But don't ask for a whisky and . . . for others there is draught Sam Smiths.

All the garages give you a good saving. But the cheapest, the Jet station **4**, is the furthest – you'd save over 12p a gallon. On the way to it you pass the old *New Inn* **7**. Pies, pasties, pressure beer and a room for kids.

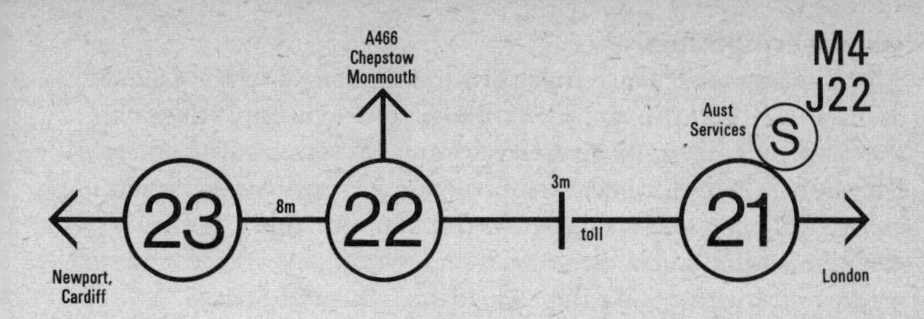

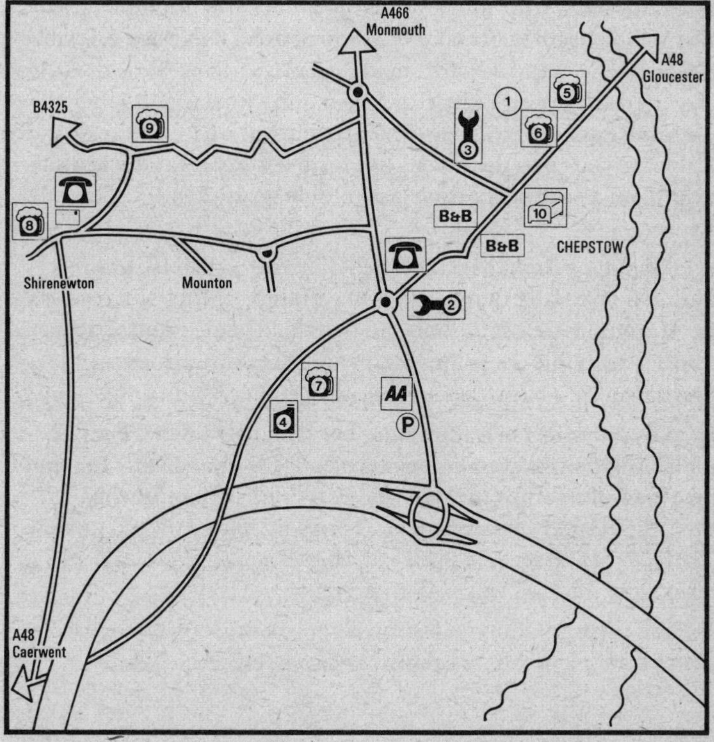

1 The Castle
2 Larkfield Garage. Hours: 8 am – 10 pm. Breakdown during normal workshop hours (Chepstow 3641). Ford dealer
3 Chepstow Service Station. Petrol hours: 8.30 am – 6 pm (till 5 pm on Sat, no Sun). 24-hr breakdown (Chepstow 2674). Leyland dealer
4 Jet Filling Station. Hours: 7 am – 9 pm (opens 9 am Sun).
5 *Ye Olde Three Tuns*, Whitbread
6 *The Five Alls*, Whitbread
7 *The New Inn*, Free house
8 *The Tredegar Arms*, Free house
9 *The Carpenters Arms*, Free house
10 *The George Hotel* (Chepstow 2365)

almost everything

J24 is very good; and Caerleon is really the place to head for. **J25** is included so that you can save a few miles by leaving or joining at a different junction if you go to Caerleon. A few negatives: do not go to Newport, which is either still suffering from World War II or, just possibly, the planners; do not take the A449 – there are no U-turns for 20 miles (this useful information is provided once you are committed to the road!); do not take the A455 to the Industrial Area.

So go to Caerleon. From **J24** follow the A48 towards Newport; after half a mile turn right before *The Royal Oak* pub. A short distance beyond the pub on the main road is the Talberth Service Station **3** – many services provided and very cheap petrol. *The Neptune* **4**, further on, is similarly cheap. On the small road to Caerleon, going down the hill, you pass *The Kings Arms* **5**, a decent pub with draught bitter. The restaurant has an interesting looking menu but is a touch expensive. Just before you cross the River Usk you find *The Ship* **6**. Chicken and scampi, but also canelloni and lasagne; not on weekend evenings, however.

In Caerleon the Romans established a fortress, called Isca, with a legion of men to keep down the unruly Silurians. Much still remains. The Amphitheatre **15**, the only one of its kind in the country, is open at most reasonable hours for a few pence. There are also excavations of the barracks, a bath, and a free museum.

There are a number of restaurants. The definitely pricey *Priory* **12** which has a short and good-looking menu. *The Copper Kettle* **11** should prove to be more convenient, particularly with children. It has longish hours and a longish menu. Take your pick of the pubs in town – *The White Hart* **8** seemed to have the best beer. *The Hanbury Arms* **7**, overlooking the Usk, was a good cheap place to stay.

The Holy Trinity Church **16** is interesting because of its modernized interior – after a fire. A Norman doorway and lovely tower.

1 Lynwood Garage and Taylors Transport Café. Hours: 5.30 am – 9.30 pm (closes 7 pm Sat, Sun)

2 Hillcroft Garage. 24-hr breakdown (day, Llanwern 2040, night, Magor 521). Workshop during normal hours

3 Talberth Service Station. Petrol hours: 7 am – 11 pm. 24-hr breakdown (Newport, day 271967, night 45300). Ford dealer

4 Neptune Service Station. Hours: 7 am – 10 pm (7 am – 9 pm Sun)

5 *The Kings Arms*, Bass Charrington. Restaurant

6 *The Ship*, Courage

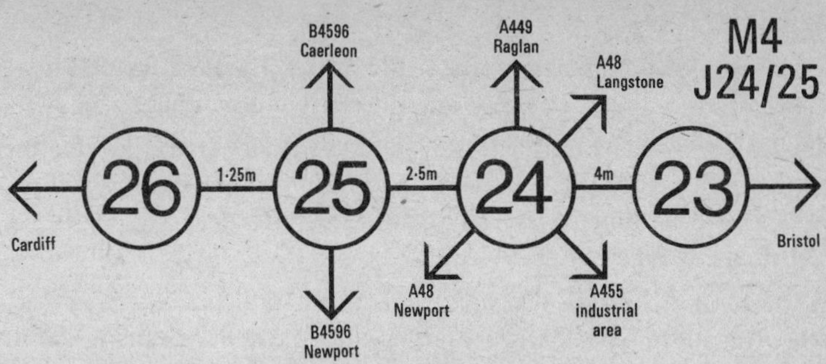

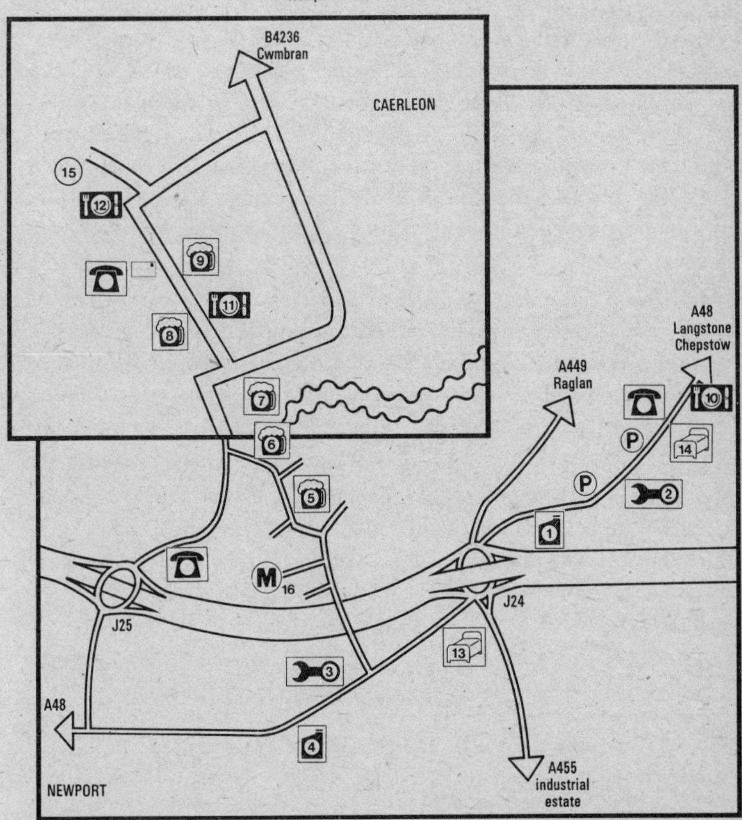

7 *The Hanbury Arms*, Bass Charrington. B&B (Caerleon 420361)
8 *The White Hart*, Courage
9 *The Bull*, Ansells
10 *The Forresters Arms and Restaurant*
11 *The Copper Kettle Restaurant*. 9 am-ish to 10 pm-ish (closed Sun) (Caerleon 420653)
12 *The Priory Hotel and Restaurant* (Caerleon 421241)
13 *The Gateway Motor Motel* (Llanwern 2777)
14 *The New Inn Motel* (Llanwern 2426). Also 24-hr petrol machine
15 Caerleon Roman Amphitheatre
16 Holy Trinity Church, Christchurch

J26 don't

If travelling towards Bristol wait for **J25** or **J24**. If travelling towards Cardiff you should have used one of the previous junctions.

But cheap petrol is available on this junction. All four garages offer a saving of at least 12p on motorway prices. The cheapest garage is the one closest to the junction, Cyril Rogers' **1**, but it is on the wrong side of the dual carriageway.

The Greenhouse **6**, at some distance from the junction, is a large and fairly pleasant pub. It has a very large walled garden with swings, and a long food menu.

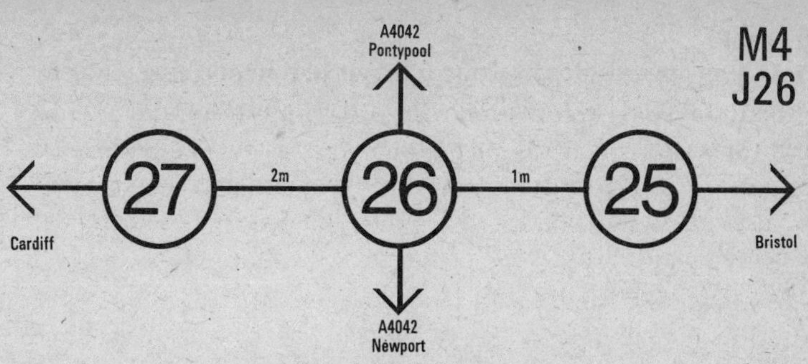

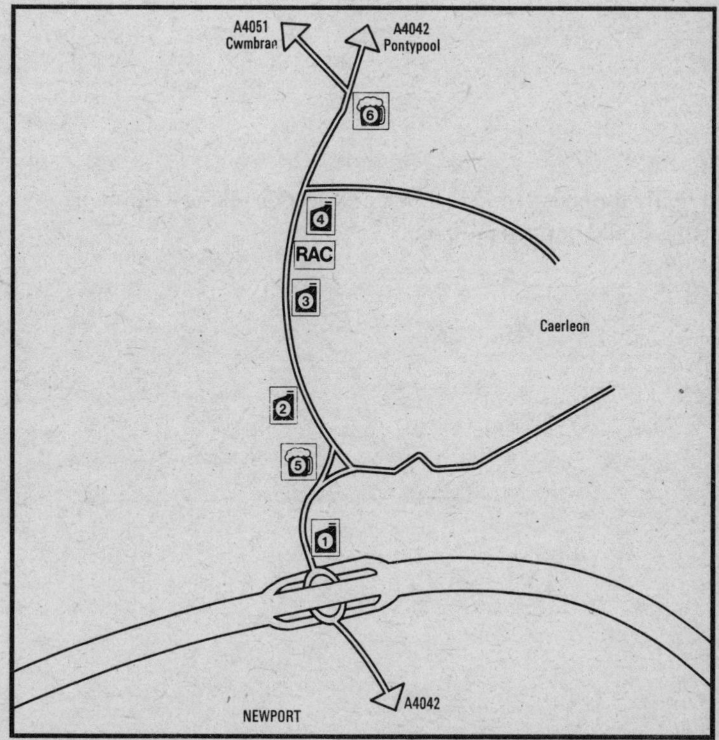

1 Cyril Rodgers' Garage. Hours: 7.30 am – 8 pm (shorter at weekends)
2 Redcastle Service Station. Fiat and Vauxhall agents
3 Malpas Service Station
4 Llantarnam Service Station
5 *The Borderer*, Courage
6 *The Greenhouse*, Courage

J27 don't

There are both garages and pubs on the A467 towards Risca, but without travelling over two miles the petrol isn't cheap and the pubs aren't special.

J28

Currently the end of the M4, but a new section taking it through to Cardiff should be open in 1978.

GUIDE TO MAP SYMBOLS

 PETROL

 GARAGE AND BREAKDOWN

 PUB

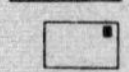 POST OFFICE

 TELEPHONE

 SHOP

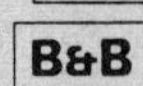

BED AND BREAKFAST

 HOTEL

 PICNIC SPOT

 FISH AND CHIPS

PARKING

RAC

AA

MUSEUM

 RESTAURANT

HOSPITAL

 WINE BAR

 POLICE STATION

 POTTERY

 SWIMMING POOL

M5

Certain junctions are not included: they are either intersections with other motorways, don't exist, or offer no real alternative services. They are listed below.

J8

J12

J15

petrol/visit (pub and restaurant)

Somebody said that the only good thing about Birmingham is that they built two motorways over the city to help you avoid it. Pity then that these stretches of motorway seem to be falling to pieces.

And it is true that there is very little to be conveniently found off these urban junctions, just endless miles of dual carriageways that all look the same. Birmingham seems to have devoted the post-war period to building tower blocks and a comprehensive road system. It would seem that they got it all wrong, except that the roads are clearly needed to cope with the vast number of heavy lorries rumbling around.

Sane advice on this junction would be not to use it. Yet there are two places worth finding, *The Manor House* **6**, and Sandwell Valley Park **8**. In both cases you stand a good chance of getting lost particularly in trying to find *The Manor House* because the planners have decided that a remarkable number of roads are going to be called the A4031. And most of these so named take you in the wrong direction – to West Bromwich town centre which is cleverly disguised in turn as a giant roundabout. For full details of why you should go to *The Manor House* see **J9** of the M6; it will be quite enough here to try and describe your route.

Off the junction take the A41 (Expressway) towards Wolverhampton. At the roundabout take the A4031, careful now, towards Walsall. After three-quarters of a mile filter left before some traffic lights and follow the one-way system to the right. When you come to what appears to be a roundabout turn left, and then second left off the next roundabout by *The Golden Lion* **5**. You will be amazed by what you see on your right.

Sandwell Valley Park is simply a very large open area in the middle of Birmingham, which is strange enough in itself. Take the A41 towards Birmingham. After half a mile there is a small turning to the left just before the Co-op Laundry. Quite a few parking spots, a Gothic chapel and a lake.

All the petrol stations listed are cheap. There is also a motel signposted off the junction – the *Europa Motor Lodge* **9**.

M5 J1

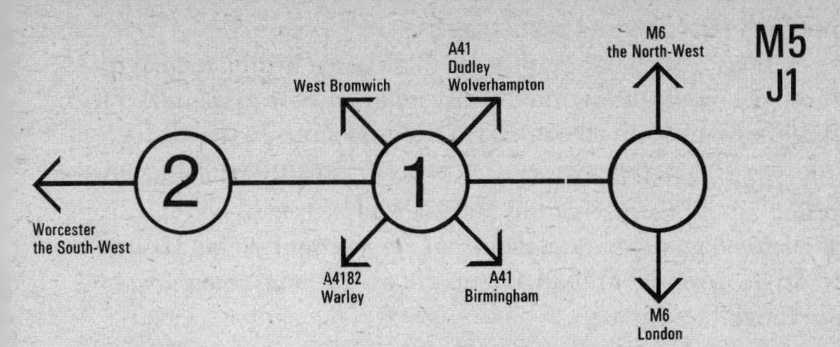

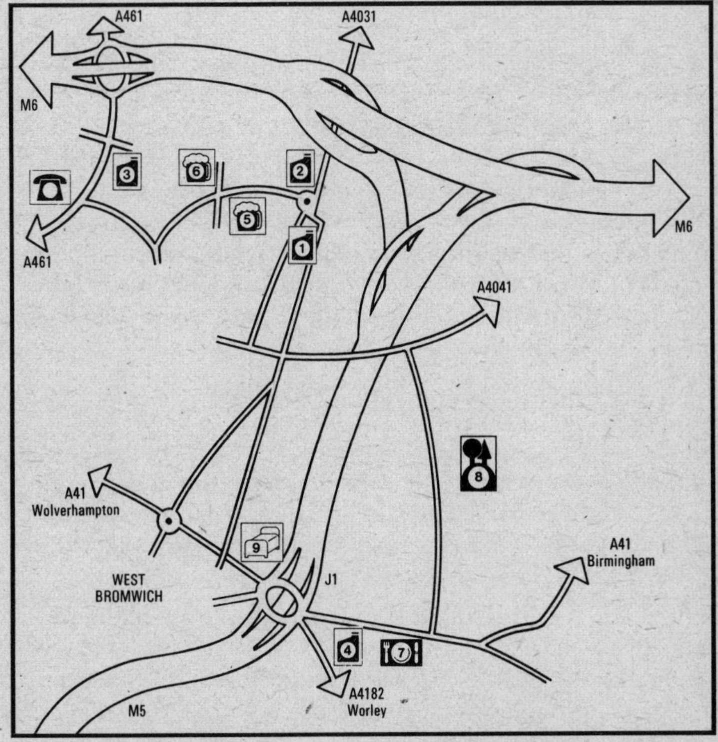

1 Stone Cross Service Station. Hours: 7 am – 11 pm (9 am – 9 pm Sun)
2 Pylon Service Station. Hours: 7.30 am – 9.30 pm
3 College Service Station. Hours: 8 am – 10.30 pm (9 am – 9.30 pm Sun)
4 Colmore Depot Service Station
5 *The Golden Lion*, Mitchells and Butlers
6 *The Manor House*, Ansells. Restaurant and steak bar (021 588 2035)
7 *The Hawthorns Grill*
8 Sandwell Valley Park
9 *Europa Motor Lodge*

J2 don't

Drive on, unless you want very cheap and very convenient petrol.

From the motorway roundabout get onto the A-road roundabout and take the first left off – the A4123 to Birmingham. On the left you will find Birchfield Service Station, open from 7 am to 9 pm. On Sundays it opens at 9 am. It has toilets and a pay-phone.

There is also a garage attached working a normal five-and-a-half-day week. The owner, Graham Germaine, says he will try and fix anything. He said it.

GUIDE TO MAP SYMBOLS

 PETROL

 GARAGE AND BREAKDOWN

 PUB

 POST OFFICE

 TELEPHONE

 SHOP

BED AND BREAKFAST

 HOTEL

 PICNIC SPOT

 FISH AND CHIPS

PARKING

RAC

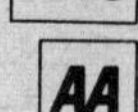

AA

MUSEUM

 RESTAURANT

HOSPITAL

 WINE BAR

 POLICE STATION

 POTTERY

 SWIMMING POOL

petrol/hotels

In both directions, coming off this junction, there are long stretches of dual carriageway with no turning points. You are entering urban Birmingham – or leaving. But you will find 24-hour petrol stations in both directions with cashiers rather than machines, and both cheap. As usual the cheapest petrol, Copes **3**, was the furthest away.

The A456 into Birmingham is the Hagley Road, renowned for its hotels. After about two and a half miles every other building is an hotel. I stayed at *The Grecian* **10** which was very friendly, although the price of their drinks was much too high.

To confuse you there are two *Black Horses* on this junction. Both are Ansells and they are not too far apart. The closest *Black Horse* **5** is just past the Heron petrol station **4**. It has draught bitter and mild, basket snacks at all times and a restaurant open every day except Sunday lunch. Standard pub grub – chips with everything – and children can be catered for. But, the landlady says, no food after 2 pm.

The other *Black Horse* **7** is in the country, not too far from Frankley Services, and has just started doing food. They are trying to find out what the custom might be. I suggested that they shouldn't do chips with anything as the smell always spreads throughout the pub. But they say that's what people want, particularly the lorry drivers who spirit themselves up from the service area. And as these service areas prove, people can only 'choose' from what they are offered – much of the time we are obliged to buy what we don't really want.

The Dog **7** is set in a piece of parkland; a pub for the young half-trendies and the ageing dogs taking their 'friends' out for a quiet drink. *The Cock and Magpies* **8** has lunchtime snacks.

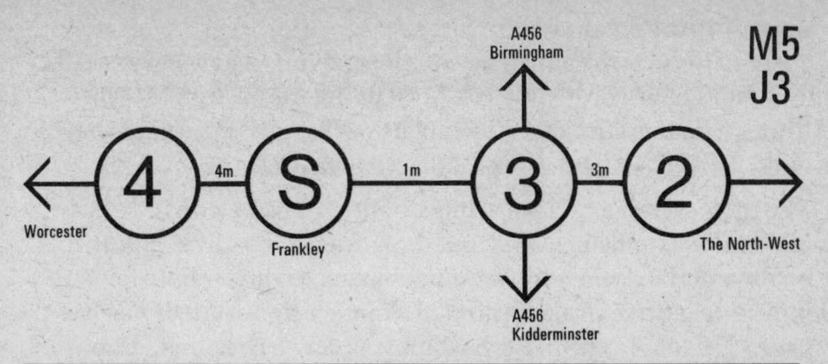

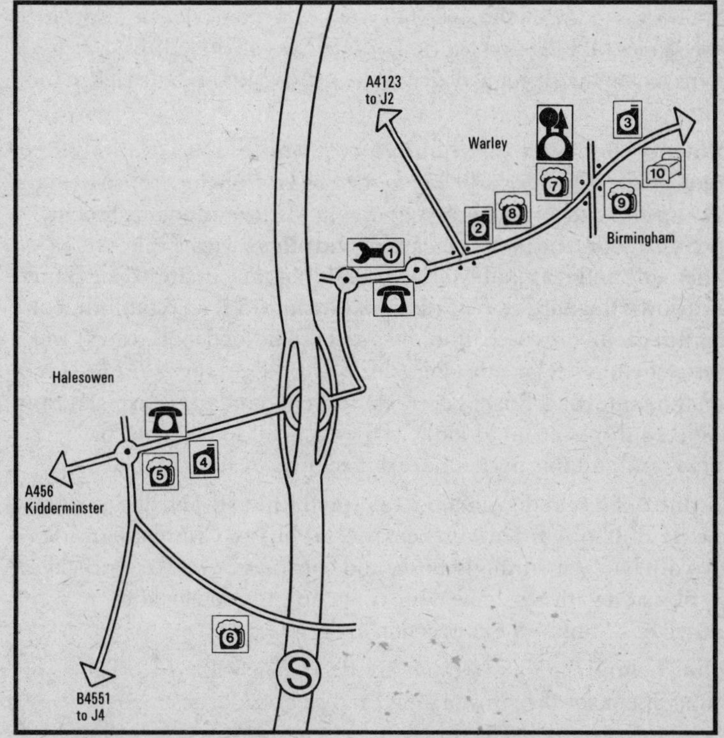

1 Browning Service Station. Hours: 7.30 am – 10.30 pm. 24-hr breakdown (day 422 2198, night 422 3946)
2 Fitzroy Motors. Hours: 7 am – 10 pm
3 Copes Garage. 24-hr petrol
4 Newbury Motors. 24-hr petrol. Leyland agents
5 *The Black Horse*, Ansells
6 *The Black Horse*, Ansells
7 *The Dog*, Bass Charrington
8 *Cock and Magpies*, Mitchells and Butlers
9 *The Kings Head*, Ansells
10 *The Grecian Hotel* (429 2145)

garage/petrol/food/picnic

A lot of variety on this junction, so it depends on what you want. All the garages have cheaper petrol. Most useful was Maron Motors **4**. Although furthest from the junction its workshop is open seven days a week – and it has a 24-hour breakdown service. Do they ever rest?

Close to this garage is Lickey Hills Country Park **14** with its heavily wooded slopes and open land, but the entrance is badly signposted. You have arrived when you see a sign saying 'eighteen-hole golf course' – just drive straight through. Another sign says *Old Rose and Crown* **12**. This is a cheap B&B which was once a coaching station for extra horses to use on the steep hill you've just come down. To get to these places take the first left (to Lydiate Ash) off the A38 to Bromsgrove; then a country drive, two crossroads and turn left at the T-junction.

A range of choices for food, quite a lot of them on or just off the A491 to Stourbridge. *The Manchester* **5** is on the B5441. Lunches from Monday to Saturday with an above average menu – chicken and mushroom quiche, savoury meat pie, macaroni, and others. Nearly all homemade and reasonably priced. Children can be catered for. Three miles down the A491 is *The Fourwinds Restaurant* **11**, an establishment for adult carnivores with time and money. The food looked good and smelt delicious – huge meat joints. It's really a 'carvery'. *The Bell Inn* **8** is on the same road. Snacks every day except Sunday and a restaurant which is only closed on Monday. There is a children's room for snacks, and suitable portions are served in the restaurant.

The pub nearest to the junction was also the nicest. The tiny *Royal Oak* **6** has a rambling garden with benches, rabbits and a stream. Inside, two plain bars with draught bitter and baps. *The Swan* **7** in Fairfield is also pleasant with Springfield bitter on tap and good looking sandwiches – unlike the conversion in the lounge.

Hiding behind the Nafta garage **3** is the *Marlgrove Motel* **13**. The management speak highly of their English breakfasts.

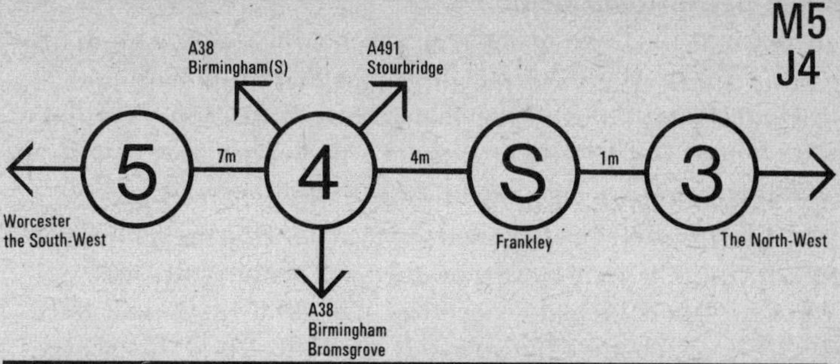

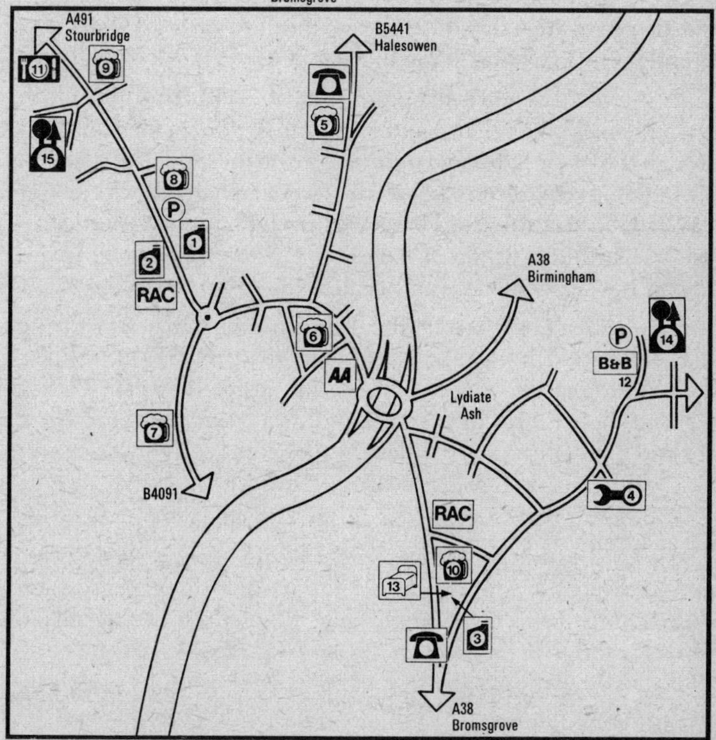

1 Bell Service Station. Hours: 7.30 am – 10 pm
2 Bell Filling Station. Hours: 7.30 am – 7.30 pm. 24-hr petrol machine
3 Marlgrove Ltd. Hours: 7 am – 11 pm
4 Maron Motors. Hours: 7 am – 9 pm. Workshop open same hours (021 445 3170). 24-hr breakdown (night, Bromsgrove 77688)
5 *The Manchester*, Mitchells and Butlers
6 *The Royal Oak*, Mitchells and Bulters
7 *The Swan*, Mitchells and Butlers
8 *The Bell Inn*, Mitchells and Butlers. Restaurant (Belbroughton 730232)
9 *The Holly Bush*, Mitchells and Butlers
10 *The Marlbrook*, Ansells. B&B (Bromsgrove 78060)
11 *The Fourwinds Restaurant*. Closed Mon, Sat lunch and Sun evening (Belbroughton 730332)
12 *The Old Rose and Crown*. B&B (021 453 3502)
13 *Marlgrove Motel and Restaurant* (Bromsgrove 72889)
14 Lickey Hills Country Park
15 Hollies Hill picnic spot

petrol/visit/pubs/snacks

As so often, the good things are not close to the junction. Also, in this case they are all in very different directions. It is worth putting an extra hour or so on your trip for The Avoncroft Museum of Buildings **16**. *The Eagle and Sun* **11** is a nice pub in a nice location with good food. *The Bowling Green* **5** is a place for those who like traditional pubs.

It is a good junction for cheap petrol. Head north on the A38 towards Bromsgrove. There are two garages, **1** and **2**, within half a mile and both offer 24-hour breakdown services. The garage at the half mile mark has longer hours – but none stay open after 9 pm. If you have decided to go to the Avoncroft Museum the third garage **3** is on the way and they will try and fix anything.

The Avoncroft Museum is signposted from the A38. After about two and a half miles take a right-hand turning to Redditch, the A4024. Through the traffic lights and the next turn on the right. On one site, a lot of buildings have been gathered that would otherwise have decayed or been destroyed. They have been faithfully rebuilt and if possible, like the old windmill, have been put in working order again. They say it will take an hour and a half of your time.

The Eagle and Sun **11** sits on the edge of the Birmingham and Worcester Canal. In Droitwich you take the Hanbury road, the B4090, for one mile. Children can be catered for, especially in good weather. There is lunch and supper seven days a week and always something hot. No chips and therefore no smell to destroy the decent beer, but there are pizzas, chicken curry or beef goulash.

There are many choices if you want to stay overnight. The range goes from *The Château Impney* **15** to *The Castle Hotel* **13** – with no disrespect to either extreme. Finding the *Impney* more than a trifle expensive and the *Castle* more than a trifle unwelcoming (though it serves a good pint of bitter), I stayed at the *St Andrews House Hotel* **12** which was quiet.

If you are staying overnight you should go to *The Bowling Green* **5**. On the south-bound sliproad of the motorway there is a sign to Stoke Works; you will find the pub after about a mile and a quarter.

Also if you stay in Droitwich and are heading south, rejoin at **J6**. Head south out of town towards Worcester and take the left-hand turn, the A4538, for Evesham.

1 Forge Garage. Hours: 7.30 am – 9 pm (later starts on Sat, Sun). (day, Wychbold 205, night Bromsgrove 33990)

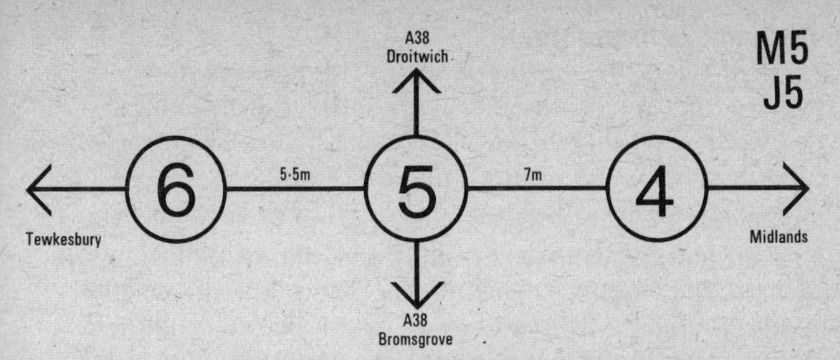

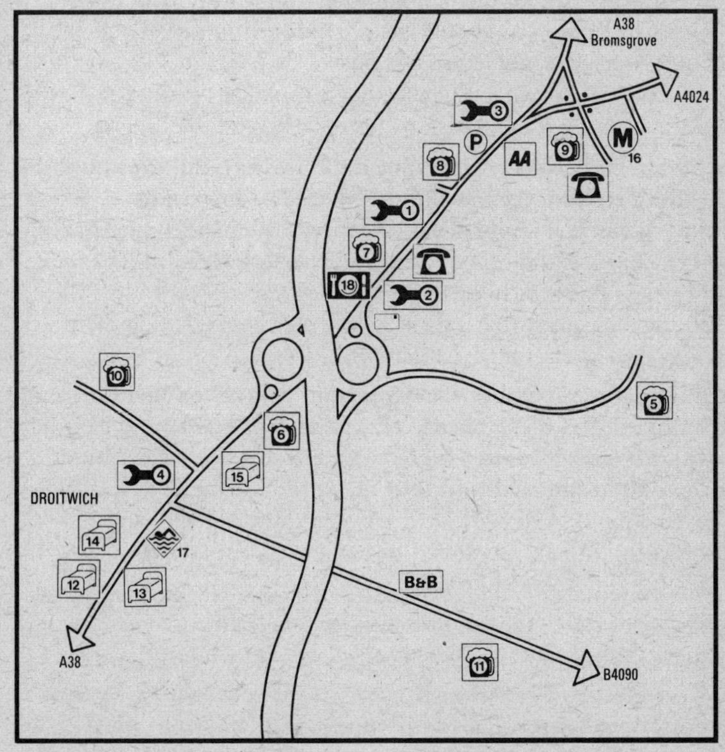

2 Wychbold Garage. 24-hr breakdown (day Wychbold 448, night Droitwich 4406 or 3911)
3 Warren Garage. Local breakdown (day Bromsgrove 32042, night Wychbold 462)
4 Droitwich Garage
5 *The Bowling Green*, Banks
6 *The Robin Hood,* Mitchells and Butlers
7 *The Crown Hotel*, Banks
8 *The Swan Inn*, Davenports
9 *The Grasshopper*, Ansells
10 *The Gardeners Arms*, Hanson
11 *The Eagle and Sun,* Mitchells and Butlers
12 *St Andrews House Hotel* (Droitwich 3202)
13 *The Castle Hotel*, Davenports (Droitwich 3104)
14 *The Worcestershire Hotel* (Droitwich 2371)
15 *Château Impney* (Droitwich 4411)
16 Avoncroft Museum of Buildings
17 Swimming pool
18 Café

pubs/petrol/overnights

Dear Rick, this is your junction really, the one you always use travelling from Manchester to Oxford. And the other way too. I wonder how many times you have turned off here without realizing, as always, what pleasures you are missing.

You should try *The Bridge* **4**. After half a mile on your normal road, the A4538 towards Evesham, take a signposted left turn to Tibberton, and then first left again in a short while. There are two Banks' pubs in the village, *Speed The Plough* **5** and *The Bridge* which sits on the Worcester and Birmingham Canal. The hand-drawn bitter in *The Bridge* is fine. Inside you should cast a hand over the pile of well-thumbed, and not so clean, seaside postcards. You should also cast your eye on the tiles which suggest that a woman of twenty is rather like Africa while a woman of sixty has come to resemble Siberia!

Another pub you could visit is *The Swan* **7**. It does mean you would have to retrace your steps slightly along the A4538 towards Droitwich, but you would make a considerable saving on petrol at the garages Copcut **1** and Martin Motors **2** just past *The Swan* **7**. So slide your Datsun in amongst the Fords and hear the cries of 'middle for diddle, old boy' and 'what's your poison, old chap?'. The landlord will 'dispense' you a pint of Marston's.

Should you travel this way with your family you have a choice of places for a visit, walk or picnic. Very close is the canal **9** and the road here is wide enough for parking. At a greater distance is Spetchley Gardens **10** (mentioned more fully under **J7**) although I daresay you know Captain Berkeley MFH already. So you could rejoin the motorway at the next junction. But somehow I can't see you taking this route so far from your routine.

So best wishes on this fairly ordinary junction, John.

PS. I know you are occasionally gripped by advanced paranoia but in this case don't worry (too much) about all the police cars you see in your rear-view mirror. They aren't necessarily following you; the HQ of the West Mercia Police is close by.

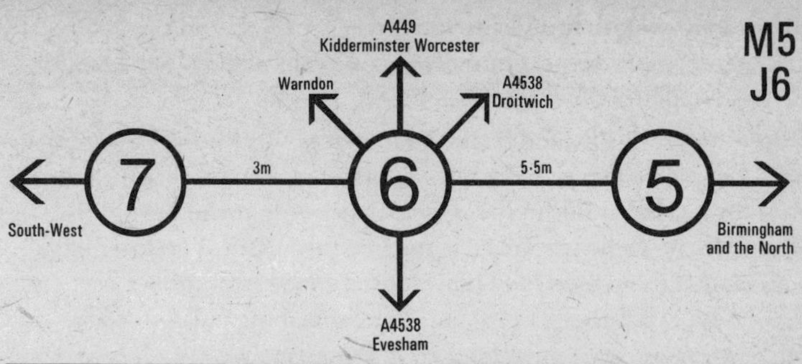

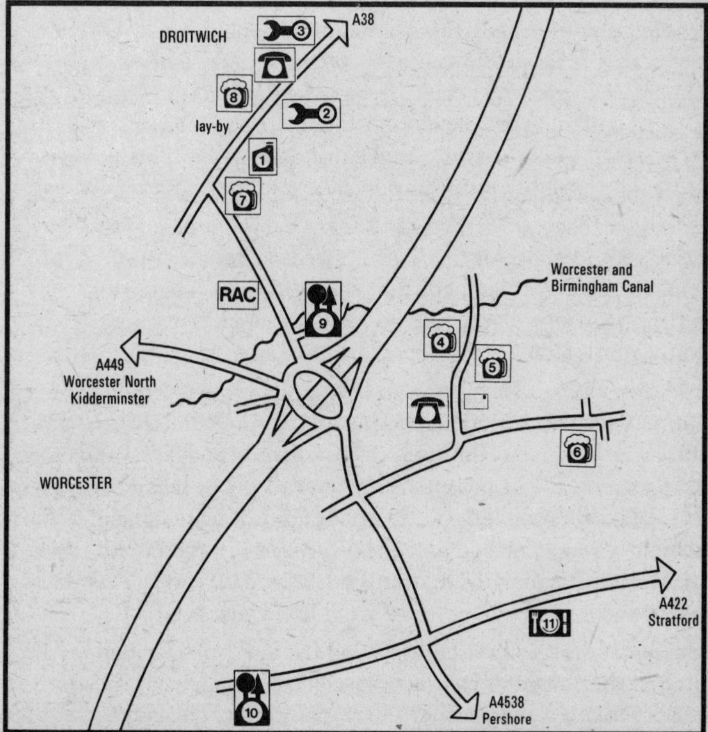

1 Copcut Filling Station. Hours: 7.30 am – 10 pm (later opening Sat, Sun)
2 Martin Motors
3 Paul Newbury Ltd. General repairs, tyres, batteries. Breakdown in working hours
4 *The Bridge*, Banks
5 *Speed the Plough*, Banks
6 *The Chequers*, Ansells
7 *The Swan*, Marston
8 *The Copcut Elm*, Mitchells and Butlers
9 Picnic spot on Worcester and Birmingham Canal
10 Spetchley Gardens
11 *The March Hare Inn and Restaurant* (Upton Snodsbury 222)

pub snack/petrol/breakdown/visit

No special recommendations for this junction, though *The Swan* **5** is very convenient.

Worcester is close by and beautiful in places. But you go there at your peril. Let me just give you two facts; first, the planners have instituted what they call a 'traffic management scheme' in town; second, I've been stuck in traffic jams every time I go there. But Worcester has a cathedral, a river, many old buildings, a good restaurant (*King Charles II*, book on Worcester 22449) and some smashing pubs – try *The Cardinals Hat* or *The Kings Head* or *The Wheatsheaf*.

There are many cheap garages between the junction and Worcester and you should be able to save at least 10p a gallon. They also get cheaper the further you get into town. The Larkhill **1** is a distance of one and a half miles, is open for long hours, has a Godfrey Davis attached for 24-hour car-hire, and has its own 24-hour breakdown service. The Redhill Filling Station **2** also has a 24-hour breakdown service.

The Swan **5** is ideally placed. One hundred yards down the dual carriageway to Worcester you take the right-hand turning to Whittington. Decent pub grub on weekday lunchtimes, a garden, a friendly landlord and a room for children.

For Marstons go to *The Sebright Arms* **6** opposite the Larkhill Service Station. A very big secluded garden and there are plans for a children's room. It has three bars, draught mild and bitter and serves cold bar snacks. More pricey sit-down meals can be had if you travel on the A44 towards Evesham. In a wide lay-by on the right after nearly three miles you will find *The Bird In Hand* **8** – an English-style steak establishment with children's portions. Further on, over the limit, and more expensive is *The Plough and Harrow* **9**.

For a visit and walk between April and October go to Spetchley Park **10**, rejoin the motorway at junction six if travelling north. There are 40 acres of garden and another 140 acres for deer. The house, owned by the Berkeley family, is not open. But even if you can't see how they live you can see the style of their death in All Saints Church – beautiful tombs.

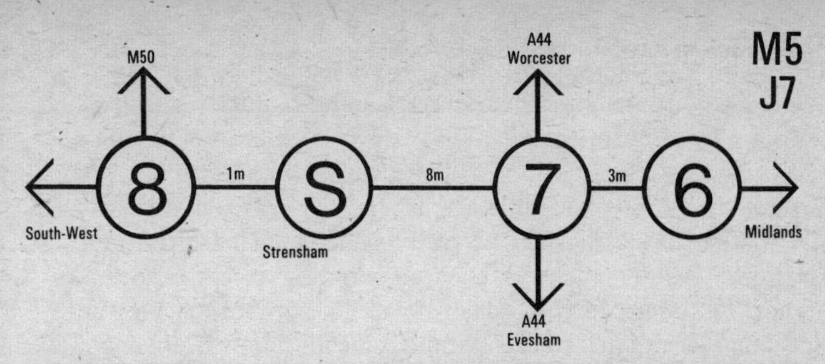

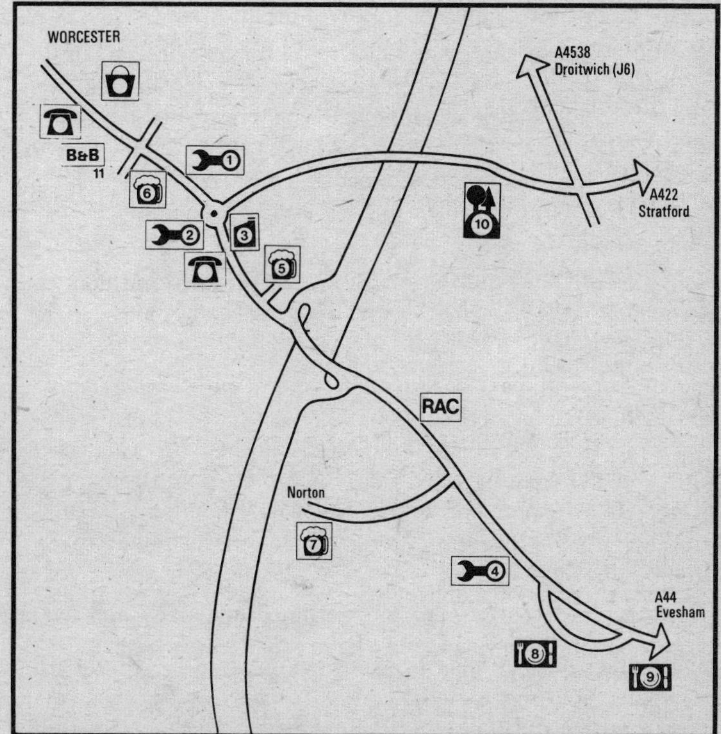

1 Larkhill Service Station. Hours: 8 am – 11 pm (8 am – 9 pm Sun). 24-hr breakdown (Worcester, day 355315, night 20545). Godfrey Davis 24-hr car-hire (Worcester 54557)
2 Redhill Filling Station. Hours: 7.30 am – 10 pm. 24-hr breakdown (Worcester, day 353777, night 356520)
3 Whittington Road Filling Station
4 Motor House Garage (Worcester 840661)
5 *The Swan*, Banks
6 *The Sebright Arms*, Marston
7 *The Retreat Inn*, Marston
8 *The Bird In Hand Restaurant* (Worcester 840647)
9 *The Plough and Harrow* (Peopleton 259)
10 Spetchley Park Gardens
11 Willesley Guest House

visit

Tewkesbury is different and it took me some time to realize why. There is a Norman abbey, two rivers, leaning Tudor houses all over the place (it's a surprise that many of them are still standing) and everywhere a feeling of the past. The town has maintained an individuality that many other English towns seem to have lost so easily – they have all grown to look the same. 'Fletchers fishing tackle and guns', Palmers, Baxters, Heywoods and Dave Perks – all names in the high streets. There is a Hepworths, Dewhurst and Co-op but they don't dominate. The simple and somehow not very obvious fact is that the chain-stores have not destroyed the town.

No really cheap petrol here (wait for **J7** or **J5** going north and **J13** going south). But if petrol is urgent there is a convenient garage, the Ashchurch **1** with fairly long hours. In town there are two garages, Graham Wright Motors **2** and Mitton Manor Garage **3**; they seem to have a lot of AA spanners between them but my car didn't need fixing. Nor should food be any problem in town as there are a number of cafés and take-aways.

The pleasure of Tewkesbury is to walk around the town and along the banks of the River Avon – the Severn also joins close by. The place to start is the 850-year-old abbey **9**.

The town also contains Gloucestershire's oldest inn – *Ye Olde Blacke Beare* **6** – which has had a continuous licence since 1308, the front bar that is. A pity then that they mainly serve Whitbread beers under pressure, but at least it serves real ale (PA on hand pump from the Whitbread Cheltenham brewery). Just down the lane is another Whitbread pub, *The White Bear*. Not special but the nice joke is that the intervening modern housing estate is called Twixtbears.

The Blacke Beare has a decent size terrace, lunchtime snacks and, if it's really pelting down, there's a centre room which children can use. Just across the river from the pub is a good place for a picnic or a walk. Also in town you will find *The Britannia* **4**, a Davenports pub which has good beer but an awful interior conversion, particularly the bar area. There is also a Wadworth pub, *The Berkeley Arms* **5** which appears to keep its own hours.

Note that you can rejoin the M5 going north by going out of town (on the A38 towards Worcester) to **J1** of the M50, which, incidentally, is worth visiting in its own right.

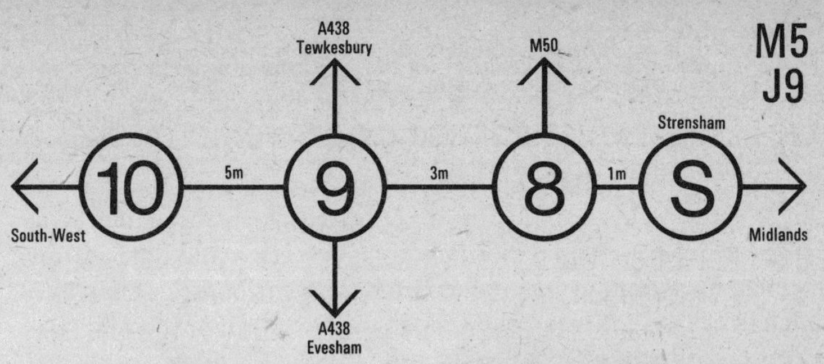

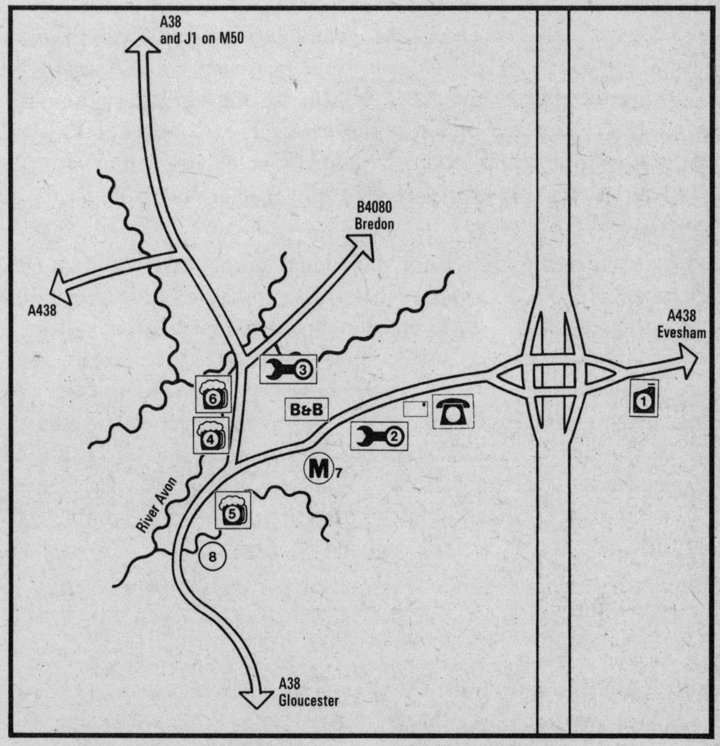

1 Ashchurch Service Station. Hours: 7 am – 10 pm (8 am – 8 pm Sun)
2 Graham Wright Motors. Breakdown and repairs in working hours (Tewksbury 292398)
3 Mitton Manor Garage
4 *The Britannia*, Davenports
5 *The Berkeley Arms*, Wadworth
6 *Ye Olde Blacke Beare*, Whitbread
7 Museum
8 The abbey

petrol/food/snacks/visit

These junctions are put together for two reasons. First, the object of attention in both cases is the town of Cheltenham. Secondly, junction 10 can only be used for southbound traffic going into Cheltenham or northbound traffic coming out of town.

Don't be put off by the official guide or by the town's reputation of being the last resting place for military types. It is a middle-class town – almost by definition since it has two Berni steak houses – but it has much to offer. All manner of shops, snack-bars, restaurants and hotels. Many walks and places to visit.

For eating both *Food for Thought* **11** (evenings only) and *The Aubergine* **13** are worth a visit; in both cases it would be wise to book. *Food for Thought* has the shorter menu and (silly to say but some description is needed) has the more 'English' of the menus. For a quicker and cheaper meal *Forrests Wine Bar* **12** is good. Excellent homemade soup for 25p and there is always a dish of the day. But look around, there are many other places.

There are two tremendous pubs, close to each other just off the paved High Street. *The Restoration Inn* **9** looks like a converted shop. Draught Burton and Ind Coope, and a nice luncheon menu with great variety of pizzas. If you're worried by your angle of vision or the state of your brain, check the slope on the floor before worrying too much. Just round the corner you will find the double-fronted Regency *Cotswold Hotel* **10**. A place of many facets depending upon the time of day and what you want. The beer is draught Wadworths – bitter and 6X. It has two bars, one definitely smarter than the other. There's good lunchtime food and a restaurant as well.

Cheltenham Services **1** has 24-hour cheap petrol, but there are many other cheap garages in town and you should be saving at least 10p a gallon.

Finally a small country pub, *The House in the Tree* **7**, on a complex route between the two junctions, should be tried.

M5 J10/11

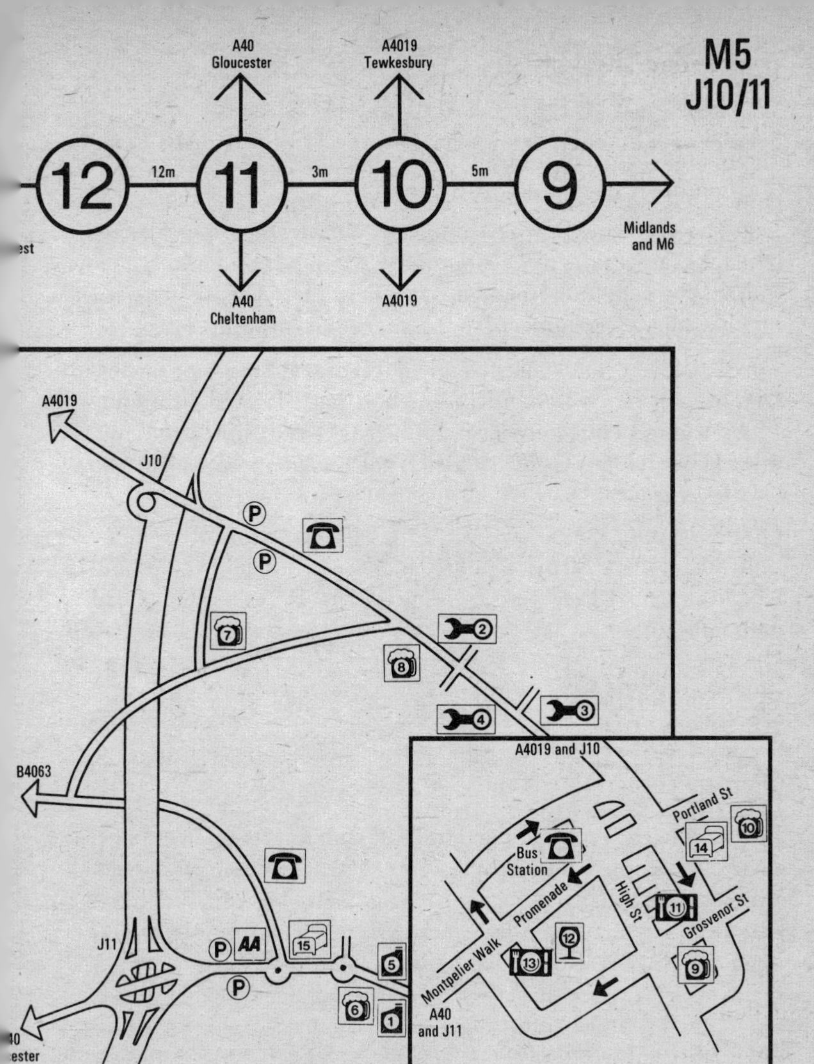

1 Cheltenham Services. 24-hr petrol
2 Autorama Garages. Hours: 7 am – 10 pm (9 am – 6 pm Sun). Cheltenham 26896
3 Waterloo Garage. 24-hr breakdown (Cheltenham 59403)
4 Haines and Strange. 24-hr breakdown
5 Castle Filling Station
6 *The Landsdown Inn*, Whitbread
7 *The House in the Tree*, Whitbread
8 *The Crosshands*, Whitbread
9 *The Restoration Inn*, Ind Coope
10 *Cotswold Hotel* (Cheltenham 23998)
11 *Food for Thought* (Cheltenham 29836)
12 *Forrests Wine Bar* (Cheltenham 38001)
13 *Aubergine Restaurant* (Cheltenham 31402)
14 *Central Hotel* (Cheltenham 24789)
15 *Golden Valley Hotel* (Cheltenham 32691)

24-hour garage and petrol/visits

If you are a bird fancier, and it's way off limits, you can go to the Wildfowl Trust **14**. It will take time and cost you money, though it gets cheaper the older or younger you are – adults £1, OAPs 75p, children 45p. You can have a picnic there but don't take dogs, chinchillas, mongooses (not birds!) or transistors. If travelling south you can rejoin the M5 at **J14**. Close to the Trust is *The Tudor Arms* **6** which has a garden and a variety of food. Also in Slimbridge and close to the main road is the Slymbridge Gallery **12**; they display the work of a number of craftspersons and you can get morning coffee.

I prefer donkeys and you can find one of them at Frampton on Severn which is also much closer to the junction than Birdland. Frampton boasts a lovely village green, Rosamundes Green, three ponds, which must be a record, two pubs, which is not, and one donkey. It is also a very lovely place.

Of the two pubs I preferred *The Bell* **4**. Within minutes of opening time the regulars, all male, poured in; it was a Sunday evening and it looked as though they were avoiding the chores. A short menu with homemade items.

Just beyond the village is the Gloucester and Sharpness Canal **13**. Park this side and walk in either direction. At the other end of the village is *The Old Vicarage Hotel* **11**. Twenty-one rooms and very secluded. It also seems reasonably priced – £5 for B&B with special rates for kids.

For garages the Fromebridge **1** and Claypits **2** seem to offer between them everything that is needed. The Fromebridge will fix your car just about anytime, but they only do light work on Sundays; they also carry a wide range of spares. Claypits has 24-hour petrol from a machine; there is also another machine on the A38 towards Gloucester. It sits most attractively outside *The Forge Restaurant* **10** – not a view I would want with my *tournedos rossini* (£3.50). But the menu did look quite nice.

If you are going to the Wildfowl Trust, picking up your cheap petrol on the way, you can take your choice of a couple of pubs on the route – *The George* **8** or *The White Lion* **7**. *The George* has quite a good looking menu and will be able to cater for children when their restaurant is built. *The White Lion* does bar snacks (scampi, etc), has a garden with swings and can put you up for the night at a very reasonable price.

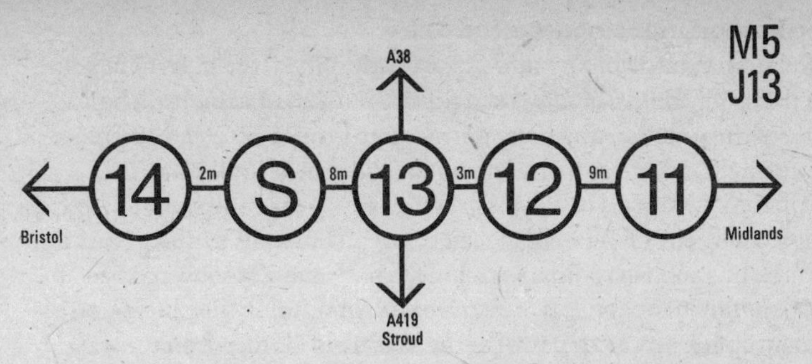

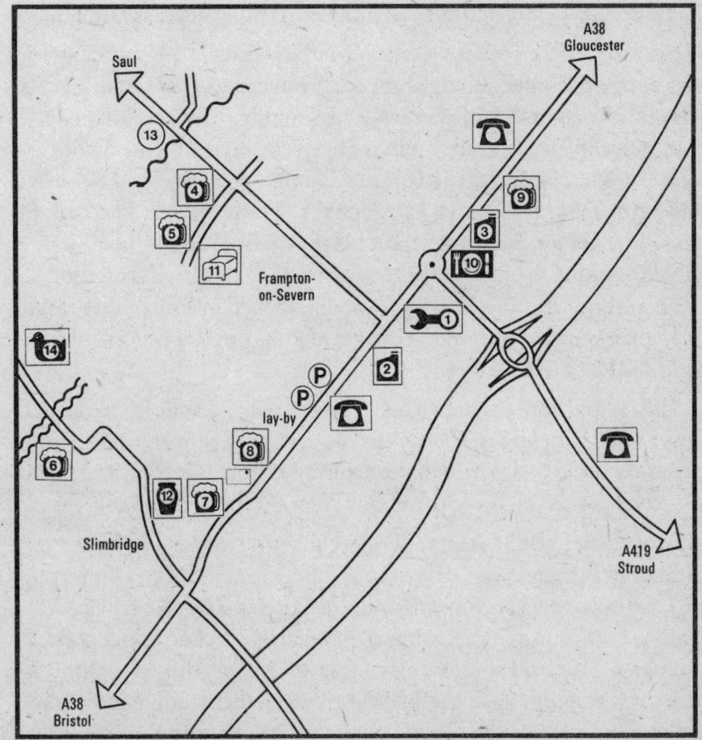

1 Fromebridge Garage. 24-hr breakdown. Motor spares and car hire. (Saul 362)
2 Claypits Garage. Hours: 8 am – 6 pm, Mon – Sat. 24-hr petrol machine
3 Garage. 24-hr petrol machine
5 *The Three Horseshoes*, Whitbread
4 *The Bell Inn*, Whitbread
6 *The Tudor Arms*
7 *The White Lion*, Whitbread. B&B (Cambridge 240)
8 *The George*, Whitbread
9 *The Whitminster Hotel*, Whitbread
10 *The Olde Forge Restaurant* (Saul 875)
11 *The Old Vicarage Hotel* (Saul 562)
12 Slymbridge Pottery
13 Gloucester and Sharpness Canal
14 The Wildfowl Trust

accommodation/food/petrol/pubs

There is no snack-bar or café for a quickie, but all the pubs have some food to offer. Both *The Huntsman* **5** and *The Gables* **7** are within half a mile of the junction and have normal pub grub. *The Gables* also has a large garden. My favourite within the three-mile limit was *The Whitehorse Inn* **6**. It is one of those increasingly rare and rather nice pubs where they haven't knocked down all the walls to make one large bar. Four smallish rooms, smashing sandwiches (bloody-red beef in thick white bread for 25p!) and a chatty lot running the place. You can also pick up cheap petrol at the Whitfield Garage **2** on the way there. Incidentally this garage specializes in trailer repairs and sells boats.

Quite a range of choices if you want to stay overnight. *The Elms* **11** has ten rooms, is extremely pleasant and reasonably priced. It is a seventeenth century house which has been converted by the owner and the outside is covered with plants. Going up-market and close to double figures you can choose between the *Newport Towers Motel* **13**, 60 rooms, and *The Park Hotel* **14**, 10 rooms. Both these hotels have restaurants which are open to non-residents and both will cater for children at reduced rates. *The Park*'s menu looked more exciting but it is closed on a Sunday evening. You can also stay at *The Gables*, *The Tudor Lodge* **12** or *Green Farm* **15**.

I wouldn't know how to choose between the two 24-hour breakdown services. The Falfield **1** is closest but the garage is almost totally obscured by broken-down vehicles. Now maybe this is bad news – but on the other hand it is living proof that they get the vehicles in.

For those of you from Masham (Yorks) thirsting for a sight of the River Severn I suggest you drive the six miles to Oldbury. There you can choose between *The Anchor* **9** and *The Ship* **10**. *The Anchor* has a lovely location by the river, a large garden, draught beer, very good food, its own wine and something awful called sheepdip. If you find it slightly over-popular with the BMW crowd go to the other end of the village to *The Ship*. Good food and good draught beer again. While I like Theakston's bitter (from Masham, Yorks) Courage's Directors is a fine beer.

If you head north along the A38 towards Gloucester for any reason, it would be worth your while to rejoin the M5 at **J13** – and you could also visit the Wildfowl Trust on the way.

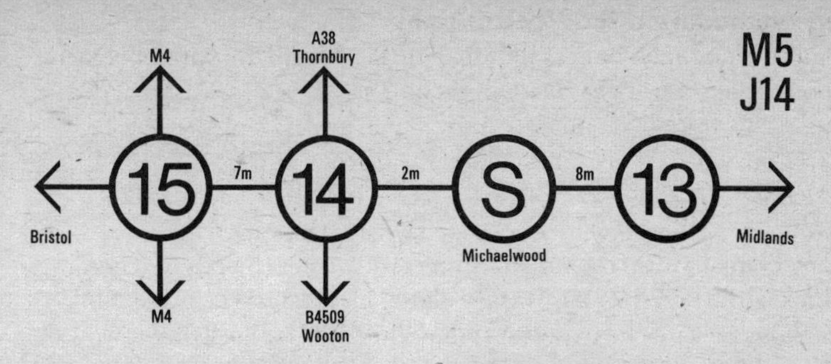

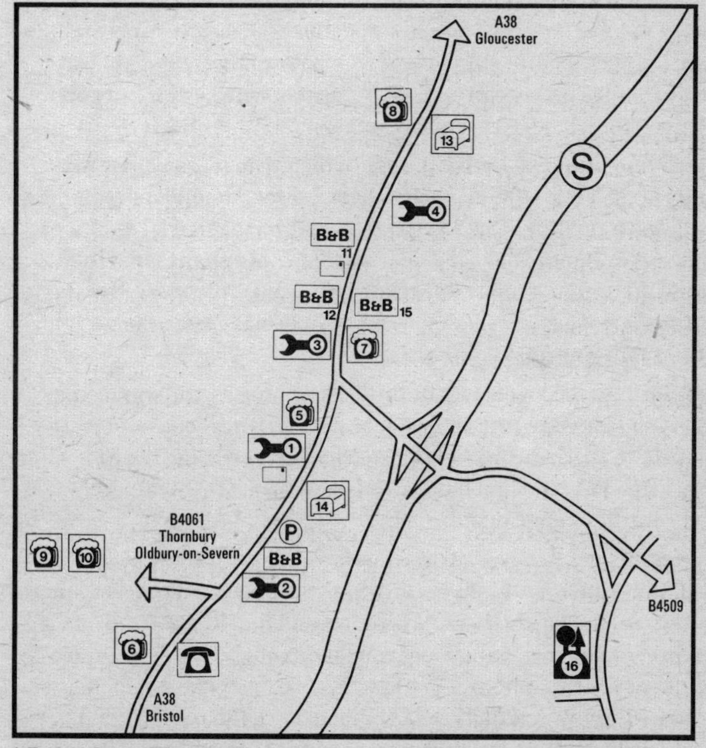

1 Falfield Garage. Hours: 7.30 am – 6 pm (9 am – 4 pm Sun). 24-hr breakdown (Falfield 286)
2 Whitfield Garage. Trailer experts (Falfield 296)
3 Stone Garage
4 Taylors. 24-hr breakdown, spares (Falfield 8333)
5 *The Huntsman,* Whitbread
6 *The Whitehorse Inn,* Whitbread
7 *The Gables Hotel and Restaurant* (Falfield 272)
8 *The Stagecoach Inn* (Berkeley 385)
9 *The Anchor,* Free house
10 *The Ship,* Courage
11 *The Elms.* B&B (Falfield 279)
12 *The Tudor Lodge Guest House* (Falfield 396)
13 *Newport Towers Motel* (Berkeley 575/6/7/8)
14 *The Park Hotel and Restaurant* (Falfield 550)
15 *Green Farm.* B&B (Falfield 319)
16 Tortworth Park. Hours: open Sun, summertime

petrol/food

Whether you are on the M5 or M4 and heading north, south, east or west take this junction for cheap petrol and fill your tank up. Within one and a half miles on the trusty A38 towards Bristol there are three cheap garages – as they are in competition with others along this urban route the prices are likely to stay low. They also have long hours.

Taking the A38 in the other direction (to Gloucester) you will find the Almondsbury Service Station **4**. It is not quite so cheap but everything else you might want on this junction is this side of the motorway. *The Rocklands* **5** in Almondsbury opens on Friday and Saturday evenings for supper and they have plans for opening on other evenings if they can attract the custom with simple but good home cooking. They also have two cheap rooms for B&B.

Two pubs of interest, both Courage, which is no real surprise in the Bristol area. Try and find *The Bowl* **7** in Lower Almondsbury built by some wise monks in 1132. Do this by avoiding the sign for such a place (down Over Lane). Take the next small turning on the left, Hollow Road, and head narrowly downwards. Cut back on yourself to the right at the bottom. *The Bowl* has draught beer, a restaurant, a garden, skittles, snacks and a car park.

The Swan **8**, in the lovely village of Tockington, has undergone the surgery so beloved of the sixties – copper and so-called comfort. It's easy to find. Take the first signposted left after crossing the M4 motorway. Take the first left which is signposted to Tockington. It has the normal range of pub grub.

The Manor House Restaurant **6** at Gaunts Earthcott is something completely different. First, realize that you are in for a time-wasting treat. Second, ring and book. Third, try and find it. Fourth, you may be able to barter for your meal if you take enough junk or antiques. Fifth, take your own booze. Sixth, when seated, try and decipher the menu. Chicken Lucretia Borgia? Fillet of Pork Pigling Bland? They are very friendly and children are welcome at lunch. In fact its quite easy to find in daylight when you are on the A38 heading north. Take the first, and signposted, right after crossing the M4.

If you are stuck for a place to stay there is B&B at *Hill Farm* **10**, which is close and cheap but has nylon sheets. If you want to pay twice as much and travel four miles take the A38 north to *The Alveston House Hotel* **9** which looks nice.

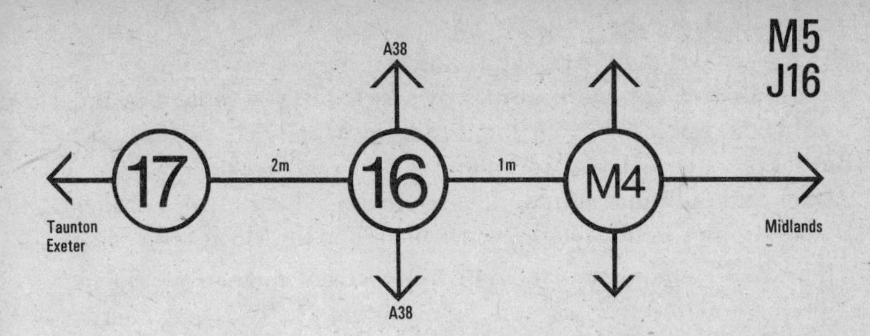

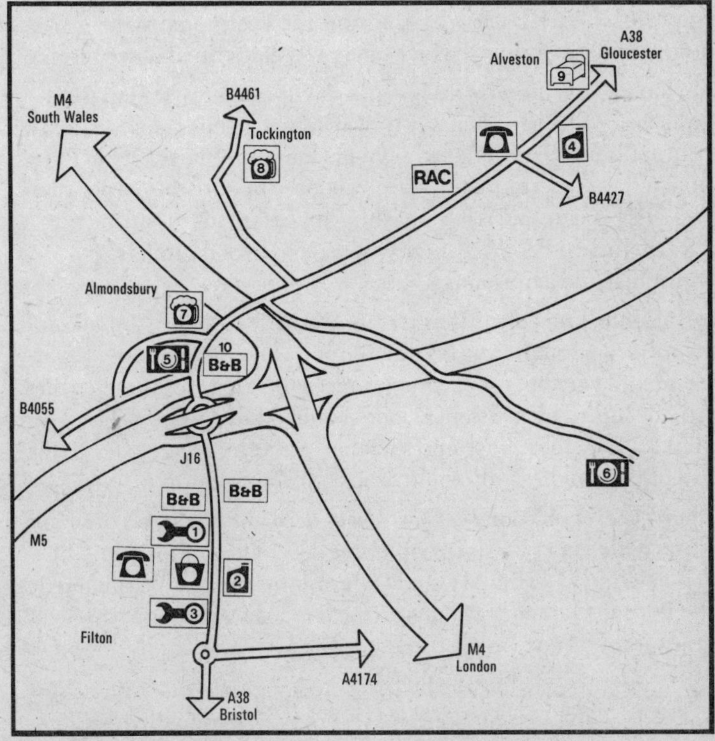

1 Patchway Service Station. Hours: 7 am – 11 pm. 24-hr breakdown (day Almondsbury 612766, night Pilning 3200)
2 Stoke Brook Service Station
3 Runway Motors. Toyota agents (Bristol 693704)
4 Almondsbury Service Station. Hours: 7 am – 9 pm
5 *The Rocklands Restaurant and Tea Room.* Hours: 10 am – 6 pm Mon – Sat. B&B (Almondsbury 612208)
6 *The Manor House Restaurant* (Winterbourne 772225)
7 *The Bowl,* Courage
8 *The Swan,* Courage
9 *The Alveston House Hotel* (Thornberry 415050)
10 *Hill Farm.* B&B (Almondsbury 613206)

visit/petrol/garage

If you were ever going to make a habit of using motorway junctions around Bristol, and there are many worse habits you could develop, it would be sensible to buy Ordnance Survey Map 172 of Bristol and Bath. For instance if you were going to use the village of Pilning for garage and pub you might want to rejoin the M4 at **J21**; or, visiting Blaise Hamlet **12** in daylight, you could rejoin the M5 at **J18**.

There are four garages on the A4018 into Bristol and petrol is cheap. The closest is Cribbs Causeway Filling Station **1**. It has long hours and a 24-hour note acceptor which, the owner assures me, usually gives petrol as well. Further on the same road you come to the Beaufort Service Station **2** which offers a 24-hour breakdown service.

If you have made the wise decision, in daylight that is, to visit Blaise Hamlet you will find a cluster of well-meaning telephone boxes just off the roundabout when you turn right to Henbury. Blaise Castle **11** is signposted from here and the Hamlet is close by. Bristol Corporation owns Blaise Castle and it is a smashing place for kids to run, picnic and waste time. All for free there is open land, woods, toilets, playgrounds and a museum.

The National Trust owns Blaise Hamlet – the entrance is a single and easily missed wrought iron gate on the one-way traffic system. Eight different and very beautiful cottages surround a green and, since they are still occupied by pensioners, one should tread decently. They were built in 1809 by John Nash and somehow strike an image of an idyllic way of life. If childless you could drop in at *The Blaise Inn* **8**.

Neither *The Plough* **5** nor *The Cross Hands Inn* **6** in Pilning can cater for children which is a pity since both serve decent food. Full details of both places in **J21** of the M4, and of the multifarious services offered by the Pilning Garage **3**. All this on the B4055 to Severn Beach – what a name for mud! You will also find *The Fox* **4** in Easter Compton on this road. Draught Courage and food.

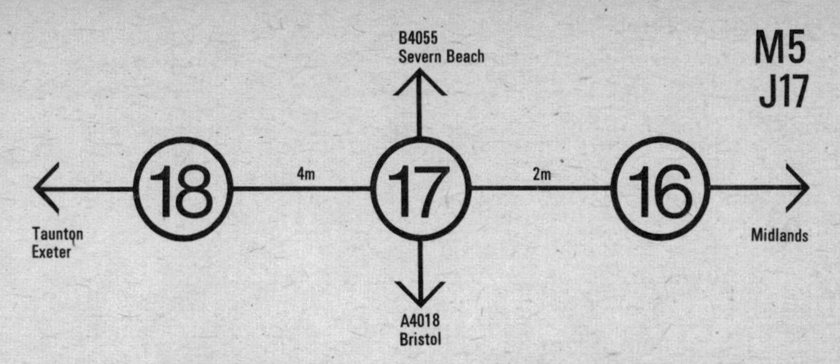

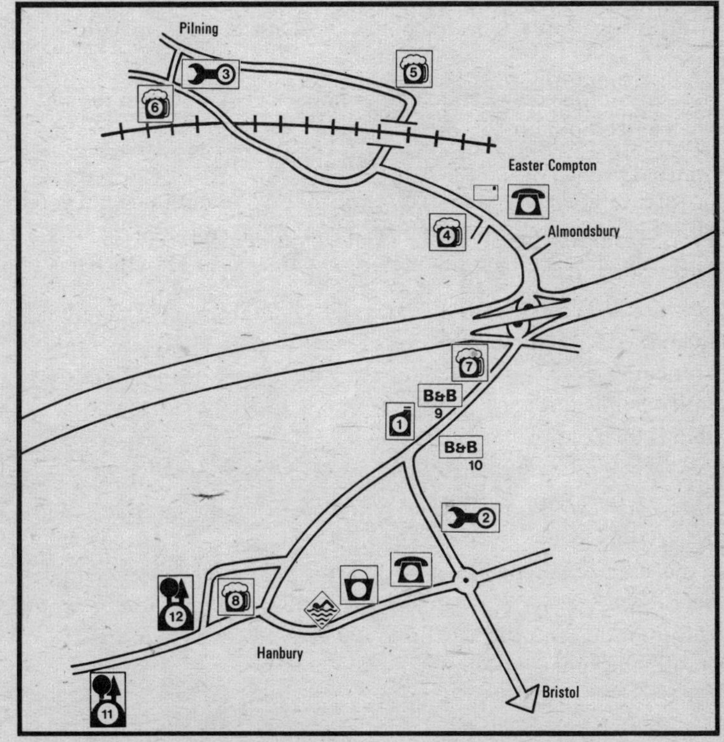

1 Cribbs Causeway Filling Station. 24-hr petrol machine

2 Beaufort Service Station. 24-hr breakdown (day Bristol 500544, night Winterbourne 774336)

3 Pilning Garage. 24-hr breakdown (day Pilning 2909, night Thornberry 412402 or Bristol 695843)

4 *The Fox*, Courage

5 *The Plough*, Wadworth

6 *The Cross Hands Inn*, Courage

7 *The Lamb and Flag*, Courage

8 *The Blaise Inn*, Courage

9 *Cribbs Lodge*. B&B (Bristol 500066)

10 *Cribbs Farm*. B&B

11 Blaise Castle

12 Blaise Hamlet

petrol

This junction serves the industrial complex of Avonmouth and unsurprisingly is not too attractive until, going in the other direction, you get to the village of Shirehampton and beyond that Shirehampton Park **14**. Smashing views, woods and a good place to walk. But the only reason for using this junction is very cheap petrol which, surprisingly, is not on the Avonmouth side of the junction.

While the Avonmouth Filling Station **3** is fairly cheap, the four on the other side of the junction are cheaper and even grumbling about how little they make on petrol sales. The Pembroke Service Station **4** does repairs during normal working hours and has a 24-hour breakdown service.

In Shirehampton you will find many shops, three Courage pubs and one fish and chip shop, *The Blue Dolphin* **13**. Of the pubs I preferred *The Lifeboat* **6** but none on this junction are very special.

There are quite a few transport cafés on the Avonmouth side but you will have to make your own choice as I couldn't face four breakfasts. There is also a Bass Charrington pub, *The Miles Arms* **11**, which has food.

M5
J18

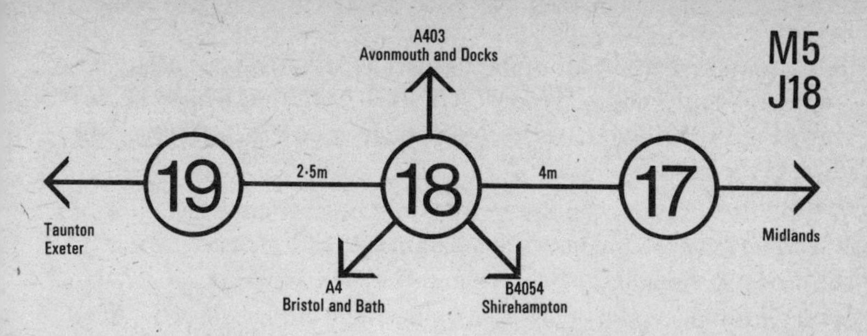

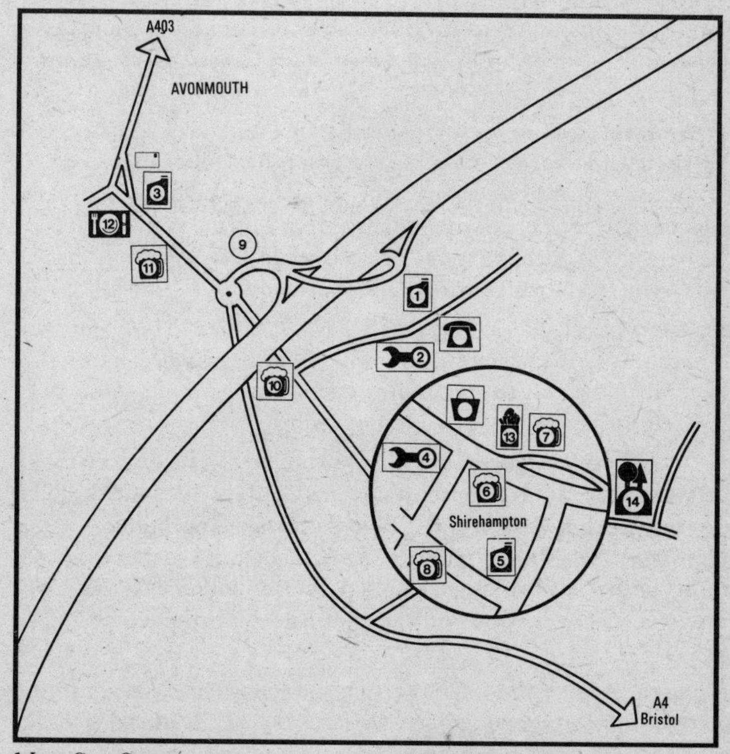

1 Long Cross Garage
2 Kingswestern Avenue Service Station. Hours: 7.30 am – 10 pm (9 am – 9 pm Sun). Repairs (Avonmouth 4102)
3 Avonmouth Filling Station
4 Pembroke Service Station. 24-hr breakdown (day Avonmouth 7396/7, night Bristol 27481)
5 Fourways Service Station
6 *The Lifeboat*, Courage
7 *The George*, Courage
8 *The Rising Sun*, Courage
9 A Courage brewery
10 *The Hope and Anchor*, Courage
11 *The Miles Arms*, Bass Charrington
12 Transport Café
13 *The Blue Dolphin*. Fish and chips
14 Shirehampton Park

Only one has survived the jump. It was 18 May 1885 when 24-year-old Sarah Ann Henley leaped feet first off the bridge. Going this way her long Victorian skirt acted as a parachute on the 250-ft fall to the River Avon below.

The Clifton Suspension Bridge **17** is four miles from the junction but if you've never seen it now's your chance. You don't have to do a Sarah Ann though, the Bridge should be seen from every angle, day and night. Price: 10p for a car, 2p for feet. On either side of the Avon Gorge there are lovely places to relieve the motorway tedium. On the far side are Clifton Downs **15** with a camera obscura on top and caves below, and not far away, in Syon Place, is *The Coronation Tap,* a proper cider pub.

On the near side is the Ashton Court Estate **14** and the Avon Gorge Forest **16** with a variety of walks. The Estate has rolling parkland, woods, a nature trail, deer park, golf – the lot. A good place to go with children, as is the Forest with its marked walks of different lengths. The entrance is not all that well marked but look for a gateway that bears some resemblance to a small Greek temple.

Another proper cider establishment is *The Black Horse* **5** in Clapton-in-Gordano. It's a long winding road but the journey is worth it to find this small, old, many roomed, dark and low-ceilinged pub. More than adequate food and draught Courage as well.

The Avon Ferry no longer runs from Pill but there's a chippy on the harbour's edge, a curry house, quite a few Courage pubs and the Pill Service Station **4** which has a 24-hour petrol machine. Both the very plain *Station Hotel* **7** and *The Kings Arms* **8**, where the youth of the locality gather, serve draught Courage. Nicer than either of these two pubs is *The George Inn* **6** on the A369 to Bristol. Draught beer and pub food.

Taking the A369 in the other direction you come to Portishead. If you want to stay overnight book in at *The Royal Hotel* **12** overlooking the Severn estuary. Two restaurants in town cater for different tastes and times – *The Merrythought* **13** for snacks and *Rolles Eating House* **10** for an evening meal from Monday to Saturday. Both are reasonably priced. The Station Garage **1** has a 24-hour car hire service to complement its breakdown service, and to help you on your penniless way they take all cards.

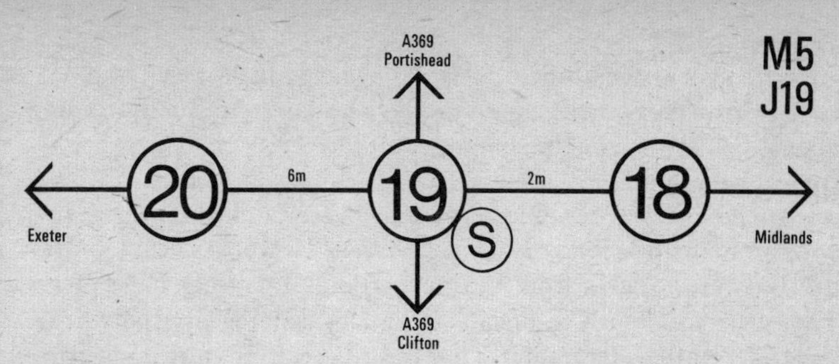

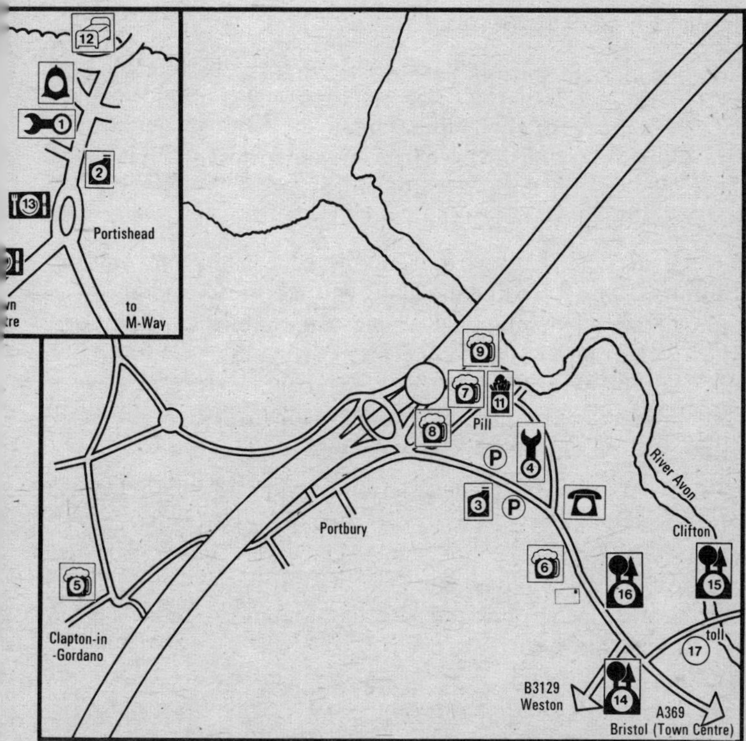

1 Station Garage (Portishead 842180)
2 Greens Filling Station. Hours: 7.30 am – 6.30 pm (9 am – 5 pm Sun)
3 Markham Filling Station. Hours: 8.15 am – 7 pm (shorter at weekends)
4 Pill Service Station. 24-hr petrol machine
5 *The Black Horse*, Courage
6 *The George Inn*, Courage
7 *The Station Hotel*, Courage
8 *The Kings Arms*, Courage
9 *The Duke of Cornwall*, Courage
10 *Rolles Eating House*
11 *The Captain's Table*. Fish and chips
12 *The Royal Hotel*, Bass Charrington
13 *Merrythought Restaurant*
14 Ashton Court Estate
15 Clifton Downs
16 Avon Gorge Forest
17 Clifton Suspension Bridge

visits/food

Clevedon is a heavy, stone-built watering hole which got left behind by the Costa del Something – or should it be Sardinia? But the coming of the M5 has put it on the commuter map for Bristol and there is a spate of new building. Clevedon has surprisingly little to offer for a town of its size. Few restaurants or pubs and some cheap garages. If you can spare the effort only *The Bristol Hotel* **7** is worth a visit – and it's a pub. There is the sea front and pier of course. Or rather, half a pier. They were apparently testing its strength by hanging large polythene bags filled with water from it. Then came the call for lunch and a part of the pier felt the call of the sea.

I was going to say give this junction a miss until I found a circuit (as on list) that would stretch your legs and offer a choice of food and cheap petrol. There might be alterations to the existing junction before this book is published so what you want to do is get on the B3130 to Nailsea. Off the junction you turn right at the first roundabout and then right at the T-junction.

You can then choose between a visit to Clevedon Court **1** or a walk up to Cadbury Camp **2**. To find the Camp you pass the Clevedon Pumping Station (which should be open to the public) and find a sign saying 'road unsuitable for motor vehicles'. It *is* suitable although narrow, but there is only parking room for about twenty vehicles at the top. From there you can walk straight on up to the Camp or cross the motorway on a fine, high bridge and pick blackberries.

Opposite Clevedon Court is the road for the pottery **3** and the Craft Centre **4** which supports a variety of trades. In the latter there is a small café which sells coffee and homemade cakes. It has a good lunch menu (not Mondays) at reasonable prices – quiche and omele omelettes. Also open Friday and Saturday evenings and a three-course Sunday lunch costs just over £2.

Alternatively you can follow the slightly complex route to the village of Kenn where you will find *The Drum and Monkey* **5**. Pressure Courage, a long cheap menu and a garden outside. The M5 is now signposted. After you cross it there is the Wayside Filling Station **6** for cheap petrol.

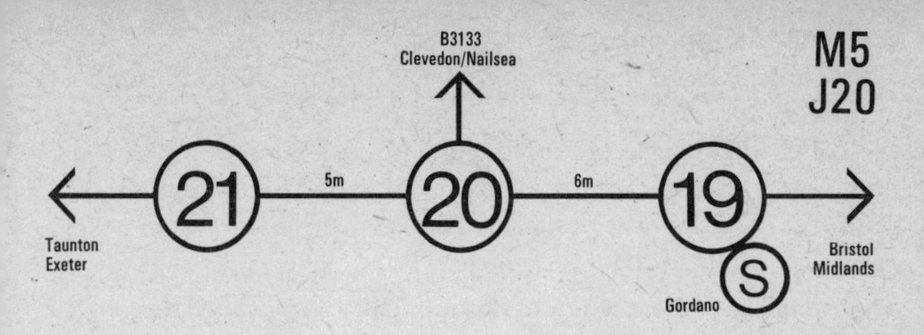

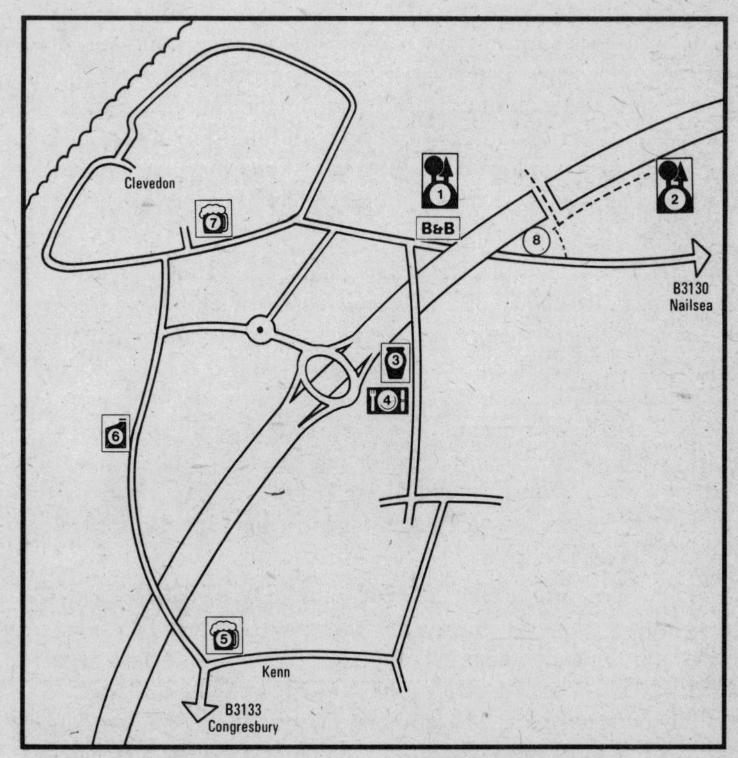

1 Clevedon Court. Hours: 2.30 – 5.30 pm Wed, Thur, Sun (Apr – Sept)
2 Cadbury Camp
3 Pottery
4 Craft Centre and Restaurant. Hours: 10 am – 5.30 pm Tue – Thur (10 am – 10.30 pm Fri & Sat, Sun lunch)
5 *The Drum and Monkey*, Courage
6 Wayside Filling Station. Hours: 8 am – 6 pm (10 am – 1 pm Sun)
7 *The Bristol Hotel*
8 Clevedon Pumping Station

accommodation/pub food

Tralee and Tresco, Ocean and Seabreeze, Deetra and Cador, and hundreds more on the road to Weston-Super-Mare. Out of season you could spend a year of your life staying in B&Bs on the A371 – and the closer you get to the town centre the more you find. There are also a number of fairly cheap garages – the closer you get the cheaper they get. But I should head for the village of Banwell.

The village hangs on the side of Banwell Hill and was sited there because of the natural flow of water out of the Mendips, but what was the village pond is now occupied by the bowling green. The church is worth a visit for its ancient font, stained glass windows and smashing chancel screen. There is also a castle at the top of the hill. A plaque on the front gate reads: 'Banwell Castle, built in the 19th century, and of no historic interest. Kindly observe that this Englishman's Castle is his Home and do not intrude.' With a bald notice like that, village gossip had the owner down as a porn merchant, but this turned out to be untrue.

Banwell offers a range of food from fish and chips **14** and pub snacks to *oysters à la gumbo* for £3.30 at *The Anvil Restaurant* **13**. It has a surprisingly long menu for a place so small. *The Ship* **10** would appear to be the locals' hostel, bar skittles being played with a lot of jibes and skill in the public bar. Snacks are available. The Menu is longer at *The Brewers Arms* **11** down past the bowling green. The pub has a nice location with two gardens and a lot of half-tree seats; dull but usual modernization inside. Eastfield House **15**, built in the early part of the last century, looks like a nice place to spend a night but it is not as large at it looks, so book.

Should you not want to take the back roads to Banwell there are two pubs within a couple of miles on the A370 towards Bristol. Both have normal pub snacks – things in baskets etc. *Palmer's Elm* **4** has a garden and children can be catered for. The landlady said 'the elm' was burning in the open fire. The landlord disagreed. *The Full Quart* **5** also has a garden and serves draught Ind Coope, christened Old Chateau by the locals.

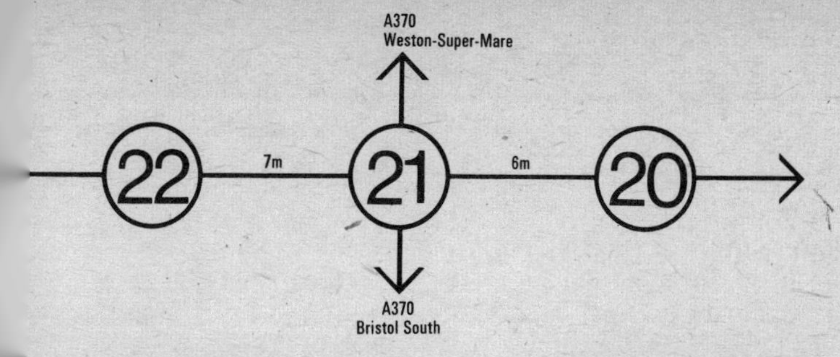

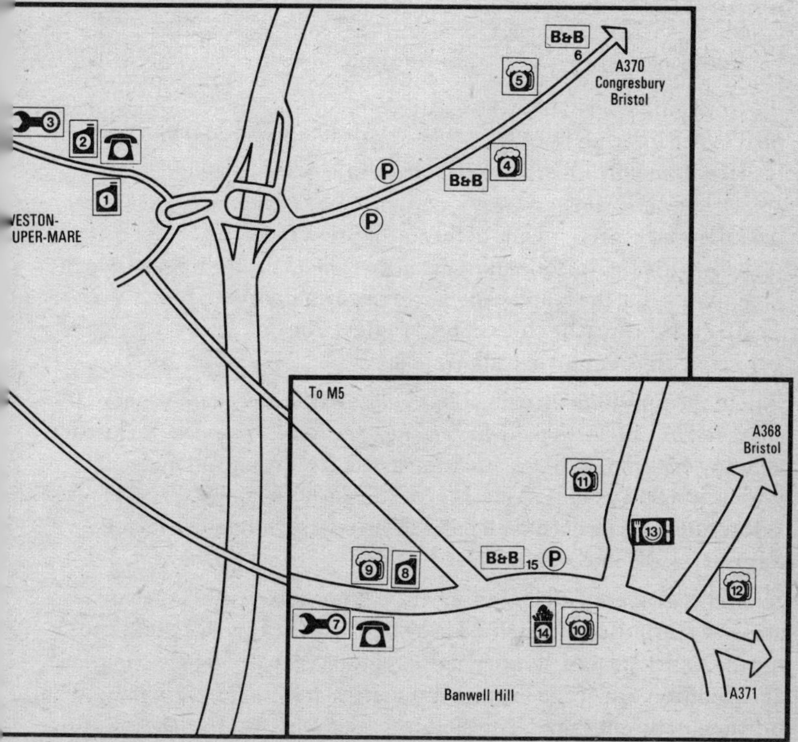

1 Worle Service Station. Hours: 6.30 am – 9 pm (8 am – 9 pm Sun)
2 New Bristol Road Service Station
3 Dawsons Garage. Weekday repairs
4 *Palmer's Elm,* Watney
5 *The Full Quart,* Free house
6 *Pool Farm.* B&B (Yatton 833138)
7 Knighcott Service Station. Breakdown and repairs in working hours (Banwell 2355)
8 Elf Garage. Hours: 7.30 am – 7 pm (9 am – 6 pm Sun)
9 *The Whistling Duck,* Free house
10 *The Ship,* Courage
11 *The Brewers Arms,* Courage
12 *Ye Olde Bell Inn,* Whitbread
13 *The Anvil Restaurant* (Banwell 822773)
14 Fish and chips (Tues, Thurs, Fri, Sat)
15 Eastfield House. B&B (Banwell 2429)

food/petrol

Very little on this junction to cause interest. A trip to Burnham-on-Sea is not advised. In high season you'll get jammed in and find nowhere to stay; in low season you'll catch cold because there's no one to keep you warm. But for children the sands are nice and there are many small eateries and lots of B&B.

You could climb to the top of Brent Knoll **12** which stands out in shapely fashion from the flat, uninteresting landscape. Myself, I would break the unwritten rules of this book and travel seven miles of the wide A38 towards Bristol and head for the hills. Axbridge, Cheddar, Winscombe, the Gorge and the Forest. It would certainly be time-wasting but it's very beautiful and there are many pubs, cafés and restaurants.

Petrol on the A38 is cheap. Biddisham Motors **1** will do repairs during normal working hours and Tarnock Garage **2** has a 24-hour breakdown service.

To take your walk or picnic to the top of Brent Knoll drive along the A38 towards Bristol for a short distance. Then take the first left which is signposted to the Knoll. About a mile down this road, past *The Red Cow* **6** and close to the church, turn right up the hill. Park on the brow – there is still a fair bit of walking to do.

There are a number of eating places close to the junction. A snack at *The Old Fox Café* **9**; a sit-down meal at *Brent House Restaurant* **7**, closed Sunday evening, or *Greystones Restaurant* **8**, closed Sunday evening, Monday and Tuesday. Neither is particularly cheap but Brent House does children's portions and has a three-course Sunday lunch for £1.50.

Travelling on the A38 in the other direction you come to the small town of Highbridge which will provide you with any shopping needs. It also has more than its fair share of antique shops. There is a market on Mondays and if you are a genuine marketeer *The Highbridge Hotel* **11** stays open till 4 pm.

Coming into Highbridge you will find a free house, *The Bristol Bridge Inn* **4**. Pub food, small car park and, a rarity for the area, draught Courage.

M5 J22

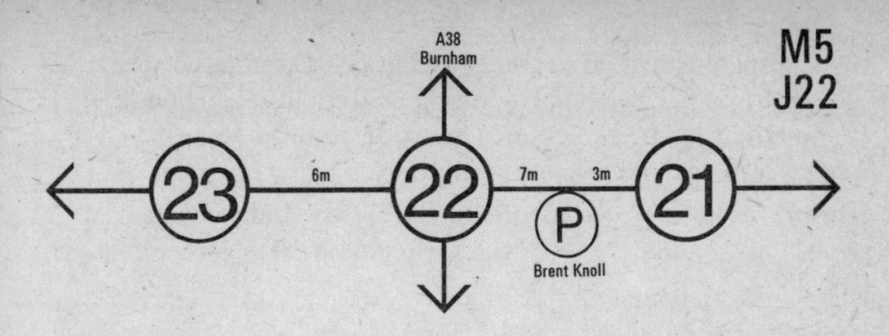

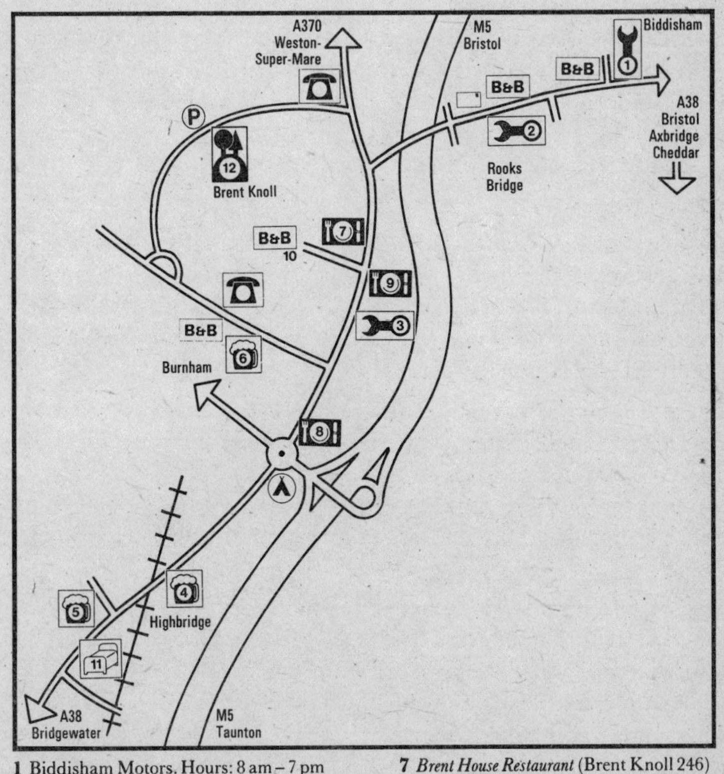

1 Biddisham Motors. Hours: 8 am – 7 pm
2 Tarnock Garage. 24-hr breakdown (Edingworth 320)
3 Brent Knoll Garage. Hours: 8.30 am – 6.30 pm (10.30 am – 1 pm Sun)
4 *The Bristol Bridge Inn,* Free house
5 *The White Hart,* Whitbread
6 *The Red Cow,* Whitbread
7 *Brent House Restaurant* (Brent Knoll 246)
8 *Greystones Restaurant* (Brent Knoll 239)
9 *The Old Fox Café*
10 *Battleborough Grange.* B&B (Brent Knoll 208)
11 *The Highbridge Hotel* (Burnham-on-Sea 783252)
12 Brent Knoll picnic spot

J23 don't

But if desperate the A38 is running alongside. If heading north take the A38 through Pawlett to Highbridge and rejoin at junction 22. In Pawlett there is a Jet garage open from 6 am to 10 pm seven days a week. *The Elms Café* and a pub are close by.

If heading south you can go through the town of Bridgwater and rejoin at junction 24. Most services available in the town. See notes on **J24**.

GUIDE TO MAP SYMBOLS

 PETROL

 GARAGE AND BREAKDOWN

 PUB

POST OFFICE

 TELEPHONE

 SHOP

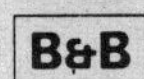

BED AND BREAKFAST

 HOTEL

 PICNIC SPOT

 FISH AND CHIPS

PARKING

RAC

AA

MUSEUM

 RESTAURANT

HOSPITAL

 WINE BAR

 POLICE STATION

 POTTERY

 SWIMMING POOL

garage/petrol/food

Good news for beer drinkers is that the smallish town of Bridgwater on the very muddy River Parrett has 73 pubs. The bad news is that most of these are owned by Whitbread. Those that aren't fall into the hands of Bass Charrington and Courage.

There seems little point in going into Bridgwater. The town provides all known chain stores and banks. There is a variety of restaurants and hotels from which you can choose. One restaurant in a nice spot is *The Watergate* **9**. It is beside the river and contains the only remaining piece of Bridgwater Castle. Steak and fish at about £2.50 for the main course. Closed on Sundays.

I didn't bother to sample the 73 pubs (or even count them) but the red sandstone pile called *The Quantock Gateway* **7** would be worth a visit should you find yourself unavoidably detained in Bridgwater. It has draught Bass, snacks, a place for children and rooms for the night. Easy to recognize when you see it, travelling out of town on the A39 towards Wembdon.

In the centre of town you will find *The Royal Clarence Hotel* **10**. A single room for about £7, a restaurant, lunch buffet and draught Bass in the Sedgemoor Bar.

But most needs can be satisfied very close to the junction. Heathfield Garage **1** offers a 24-hour breakdown service and they will try and fix rather than tow; 24-hour petrol from Westways Garage **3** with a machine that takes 50p, £1 and £5; Woods Filling Station **2** opens at 6.30 am six days a week because it's right next door to *Graham's Transport Stop* **8** which would be a very good place to have breakfast or that kind of meal.

Also very close to the junction is *The Compass Inn* **4**. All beer on pressure and no room for kids but a fair range of food – chicken curry, Gloucester sausage and the inevitable scampi in basket. But I much preferred the atmosphere in *The George* **5** in the village of North Petherton. It will soon have a dining area and possibly some accommodation. There's a children's room, a small parking area, and pressured beer.

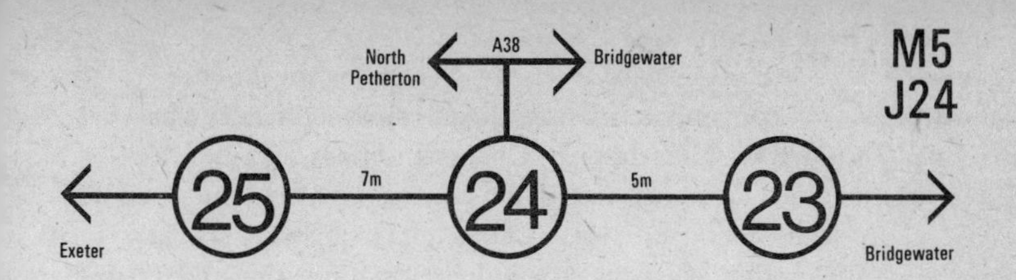

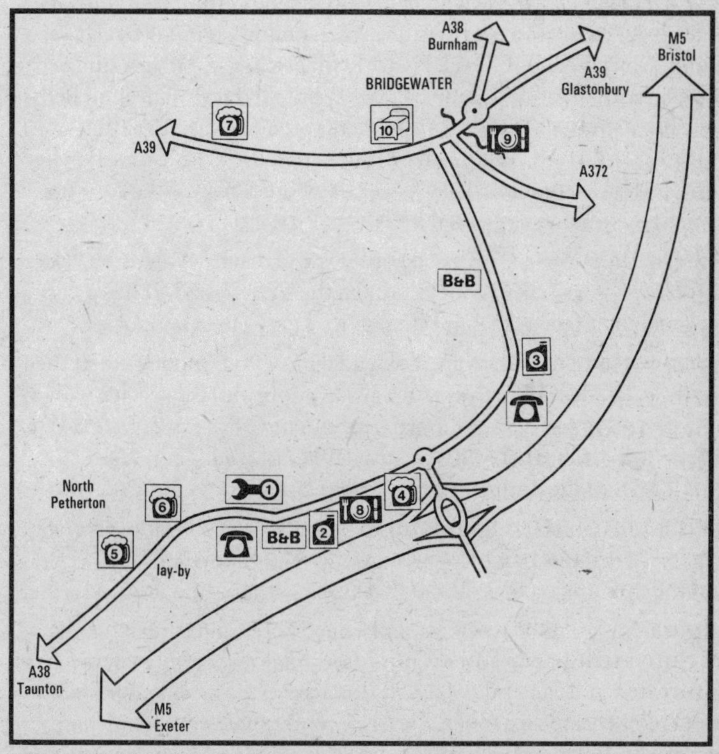

1 Heathfield Garage. 24-hr breakdown (Bridgwater 662230)
2 Woods Filling Station. Hours: 6.30 am – 8 pm weekdays
3 Westways Garage. 24-hr petrol machine
4 *The Compass Inn,* Whitbread
5 *The George,* Whitbread (Bridgwater 662330)
6 *The Clarence,* Whitbread
7 *The Quantock Gateway,* Whitbread (Bridgwater 3592)
8 *Grahams Transport Stop.* Hours: 6 am – 10 pm (open till 1 pm Sat, closed Sun)
9 *The Watergate Restaurant.* Closed Sun. (Bridgwater 3847)
10 *The Royal Clarence Hotel* (Bridgwater 55196)

garages/hotels/pubs and pub food

Apart from *The Blackbrook Inn* **5** which sits right on the junction, nothing is very convenient but nonetheless most services can be found. *The Blackbrook* has draught Ushers and Bass, a garden, a children's room, a restaurant and bar snacks, but a homemade Scotch egg at 70p seemed a bit expensive unless it has some very special ingredient! Another Watneys pub which sells interesting and unusual food (steak in Stilton, smoked mackerel) is *The Crown* **7** in Creech Heathfield. It's two and a half miles away and a bit difficult to find but it's worth a visit for those who believe (correctly) that most pub food comes in a basket and is generally awful. Follow signs for Creech St Michael and then for Creech Heathfield. It's at the end of a small road amongst a lot of modern bungalows. A thatched pub with thatched dovecote to match. I was told by a naval type there that Watneys Starlight could only have been introduced in the West Country where there is so little choice of decent beer. Any other part of the country, he claimed, would have rejected it.

While on the subject of pubs one other is worth a brief mention. *The Nags Head* **6** is a small Watneys pub on the Yeovil road. It has a very nice garden, bar snacks, bar billiards and very clean lavatories.

A lot of hotels to choose from. You can whack your money out at the grand *Castle Hotel* **13** in the centre of Taunton, and the service will be good, or you can stay at the more convenient *Creech Castle Hotel* **11** for half the price. Cheaper still and smaller is *The White Lodge Hotel* **10**. B&B is £5 and the dining-room is rather splendid.

The Thornfalcon Garage **1** seems to provide good all round service with its workshops being open longer (8 am to 9 pm six days a week) than the forecourt. Cheapish petrol and a 24-hour breakdown service.

Taunton has all the shops you might need and, quite a rarity, a 24-hour attendant-operated garage, Dunns Motors **2**, almost in the centre of town. Finally if you want to waste time and spend money there is *The Quorum Restaurant* **14**. It claims to have an 'Edwardian atmosphere' and certainly there were candles on the table and serving persons wearing long white aprons and nice smiles. Pleasant, pricey and book – but never on a Sunday.

M5 J25

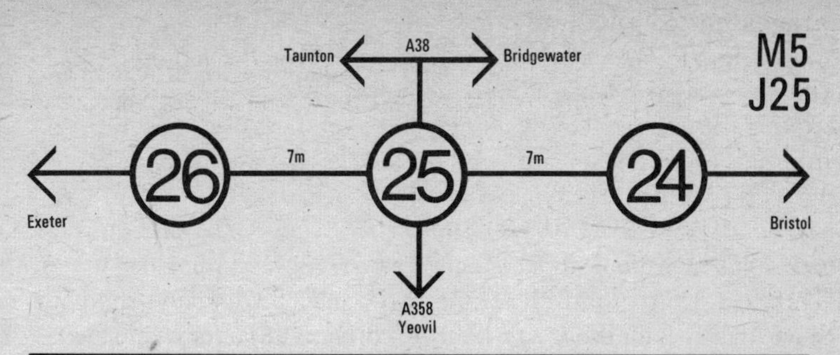

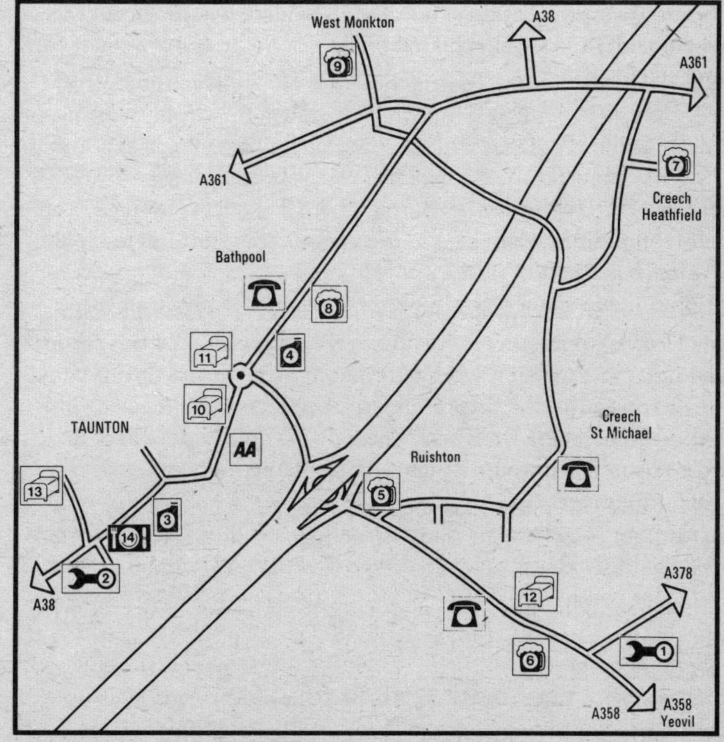

1 Thornfalcon Garage. 24-hr breakdown (Taunton, day 442205, night 443065 or 76595)
2 Dunn's Motors. 24-hr petrol and breakdown (Taunton 2607). Fiat and Citroën agents
3 Autorama. Hours: 6.30 am – 12 pm (opens 8 am Sun)
4 Central Service Station
5 *The Blackbrook Inn*, Watney (Taunton 442245)
6 *The Nags Head*, Watney
7 *The Crown*, Watney
8 *The Bathpool Inn*, Whitbread
9 *The Monxton*, Watney
10 *The White Lodge Hotel* (Taunton 3287)
11 *The Creech Castle Hotel* (Taunton 3512)
12 *The Falcon Hotel* (Henlade 442502)
13 *The Castle Hotel* (Taunton 2671)
14 *The Quorum Restaurant* (Taunton 88876)

picnic/pub/overnight/breakdown

The best thing about this junction is the Wellington Monument **13**. The second best is *The Half Moon* **5** pub with the nicest glass of Whitbread I've ever tasted.

The Wellington Monument, guarded by the National Trust, stands high in the Blackdown Hills. Given its size and obviousness, directions are hardly necessary. Superb views – minute things crawling on the motorway – grassland, slopes and woods.

Since you've come so far and if you're childless go to *The Half Moon* which looks down the other side of the Blackdown Hills. It's in a place called Clayhidon and there is bar food.

Taking the spur road off the junction to Wellington you come to a roundabout. The A38 is signposted into town. But the first turning off this roundabout is, in fact, the Wellington by-pass which is called the A38 at its other end. If, for instance, you were planning to stay the night you could go to *The Beam Bridge Hotel* **9** along the by-pass. You would then continue on the A38 towards Cullompton and rejoin the motorway on **J27**.

Other places to stay would be *The Blue Mantle House Hotel* **11** or *The Cleve Hotel* **10**, both near the centre of Wellington. *The Cleve* is set on a hill amidst a lot of lovely land. The new management is trying to take it up-market – the certain presence of company-financed businessmen. Single B&B starts at £6.50 so you'd better check the prices. The garden would be lovely for kids and there are reduced rates for them. *The Blue Mantle* is considerably cheaper and again there are special rates for children but there are only eight rooms so it would be best to book in season. Even cheaper and right next-door, but not for children, is *The Three Cups* **7**. There's no cooked breakfast but what do you expect for £2.50 – and you do get cornflakes, toast and tea. *The Three Cups* also has draught Trophy and Huntsman.

For cheap petrol and breakdown service the family-run Chelston Motors **1** seems satisfactory. 24-hour petrol can be found in the centre of Bridgwater at the St John's Service Station **2**. Turn right before you get to the traffic lights opposite a garage called Richardsons which also operates a 24-hour breakdown service.

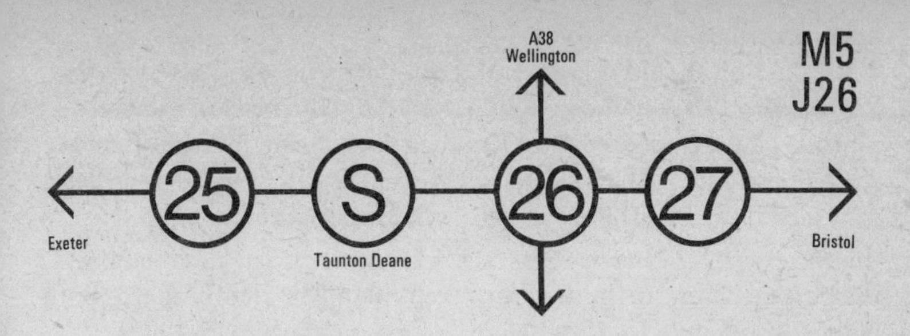

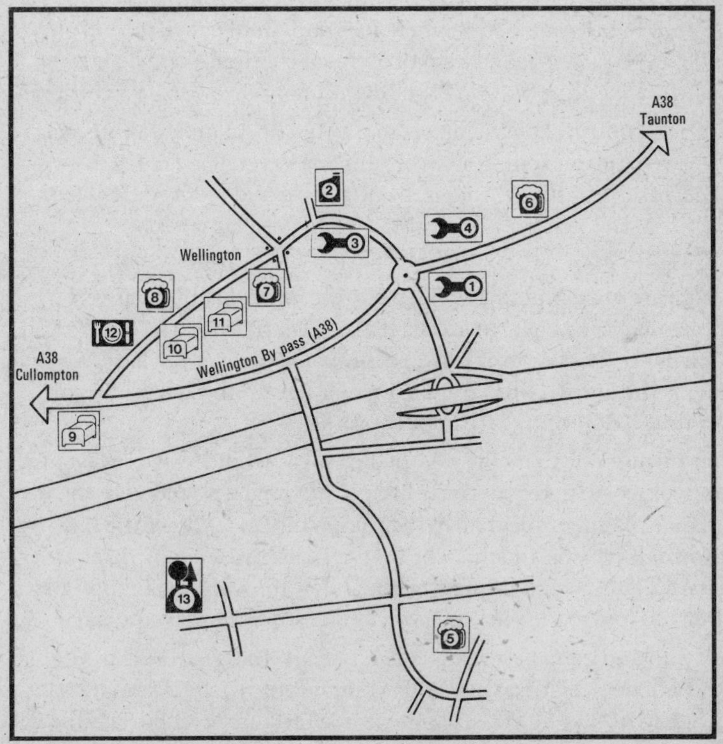

1 Chelston Motors. Hours: 8 am – 9 pm (10 am – 7 pm Sun) 24-hr breakdown (Wellington 2075)
2 St John's Service Station. 24-hr petrol machine
3 Richardson's Garage. 24-hr breakdown (Wellington, day 4181, night 2068 or 2444)
4 Piccadilly Garage. Repair service during normal working hours
5 *The Half Moon*, Free house
6 *The Blackbird*, Watney. B&B (Bradford-on-Tone 273)
7 *The Three Cups*, Whitbread. B&B (Wellington 2066)
8 *The Barley Mow*, Watney
9 *The Beam Bridge Hotel* (Greenham 672223)
10 *The Cleve Hotel* (Wellington 2033)
11 *The Blue Mantle House Hotel* (Wellington 2000)
12 *The Farmhouse Café*
13 Wellington Monument

accommodation/pub food

This junction should be used with **J28** since some of the best places are midway between the two or on that route. But beware – the planners have purloined the A38 which used to run from this junction to Cullompton via Willand. In fact the road is still there but they have renamed it the B3181 for reasons best known to themselves.

On this road *The Verbeer Manor Hotel* **14** is worth a visit and reputedly the best mechanic in the area runs the Willand Service Station **5**. Both of these are covered in **J28**. Before you reach either you pass *The Halfway House* **7**. Watneys pubs are not lightly recommended but *The Halfway* has decent food (homemade soup, Budleigh Salterton pie and Devon pasties); and a small room for children. Next door is the Culm Vale Filling Station **2**, one of the many cheapish garages here.

There is quite a choice of places to stay but no luxury establishments. Towards the unexciting town of Samford Peverell is *The Green Headlands Hotel* **10** – 11 rooms, £4.50 a night and reduced rates for children. In town is *The Merriemeade Hotel* **9**. It has ten rooms, a restaurant and a large garden which has a snack bar in summer.

There are also a number of B&B places: *Higher Elms* **11** was very pleasant. Mr Palmer runs a clean market garden (no pesticides) and his wife cooks a fine breakfast. So buy your seasonal veg here. Next door is the Lamb Hill Garage **1** and *The Lamb* pub **6** where they are building a dining area for normal pub fare.

The picnic spot **15** on the edge of the (once) Grand Western Canal is not too easy to find nor is it really special, but if it's a nice day and the kids are playing volleyball in the back of the car . . . Take the A373 towards Tiverton and then the first right. Right again by *Ayshmeade Farm* **12** (B&B) and the next right. Follow the winding, bumpy and often narrow road. The road widens and straightens by the canal.

For pub and games fanatics its *The Ayshford Arms Hotel* **8**. Darts, table football, pool, skittles (but bring your own team), ten Dalmations, eleven Muscovy ducks, six bedrooms, a restaurant, children's room, draught Ind Coope and Huntsman, bar snacks and one ghost. But it's four and a half miles from the junction.

1 Lamb Hill Garage. Hours: 8 am – 7 pm (opens 9 am Sun)
2 Culm Vale Filling Station. Hours: 8 am – 9 pm (opens 9 am Sun)
3 Kellands Garage. Hours: 7.30 am – 10 pm Daytime breakdown (Samford Peverell 820264)

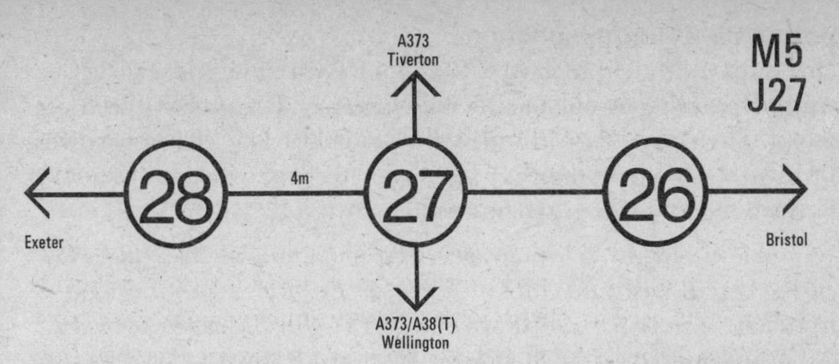

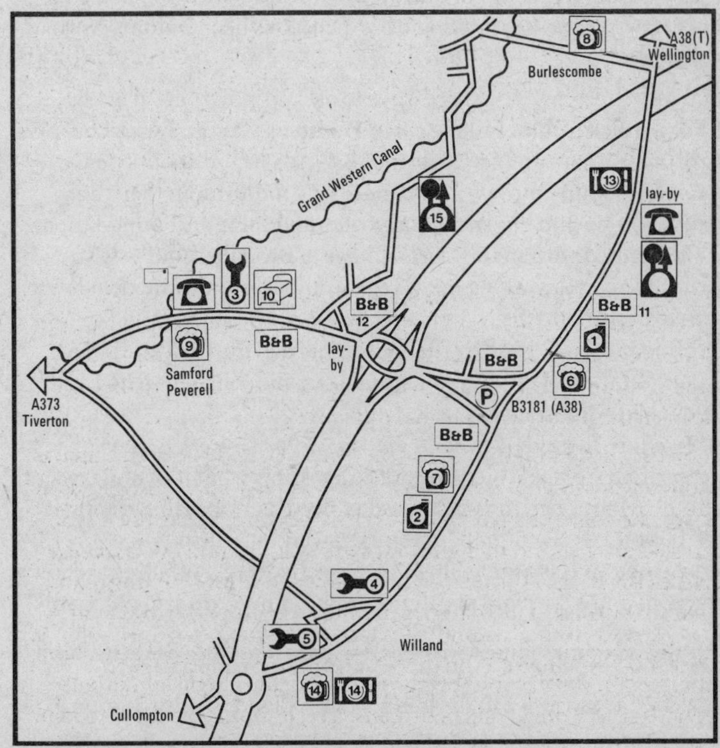

4 Willand Garage. Possible 24-hr breakdown (Samford Peverell 820224)

5 Willand Service Station. Hours: 7 am – 10 pm. Virtual 24-hr breakdown (Cullompton 2282)

6 *The Lamb*, Free house

7 *The Halfway House*, Watney

8 *The Ayshford Arms Hotel* (Greenham 672319)

9 *The Merriemeade Hotel*. Whitbread free house (Samford Peverell 820270)

10 *The Green Headlands Hotel* (Samford Peverell 820255)

11 *Higher Elms*. B&B (Craddock 40237)

12 *Ayshmeade Farm*. B&B (Samford Peverell 820464)

13 *Morgans Transport Café*. Hours: 6 am – 7 pm (open till 10 pm Sat, closed Sun). B&B (Greenham 672273)

14 *The Verbeer Manor Hotel*

15 Grand Western Canal

petrol/food/accommodation

No doubt the dull little town of Cullompton was once choked with traffic streaming through to the West Country. It must have been awful. Then came the M5 and took most of the traffic. The town died a little (at the moment there is a suggestion that the whole town should be declared a service area!) but remains awful.

It does however provide many services, shops and banks. Quite a few eating places. Fish and chips at *The Crown Fish Bar*, take-away food from *Kev's Kitchen*, or a sit-down at *Goffey's Coffee Bar and Restaurant* **9**. All tastes catered for. Well, maybe. Just outside town and going up-market is *The Inglenook Restaurant* **8** which looks like its name. Normal English fare.

But really there are only three ways to use this junction – if at all.
1. For a quick fill-up. Fill the car at Whittens Garage **1** with cheapish petrol and drop in at *The Showmen* pub **4** – it's where about twenty showmen rest up for the winter months. In the autumn they run a small fair. The pub has snacks, a garden and some accommodation.
2. *The Drewe Arms* **5** in the lovely village of Broadhembury. It's a journey of six miles; along the A373 towards Honiton and then left at the first sign giving the right name. *The Drewe Arms* is a large, rambling pub with good draught beer, normal pub food and some accommodation. The village is spread out and full of thatched and whitewashed houses.
3. My choice would be to go to *The Verbeer Manor Hotel* **6**. An extraordinary place which doesn't really know what it is, and it is not an hotel. Mentioned in the Domesday Book as Firbeare Manor it is part Tudor, part Georgian, part modern and still being reconstructed. It is a smashing place for children, has large gardens, a playroom and a special kids' dining-room. There are also pheasants and geese wandering around. The food looks good, is reasonably priced and homemade. And there's an antique shop attached.

Opposite the entrance to the hotel is the Willand Service Station **3**. The garage has a café attached and also sells everything from fresh brown eggs to Sugar Puffs. Charlie Goff is reputed to be the best mechanic in the area and is virtually on call for repairs at any time though his wife would prefer you not to ring at 3 am.

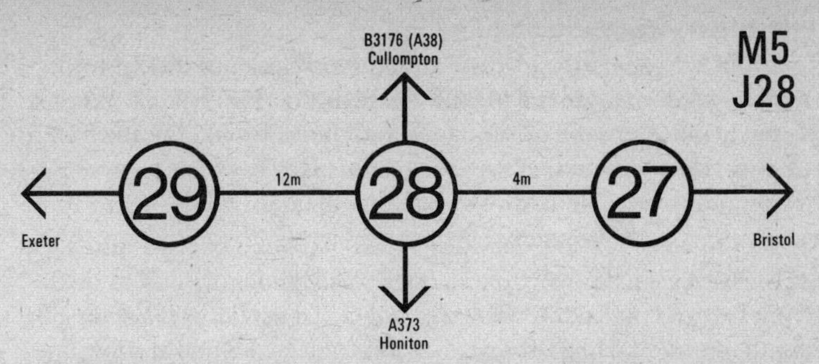

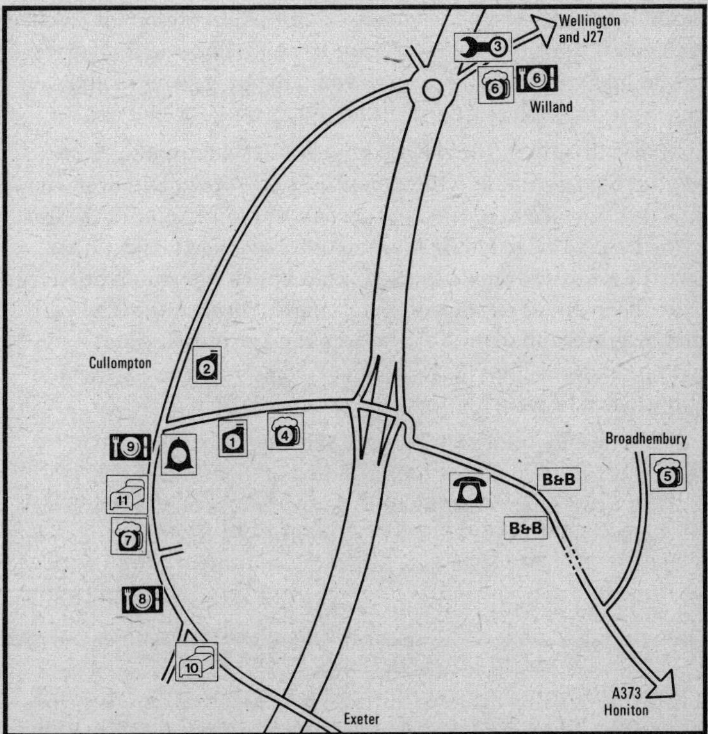

1 Whittens Garage. Hours: 7 am – 9 pm (8 am – 8 pm Sun). Car hire
2 Culm Garage
3 Willand Service Station. Hours: 7 am – 10 pm. Virtual 24-hr breakdown service (Cullompton 2282)
4 *The Showmen*, Watney. (Cullompton 2317)
5 *The Drewe Arms*, Whitbread and Bass. (Broadhembury 267)
6 *The Verbeer Manor Hotel*
7 *The Bell Inn*, Whitbread
8 *Inglenook Restaurant*
9 *Goffey's Coffee Bar and Restaurant*
10 *The Cullompton Hotel* (Cullompton 2272)
11 *The Manor House Hotel* (Cullompton 2281)

J29/30 everything

Junction 30 is one of the nicest in the country (junction 29 is only for traffic getting on to and off the A30 towards London) but it is complex. Not only is the motorway service area off the motorway but the planners have built a whole system of feeder roads which they desperately want you to use – and their route is usually longer. So on the Exeter side of the junction ignore the signs and use the map.

If you want a good break from the motorway, move directly to Topsham and pass Exeter Services. The village is largely unspoiled, has all manner of shops, too many good pubs to mention and lovely walks along the River Exe. Some say it's the oldest port in the country. *Peter Fender's* **11** café, restaurant, wine bar and shop is extremely pleasant and you might discover to your advantage what exactly a 'free vintner' can do. Good coffee and a wide range of cheeses.

Just outside Topsham, on the road signposted to Exmouth, is *The Bridge Inn* **6**, on the bank of the River Clyst – complete with weir and swans. It's an ancient pub – the masons who built Exeter Cathedral are said to have lodged here. Many small rooms and one large bar where the grain was once stored – the landlord's grandfather brewed his own beer. Now you can only get draught Theakstons, Wadworths, Worthington and Badger. Ploughman's and pasties for food.

Two pubs in the area have good food. *The Blue Ball* **8** is close by the junction on the back road to Topsham. Mackerel with gooseberries or mustard sauce for under £1. There is a garden. Further afield is *The Diggers Arms* **7** in Woodbury Salterton. It was once called the Salterton Arms but an Australian landlord left his mark 25 years ago. Home-cured ham, crab sandwiches and draught Bass. An interesting pub.

C&P Motors **1** is highly rated locally as a good garage. They have a 24-hour breakdown service but the mechanics will fix your car on the spot if they can. Even with the charge of a night call this could be cheaper than staying in one of the expensive motels which litter the roads around Exeter.

If you need to stay the night there are many B&Bs and cheapish hotels on the main road into Exeter. Out of town too there are many B&Bs. The two I liked the look of were *Newcourt Barton Farm* **14** and *Ivington Farm* **13** – both peaceful working farms.

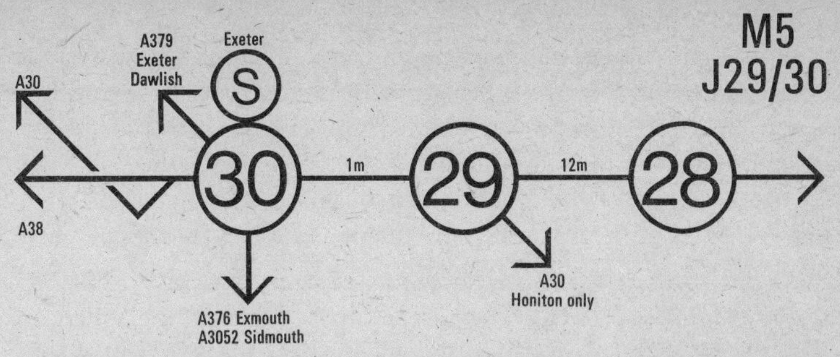

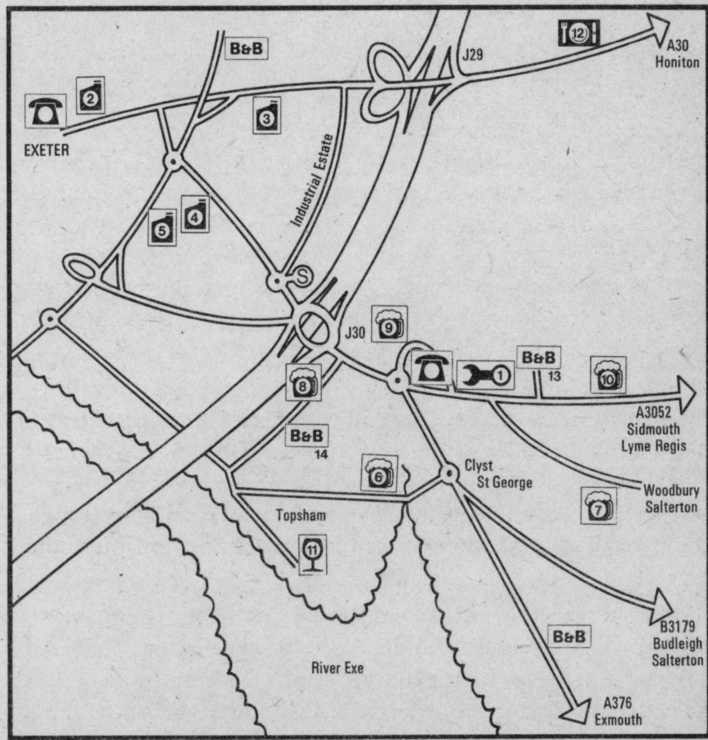

1 C&P Motors. 24-hr breakdown (day Topsham 4425, night Exeter 66567)
2 Supreme Heavitree Filling Station. 24-hr petrol (except Tues and Weds nights)
3 Standfield & White. Hours: 7.30 am – 7 pm
4 Middlemoor Service Station
5 Exeter Service Station. Hours: 7 am – 10 pm (closes 9 pm Sun)
6 *The Bridge,* Free house
7 *The Diggers Arms,* Free house
8 *The Blue Ball,* Whitbread
9 *The Half Moon,* Whitbread
10 *The Cat and Fiddle,* Whitbread
11 *Peter Fender.* Wine bar, shop, restaurant
12 *The Black Horse Transport Café.* Hours: 6 am – 11 pm (open till 7 pm Sat, 11 pm Sun). B&B (Exeter 67681)
13 *Ivington Farm* (Topsham 3290)
14 *Newcourt Barton Farm* (Topsham 3176)

M6

Certain junctions are not included: they are either intersections with other motorways, don't exist, or they offer no real alternative services. They are listed below.

J5

J6

J8

J10

J16

J25

J30

J41

Nothing is very convenient on this junction and there is little to recommend. The petrol at VP Motors **1** and Brownsover **2** is cheap but you have to travel a distance of two miles to get it. The only place really worth a visit is *The Stag and Pheasant* **7** in the small village of Newton. Heading towards Rugby, take the first left turning after almost exactly one mile; travel slightly more than that distance along this small road to the crossroads where you turn left. *The Stag* has a long and varied menu written, bistro-style, on a blackboard. Chili con carne, moussaka, spaghetti, and all the other more usual things; lunch from Monday to Friday and evenings from Tuesday to Saturday; reasonable prices too. A dining area where children can eat, a large field out the back, and skittles.

To the north of the junction there is very little – and what there is, is expensive. Petrol at the Gibbetts Cross Garage **3** was *more* expensive than the motorway service areas when I was there. For this reason alone, as a rarity, it is included in the list. *The Hay Waggon* **6** also seems expensive. Its beer, Ruddles and Hook Norton, is overpriced. So is its food which is largely of the deep-fried variety – at least that's what the pub smells of. I really don't understand why pubs selling good beer can deaden the smell/taste with the all-pervasive oil of deep-fried chips. *The Hay Waggon* is a modern pub of the heavy stone variety which for my money doesn't come off, and this is a pity since it is set in an ideal place and in an area where there is so little else. No children, and closed Saturday lunchtime.

There are a number of nice and useful places in Rugby, as well as cheap petrol, but the town centre is more than three miles from the junction. Fit-a-Screen **4** run a 24-hour service for windscreens and breakdowns. Both *The Three Horseshoes Hotel* **13** and *The Andalucia Restaurant* **11** were pleasant places, although I don't think a restaurant like that should serve tinned consommé soup without, at least, indicating that fact on the menu. As the name suggests, Spanish fare with some very good-looking main dishes.

M6
J1

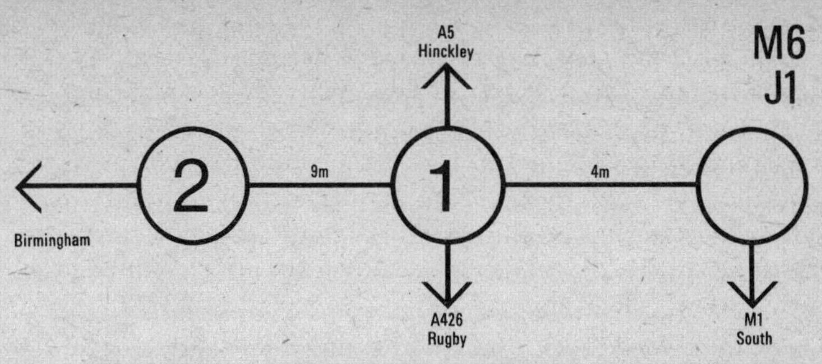

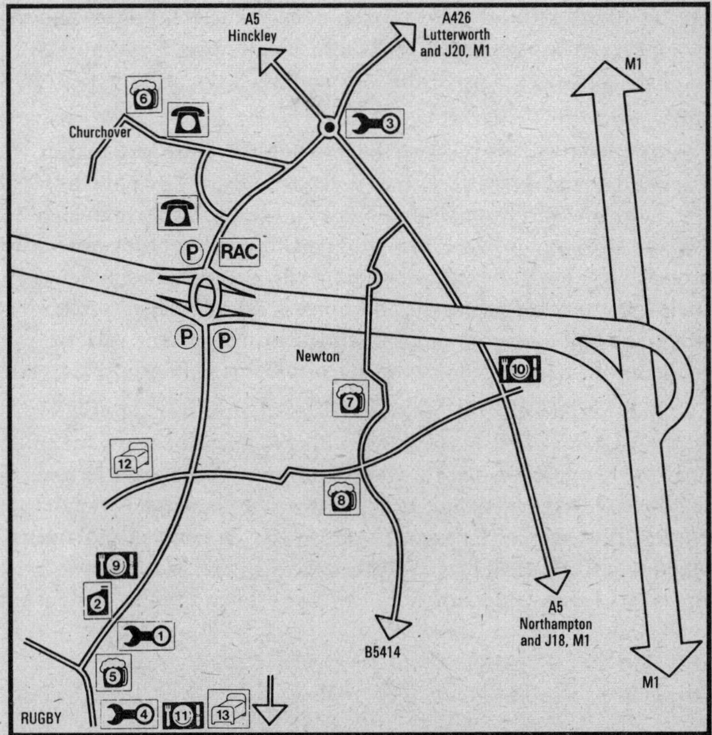

1 VP Motors. Hours: 8 am – 9 pm (open till 6 pm Sat, 10 am – 2 pm Sun). Breakdown in normal working hours (Rugby 4727). Toyota agent
2 Brownsover Service Station. Hours: 7 am – 9 pm (opens 9 am Sun)
3 Gibbetts Cross Garage
4 Fit-A-Screen. 24-hr breakdown and windscreen service (Rugby 72153)
5 *The Avon Mill*, Mitchells and Butlers
6 *The Hay Wain*, Free house
7 *The Stag and Pheasant*, Watney
8 *The St Thomas Cross*, Free house
9 *The Glebe Café*
10 *The Watling Street Transport Café*. Hours: 7.30 am – 5 pm, Mon – Fri
11 *The Andalucia Restaurant* (Rugby 76404)
12 *The Brownsover Hall Hotel* (Rugby 73138)
13 *The Three Horseshoes Hotel* (Rugby 4585)

visit/petrol/pubs

The village of Brinklow is included on this junction because it is worth visiting in its own right. It's on the Fosse Way, and you might find that Coombe Countryside Park **15** is worth a visit – in which case you can do a round trip taking in Brinklow. There are over 200 acres of parkland at Coombe; there's a lake, Birdland and many walks. During the summer season, Easter to the end of September, there is a charge for entry to the park and the many other activities which go on; out of season it's free.

The Potters Green Service Station **2** has the cheapest petrol on the junction but its position is not entirely convenient. It keeps long hours and appears to be a good garage. The Brinklow Service Station **4** is only slightly more expensive and you would clearly buy your petrol there on the round trip.

There are two very nice pubs on the junction. *The Red Lion* **6** in the village of Barnacle is set back from the road with a long front porch. Decent food too – things like faggots and mushy peas and homemade steak and kidney pies. Good beer and bad music. The best beer is at *The Old Plough* **7** – draught Bass. A plain village pub with simple snacks. On the other side of the junction *The Mount Pleasant* **8** sells a very good looking ploughman's lunch and draught bitter. A large garden out the back, too, for those warm weather kids.

Brinklow is a spread out village with a wide main street. The Oxford Canal runs to the north of Brinklow with a short spur coming into the village. *The Fosse Restaurant* **12** would be the place to take the kids. Straightforward English food much of which is homemade – including the cakes and scones. *The Raven* **10** is the most pleasant pub of the comfortable variety with the best beer, and *The Dun Cow* **11** has a long and average pub menu.

1 Mount Pleasant Service Station. Hours: 7 am – 9 pm (opens 9 am Sun)
2 Potters Green Service Station. Hours: 8 am – 10 pm (10 am – 9 pm Sun) 24-hr breakdown (Coventry, day 614570, night 455873)

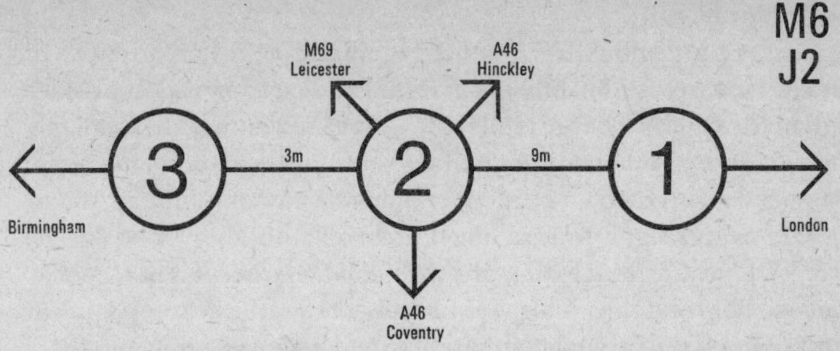

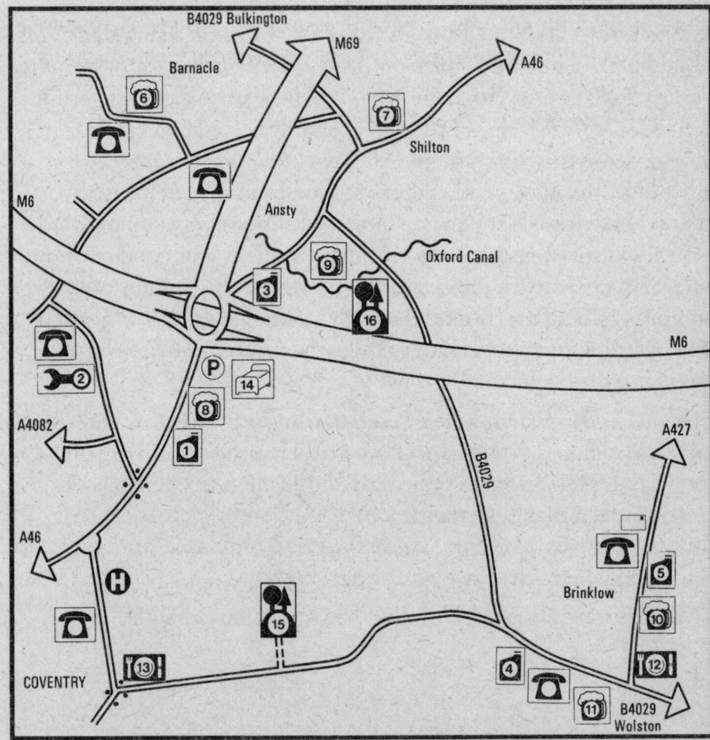

3 Cater Sports Services. Hours: 8.30 am – 6 pm (shorter at weekends)
4 Brinklow Service Station. Hours: 7 am – 7 pm (opens 8 am Sat, 9 am Sun, closes later in summer)
5 Brinklow Garage. Hours: usually 9 am – 8 pm but slightly irregular (opens around lunchtime Sun)
6 *The Red Lion*, Mitchells and Butlers
7 *The Old Plough*, Bass Worthington
8 *The Mount Pleasant*, Marston
9 *The Crown Inn*, Mitchells and Butlers
10 *The Raven*, Ansells
11 *The Dun Cow*, Mitchells and Butlers
12 *The Fosse Way Restaurant*. Closed Mon, Sun and Tue evenings
13 *The Vineyard Restaurant*. Steak bar (Coventry 454159)
14 *Eurocrest Motel*
15 Coombe Countryside Park
16 Oxford Canal – walk

petrol/pubs

Many are the devious arts practised by a certain brewery to entice the unwary into its establishments. Painting the exterior of a canal-side pub in the style of a barge is all right – even interesting, although the interior doesn't follow through. But to exclude the name of the beer sold inside with such an attractive come-on exterior is unfair. And to have two large signs – one saying 'Pub Food', the other 'Food At The Bar' – suggesting that food is always available, when it is not, goes a long way beyond the unfair. *The Cutalong Inn* **9** is the Watney's pub at fault. A good pub in such a situation would have a lot going for it.

The A444 towards Nuneaton is a wide fast road with a single turn-off for Bedworth in its three miles – and since Bedworth has a new traffic scheme which causes jams, the A444 is of little use except for getting you to *The Griff House Hotel* **10** – a reasonably priced hotel in largish gardens. So on this junction take the A444 towards Coventry – but don't go to Coventry – and at the first roundabout head for Bedworth on the B4113. Just after you cross under the motorway you will find the rather surprising *Black Horse* **4** on the right. It sells good beer and is surprising because it looks as though five different minds took part in its conversion. Just beyond that is Whitehall Motors **1** which sells cheap petrol; attached to it is a garage which runs a 24-hour breakdown service.

Between *The Black Horse* and Whitehall Motors is a narrow lane down which you will find *The Boat* **5**. Don't go there unless you are genuinely interested in seeing what a very small old-fashioned pub looks like. A couple of dozen makes a crowd.

Close to the junction is a *Novotel Hotel* **11**. Its grill room is open from six in the morning till midnight; a full breakfast would cost about £1.70; steaks are about £2 and there are reductions for kids.

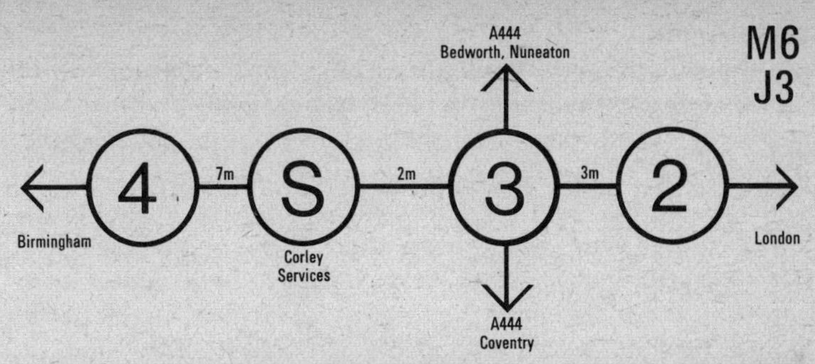

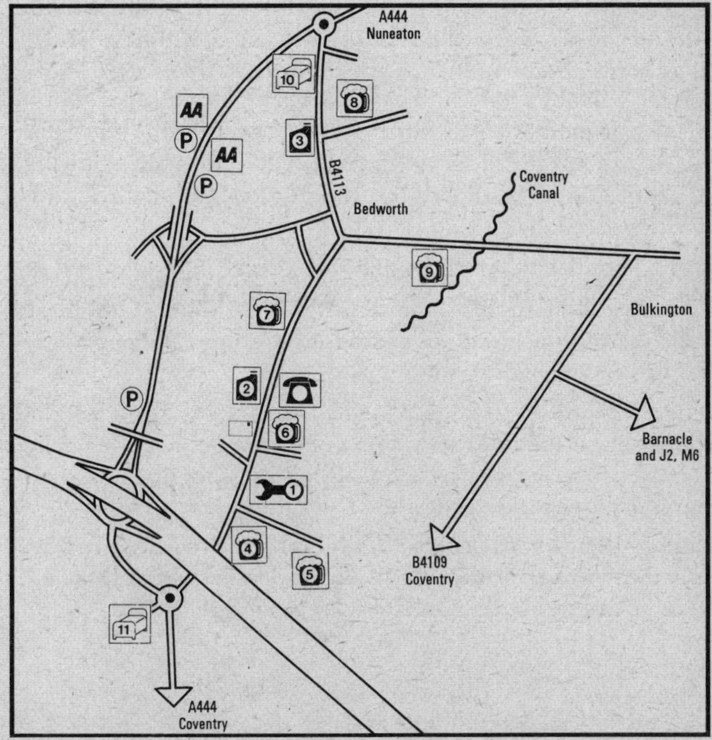

1 Whitehall Motors. Hours: 7 am – 7 pm (shorter at weekends). 24-hr breakdown (Coventry 311395)
2 Heron Service Station. Hours: 7 am – 11 pm (9 am – 10 pm Sun)
3 Orchard Garage. 24-hr petrol machine
4 *The Black Horse*, Mitchells and Butlers
5 *The Boat*, Ansells
6 *The Lord Raglan*, Ansells
7 *The Bull*, Mitchells and Butlers
8 *The Miners Arms*, Marston
9 *The Cutalong Inn*, Watney
10 *The Griff House Hotel* (Nuneaton 382984)
11 *Novotel Hotel* (Coventry 88833)

J4 don't
A complex, messy and uninteresting junction. The sensible advice is don't, yet the small town of Coleshill is quite attractive.

This is a double junction, first with the M42 going to the south – Coventry and Warwick; then with the A446 heading north for Lichfield. Many dual carriageways hurrying importantly around the place but seemingly under-used. Someone could have a big plan for the future on this junction.

Anyway, if you want to go to Coleshill take the A446 towards Lichfield; after quarter of a mile take the B4117 forking off to the right. At the far end of town, by the river, you will find cheapish petrol at the Bridge Service Station and the attractive looking *Wheatsheaf* (Mitchells and Butlers) which has food. Climbing back up the hill into town on the crossroads with the A47 you will find the very plain *Green Man* selling real ale. Turning right at that crossroads you will find *The Bell Inn,* a Davenports inn, within a couple of hundred yards. Sandwiches and snacks.

There is also a Chinese restaurant and an Ansells hotel, *The Swan,* in town. Coleshill is probably the place to come for some shopping and a quick snack.

GUIDE TO MAP SYMBOLS

 PETROL

 GARAGE AND BREAKDOWN

 PUB

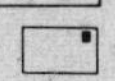 POST OFFICE

 TELEPHONE

 SHOP

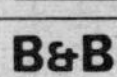

BED AND BREAKFAST

 HOTEL

 PICNIC SPOT

 FISH AND CHIPS

PARKING

RAC

AA

MUSEUM

 RESTAURANT

HOSPITAL

 WINE BAR

 POLICE STATION

 POTTERY

 SWIMMING POOL

petrol/hotels

Unless you want to stay in a pricey hotel/motel, and you have a choice of three, this junction is not for you. Cheap petrol is available at all the garages listed.

But on a good clear day you could go to Barr Beacon **12** and survey the City of Birmingham. Marvel at the fact that they haven't built on land roundabout – though on a windy day you would understand why – apart, that is, from the marching pylons. There's a war memorial with a green cupola and a kids' playground on top. To get there, just head for the highest point: either take the A34 to Walsall and turn right immediately after *The Post House* **9**, or take the A34 to Birmingham, turn left at the traffic lights and then left again, after half a mile, at the roundabout.

Three of the hotel chains have places on this junction – THF, Crest **10** and Greenall Whitley **11**. They have hundreds of beds between them and cater for the business trade – and their prices show this. At weekends they may well have empty rooms and cheaper rates. I wouldn't really know how to choose between these three establishments. *The Post House* is the nearest and is shielded from the motorway by a great bank of earth. It has a buttery, open from 7.30 am to 10.30 pm for light meals and snacks. It's more expensive than *The Crest* but somehow charges very little for sharing children. *The Barr* is the cheapest and furthest away.

The pub food hereabouts is very standard. *The Bell Inn* **8** is the most convenient but only the distant *Three Crowns* **7** can really cater for children. It serves lunches during the week and bar snacks all the time except Sunday. It also has five bedrooms to let at £6 for B&B.

The Three Crowns Garage **1** is nearby and while it doesn't sell the cheapest petrol on the junction it seems to provide just about every other service. Finally, it would be wise to fill up with petrol if you are heading towards London – there are not too many cheap garages for some distance.

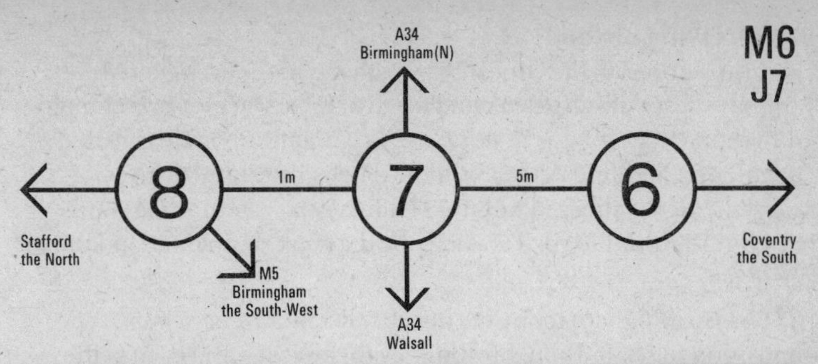

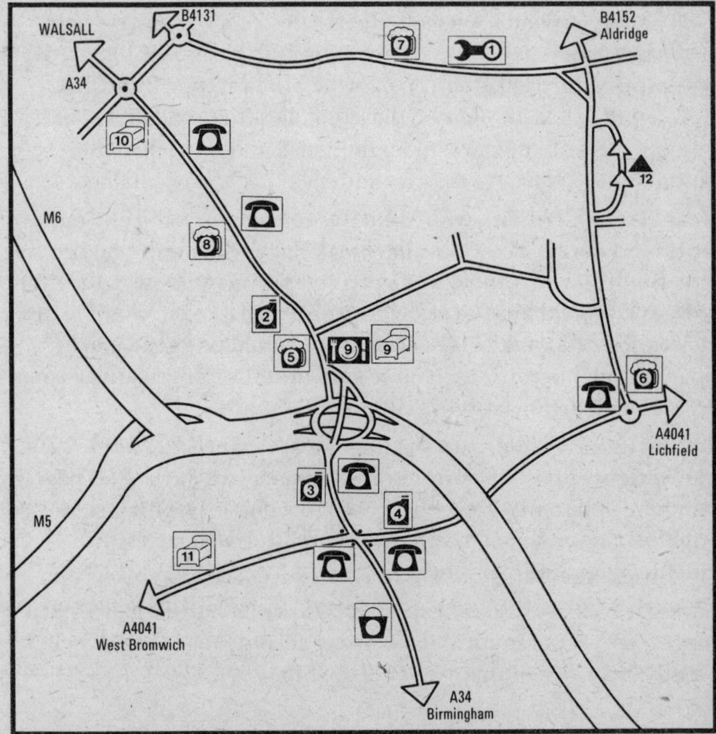

1 Three Crowns Garage. Hours: 8 am – 9 pm plus 24-hr machine. 24-hr breakdown (Aldridge 53232). Leyland agent
2 Tame Service Station. Hours: 8 am – 11 pm (opens 9 am Sun)
3 Gateway Self Service
4 Sundial Garage
5 *The Beacon*, Mitchells and Butlers
6 *The Old Horns*, Mitchells and Butlers
7 *The Three Crowns*, Mitchells and Butlers (Aldridge 23951)
8 *The Bell Inn*, Mitchells and Butlers
9 *The Birmingham Post House and Buttery* (021 357 7444)
10 *The Walsall Crest Motel and Restaurant* (Walsall 33555)
11 *The Barr Hotel*, Greenall Whitley. (021 357 1141)
12 Barr Beacon

petrol/visit/pub food

Congratulations to the City of Birmingham, to the architect Mr James Roberts (if still alive), and to Ansells Brewery for preserving and finding a use for *The Manor House* **9**. To come upon this moated and ancient building in the middle of a housing estate causes amazement and shock. The Great Hall, now a restaurant, is dated between 1290 and 1310; it is said to be the most complete of its kind in existence.

In 1952 Birmingham took over this derelict hulk. There was opposition to restoration, presumably to the cost – and even in those far-off days inflation took its toll. But the decision was clearly right. *The Manor House* is not an easy place to find. Take the A461 towards Wednesbury; turn left after you pass the Mobil station **2** and just before a pub called *The Park* on the left. Follow this road for about three-quarters of a mile, go under the canal, and turn left at the roundabout.

To eat at the restaurant, with its interesting menu, would obviously take time. There is also a Cavalier Steak Bar and some decent beer there. But if all you wanted was a predictable Cavalier steak then you need do no more than stop at *The Jockey* **7** which is much closer to the junction. Next door is *The Cottage* **6** which would be a good place to stop in summer because of its large garden at the front. Standard pub food and a garden 'servery' on summer weekends.

Just past these two pubs, up Vicarage Road, is *Ye Olde Leathern Bottel* **8**. Turn right opposite the graveyard in Brunswick Park **12**. It has been there apparently since 1510, though it doesn't look it inside or out. A lot of rooms, good beer and a heavy trade in businessmen munching giant rolls for lunch.

All the garages listed sell cheap petrol. I have included a lot so that if you were travelling south and wanted to get onto the M5 you could fill up on the way. See the map for **J1** of the M5.

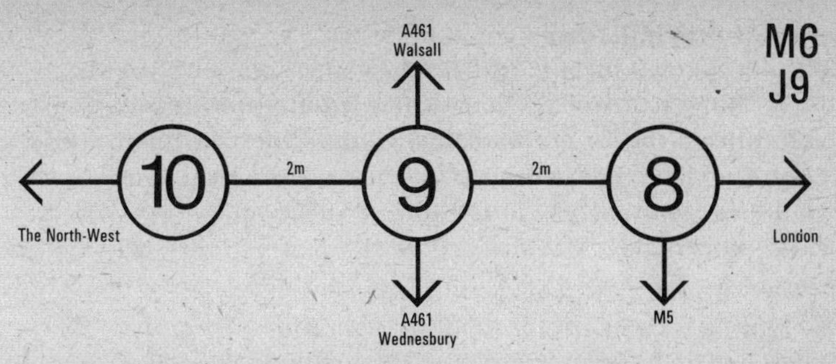

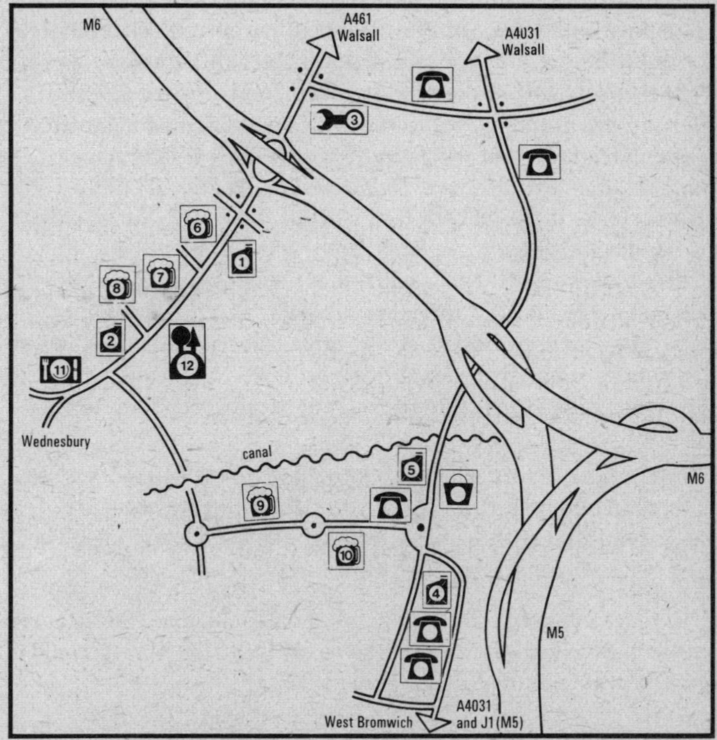

1 College Service Station. Hours: 8 am – 10.30 pm (9 am – 9.30 pm Sun)
2 Wood Green Service Station. Hours: 8 am – 10 pm
3 Grange Garage. Hours: 7.30 am – 9 pm (opens 9 am Sun). Windscreen service every day until 9 pm
4 Stone Cross Service Station. Hours: 7 am – 11 pm (9 am – 9 pm Sun)
5 Pylon Service Station. Hours: 7.30 am – 9.30 pm
6 *The Cottage,* Mitchells and Butlers
7 *The Jockey,* Ansells. Cavalier Steak Bar
8 *Ye Olde Leathern Bottel,* Mitchells and Butlers
9 *The Manor House,* Ansells
10 *The Golden Lion,* Mitchells and Butlers
11 *Bamboo Hill.* Take-away
12 Brunswick Park

petrol/pub snacks/pubs

Whether going north or south it is very simple to exit on one of these junctions and return on the other if, that is, you want anything on offer in the direction of Cannock. All three garages have cheap petrol, that at Longford **2** being the cheapest but not by too much. The mechanics at Hilton **3** appeared helpful and keep very long hours. Their house is next to the garage.

Now a plain description of four pubs so that you can choose. *The Wheatsheaf* **5** is very close to junction 11. It is a bare pub with two bars. Small open fires in winter, no carpet, real ale and rolls – a workingmen's pub. *The Elms* **6** has a lunchtime business clientele. It has moulded radiators. The tables, chairs and lights are also moulded. There are moulded half-tables in front of mirrors. The colours are green and lilac – in a synthetic material. A strong smell of cooking. Bar snacks and a restaurant. Children allowed into the restaurant, even to eat snacks. *The Four Crosses* **4** is an old building with an exterior made dirty by the lorries passing on the A5. Two bars inside. One bar has been converted to the comfortable. In the public bar three high-backed benches surround a wide open fire. Scrubbed tables and many brass adornments. Sandwiches. Finally, another Banks pub, *The Spread Eagle* **8**. A very large roadhouse. The public bar is plain and straight. The lounge has more of a curve and carpet. Pillars and a raffle ticket system for standard pub food. Some deep-fried food and no coaches.

Behind the late Victorian façade of Moseley Old Hall **10** hides a late Elizabethan building. Famous, and probably preserved because Charles I hid out here after his defeat at the battle of Worcester. The hiding place remains, along with some lovely panelled rooms.

M6 J11/12

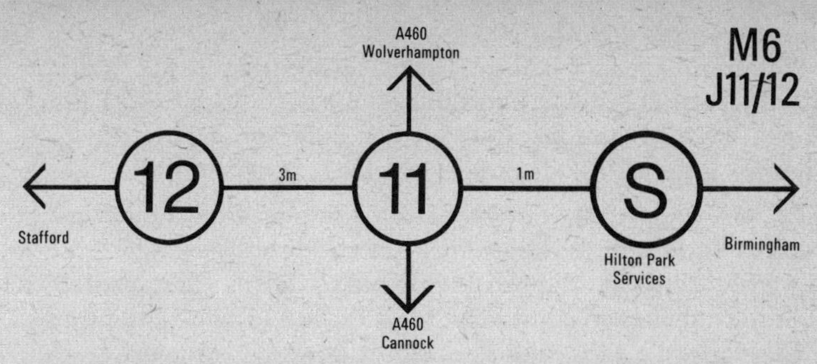

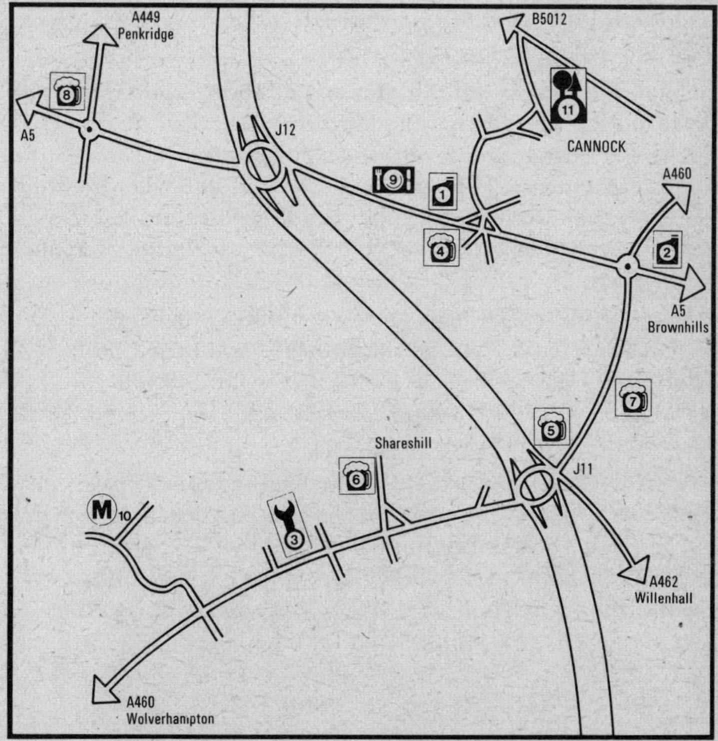

1 Four Crosses Service Station. Hours: 8 am – 8 pm (opens 9 am Sun)
2 Longford Filling Station. Hours: 7 am – 9 pm. 24-hr petrol machine (£1 notes)
3 Hilton Service Station. Hours: 8 am – 7 pm. General repairs till 10 pm every day (Wolverhampton 732566)
4 *The Four Crosses*, Banks
5 *The Wheatsheaf*, Banks
6 *The Elms*, Mitchells and Butlers
7 *The Star and Garter*, Ansells
8 *The Spread Eagle*, Banks
9 *Holly's Transport Café*. Open 24 hrs
10 Moseley Old Hall. National Trust. Open 2 – 5 pm Wed, Thur, Sat, Sun (March – Nov)
11 Shoal Hill picnic spot

garages/petrol/B&B

This is a functional junction. If travelling north look at **J14** for details of the centre of Stafford. If travelling south go through Penkridge and rejoin at **J12**. In this case you will waste little time and save a lot of money on petrol. All the garages listed sell cheap petrol.

You buy your petrol, you have a snack, you quench your thirst and you drive on – unless you are in dire mechanical straits. All three garages offering breakdown services seemed helpful, and all will try to get you moving rather than tow. One garage told me a tale (and had bills to prove it) of a motorist who broke down *off* the motorway. He was towed *onto* the nearest service area. It cost him over £30 to get off again and that was before any repair work.

For food, *The Garth Hotel* **6**. Above average pub food and a restaurant open at normal times except Sunday evening; snacks at all times. Children of the right size pay half in the restaurant and there is a room for kids to eat snacks. The right size means that the landlord does not believe that children who resemble giant gannets eat any less than adults. There are eight bedrooms but they are usually full – certainly in the week.

Further into town is *The Royal Oak* **7** which offers a similar range of services. Children allowed in at lunchtime for snacks or a meal. Between these two hotels is the Rising Brook Garage **2**. They specialize in tyres, batteries and general repairs; what's important is that they are open on Sunday mornings.

In Penkridge, *The Littleton Arms* **9** serves food and you can have a nice pint of beer in *The White Hart* **8**. The canal **12** is a good place to stretch your legs although you can still hear the motorway. To get there, take the first right, signposted to Acton Trussell, off the main road to Stafford. Through the village past the church and right at the T-junction, signed to Penkridge. Lots of parking space.

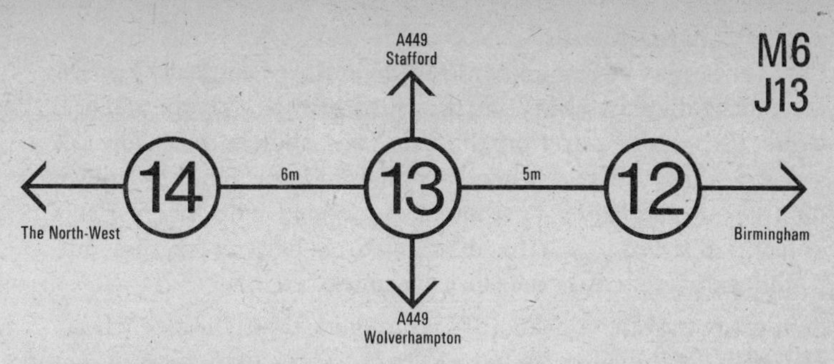

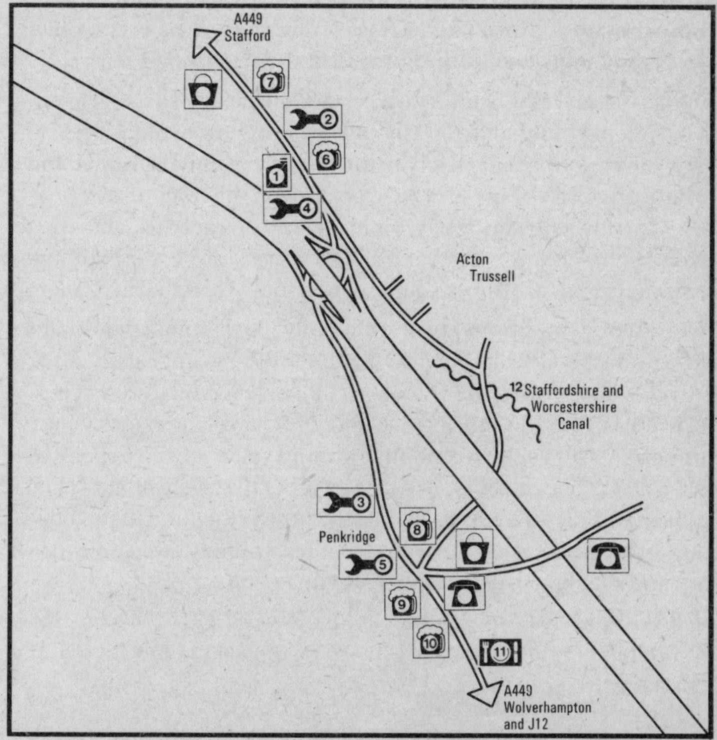

1 Acton Gate Service Station and Snack Bar. Hours: 7.30 am – 8 pm (shorter at weekends)
2 Rising Brook Service Station. Hours: 9 am – 9.30 pm. Workshop: 9 am – 6 pm (half-day Sat, Sun)
3 Dunn's Garage. 24-hr breakdown (Penkridge day 2260, night 2047)
4 Moss Pit Garage. 24-hr breakdown (Stafford 52119). Renault agent
5 Hodsons. Hours: 7.30 am – 8 pm (9 am – 5 pm Sun). Breakdown in working hours (Penkridge 2244)
6 *Garth Hotel*, Banks. B&B (Stafford 51402)
7 *The Royal Oak Hotel*, Bass Worthington. B&B (Stafford 58402)
8 *The White Hart*, Mitchells and Butlers
9 *The Littleton Arms*, Mitchells and Butlers
10 *The Railway*, Ansells
11 *Sunset Hotel and Transport Café*
12 Staffordshire and Worcestershire Canal

petrol/pub food/pubs

On Wednesday 17 September 1642, good King Charles I slept in a lovely Elizabethan building in the centre of town. I doubt that he would do it now. Apart from the fact that the hotels are usually full on a Wednesday, the road system in Stafford is at the time of writing in a terrible mess and almost permanently jammed. They say (a friendly policeman late at night) that it's going to get better when the giant roundabouts that litter the place are connected up.

So is it worth going to Stafford? If you could stay at the lovely *Vine Hotel* **9**, have a meal at *The Curry Kuteer* **11**, if you like Indian food, and drink a pint of ale at *The Malt 'n Hops* **7**, then the answer is yes. Cheap petrol is available, too, at the Foregate **2** and Attwoods **4**.

The Vine Hotel is right behind the Crown Court in the centre of town. It is a surprising building to find in such a place – low, whitewashed and partly covered by a vine. B&B is reasonable and children under ten are half-price. There are also kids' portions in the restaurant, open from Monday to Friday, and a room for them to eat bar snacks (none at Sunday lunchtime). The rates at *The Swan Hotel* **8** in the high street are similar. Kids are only a couple of pounds extra if sharing a room.

If you entered town from **J14** (incidentally, ignore the sign to Stafford off the roundabout; take the next turning – the unsignposted A5013) Attwoods Garage is at the other end of town (as if you were leaving, southwards, for **J13**), stuck in the middle of one of the giant roundabouts. On your second time around you might also spot *The Malt 'n Hops*. The prices for beer are high but that's the price of choice maybe – Ruddles, Holdens, Marstons, Sam Smiths and more. Food, on the other hand, is very reasonable. Meals for lunch during the week and snacks always available. Room for kids.

Izack Walton left a small cottage at Shallowford **12** to the town. He never lived there and it is now a one-room museum. Only for rod-and-tackle fanatics.

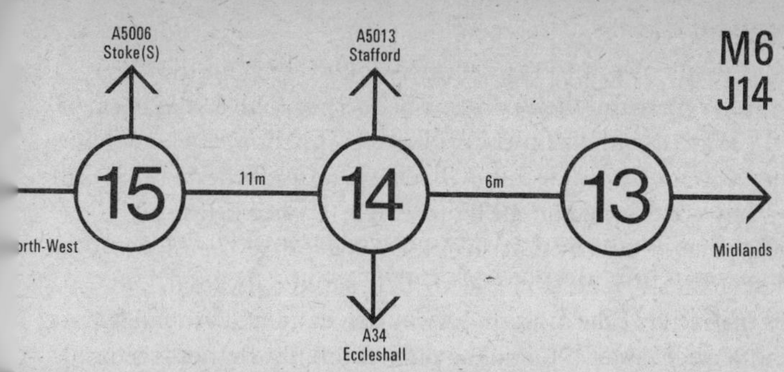

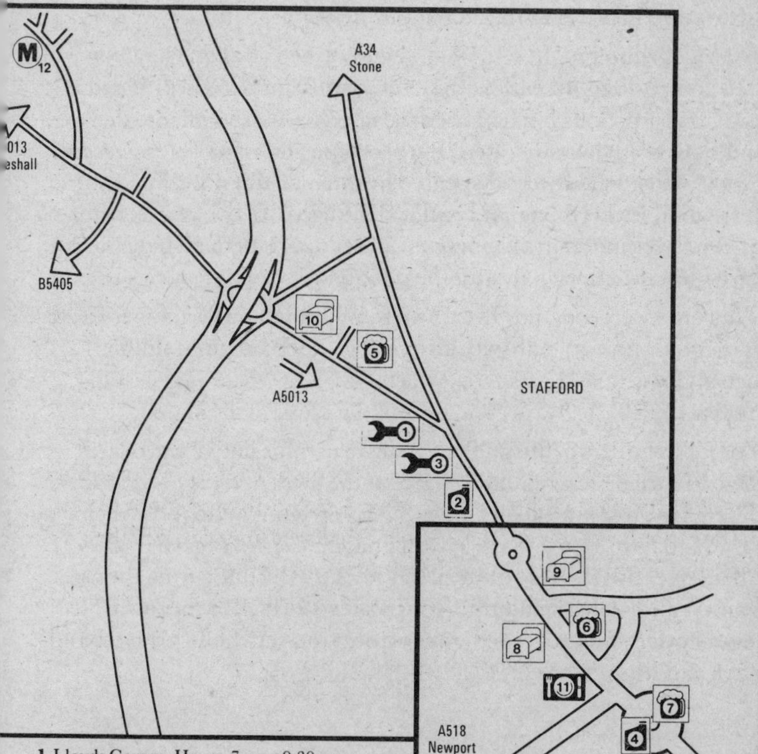

1 Lloyds Garage. Hours: 7 am – 9.30 pm (shorter at weekends). 24-hr breakdown (Stafford 51331). Ford agent
2 Foregate Service Station. 24-hr petrol
3 National Tyre Service Centre. Tyres and batteries
4 Attwoods. Hours: 8 am – 10 pm (9 am – 4 pm Sun)
5 *Holmcroft Inn*, Banks
6 *The Bear Inn*, Banks
7 *The Malt 'n Hops*, Free house
8 *The Swan Hotel* (Stafford 58142)
9 *The Vine Hotel*, Banks (Stafford 51071)
10 *The Tillington Hall Hotel*, Greenall Whitley (Stafford 53531)
11 *The Curry Kuteer Restaurant*
12 Izack Walton's House/Museum. Open 10 am – 1 pm, 2 – 5 pm (Thur – Sun)

Dear Mr Rodgers,
You, as Minister of Transport, set up a wide-ranging inquiry into motorway services and their prices. The real problem is that because most people are terrified of turning off at any junction, not knowing what they will find, how far they will have to go and whether they will get lost, they are trapped on the motorways. It is not so much monopoly practice as fear that gives the service areas their trade. One journalist wrote: 'Prices, to me, seem high, service abysmal, and facilities primitive. Like most motorway drivers, I unfortunately have to use the service areas.' Nor do the public complain – there seems little point in complaining about the inevitable.

On a wet winter night some years ago I turned off at this junction with two companions in search of a small country pub. We'd dithered at previous junctions but had been too nervous to drive off into the unknown. But here we'd seen the beckoning lights of *The Post House* **7**. Apparently drinks were dispensed from a machine only. We retreated. It was then that I realized the need of a book to list the alternatives junction by junction. This is it. Not perfect, but it does provide a range of choices for the public.

This junction is not, however, worthy of the name alternative. There is no small country pub with an open fire, good beer and simple decent food.
Yours J.S.

But for members of the public having to use this junction, you will save £1 buying ten gallons of petrol at the Swift Service Station **1**. There is a garage attached to the Swift and it might be able to help you out. If you are forced to stay overnight, *The Clayton Lodge* **6** is fairly attractive. But it is also quite pricey and usually full during the week. With your kids, on a fine day, you could go to Trentham Park **8**. Again pricey but it seems to support almost every known outdoor park activity, and there is a lovely lakeside walk.

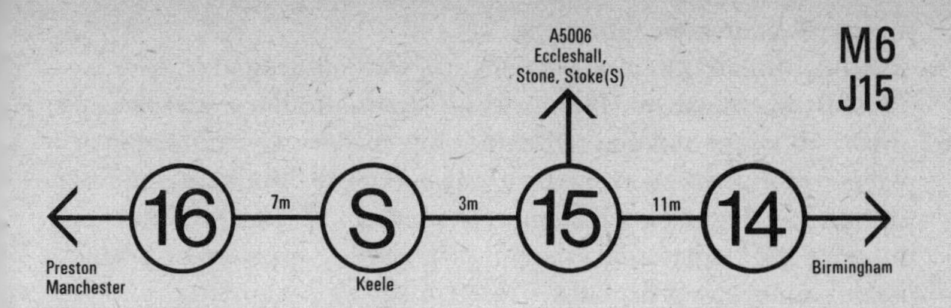

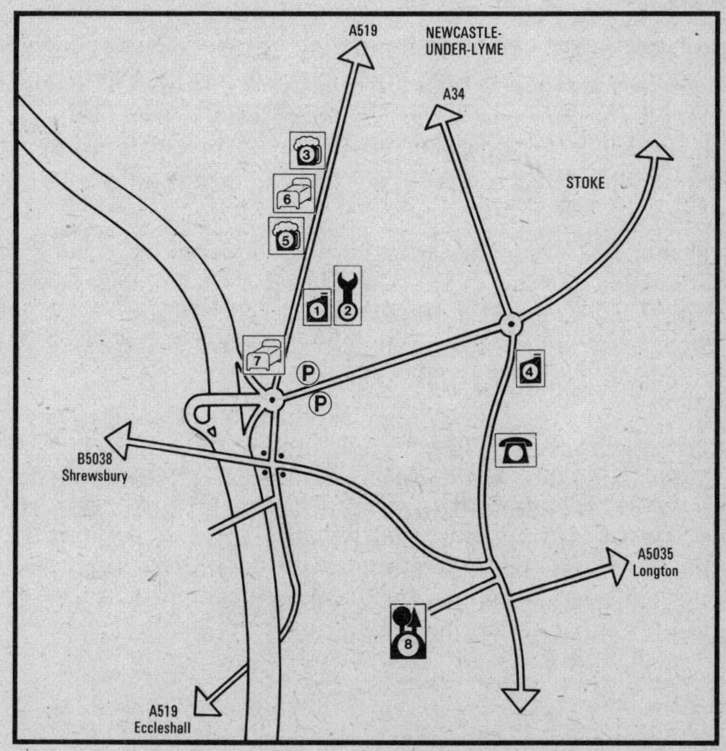

1 Swift Service Station. Hours: 7.30 am – 11 pm (shorter at weekends)
2 Swift Service Station Garage. 24-hr breakdown (day Newcastle 627838, night Betley 417)
3 Clayton Service Station
4 Handford Service Station
5 *The Copeland Arms*, Ansells
6 *The Clayton Lodge Hotel* (Newcastle 613093)
7 *The Post House Hotel* (Newcastle 625151)
8 Trentham Park

restaurants/overnights/pubs

The territory around this junction is the stalking ground of the Cheshire businessmen. They work on expense accounts and are provided, for their money, with thick pile carpets. There are many places to stay but you are going to pay about £10 – and that's without supper. For that reason I include *Holford Farm* **14**. It's three miles on the A534 to Congleton – turn right just before a very sharp left-hand bend. Four cheap bedrooms.

The petrol at any of the first three garages listed will save you nearly 10p a gallon. The closest garage, Hills **4**, is more expensive. It's within a hundred yards of the junction and is disguised as a car graveyard – it is also very overgrown.

While watching your car being given the treatment in the Old Smithy Garage **2**, you can repair to *The Legs of Man* **6** just across the road. Good beer and the normal range of pub snacks. There is also a restaurant (the landlord is cook) which has children's portions and prices.

Remember that everything on this junction is a bit expensive. But if you deserve a treat stay at *The Old Hall Hotel* **10**. The building is large, beautiful, half-timbered and listed as Grade 1. The fourteen bedrooms have been well done-up. There is a restaurant serving traditional English food and Boddingtons beer.

In the town square are two extraordinary Saxon crosses, said to date from the eighth century. They reach for the heavens as you move gracefully across the square after an excellent pint of Robinsons at the sparse *Crown Hotel* **8** and down the old coaching road to *The Lower Chequer* **9**. It's said that the maids and servants drank down here in this ancient half-timbered building. Secret tunnels, or claims for them, abound. The last time they dug for one in the cellars of the Old Hall they only managed to flood the place.

The Bluebell **7** is quite a distance from the junction – a journey only worth making on a fine day to sit in the lovely garden. The same is true of the picnic spot **15**, an area of silver birch trees.

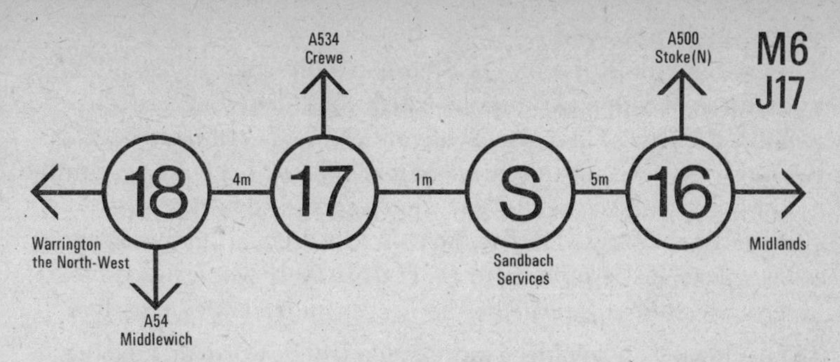

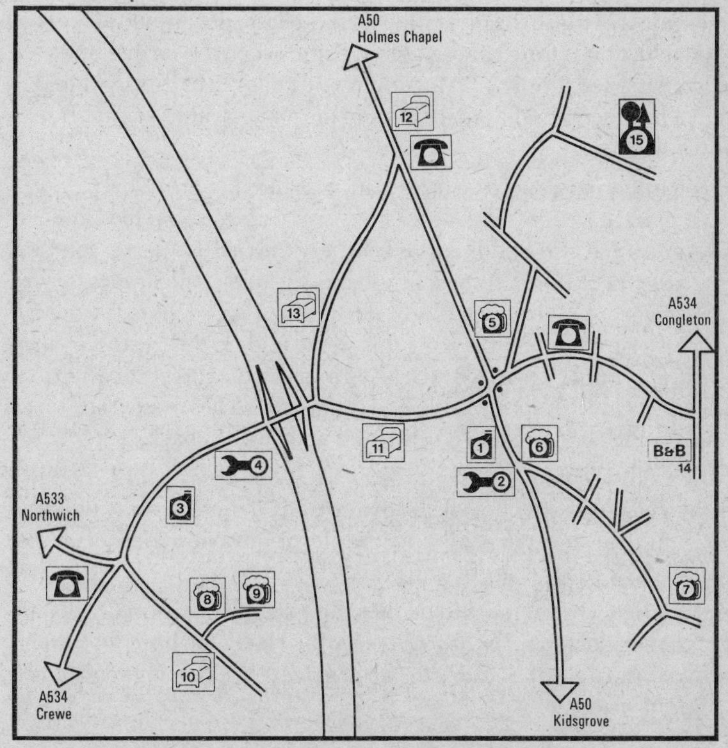

1 Four Ways Garage. Hours: 7 am – 8 pm
2 The Old Smithy Garage. 24-hr breakdown service (Smallwood 334)
3 Heron Service Station. Hours: 7 am – 11 pm (8 am – 10 pm Sun)
4 Hills Garage. Hours: 8 am – 10 pm. 24-hr windscreen service (Sandbach 2498)
5 *The Rose and Crown,* Ansells
6 *The Legs of Man,* Robinsons. Restaurant (Smallwood 332)
7 *The Bluebell Inn,* Greenall Whitley
8 *The Crown Hotel,* Robinsons
9 *The Lower Chequer,* Ansells
10 *The Old Hall,* Free house. Restaurant and hotel (Sandbach 3757)
11 *The Chimney House Hotel and Restaurant* (Sandbach 4142)
12 *The Bears Head Hotel and Restaurant* (Holmes Chapel 35251)
13 *The Saxon Cross Motel* (Sandbach 2636)
14 Holford Farm. B&B (Smallwood 427)
15 Brereton Heath picnic spot

petrol/visit/pub food

The Cotton Filling Station **1** is almost on the junction and, while not as cheap as the other two garages listed, you still save nearly 10p a gallon. In Holmes Chapel you will find *The Good Companions* **5** which has food on weekdays and can cater for children. There is a restaurant at *The Old Vicarage Hotel* **11** if you want a good sit-down meal, and children are cheaper. They do have three bedrooms but these appear to be expensive. Better to go to *The Holly Lodge* **10** where they have invented a children's tariff they don't even understand themselves.

Time allowing and children ranting, it might be worth making the five-mile trip to see the mysterious radio-telescopes at Jodrell Bank **14** – listen to noises from space made at a time when the earth didn't exist. Afternoons only. 50p for adults and children half-price. I find that a bit steep for what there is – and the planetarium is extra. But you only go once.

If you intend to travel that far, go through the village of Goostrey. Two pubs there. *The Olde Red Lion* **7** serves very good bar food and has a restaurant – also Boddingtons beer. *The Crown* **8** also serves food and can cater for children. It has three bars, reflecting, one supposes, the class divisions in the village, and serves draught Pedigree. It would also be wise if you were making this trip to pick up the cheapest petrol at the Discount Centre **3** which also gives you the choice of eating at *The Swan Hotel* **6**. Normal pub food from sandwiches to steaks. Guns on the walls, budgies down below and a garden out back.

Now a silly recommendation: *The Yellow Broom Restaurant* **12**. You'll never get in unless you book in advance, and if there are only two of you you'll never get in at all since they have only one table for two. But I'm told it's good. So if you can plan . . .

In Middlewich, not marked on the map, you will find two nice places. On the edge of town *The Boars Head* **9** which has good beer, food and bedrooms. In town, *Franco's Italian Restaurant* **13**. Evenings only and children welcome.

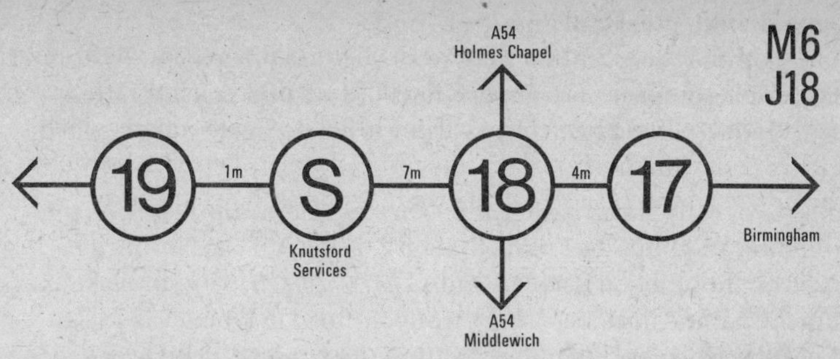

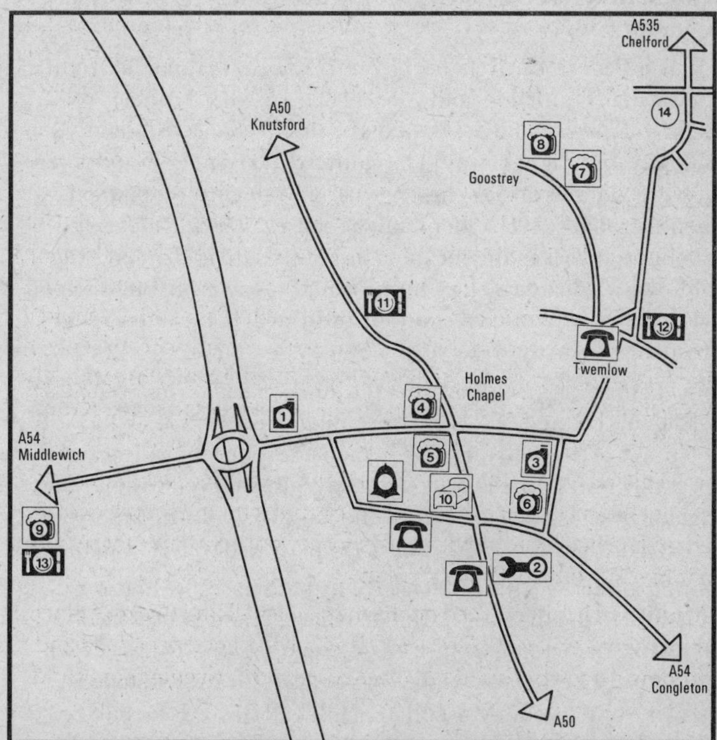

1 Cotton Filling Station. 24-hr petrol
2 Baldwin and Parker. Hours: 8.30 am – 8 pm (closes 5 pm Sat, Sun)
3 Manor Discount Centre Filling Station. Hours: 7.30 am – 7 pm (shorter at weekends)
4 *The George and Dragon,* Robinsons
5 *The Good Companions,* Watney
6 *The Swan Hotel,* Sam Smith
7 *The Olde Red Lion Inn,* Free house
8 *The Crown,* Marston
9 *The Boars Head Hotel,* Robinsons (Middlewich 31919)
10 *The Holly Lodge Hotel* (Holmes Chapel 37033)
11 *Old Vicarage Hotel and Restaurant* (Holmes Chapel 32041)
12 *The Yellow Broom Restaurant* (Holmes Chapel 33289)
13 *Franco's Restaurant* (Middlewich 3204)
14 Jodrell Bank. Open March 18 – Oct 31 every afternoon (Sun afternoons only in winter)

petrol/hotels/restaurants/pub food

One of those very rare junctions where one has to leave good places off for reasons of space and range. Knutsford is a middle-class retreat with good food and beer and a variety of hotels; but first those places closer to the junction.

The two really cheap garages are Northern Caravans **1** right on the junction and Plumley Filling Station **2** on the A556 to Northwich. Also on the junction is a plain pub, *The Windmill* **5**, with simple rolls at lunchtime and good beer. Further up the road in Plumley is *The Smoker Inn* **6**, a very old pub with attractive bar food, good beer and a restaurant.

In Lower Peover, turn left just before *The Smoker Inn* and then right at the eventual T-junction, and you will find, up a hard cobbled road, *The Bells of Peover* **7** and St Oswald's Church – connected, rightly some would say, by a right of way. The church dates from 1269 and is very lovely. It contains an oak chest hewn from a single piece of wood which is probably even older than the church. *The Bells of Peover* (pronounced Peever and meaning bright stream) is an interesting building with nice gardens. Once you find your way in, there is good beer, bar snacks, a rated restaurant and a large and antique room with an open hearth.

Going in the other direction from the junction and turning left at the traffic lights on the A50, you will eventually come to *The Kilton Inn* **8**. A good range of food starting with homemade soup for just 16p and then a lot of different salads. You could then really ruin your whole time schedule by a visit to Tatton Hall and Park **16**. Only the super-rich and extraordinary could have built the place and collected all the stuff.

Another kind of wealth and eccentricity built the coffee house in Knutsford in the shape of an Italian palace. It now houses *La Belle Epoque* **15**. An incredible place – just go and see. *The Rose and Crown Hotel* **12** is the best place to take kids for food – a range of stuffed potatoes – and to stay. Most other places will feed kids for half-price. A cheap hotel for a family overnight would be *The Heatherfield* **13**.

1 Northern Caravans. Hours: 7.30 am – 10 pm (opens 8.30 am Sun)
2 Plumley Filling Station. Hours: 8 am – 8 pm (later opening Sat, Sun)
3 Orchard Service Station. Hours: 8 am – 6 pm (closed Sun)
4 Cheshireways Filling Station. Hours: 7 am – 11 pm. 24-hr petrol machine
5 *The Windmill*, Robinson
6 *The Smoker Inn*, Robinson (Lower Peover 2338)
7 *The Bells of Peover*, Greenall Whitley. Restaurant (Lower Peover 2269)

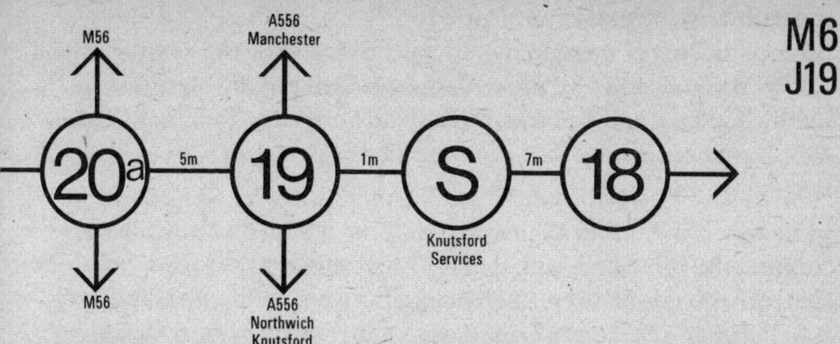

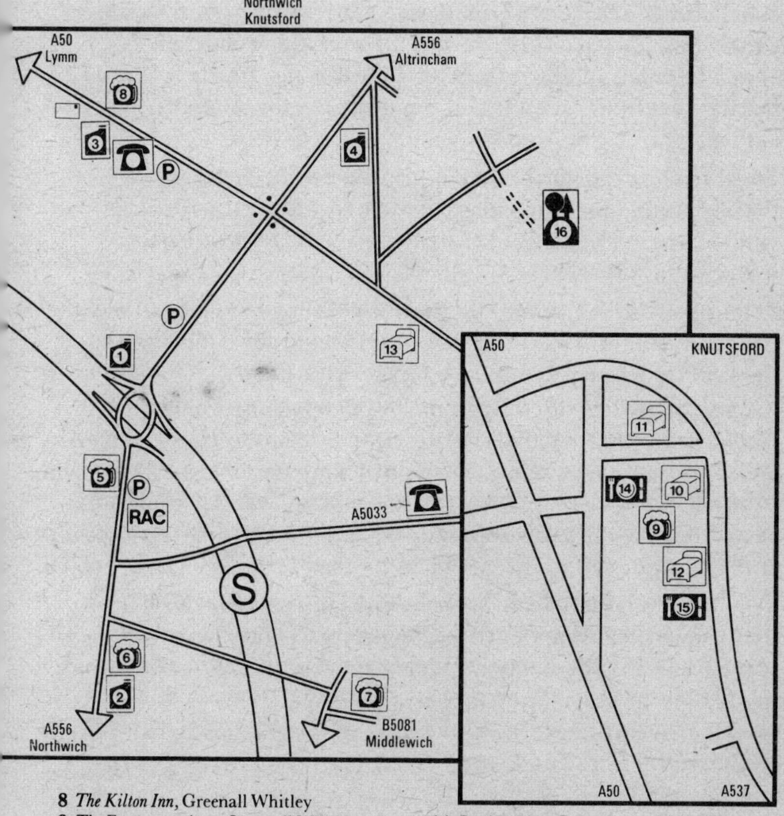

8 *The Kilton Inn*, Greenall Whitley
9 *The Freemasons Arms*, Greenall Whitley. B&B (Knutsford 2368)
10 *The Royal George*, Watney. (Knutsford 4151)
11 *The Angel Hotel*, Greenall Whitley. (Knutsford 52627)
12 *The Rose and Crown Hotel* (Knutsford 52366)
13 *The Heatherfield Hotel* (Knutsford 3428)
14 *David's Place*. Restaurant. Closed Mon (Knutsford 3356)
15 *La Belle Epoque*. Restaurant and brasserie (Knutsford 3060)
16 Tatton Hall and Park. House open May – Sept in afternoons. Grounds open all year (Knutsford 3155)

pub food/walk/petrol

A good but spread out junction. If you just wanted some cheap petrol and food you would take the A50 towards Warrington. Petrol at Oulton Court **1** and a snack or reasonably priced grill at *The Dog and Dart* **10**. There is also a place to walk along the canal **16**. Parking is easy but the steep and slippery steps are not.

With time on your side the village of Lymm is worth a visit. The oldest commercial canal in the land, the Bridgewater runs through the centre of town. It is a very good place for a walk, with a lot of heavy old stone bridges. *The Golden Fleece* **5** has a garden which overlooks the canal. The pub has a varied menu with everything under £1. *The Spread Eagle* **6** is another hotel without bedrooms. It sells Lees real ale, has bar snacks and a restaurant, and can cater for children if they are eating.

The Jolly Thresher **8**, further afield, also has decent food with a dish of the day, and can accommodate children. If you are travelling north it would be worth looking at **J21** because you can return to the motorway via Warburton.

Out of town is the Lymm Dam **15** which has created a nice lake. A place to picnic or walk. It's right by the church which is built on a soft red sandstone outcrop. Just past the church are two genuine hotels. *The Church Green Hotel* **7** has food six days a week (not Monday) and children, if eating, are welcome. It has two cheapish rooms, each with their own shower and TV. If you want a real hotel you have to cross the road to *The Dingle* **14** but you also pay real prices. Children are £2 extra in your room but half-price in the restaurant with its long à la carte menu.

Down the road from these three places is the Central Garage **2**. Its petrol could be cheaper but it keeps long hours and will undertake just about any mechanical repairs – as always, within reason. But which motorists are?

1 Oulton Court Service Station. Hours: 8 am – 10 pm (8 am – 5.30 pm Wed, Sat, Sun) Howarth Motors. VW and Audi agents

2 Central Garage. Hours: 8 am – 8.30 pm (opens 9 am Sun). Summer hours longer. All repairs carried out in normal hours

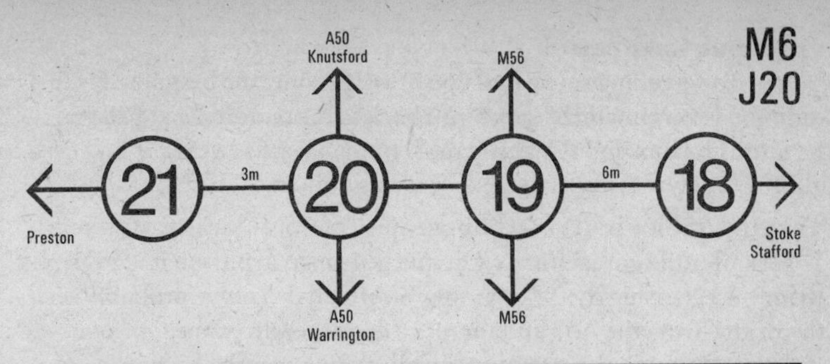

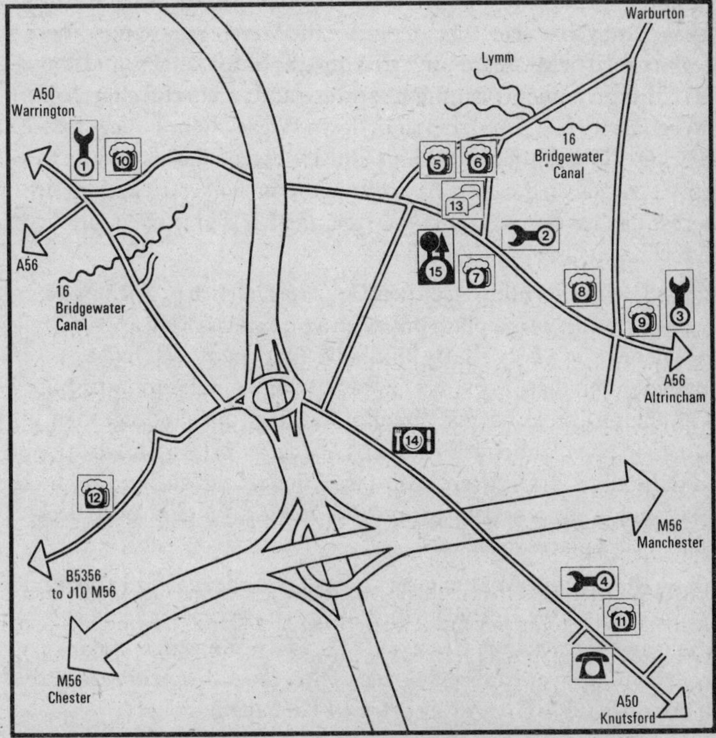

3 Avenue Motors. 24-hr breakdown (Lymm, day 2447 or 5900, night 2447). Tyre specialists

4 High Legh Filling Station. Hours: 7.30 am – 7 pm (closed Sun). Breakdown and repairs (Lymm 3517)

5 *The Golden Fleece Hotel*, Greenall Whitley

6 *The Spread Eagle Hotel*, Lees. Restaurant closed Sun, Mon

7 *The Church Green Hotel*, Greenall Whitley (Lymm 5575)

8 *The Jolly Thresher*, Hydes

9 *The Wheatsheaf*, Hydes

10 *The Dog and Dart*, Greenall Whitley

11 *The Bears Paw Inn*, Greenall Whitley

12 *The Thorn*, Greenall Whitley

13 *The Dingle Hotel*. Restaurant closed Sat lunch Sun evening (Lymm 2297)

14 *Poplar Transport Café*

15 Lymm Dam picnic spot

16 Bridgewater Canal

visits/pub food/petrol

If you are travelling south and you have the time, the best plan for this junction is a tour which brings you back to the motorway at **J20** via Lymm. The tour should satisfy most human wants (we can't guarantee everything!) and will cost a minimum of 5p.

Take the A57 for Irlam and buy cheapish petrol at Jackson Brothers **1**. Just after the garage turn right and go over Warburton High Level Bridge **15** crossing the Manchester Ship Canal. You've probably seen the bridge from the A57 and there is a good view from the top. You then spend your 5p on crossing the toll bridge over the River Mersey. If observant you will feel cheated since the Mersey is no longer there – just flat green fields. It was diverted into the Ship Canal round about 1894. Make a point of visiting the strange and wonderful church of St Werburgh **16**. Turn sharp right down Wigsey Lane having crossed the bridge. If it's shut or you can't find a leaflet on the history, go to the first cottage in the lane. Apart from the ancient church, there are interesting gravestones and a yew tree which is said to have supplied the archers at Crécy and Agincourt.

For food, without children, either *The Green Dragon* **6** or *The Saracen's Head* **5**. The *Dragon* is a plain pub with a nice range of cheap sandwiches and a very chatty landlady. *The Saracen's* has had a conversion but there are still a few old bits and pieces around. Quite a decent menu – steak barms, pizzas and cottage pie – and a garden. For a good cheap lunch try *The Bollin Restaurant* **12**. An à la carte menu and reductions for children. Also a traditional English Sunday lunch for £2.50. For the best beer around, *The Railway* **7** is close by. Check **J20** for other places in Lymm.

Taking the A57 into Warrington you will find cheap petrol at both the Woolston **4** and the Heron **3** which always has a cashier on duty. Nearby is *The Paddington House Hotel* **13**. The restaurant is open every day and children are half-price. Its nightly rates are not unreasonable but opposite is *The Grange Guest House* **14** at half the price.

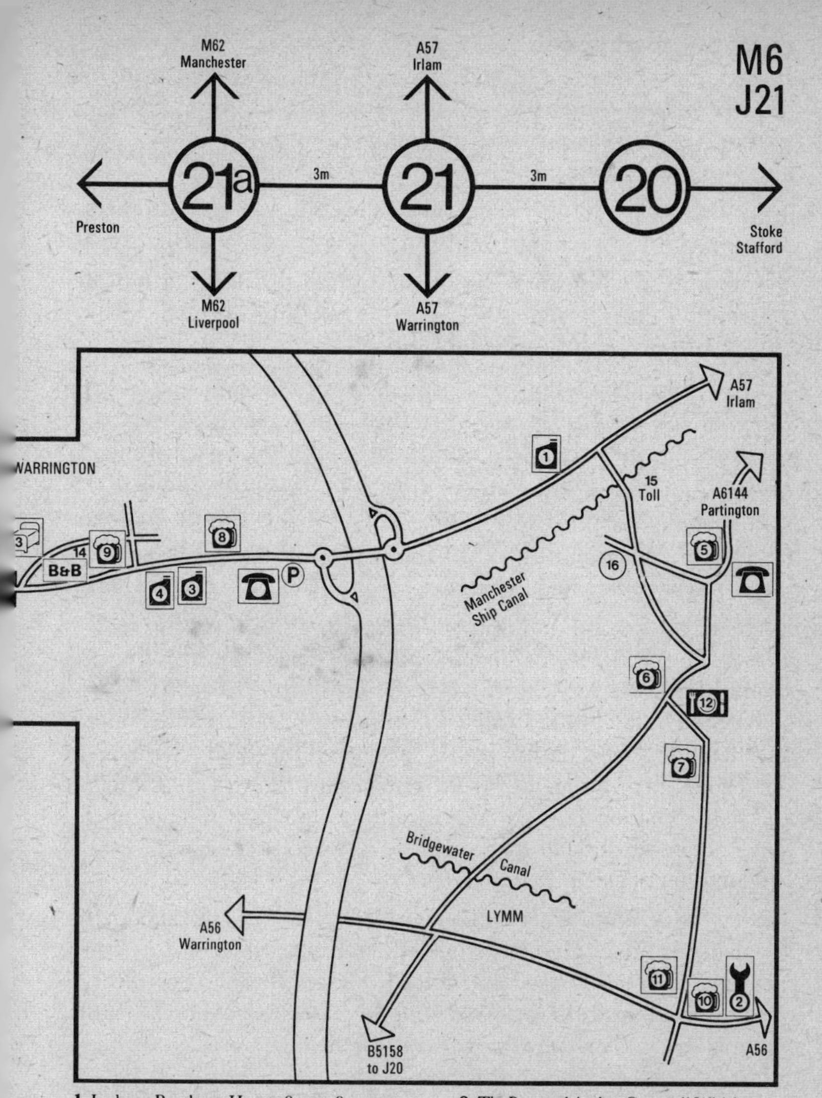

1 Jackson Brothers. Hours: 8 am – 8 pm
2 Park Garage. Hours: 8 am – 8 pm (closed Sun). Avenue Motors. 24-hr breakdown (Lymm, day 2447 or 5900, night 2447). Tyre specialists
3 Heron Service Station. 24-hr petrol
4 Woolston Service Station
5 *The Saracen's Head*, Greenall Whitley
6 *The Green Dragon Hotel*, Bass Charrington
7 *The Railway*, Boddingtons
8 *The Rope and Anchor*, Greenall Whitley
9 *The Dog and Partridge*, Greenall Whitley
10 *The Wheatsheaf*, Hydes
11 *The Jolly Thresher*, Hydes
12 *The Bollin Restaurant*. Closed Mon (Lymm 3657)
13 *The Paddington House Hotel and Restaurant* (Warrington 816767)
14 *The Grange Guest House* (Warrington 812340)
15 Warburton High Level Bridge
16 Warburton old church

food/petrol

This junction is written out of guilt for those travelling south having just passed through the deserts around Wigan. Let it also, therefore, be a warning to those travelling north. For those who only want cheap petrol; wait for **J23**. If you want food and petrol, get off here and rejoin at J23.

One note to complicate the whole issue. There is a Heron 24-hour petrol station with cheap prices just across the M62. Take the A49 for Warrington, cross **J9** of the M62 and it's soon on the right with a self-service cashier on permanent duty.

The two recommendations which appear on this junction and on J23 are A and B **1** and *The Traveller's Rest Inn* **5**. The garage has cheap petrol and the pub has good, cheap, homemade food, a garden and a dining room for children. So it is very easy for you north-bounders to go to the pub, cross over to the garage and then rejoin the motorway by using the A49.

The two new entries in the chart are *The Swan* **3** and *The Plough* **4**. *The Swan* is newly converted, and proudly so, to a Jacobean style. But in spite of this historical pretence it is trying to serve decent lunches, during the week, for under £1. *The Plough* is worth a visit since someone undoubtedly has a plan to change it into a Jacobean, if not a Saxon, paradise. Not totally unspoilt, but a simple country pub offering real ale on hard wooden seats. Not for the beaten copper and comfort brigade.

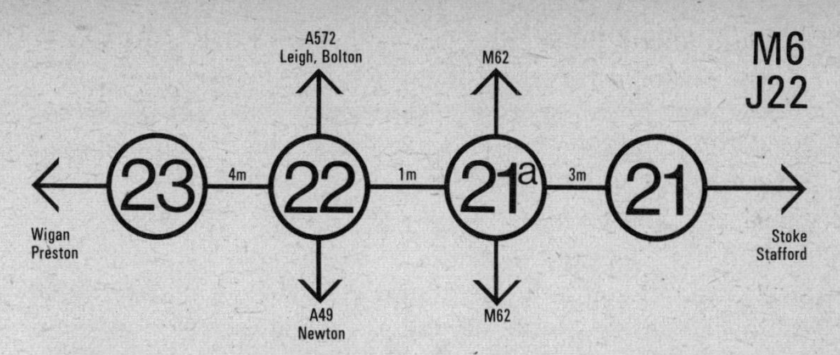

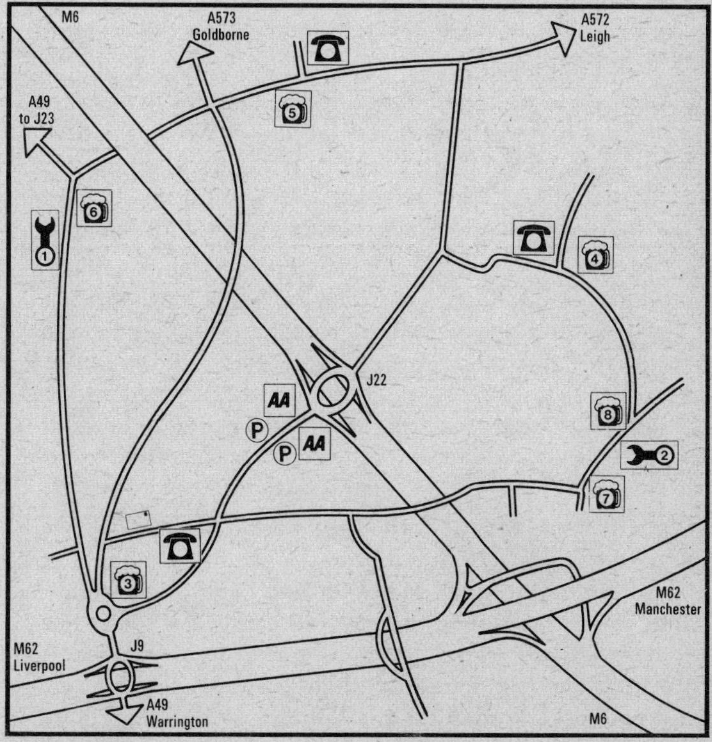

1 A and B. Hours: 8 am – 8 pm. Breakdown in working hours. Car and van hire. (Newton-le-Willows 4411). Volvo, Citroën, Daf and Datsun agents
2 Birchall's Garage
3 *The Swan*, Wilsons
4 *The Plough*, Greenall Whitley
5 *The Traveller's Rest Inn*, Greenall Whitley
6 *The Leigh Arms*, Tetley
7 *The Horseshoe*, Tetley
8 *The General Eliot*, Tetley

petrol/pub food/pubs

Most of what follows is about **J23** which connects with the old main road between Manchester and Liverpool, the A580. **J24** can only be used for getting off southwards and getting on northwards. But it does have some use for those dedicated to interesting pubs.

Very cheap and very convenient petrol available at **J24**. Right beneath the motorway is the Haydoc' Island Service Station **2**. Do not get too confused by the very compl. . roundabout much bedecked with traffic lights, nor by the neon sign in the garage (at least when I was there) proudly announcing that drunks are served. A and B **3** also appears to be a useful place. The petrol is cheap and they have a car and van hire service.

Quite a choice of pub restaurants. The place to take kids for food is *he travellers Rest Inn* **10**. Perhaps not the most convenient place to get to, but it is easy to rejoin (or come off) at **J22**. There is homemade food – steak and kidney, or Lancashire hot pot with red cabbage; and only 50p each. A dining area for children and a garden for the summer.

The Queen Anne **7** is different. An up-market conversion with slightly smoked-glass doors, tasteful, pastel nudes (female) on the wall and, the big give-away, a gas log fire. The chipped porcelain of the gents was also a let-down having gone through a lovely wooden door called Romeo. The menu looked good – items like spare ribs with sweet and sour sauce. But the ribs were very spare and the potatoes under-cooked. Too much style and not enough performance. But worth trying once.

On the road from **J23** to **J24** – the A49 via Ashton – is another restaurant, *The Bay Horse Hotel* **5**, popular with the lunchtime business trade. Just before it you will find *The Colliers Arms* **6**. To go there, you should belong to that group of people who believe that most pub conversions carried out by the breweries are close to vandalism. A very plain and simple pub with hard-backed wooden seating. Not too far away, in the centre of Ashton, is *The Kings Arms* **4**. Larger and more comfortable and, again, with real ale.

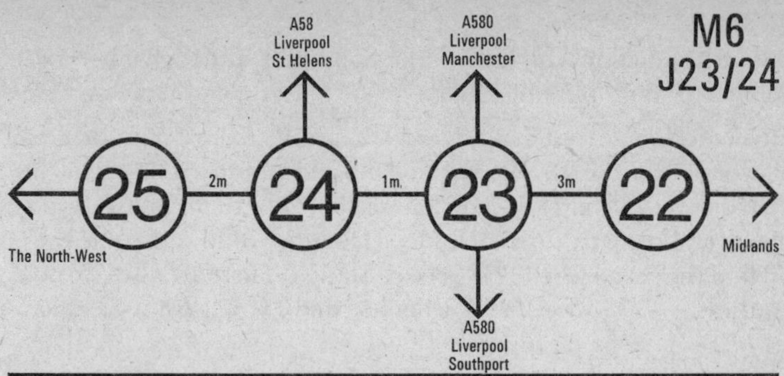

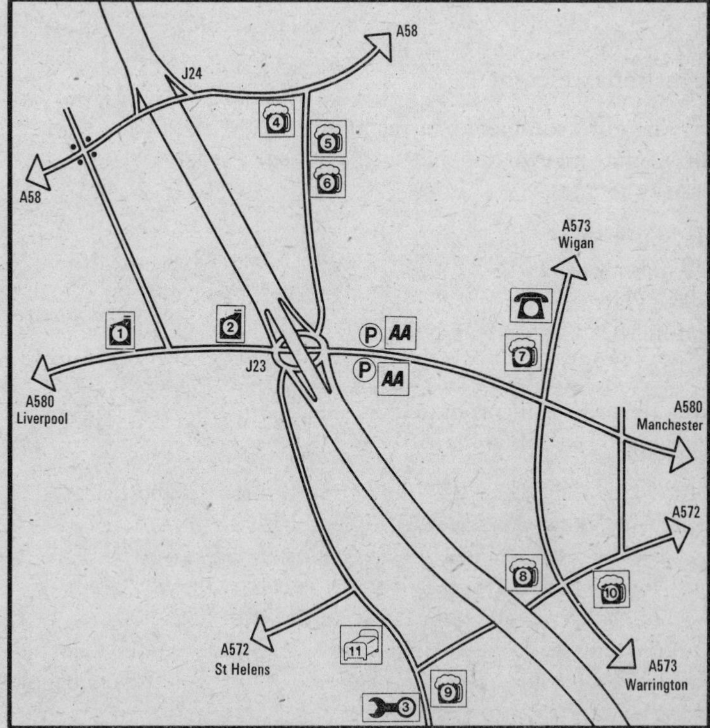

1 Telegraph Service Station. Hours: 7 am – 11 pm (8 am – 9 pm Sun)
2 Haydock Island Service Station. Hours: 7 am – 11 pm (7 am – 9 pm Sat, 8.30 am – 11 pm Sun)
3 A and B. Hours: 8 am – 8 pm. Breakdown locally on 5½-day week. (Newton-le-Willows 4411). Volvo, Daf, Citroën and Datsun agents
4 *The Kings Arms,* Tetley
5 *The Bay Horse Hotel*, Greenall Whitley. Restaurant
6 *Colliers Arms*, Burtonwood
7 *The Queen Anne*, Greenall Whitley
8 *Bulls Head*, Tetley
9 *The Leigh Arms*, Tetley
10 *The Traveller's Rest Inn*, Greenall Whitley
11 *Kirkfield Private Hotel*

J26 don't

This is the junction with the M58 for Southport, although it never gets there, being only four miles long.

But off the double roundabout beneath the M6, there is one other road that comes off – the A577 to Up Holland and Wigan. At the top of the slip road you will find a T-junction controlled by traffic lights. If you need petrol urgently turn left for Up Holland; within half a mile you will find the cheap Orell Post Service Station. There are also two pub restaurants – *The Mount Inn,* a Schooner, and *The Stag Inn,* a Cavalier.

But the real advice for this junction, and that is why there is no map, is don't.

suggestions welcome

If you have any comments, corrections,
or up-to-date information that you have discovered,
please write to:

John Slater
c/o Pan Books Ltd
Cavaye Place
London
SW10 9PG

so that they can be incorporated in
future editions of this guide.

GUIDE TO MAP SYMBOLS

 PETROL

 GARAGE AND BREAKDOWN

 PUB

POST OFFICE

 TELEPHONE

 SHOP

B&B BED AND BREAKFAST

 HOTEL

 PICNIC SPOT

 FISH AND CHIPS

PARKING

RAC

AA

MUSEUM

 RESTAURANT

HOSPITAL

 WINE BAR

 POLICE STATION

 POTTERY

 SWIMMING POOL

petrol/restaurants

Smile please, if you're coming from the north, because you are entering Greenall Whitley land. *The Tudor* **6**, *The Forresters* **7** and *The Hesketh Arms Hotel* **8** are all quite pleasant but it's not worth a special trip. When they have slightly special food and can cater for children there will be reason.

One could almost say that this junction has a lot of promise but doesn't quite make it. The junction, particularly in the direction of Standish, has an awkward shape – a piece of dual carriageway that soon withers and climbs to a minor T-junction. Yet a lot is available. *Cassinelli's Motor Inn*, **1** and **12**, is a motel, restaurant and garage. The petrol is quite cheap, the rooms are pricey and the restaurant would cost about £4 a head. But the menu has a very definite leaning to the Italian and that's not a bad thing near Wigan. There are also children's portions and prices.

Across the road from *Cassinelli's* is competition in the form of *The Black Horse Restaurant* **13** which, in spite of its name, also has the Italian connection. A similar kind of price and, again, children's portions.

The town of Standish has many shops and a delicatessen **11**, again unusual for this area, which has a good range of cheese and salami. Just beyond it is the Delph Service Station **2** which appears to be a straight garage. The owner seems more than slightly doubtful of the modern world but will tell you the worst about your car – which is always better than false hope.

As is so often the case, the cheapest petrol is not close to the junction. The closest garage, the Crow Orchard **3**, is the most expensive and is only included for convenience although you will still make a saving. In the direction of Parbold you will find the cheap and strangely named Thames Rico Service Station **5**. Opposite is *The Dicconson Arms* **9** which has snacks at all times and can cater for children. Even further afield is the Foxfield Garage **4** which has the cheapest petrol of all and also supports many AA spanners, but it is on the road to nowhere.

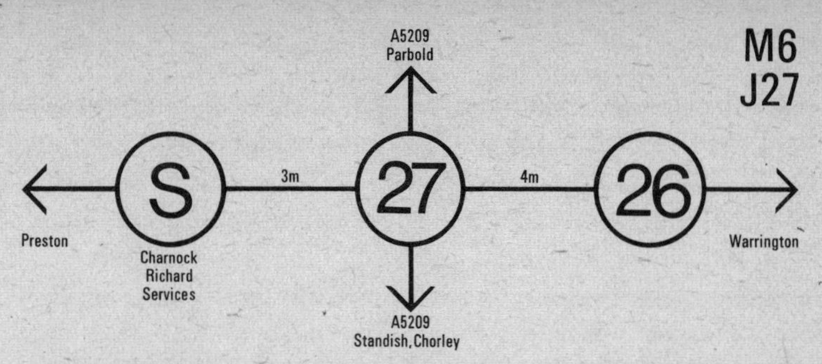

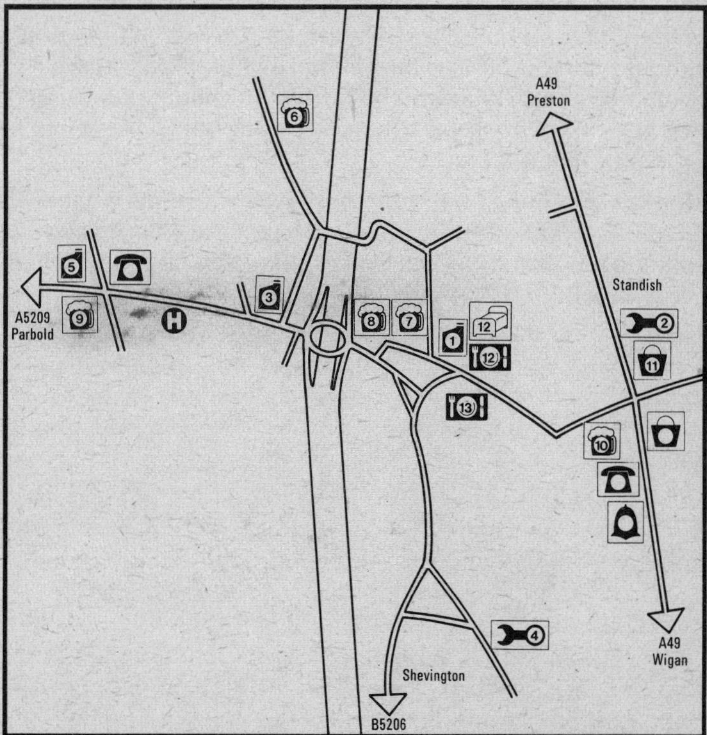

1 Motor Inn Service Station. Hours: 6 am – 9 pm (7 am – 9 pm Sat, Sun)
2 Delph Service Station. Hours: 8 am – 8 pm. 24-hr breakdown (Standish 422899)
3 Crow Orchard Service Station. Hours: 7 am – 10 pm (8 am – 10 pm Sat, Sun)
4 Foxfield Garage. Repairs (Appley Bridge 2626)
5 Thames Rico Service Station. Hours: 7 am – 9 pm (opens 9 am Sun)
6 *The Tudor Inn*, Greenall Whitley
7 *The Forresters Arms*, Greenall Whitley
8 *The Hesketh Arms Hotel*, Greenall Whitley
9 *The Dicconson Arms*, Burtonwood
10 *The Dog and Partridge*, Tetley
11 Standish Delicatessen
12 *Cassinelli's Motor Inn and Restaurant* (Standish 421504)
13 *Black Horse Restaurant* (Standish 423763)

petrol

Not too much joy on this junction. If travelling north wait for **J32**, **J33** or **J35** depending on what you want. Travelling south you are in for a fairly bleak stretch but **J23** and **J21** are worth waiting for.

Cheap petrol is available at this junction. Closest is Clayton Brook **1**, which has a transport café attached, opening on weekdays at 7 am. Breakfast is about 50p.

The only unexpected offer on this junction was three oysters for 60p at *The Old Hob Inn* **5**. Since oysters and I have not really been travelling companions since a long night in Blackpool and a long afternoon in a Britanny ditch, I simply report the offer. The *Inn* also has fresh salmon sandwiches for 35p. So, if unattended by children, it looks a good place to stop for snacks. It is a low thatched building only a quarter of a mile away. You can choose between the lounge and super-lounge for food. But not Saturday lunchtime or Monday evening.

A whole range of pubs here, particularly as you drive into Bamber Bridge. There is also a businessman's restaurant at *Cuerden Manor* **12** – Jags and BMWs indicate the style, or lack of. *The Pines Hotel* **13** has 21 bedrooms but its prices seem rather high.

M6 J28/29

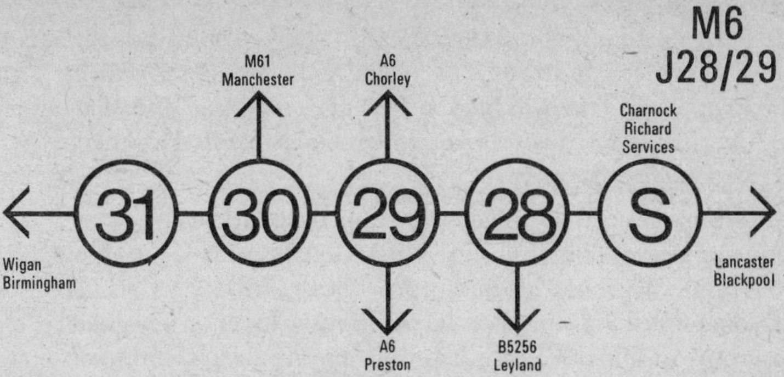

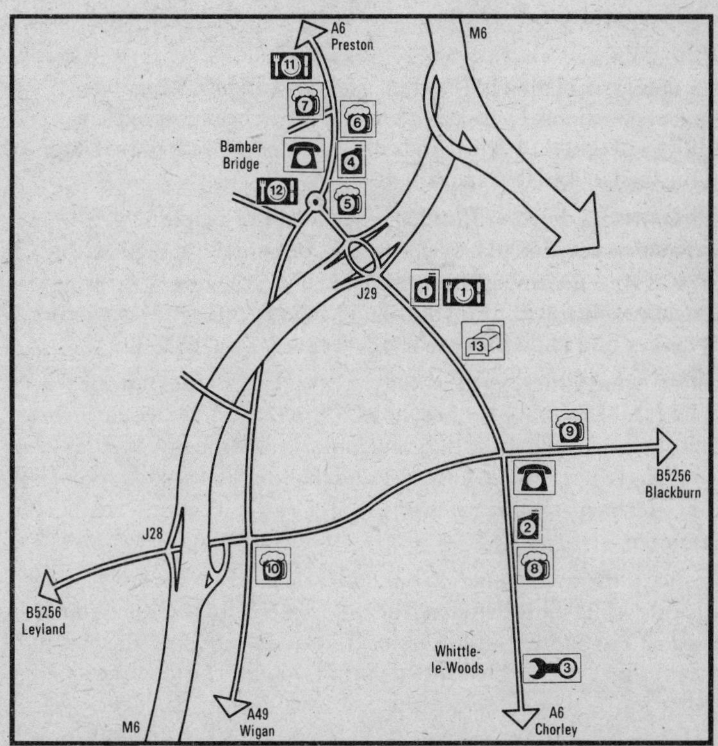

1 Clayton Brook Filling Station. Hours: 7 am – 9 pm (opens 8 am Sat, 9 am Sun)
2 Half Way Garage. Hours: 7 am – 10 pm (8 am – 9 pm Sat, 9 am – 10 pm Sun)
3 Swansea Garage. Workshop
4 Bamber Bridge Service Station
5 *The Old Hob Inn,* Matthew Brown
6 *Ye Olde Original Withy Trees,* Burtonwood
7 *The Withy rees Hotel,* Boddingtons
8 *The Half Way House,* Burtonwood
9 *The Lord Nelson,* Matthew Brown
10 *The Hayrick,* Greenall Whitley
11 *The Pear Tree,* Duttons Fish Restaurant
12 *The Cuerden Manor Restaurant* (Chorley 39447)
13 *The Pines Hotel* (Chorley 38551)

petrol/visit/pubs

Chief Seattle, that wise old Indian, said: 'Man did not weave the web of life. He is merely a strand in it. Whatever he does to the web, he does to himself.' That was back in 1854 before he was railroaded by the Americans. Two contrasting works of man, Samlesbury Hall **13** and *The Trafalgar* **5**, prove his point.

Samlesbury Hall, as far as I can make out from the cheap and confusing guide book, seems to have started life somewhere about 1309. It is a very imposing mixture of styles with a lovely Great Hall and some smashing windows. It now seems to function as a giant bazaar. Most things were for sale and there are always exhibitions – from one of which I pinched Chief Seattle's words. There is also a tea room.

The other work of man is *The Trafalgar* – a roadhouse of gigantic plastic proportions. I suppose one day it might be preserved as a tribute to all that is tasteless and characterless. The car park is large and the food looked decent enough.

In comparison, the *Little Chef* **12**, based on the principle of convenience food and plastic decor – I hope I got the adjectives the right way round – seemed pleasant. Run by four young ladies who spent more time cackling on the phone than serving. Still they were very smiley and I had a nice cup of coffee.

I wonder what Chief Seattle would have said about the claim of *The Tickled Trout* **11** to have the best hotel site in Britain. He would have probably just looked up at the great motorway in the sky. Friends who have stayed there say it is very nice and that the food is good. But it is pricey. B&B will cost you at least £13 and Vatman will still want his percentage.

Two nice pubs on the junction but both at some distance and neither really providing for the stomach or children. *The Myerscough* **8** and *The Nabs Head* **7** at Samlesbury Bottoms. But if you've been to the Hall at the right time, a quick dash down the hill wouldn't be too time wasting.

For cheap petrol you need go no further than the Riverside Filling Station **3** which is right next to *The Tickled Trout* – just off the motorway. The Five Barred Gate **2** is also cheap.

M6 J31

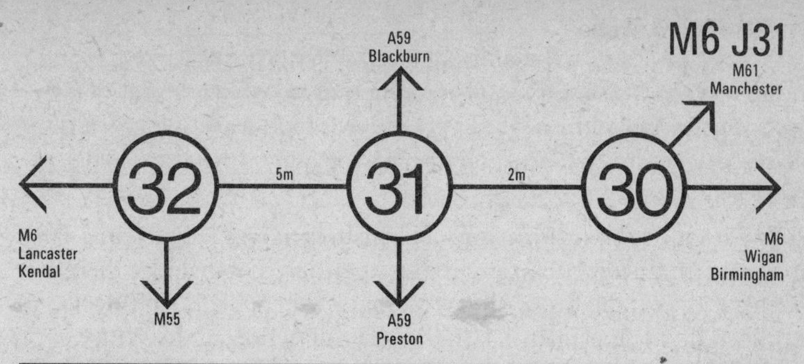

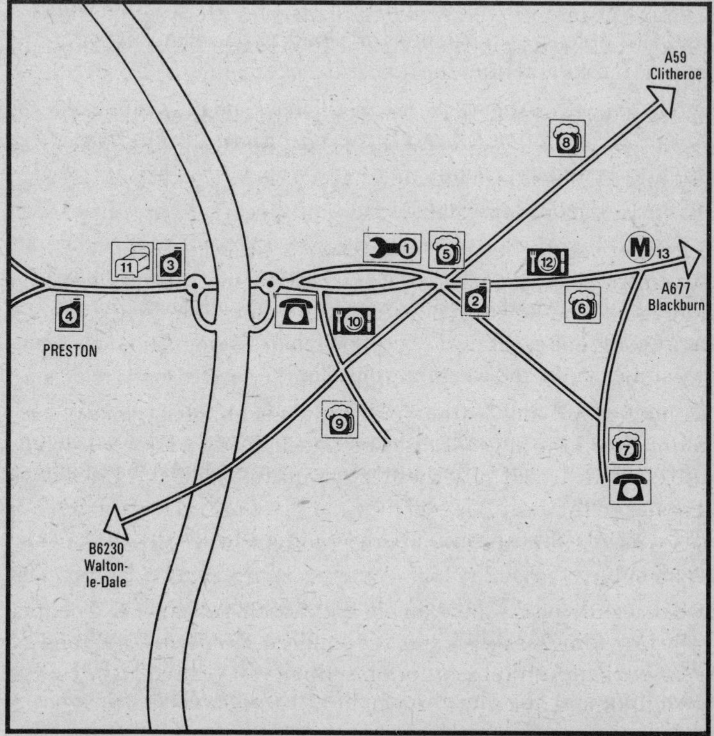

1 Samlesbury Service Station. Hours: 7.30 am – 10 pm (opens 8.30 am Sat, Sun). 24-hr breakdown (Samlesbury 204 or 658)
2 Five Barred Gate Service Station. Hours: 8 am – 10 pm
3 Riverside Filling Station. Hours: 7 am – 10 pm (later start on Sat, Sun)
4 Telegraph Service Station
5 *The Trafalgar*, Matthew Brown
6 *The Half Way House*, Whitbread
7 *The Nabs Head*, Thwaites
8 *The Myerscough*, Robinson
9 *The New Hall Tavern*, Whitbread
10 *Duttons Restaurant*
11 *The Tickled Trout Hotel and Restaurant*
12 *Little Chef*
13 Samlesbury Hall. Open 11.30 am – 5 pm except Sun

petrol/pub/shops

Correctly, **J32** is with the M55. But a short distance down this motorway (to Blackpool) is its first junction. So what follows is a description of **J1** of the M55. There are two good reasons for turning off here – very cheap petrol and a revival of your faith in a great British institution.

You will save at least 10p at any of the listed garages and the price is likely to remain low because of the competition. For instance there are three garages at the Broughton crossroads, where the B5269 meets the A6. The cheapest petrol is in the other direction, at the Withy Trees **5**. Here you can save about 15p a gallon. But it's hardly worth going so far unless you need shops or a bank or one of the many telephone kiosks that litter the roadscape like confetti.

Travelling north on the A6 there is *The Barton Café* **11**, *The Brass Knight Restaurant* **12** and *Barton Grange Hotel and Restaurant* **13**. The hotel is reasonably priced but usually very full.

Plastic and beaten copper, fake beams and fat carpets, pressure pumps and chickens laid to rest in baskets – whose idea of delight are these? But these are the fashions that dominated the conversions of the sixties whiz-kid interior designers – and they all seem to have copied each other.

A nice pub with good beer and simple home-prepared food is a licence to print money. Without too much wit or imagination it would be possible to organize (not design) something along these lines. But the big brewers have got it wrong almost every time. Maybe they don't want our money.

So if you need a restoral of your faith and a restorative too, go to *The Plough* **6** at Eaves in Cuddy Hill. Even the names sound right. But it is four-and-a-half miles away and half that distance is along narrow roads. It is a rough building with seats outside staring across the flat Lancashire plain. Inside, two nice rooms with Theakstons, Boddingtons and Thwaites on draught. Nice sandwiches and other snacks. Follow the B5269 for Elswick from the Broughton crossroads. Just after the left turn for Preston (B5411) take the signposted road to the right.

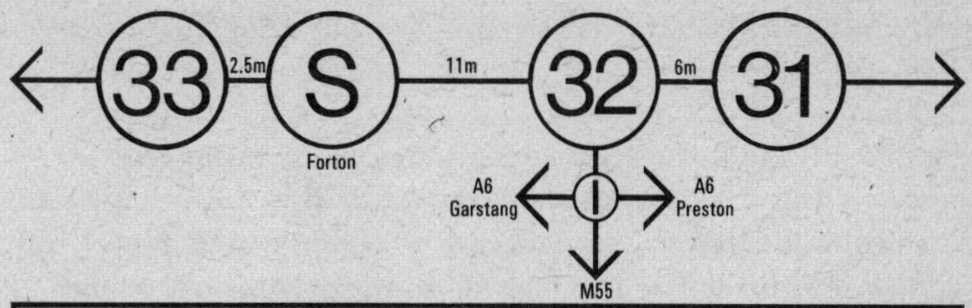

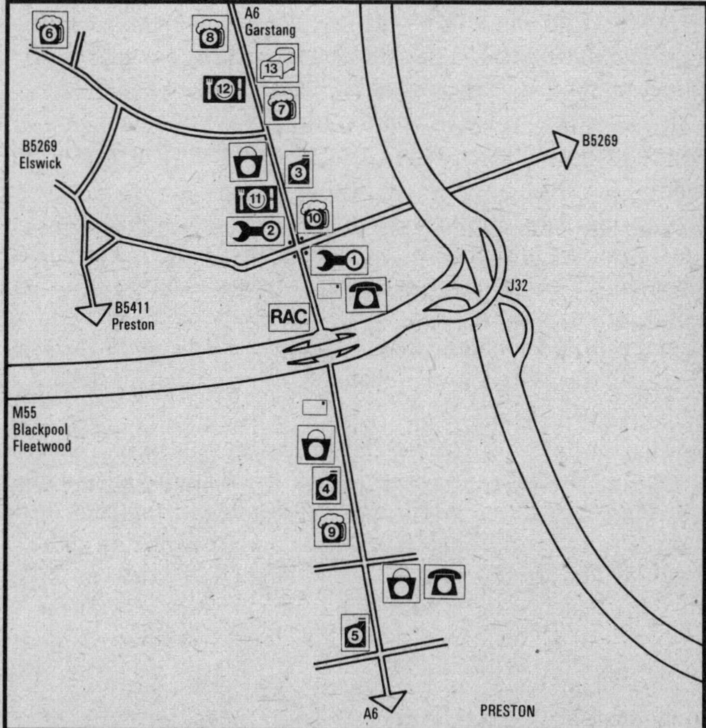

1 Broughton Garage. Hours: 9 am – 9 pm
2 International Service Station. 24-hr breakdown. Workshop (Broughton 717116). Ford agent
3 Kinders Service Station
4 Black Bull Service Station. Hours: 7 am – 11 pm (open till 10 pm Sun)
5 Withy Trees Service Station
6 *The Plough at Eaves*, Free house
7 *The Boars Head*, Whitbread
8 *The White Horse*, Matthew Brown
9 *The Black Bull*, Bass Charrington
10 *The Shuttleworth Arms*, Greenall Whitley
11 *The Barton Café*
12 *The Brass Knight Restaurant*
13 *Barton Grange Hotel*. Restaurant (Broughton 862551)

'Half of bitter, please.'
'We only sell mild.'
'Oh well, half of mild then, please.' Pause. 'Why don't you sell bitter?'
'There's no demand for it, dear.' Clearly the demand wasn't quite enough.

A loud family quarrel in another pub, and a garage owner who couldn't tell me when he closed. He explained three times that since he ran a non-union place he could close any time he liked. Fine, I said, but not too useful for the travelling public who want some certainty in their dealings with the motor trade.

There is no cheap petrol close to this junction, though as you travel southwards towards Garstang it gets cheaper, for instance at the Cabus Garage **1**. If you were going south anyway you would then easily rejoin the motorway at **J32**. Northbound travellers reverse the process.

All the eating places are on this stretch of the A6 too. Ordinary food at ordinary prices and all three places can cater for children. Furthest is *The New Holly Hotel* **10** and it seems to offer most – snacks at all opening times, a restaurant and an extensive wine cellar. Also very reasonably priced double bedrooms. *The Spinney Restaurant* **9** also has three cheap rooms. It is open from midday till nine at night and has children's portions.

Closest to the junction is *The Bay Horse* **6**, and it would be my choice for a glass of Mitchells and a decent snack in a pleasant country pub. To get there take the second left off the A6 heading south. It is actually signposted along with *The Foxholes* **11**. For the latter you turn under the railway line before getting to the pub. And I would choose to stay in this old-fashioned and isolated hotel – but it is stuck between the motorway and the London–Glasgow mainline. A bit noisy. Children yes, dogs no.

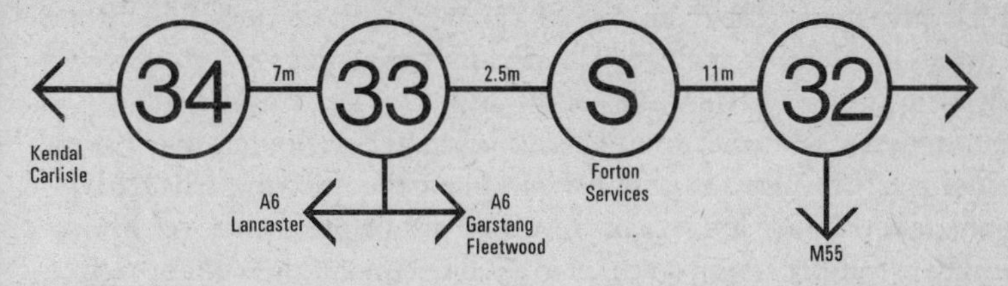

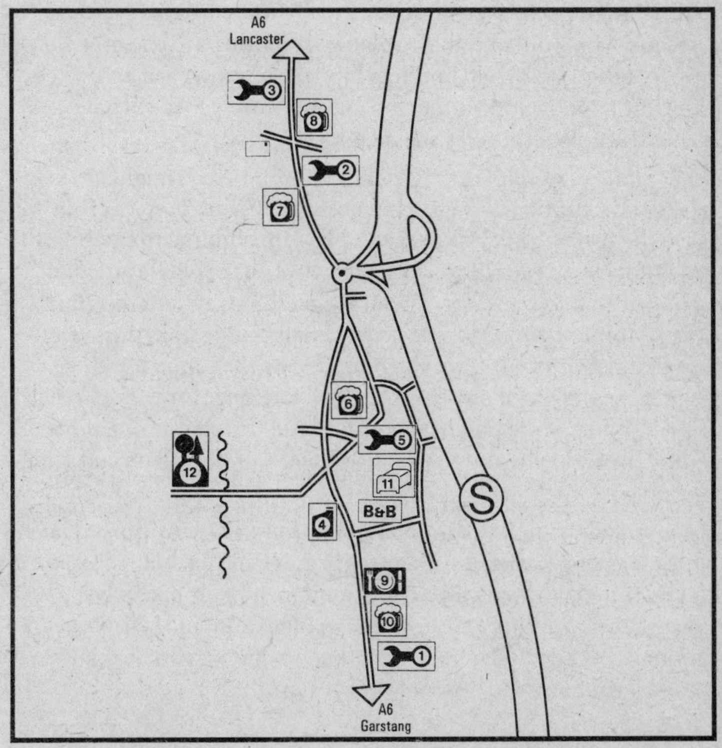

1 Cabus Garage. Hours: 8 am – 7 pm (closes 6 pm Sat, Sun). Breakdown in normal working hours (Forton 791417)
2 Burgess Garage. Repairs in normal working hours
3 Fisher Hargreaves. Datsun agent
4 Pennine Filling Station
5 Bayhorse Workshop. 24-hr breakdown (Forton 791769)
6 *The Bay Horse,* Mitchells
7 *The Plough Inn,* Boddingtons
8 *The New Inn,* Mitchells
9 *The Spinney Restaurant.* B&B (Forton 791254)
10 *The New Holly Hotel,* Thwaites (Forton 791568)
11 *The Foxholes Hotel* (Forton 791237)
12 Lancaster Canal, walk or picnic

Dear Russell Harty, what can one say about the junction you have chosen to live your life off – well, quite a long way off? It's awkward and unattractive even on the banks of the River Lune. There's an old toll bridge across the river. An old, rusting, narrow bridge that no one wants – no one even collects tolls anymore. Warnings abound about the weight, size, privacy and condition of the road. But you could have a picnic or a walk down there **13**. I somehow doubt that you've ever been there. Less than half a mile along the A683 towards Kirkby Lonsdale you turn left on a narrow road just before a white cottage and very much before you come to a red telephone kiosk on the right. Well, you might have been there to go to *The Manor House Restaurant* **11**, because you would be able to plan your journeys to book the necessary table. It's an old building in a lovely setting just across the bridge, but I don't suppose that too many ordinary folk will have a chance to sample the interesting menu.

Further along your road through Caton I suppose you might have stopped at the Station Garage **4** but not at *The Station* **6**. A lot of old brass in the two large bars and even a place for children to eat. But the petrol is not cheap – for the only cheap petrol on the whole junction you have to go into Lancaster and brave the one-way system to find Marvell Motors **1**. Good for the pocket but it could strain the brain. But problems with your tyres can be solved by the Caton Road Garage **2**. Any tyres for any car, British or foreign, at any time. Well that's what they say and with (they say) 12,000 in stock it should be possible. Breakdowns and repairs in normal working hours and some saving on petrol.

You've passed the signs for the *Scarthwaite Hotel* **12** many times. Have you ever been in? Rather a strange place that looks as though it has been undergoing changes all its life – they are now, apparently, building a restaurant. There are large gardens and some fairly cheap bedrooms. But I do wish you'd let me know what you think about this junction. Trouble is you probably never stop.

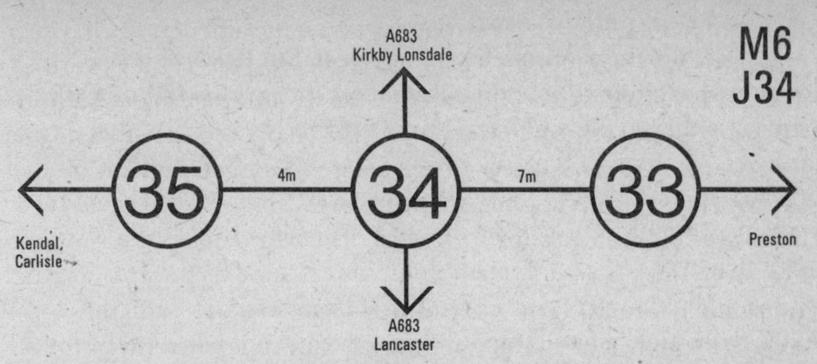

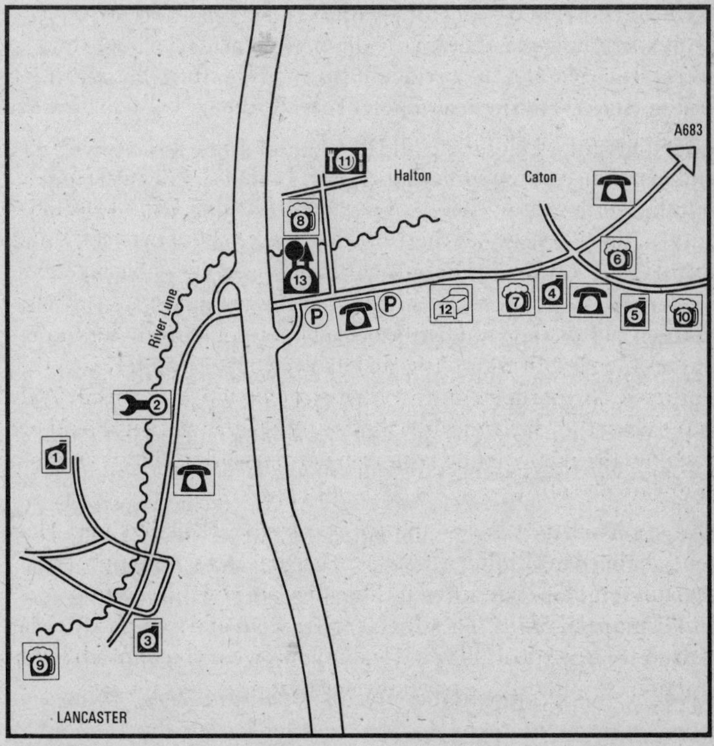

1 Marvell Motors. Hours: 8 am – 9 pm
2 Caton Road Garage. Hours: 8 am – 7.30 pm. Tyre specialists (Lancaster 2917)
3 Pye Motors. 24-hr petrol machine
4 Station Garage. Hours: 8.30 am – 6.45 pm (shorter hours Sat, Sun)
5 Brookhouse Garage
6 *The Station*, Mitchells
7 *The Ship Hotel*, Yates and Jackson
8 *The Greyhound Hotel*, Youngers
9 *The Wagon and Horses*, Hartleys
10 *The Black Bull*, Yates and Jackson
11 *The Manor House Restaurant*. Evenings, Mon – Sat. (Halton 811377)
12 *The Scarthwaite Hotel* (Caton 770267)
13 River Lune picnic spot

garages/visits/pubs/overnights

The perfect junction, of course, doesn't exist. But this is a very good junction apart from the fact that it is rather spread out and you have to travel a mile on the motorway spur (to **J35A**) before anything happens. All three garages offer mechanical services during normal working hours. Charlie Oates **1** has the cheapest petrol and locals say he is very helpful. Brookbank Garage **3** is the place to go for a blow-out or new tyre.

A museum in the old Carnforth Railway sheds complete with the Flying Scotsman, a turntable, and British Rail-style cafeteria and lavatories. More mysteriously they have a picnic spot and a greenhouse selling pot plants and hammocks! An ideal place to take diesel and electric children to savour the good old smells and feel the grease and coal. That's Steamtown **11**.

Rather different is Leighton Hall **10**. A Gothic-fronted house with a long and lovely curving driveway. Members of the family will guide you round the house, and eagles, weather permitting, will strafe the grounds. But to explain when it is open, what it will cost and what you will get is very complex, but it's worth driving there to get turned away. For free walks or picnics try the Lancaster Canal **12** or the Capernwray Forest picnic area **13**. Benches supplied.

A number of very nice pubs in the area. *The New Inn* **4** on the lovely village of Yealand Conyers. You can't dress a pub with furniture and oddments in a day. It has to grow over time. This will be one of the great pubs when its bareness fills out. Snacks at all times; children only outside on benches. *The Black Bull* **7** in Warton has bar snacks at all times, seventeen different homemade chutneys, six mustards, a place for children and Forfar Bridies. *The Eagles Head Hotel* **6** also has cheap food and snacks at all times. There is a dining area for kids and a few rooms to let. *The Shovel* **5** in Carnforth is a friendly local with a fine darts room.

For year-round accommodation try *The Holmere Hall Hotel* **8**. Nine reasonably priced rooms and good snacks and food at most decent hours of the day. Children's rates.

1 Charlie Oates Ltd. Hours: 8 am – 8 pm. Breakdown in normal working hours (Carnforth 2460)

2 Warton Hall Garage. Hours: 8 am – 7 pm (10 am – 6 pm Sun). 24-hr breakdown (Carnforth 2107)

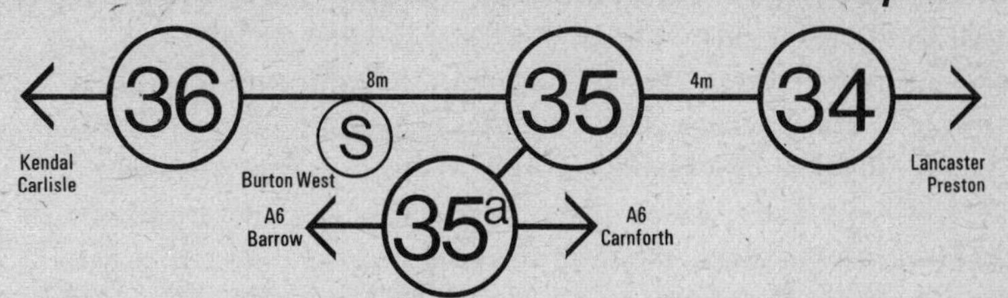

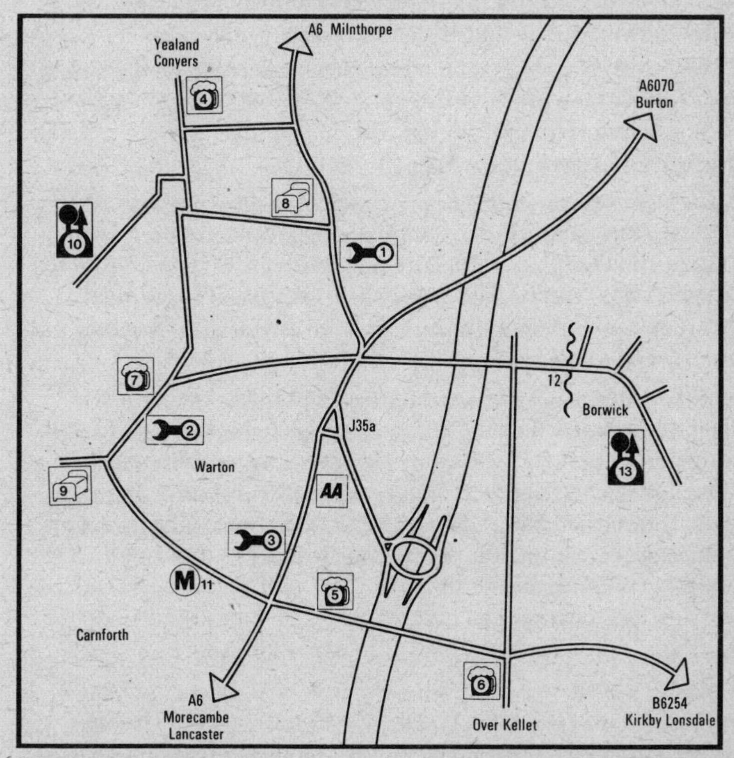

3 Brookbank Service Station. Hours: 8 am – 9 pm (opens 9.30 am Sun). Tyres and batteries. (Carnforth 2609)
4 *The New Inn*, Hartleys
5 *The Shovel*, Boddingtons
6 *The Eagles Head Hotel*, Mitchells (Carnforth 2457)
7 *The Black Bull*, Mitchells
8 *The Holmere Hall Hotel* (Carnforth 2931)
9 *The Warton Grange Hotel* (Carnforth 2895)
10 Leighton Hall. Hall open Wed and Sun afternoon (May – Sept). Grounds every day except Mon and Sat
11 Steamtown Railway Museum. Open daily 9 am – 5 pm
12 Lancaster Canal
13 Capernwray Forest picnic area

petrol/garage/walk

On this junction you can walk along the edge of a canal killed by the motorway, or go to the town of Milnthorpe, gateway to the Lakes, that hasn't yet realized that it's been reprieved by the M6.

But first the Canal Garage **1** which sits/hides under the motorway. All services at all times of day or night with a saving on petrol (if you haven't filled up very cheaply at **J32** or can't wait that long) of about 7p a gallon. Close by, as the name suggests, is the Lancaster Canal **10**. In both cases take the A65 towards Kirkby Lonsdale and then take the first left off the roundabout – the A65 to Kendal. There is a large lay-by on the left just after crossing the canal bridge.

I wonder who was responsible for taking the decision to culvert the canal rather than to bridge it. The additional cost was only a few tens of thousands of pounds. The loss, except to the families of swans and ducks, quite a few miles of canal.

Also close to the junction is *The Plough* **3**. The usual pub food and snacks at all opening times. Children can be catered for and there is limited and cheap accommodation. There is a special Sunday lunch for £1.50. *The Crooklands Hotel* **8** is even closer but in an entirely different league. A small, fairly expensive and pleasant hotel with a decent restaurant attached.

Now for Milnthorpe and more particularly how to get there. It's probably only worth making the journey if travelling south, because you can easily rejoin at **J35** and pick up cheap petrol just outside the town. Off the A65 roundabout take the A6070 to Holme. Then first right, signposted to Milnthorpe and Millness – a narrow road. Left fork and left at the crossroads with the B6385. I couldn't see a signpost.

Reasons for going to Milnthorpe. Cafés with names like *The Flying Dutchman and Monarch*, a restaurant called *The Bila* **9**, and pubs called *The Coach and Horses* **3** and *The Cross Keys Hotel* **4**. When I was there, the publican in the *Cross Keys* was trying to heat two enormous rooms with half a log and three customers. But some would cross mountains to drink the beer.

M6 J36

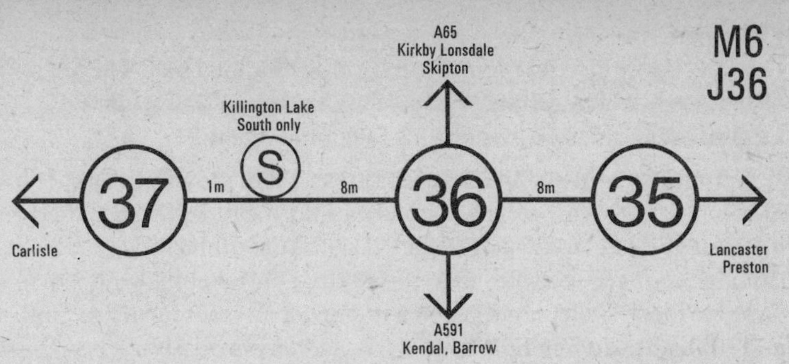

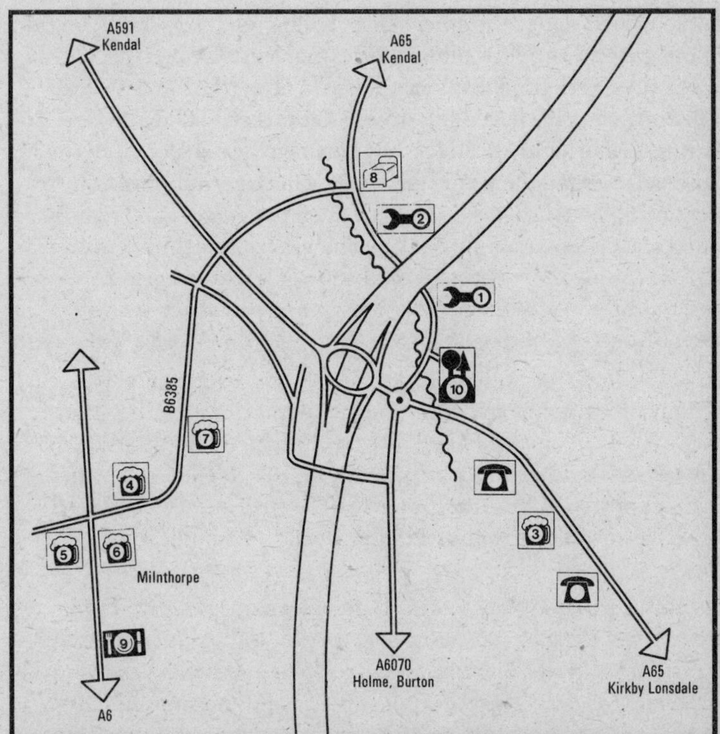

1 Canal Garage. 24-hr petrol and breakdown. (Crooklands 401/2)
2 Crooklands Motor Company. Hours: 8 am – 10 pm. 24-hr breakdown (Crooklands 414)
3 *The Plough,* Vaux (Crooklands 227)
4 *The Coach and Horses,* Mitchells
5 *The Cross Keys Hotel,* Hartleys
6 *The Bulls Head,* Vaux
7 *The Station Hotel,* Yates and Jackson
8 *Crooklands Hotel and Restaurant* (Crooklands 432)
9 *The Bila Restaurant*
10 Lancaster Canal walk

J37 don't

Don't. Or only for a picnic on the edge of Killington Lake. The town of Sedbergh, although on the edge of the Yorkshire Dales, is not attractive enough to justify driving four and a half miles.

When asked about attractive service areas, Killington Lake Service Station was always top of my list. A beautiful location, small and tidy buildings and not too much traffic – it's on the southbound carriageway only. Now it's extremely tatty – portakabins propped up on stone blocks, telephone kiosks without doors, grass turned to mud and rubbish everywhere. The petrol is also very expensive.

For your picnic go to the other side of Killington Lake where you can sit and gaze at one of the minor glories that existed when the motorways were young. It's easy to get to. Take the A683 towards Sedbergh, then the first right turning signposted to Old and New Hutton. Go straight ahead for the Old when the road forks. It's quite a narrow road but the verges are wide by the lake and you can turn at the end.

GUIDE TO MAP SYMBOLS

 PETROL

 GARAGE AND BREAKDOWN

 PUB

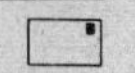 POST OFFICE

 TELEPHONE

 SHOP

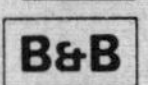

BED AND BREAKFAST

 HOTEL

 PICNIC SPOT

 FISH AND CHIPS

PARKING

RAC

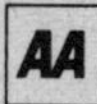

AA

MUSEUM

 RESTAURANT

HOSPITAL

 WINE BAR

 POLICE STATION

 POTTERY

 SWIMMING POOL

pub food/accommodation

To get the motorway through this valley, after river, road and rail had got there first, is a spectacular engineering feat. Best observed from the A685 through Tebay **9**. A nice spot to have a picnic is on the banks of the River Lune **8**. Take the A685 towards Brough. Buy the cheapest petrol hereabouts, a saving of about 7p, at the Lune Valley Service Station **2**, which also seems to double up as a general store. Opposite the garage is the B6261 to Orton and a little way up this road is a lay-by alongside the Lune.

The Barnaby Rudge **6** serves rather good food. It's about a mile from the junction through the village of Tebay. It's been recently rather well converted with a restaurant gallery overlooking the main bar area. A slight pity that so many of the chairs are the same – it looks like the kind of place that needed to grow, with individual pieces of furniture. Pity, too, that a free house has such a limited range of pressure beers. But the food makes up for most: homemade soup for 35p and homemade beefburgers for just over £1. Food at all opening times and decent children can be catered for. There is also a smashing pool room.

Just before *The Barnaby Rudge* is *The Junction Hotel* **5** which is open all day for simpler food. This hotel also has ten rooms at very reasonable rates. *The George Hotel* **7** in Orton village has seven rooms and is only slightly more expensive. It has bar snacks at most times.

The garage close to the junction, Diesel Services **1**, provides a 24-hour service, but its prices are so similar to the service areas that it's hardly worth pulling off for that. Well, you could save a couple of pence, but it's none too attractive.

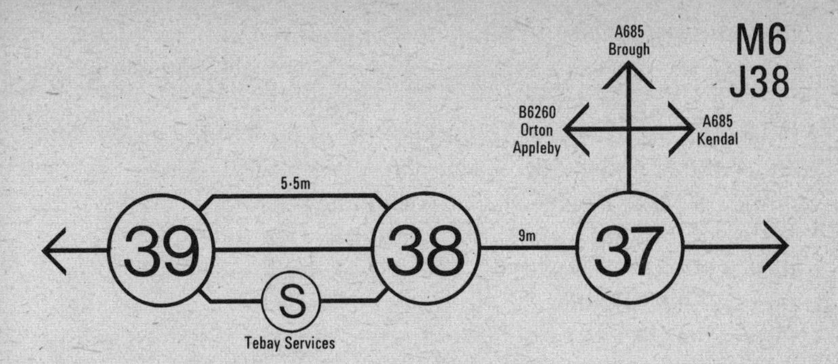

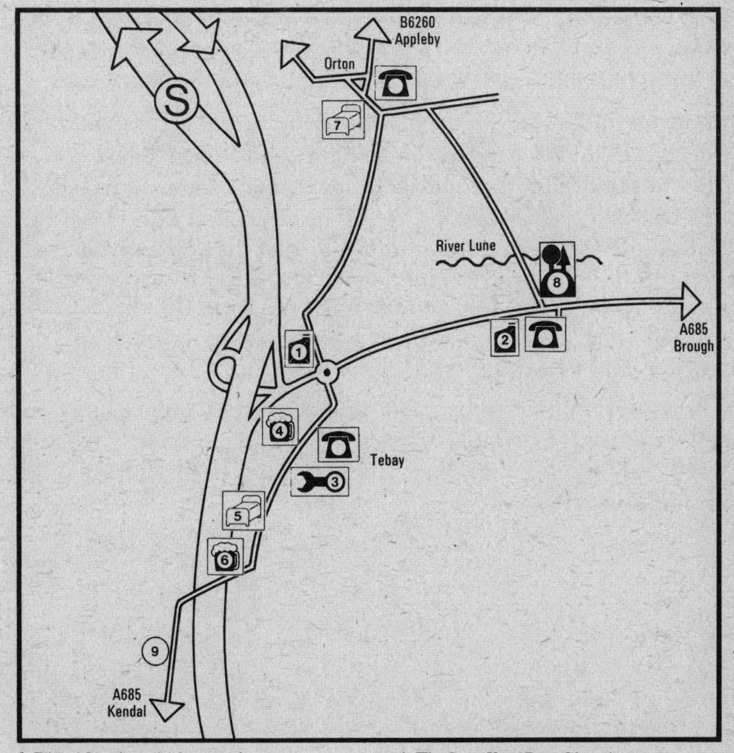

1 Diesel Services. 24-hr petrol

2 Lune Valley Service Station. Hours: 7.30 am – 9 pm (slightly shorter at weekends)

3 Grants Garage. Hours: 8 am – 7 pm (closed Sun). Breakdown in normal working hours

4 *The Cross Keys,* Bass Charrington

5 *The Junction Hotel,* Free house (Orton 232)

6 *The Barnaby Rudge,* Free house

7 *The George Hotel,* Youngers (Orton 229)

8 River Lune picnic spot

9 Motorway spotters spot

sheep and Shap

Unless you are after sheep in some form or fashion, this junction is not for you. A visit to the strip-town of Shap should not really be on anyone's list of great things to do. Though one could stand and wonder about the days, not so long ago, when the heavy lorries hammered through Shap on the A6. How did people cope? Maybe Whitbread consoled them – and there's a lot of it about. There are quite a few reasonably priced B&Bs and *The Greyhound Hotel* **3** has ten rooms and serves bar food at all opening times. They have one family room.

Two suggestions for sheep spotters. Take the road for Hardendale **8** – a road going nowhere which gets narrower as you climb the hill. Stop just after a mile on the brow. Here you can adjust your seat to avoid looking at the motorway, cement works or pylons. A pleasant place.

Not such an interesting place but a lot of empty land, apart from sheep, can be found on the B6261, signposted for Orton. But for a really strange experience – and this is for genuine motorway freaks only – continue on this road to Orton. You can now drive between the two parts of the motorway. Continue through Orton on the B6260 for **J38**.

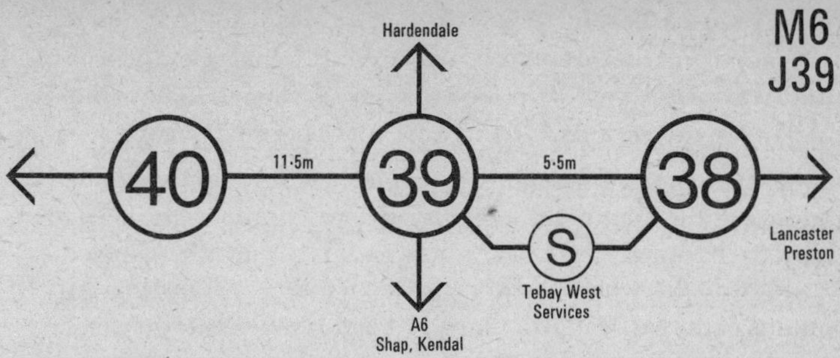

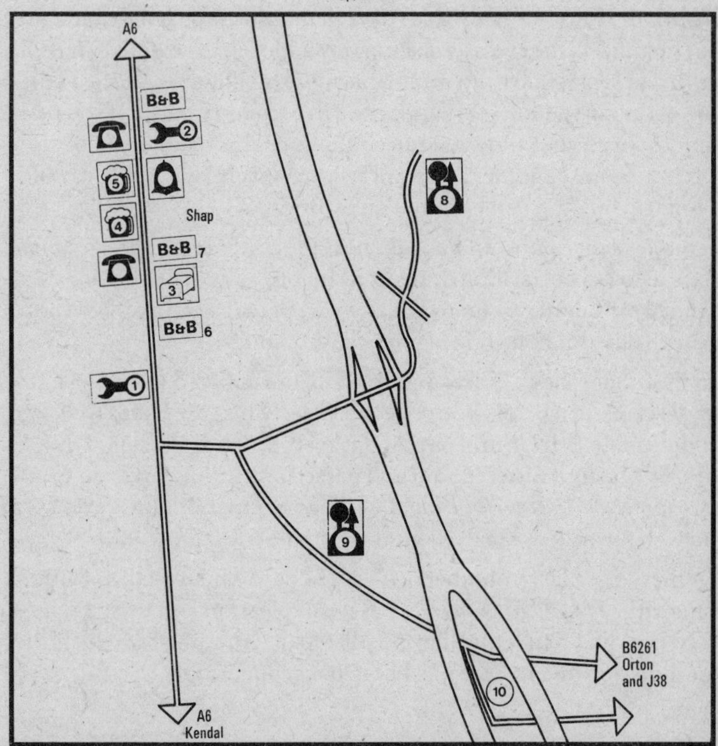

1 Fell Garage. Hours: 8 am – 7 pm (9 am – 6 pm Sun). Breakdown during these hours and repair work. (Shap 219)
2 T. Simpson & Sons. 24-hr breakdown if mechanics at home (Shap, day 212, night 236 or 311)
3 *The Greyhound Hotel*, Whitbread (Shap 208)
4 *The Crown Inn*, Whitbread
5 *The Bulls Head*, Whitbread
6 *Brookfields*. B&B (Shap 397)
7 *Rocklands*. B&B (Shap 345)
8 Hardendale picnic spot
9 Orton Road picnic spot
10 Motorway spotters spot

visits/picnics/hotels

Not a good junction for petrol – you are only saving a few pence on motorway prices. Nor is the food too special, though some of the hotels have restaurants and there are snack bars in Penrith.

Historically many important routes met here. Broughton Castle **12**, and the earlier Roman settlements, are simple proof of the need to guard such routes. The castle is only one and a half miles along the A66 to Brough – where the River Eamont meets the Lowther. Much remains of the castle, particularly its very complex gate defences.

Dalemain House **11** is also old, though the pink sandstone frontage that first meets the eye was fashionably added in the eighteenth century. It costs 60p to go round the house (children half price) but part of the surrounding grounds are a free 'country park'. If you really want to waste your time you can continue on this road, the A592, to Ullswater – just another couple of miles. A lovely lake and you could take a trip on the steamer from Pooley Bridge.

A couple of nice pubs. In Penrith, near the castle **13**, is *The Agricultural* **5**, a Victorian pub selling draught Marstons. The town should be avoided on Tuesdays – market day – except that *The Agricultural* is open all day (for bona fide pigmen only, of course).

On the other road to Ullswater, the B5320, *The Gate* **3** stands in a small lay-by just before you cross a bridge. 'This gate hangs well, and hinders none, refresh and pay, and travel on,' reads the sign. I did, with Theakstons bitter. I paid and passed on and hindered none on my way to *The Queens Head* **6** in the village of Tirril. It's an ancient pub and well furnished. Food, rooms to let and Tetleys.

But there are a large number of places to stay as indicated, and others in Penrith. *The Old Mansion House* **8** seems pleasant and reasonable. A listed building that had fallen into disrepair. Now plushly refurbished – perhaps too much so for me, but it looks comfortable.

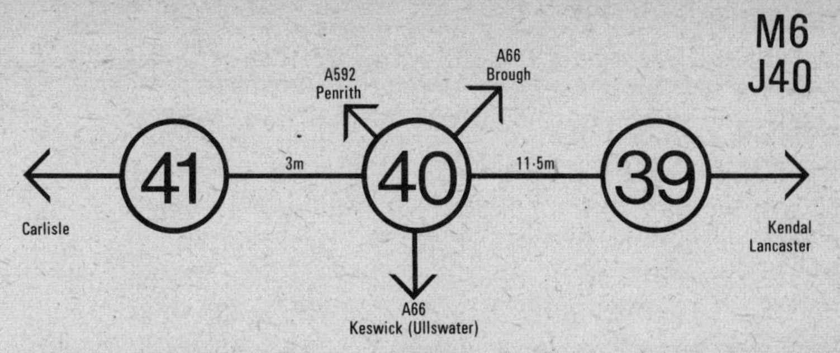

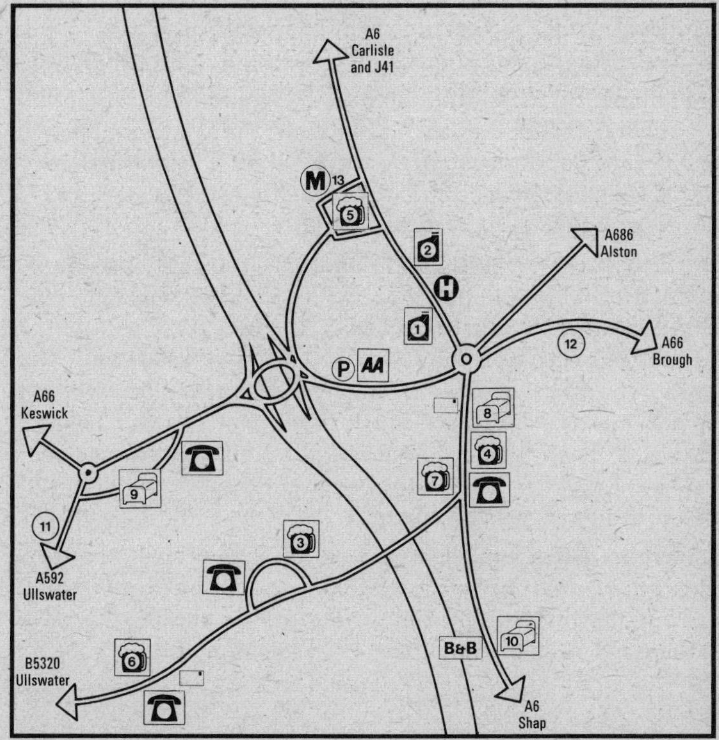

1 Bridge Lane Service Station. Hours: 7.30 am – 11 pm every day (closes 10 pm Sun)
2 Tynefield Service Station. 24-hr petrol machine
3 *The Gate Inn*, Free house
4 *The Beehive*, Whitbread
5 *The Agricultural*, Marston
6 *The Queens Head*, Tetley (Penrith 3219)
7 *The Crown Hotel*, Whitbread (Penrith 2566)
8 *The Old Mansion Hotel* (Penrith 5628)
9 *The Limes Private Hotel* (Penrith 3343)
10 *The Clifton Hill Hotel* (Penrith 2717)
11 Dalemain Country Park. Open every afternoon except Fri
12 Brougham Castle
13 Penrith Castle

Even those who live in Carlisle could not call their strung out town attractive or interesting. The M6 is really serving as a three-lane by-pass.

This junction offers very little. The petrol is pretty expensive but very convenient at the Golden Fleece **1**. The petrol does get slightly cheaper as you drive into Carlisle on the A6 and after a couple of miles there are quite a few B&Bs and hotels. But then *The Carrow House Hotel* **7** with fourteen rooms is almost right on the junction. You take the first right off the A6 into the town and then right again. It has a restaurant which is open to non-residents and has children's prices.

Close to the junction there are two very attractive villages, Wreay and Scotby, each with its own village pub (**4**, **5**). To get to Wreay you take the un-numbered road off the roundabout, signposted to Dalston. Turn left at the first crossroads and dip under the motorway. It has one small and one extra-small church; the larger of the two has very unusual windows. Both in the Parish of St Cuthbert Without – and I haven't thought of the joke line yet.

Scotby is a more normal-looking English village, with houses spread out round a large green equipped with the obligatory and impressive tree. A Courage pub, suitably named, is close by.

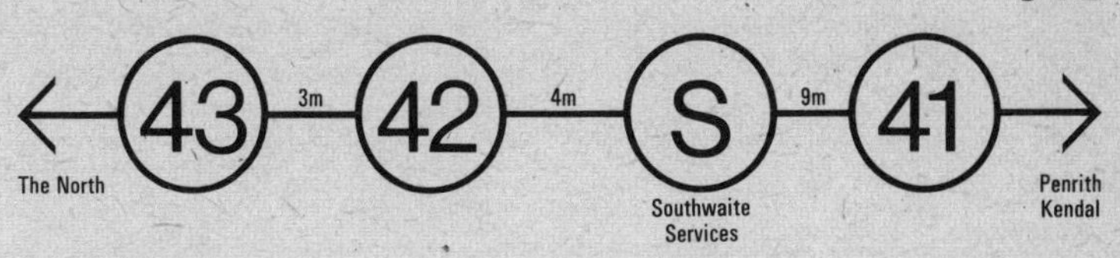

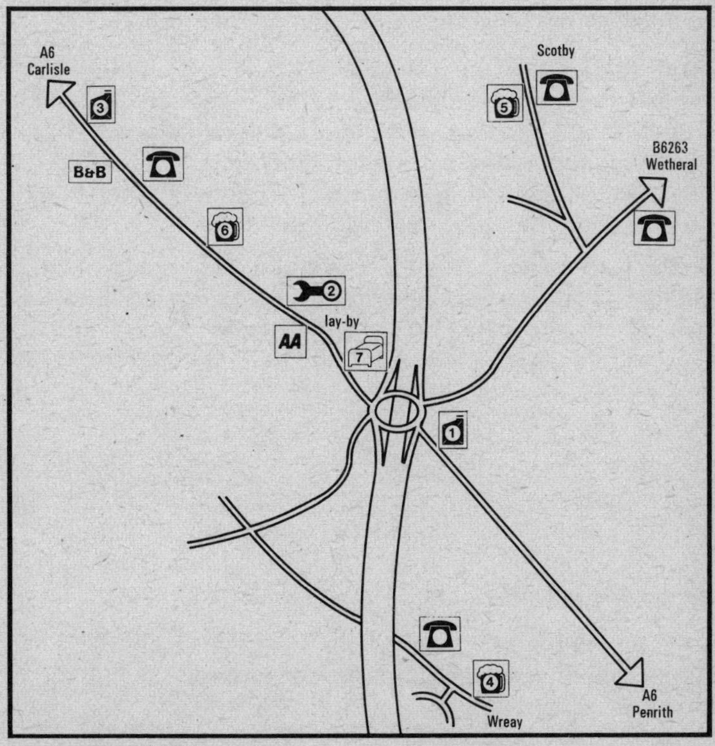

1 Golden Fleece Filling Station. Hours: 7 am Mon – 8 pm Sat (8 am – 8 pm Sun). Almost 24-hr petrol

2 Carleton Service Station. 24-hr breakdown (Carlisle, day 27287, night 29439)

3 Peterville Bridge Service Station. 24-hr petrol machine

4 *The Plough Inn*, Youngers

5 *The Royal Oak*, Courage

6 *The Green Bank*, Youngers

7 *The Carrow House Hotel* (Carlisle 32073)

Don't use **J43**, though there are two garages within a mile on the A69 going into Carlisle.

J44 is the end of the motorway and connects with the A7 and the A74. The latter has better services as it is the main trunk route to Glasgow.

If you are in urgent need of petrol there is a 24-hour garage within a short distance on the A7 into Carlisle. There is also a telephone kiosk near by.

For food and/or a bed there is a *Crest Motel* right on the junction. Much cheaper would be *Newfield Grange* (Carlisle 23066) about half a mile into town on the left and well set back from the road.

suggestions welcome

If you have any comments, corrections,
or up-to-date information that you have discovered,
please write to:

John Slater
c/o Pan Books Ltd
Cavaye Place
London
SW10 9PG

so that they can be incorporated in
future editions of this guide.

GUIDE TO MAP SYMBOLS

 PETROL

 GARAGE AND BREAKDOWN

 PUB

 POST OFFICE

 TELEPHONE

 SHOP

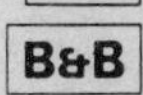

BED AND BREAKFAST

 HOTEL

 PICNIC SPOT

 FISH AND CHIPS

PARKING

RAC

AA

MUSEUM

 RESTAURANT

HOSPITAL

 WINE BAR

 POLICE STATION

 POTTERY

 SWIMMING POOL

M18
M32

visit/petrol

Roche Abbey **12**, more correctly the abbey of St Mary of Roche (of the rock), is a lovely place to visit. What remains of the abbey lies in a deep and narrow valley crossed by a stream – in fact the stream was an integral part of the building. To get there take the A634 to Blyth, pass by Maltby and wait for the signpost to the right.

It was founded in 1147 for Cistercian monks by Richard de Bully and Richard, son of Turgis – owners of the land either side of the stream. When it was suppressed in the 16th century it was valued at only £224 2s 5d – which is hard to believe given the large area still covered by buildings. As soon as the monks left the locals set to. A contemporary account says: 'All things of price were either spoiled, or carped away, or defaced to the uttermost . . . it seemeth that every person bent himself to filch and spoil what he could.'

The petrol on this junction is very cheap. The Kilns Service Station **2** is the closest to the junction and is slightly more expensive than the other two garages listed. None of the pubs are really worth visiting.

M18 J1

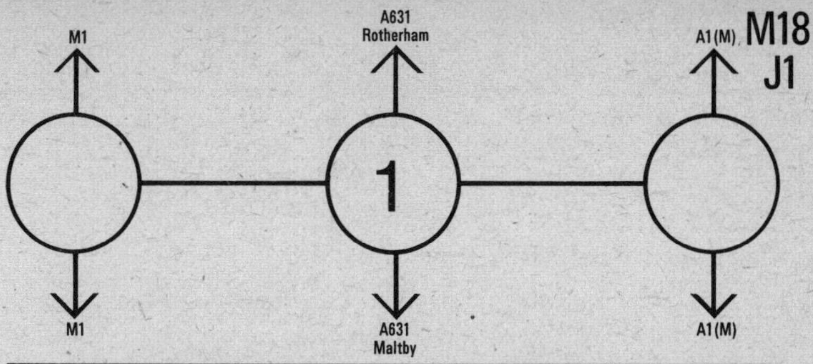

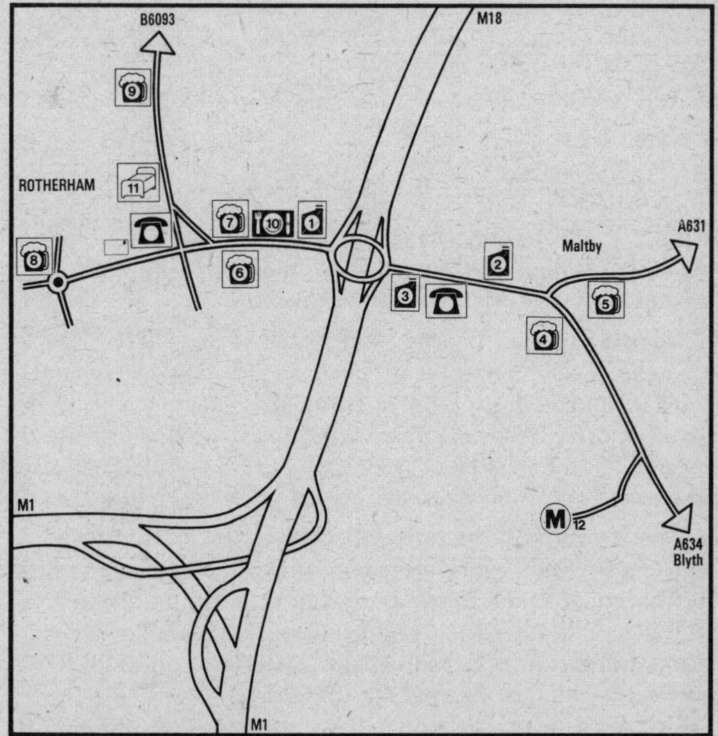

1 Whiterose Service Station. Hours: 8 am – 7 pm (shorter at weekends)
2 Kilns Service Station. Hours: 7.30 am – 10 pm (9 am – 9 pm Sun)
3 Steering Wheel Service Station. Hours: 7 am – 10 pm (opens 8 am Sun)
4 *The White Swan*, Bass Charrington
5 *The Don John*, Whitbread
6 *The Travellers*, Bass Charrington
7 *The Bell Inn*, Whitbread
8 *The Masons Arms*, Whitbread
9 *The Cavalier*, Bass Charrington
10 *Little Chef*. Open 24 hrs
11 *The Elton Hotel*
12 Roche Abbey

petrol/pub food

The M32 is only a spur road to the centre of Bristol and cheap petrol is available as soon as you come off the motorway, so I doubt whether many will feel the need to use this junction. Yet there are one or two nice places worth listing. Three simple rules for this junction: all the listed petrol is cheap – a saving of at least 10p a gallon; virtually all the pubs are Courage; the M32 separates the industrial Filton from the urban and semi-rural Frenchay.

Frenchay common, village and moor **12** are smashing. Once it must have been an area of dissent, since both the Quaker Meeting House (1673) and the small eighteenth-century Unitarian Chapel easily predates the Anglican Church. *The White Lion* **4** sits on the edge of the common. The food is above average – smoked mackerel, French bread and small salad for 65p. There is no room for children inside but in decent weather the common is surely large enough.

There is a pub in Iron Acton, *The White Hart Inn* **8**, which is worth visiting for its food. But it is five miles and it is Courage – although you can buy very cheap petrol on the way at the Winterbourne Motor Services **1**. *The White Hart* sells moussaka and curried prawns, avocados and jellied eels, and a lot more besides.

Much closer to the junction are *The White Horse* **5** and *The Hambrook* **6**. Although now a free house the latter once belonged to Courage and still sells Courage Directors bitter. It's amazing how much free choice the consumer has! And once there was Georges, and Bristol United Breweries and Simmonds and no doubt others. Now they are all Courage and that's only a part of Imperial Tobacco. Progress.

The White Horse has a nice garden and *The Hambrook* looks as though it could have been nice with more money spent on it. Better than either is the very small *Star Inn* **7** with its well kept beer. For the *Eurocrest Hotel* **11** one can only say that is rather like a glorified holiday camp without the pleasure of the redcoats – and it will cost you £11 before you even get your mouth round a piece of toast.

M32
J1

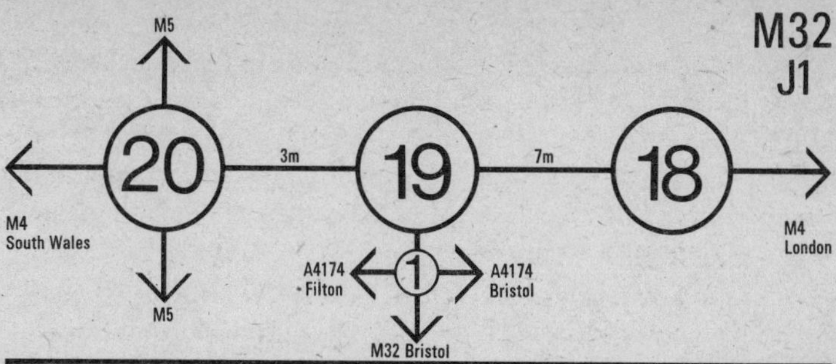

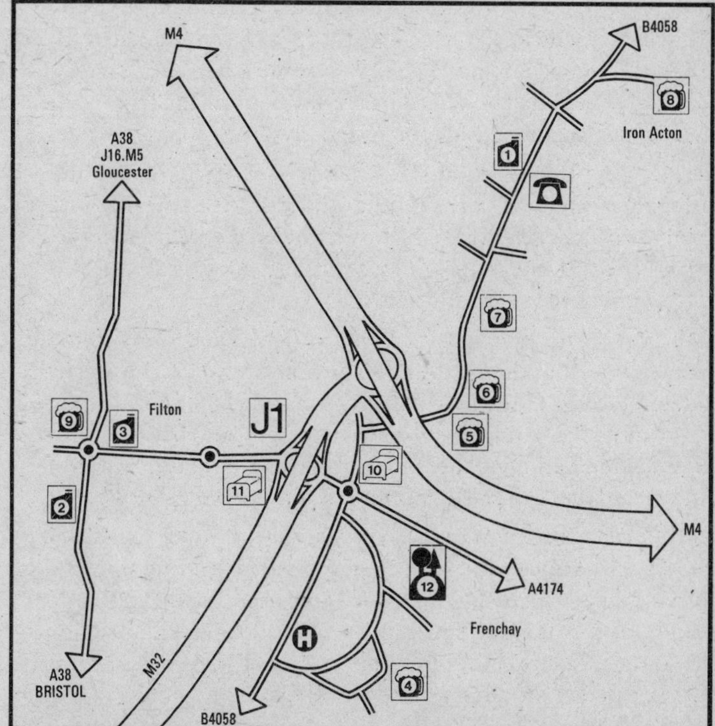

1 Winterbourne Motor Services. Hours: 7.30 am – 9 pm (9 am – 7 pm Sun)
2 Elm Park Service Station. BMW and Renault agents
3 Filton Central Filling Station. Hours: 7 am – 11 pm (8 am – 10 pm Sun)
4 *The White Lion*, Courage
5 *The White Horse*, Courage
6 *The Hambrook*, Free house
7 *The Star Inn*, Courage
8 *The White Hart Inn*, Courage
9 *The Plough*, Courage
10 *The Hambrook Grove Guest House (Bristol 571220)*
11 *Eurocrest Motel* (Bristol 564242)
12 Frenchay Common

M50

Certain junctions are not included: they are either intersections with other motorways, don't exist, or offer no real alternative services. They are listed below.

J2

J4

picnic/petrol/pubs

This is an interesting junction. Brockeridge Common **12** can be used for the grazing of cattle or sheep by those people who own strips of land in England's largest and oldest (mentioned in Domesday) water meadow, which is close by. If you want to know more about it, stay with the Halling family at *Brockeridge Farm* **11**. They only have three rooms and it's very cheap – and anyway you would probably need at least two days to understand the complexity of the water meadow. The road to the common and the farm is actually off the southern spur of the motorway junction – so if you're coming from the M5 take the small, catttle-gridded road on the left before you come to the roundabout.

Technically you are only allowed to picnic within fifteen yards of the open road. Driving further on you come to the lovely Twyning Green. There you can either have a drink in the plain but nice *Village Inn* **6**, or carry on down to *The Fleet Inn* **7** overlooking the River Avon. Very pleasant in summer with decent food – home-cooked meats – which can be eaten on the terrace. You can take a walk along the Avon on the footpath to the right.

The Twyning Service Station **1** has reasonably cheap petrol and would seem to be a good place to go for light repairs in normal working hours. The cheapest petrol is furthest from the junction at Grove House Service Station **3**. The garage keeps fairly short hours and it would hardly be worth going that far unless you wanted a pint of Marstons in the plain *Horse and Groom* **10** or unless you wanted to take a trip to the beautiful town of Upton-upon-Severn – about five miles from the junction. You can see the town in the distance in the form of a green-cupolaed red tower. It looks like an early Water Board effort but is in fact an old church tower with a later addition on top. Nice pubs in town.

For an early breakfast try *The Olde Hutte Café* **5**. You might not be able to see it as it will certainly be surrounded by lorries.

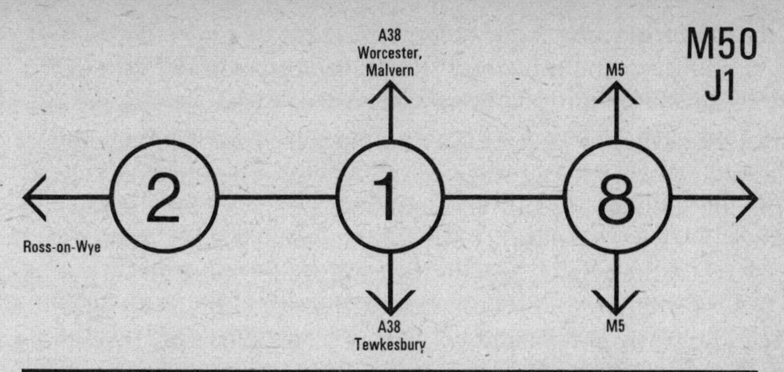

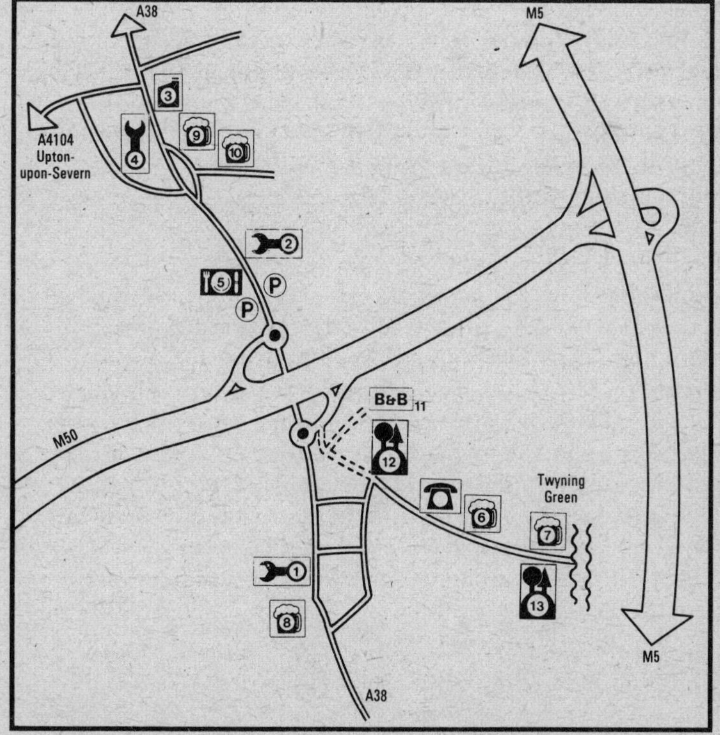

1 Twyning Service Station. Hours: 8 am – 9 pm. Light breakdown (Tewkesbury 294212) and workshop
2 Stratford Bridge Garage. 24-hr breakdown (Upton 2657)
3 Grove House Service Station. Hours: 8 am – 6 pm (9 am Sat, no Sun)
4 Ryall Garage
5 *The Olde Hutte Café*
6 *The Village Inn*, Whitbread
7 *The Fleet Inn*, Whitbread
8 *The Crown*, Ind Coope
9 *The Blue Bell*, Bass Charrington
10 *The Horse and Groom*, Marston
11 *Brockeridge Farm*. B&B (Tewkesbury 292554)
12 Brockeridge Common
13 River Avon walk

The advice at this junction should be to stay on the motorway. There is nothing conveniently close to the junction except *The Roadmaker* **5** – one of many Whitbread pubs in the area.

But the town of Newent is quite pleasant and it has a small hotel, a good restaurant and a garage that seems to provide everything. The garage is Bennions **2** and they supply 24-hour petrol and run a 24-hour breakdown service. The petrol gives you some saving on motorway prices but it wouldn't be worthwhile coming all the way to Newent for just that. The restaurant is *Bistro One* **11**; it looked good but I was there on a Sunday when it was closed. You would need time and money on your side to enjoy the meal.

The hotel is *The George* **8**. It has ten rooms, and a double room with breakfast is £10. None of the pubs in town seemed special, though *The Crown Inn* **9** in Aston Crews serves Wadworths. It's quite a long way off the beaten track. You take the B4222 signposted to Mitcheldean off the B4221 travelling towards Newent.

If you wanted to stay overnight at *The George* and eat at *Bistro One* it would be wise to book in both cases.

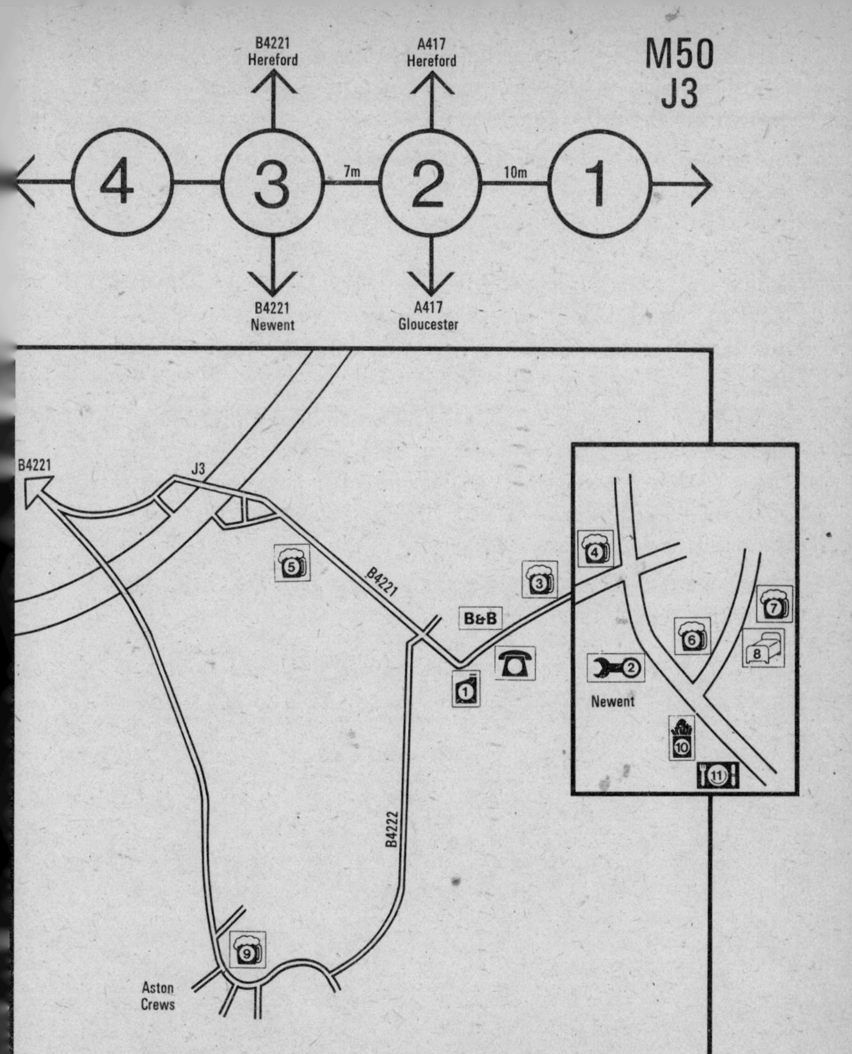

1 Kilcot Garage
2 Bennion's Garage. Hours: 8 am – 7 pm (closed Sun). 24-hr note acceptor. 24-hr breakdown (Newent 820333)
3 *The Kilcot Inn*, Whitbread
4 *The Kings Arms*, Whitbread
5 *The Roadmaker*, Whitbread
6 *The Red Lion*, Whitbread
7 *The Black Dog*, Whitbread
8 *The George Hotel*, Free house (Newent 820205)
9 *The Crown Inn*, Free house
10 Fish and chips
11 *Bistro One Restaurant*. Closed Sun, Mon lunch (Newent 820896)

M56

Certain junctions are not included: they are either intersections with other motorways, don't exist, or offer no real alternative services. They are listed below.

J1

J2

J3

J4

J5

J6

J8

J9

J11

J13

J14

healthy walks

If you are travelling from Manchester and want to take the M6 south, leave at this junction. Do not, whatever you do, use the M56 to join the M6 for that direction otherwise you end up in a real tangle – horrifically heading northwards for Birmingham! This junction also overlaps with **J19** of the M6, so take a look at that map.

For walks you have the lovely Dunham Park **8**, full of deer, the always interesting Bridgewater Canal, and Tatton Park **9** with its amazing Hall. This last one will cost you money unless you are on foot – and it just so happens that it is impossible to park near the entrance.

One of the nice entrances to Dunham is over a narrow bridge right by *The Swan with Two Nicks* **5**, which is a good pub to stop at in the summer. In the winter *Ye Olde Number 3* **3** always has a log fire going. *The Kilton Inn* **6** is the place for decent food. Homemade soup for 16p and a lot of different salads. *The Swan Hotel* **7** has a restaurant but is quite an expensive place to stay during the week. Its weekend rates are much more reasonable.

Cheap petrol at the Bowdon Filling Station **2** and a petrol machine at Cheshireways **1**.

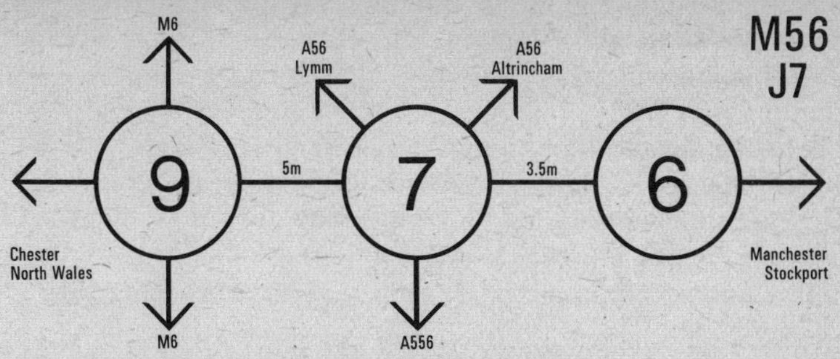

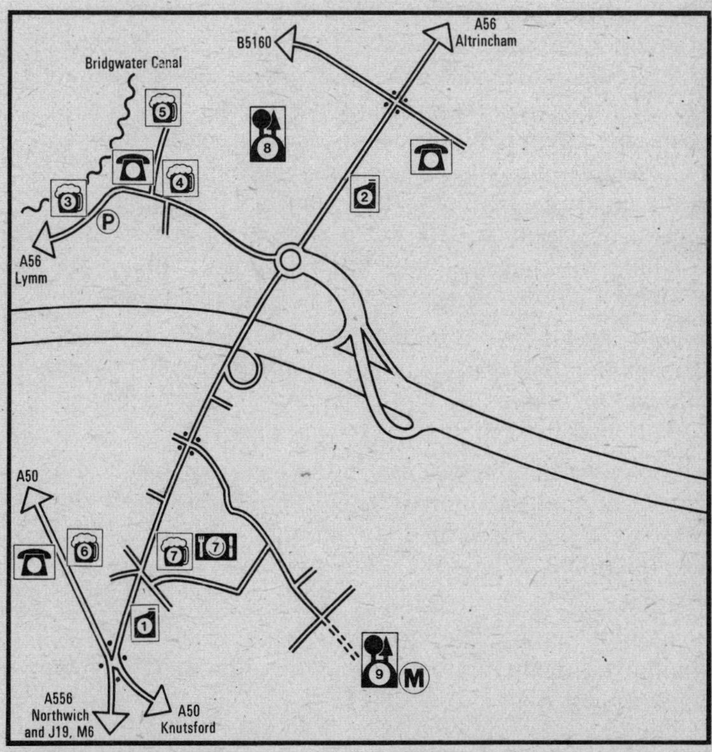

1 Cheshireways Filling Station. Hours: 7 am – 11 pm. 24-hr petrol machine
2 Bowdon Filling Station
3 *Ye Olde Number 3,* Courage
4 *The Stanford Arms,* Whitbread
5 *The Swan with Two Nicks,* Whitbread
6 *The Kilton Inn.* Greenall Whitley
7 *The Swan Hotel.* Restaurant. (Bucklow Hill 830295)
8 Dunham Park
9 Tatton Park and Hall

'I'm shopping for the wife.'
'Do you have a list?'
'No, I always stand like this.'
One of Greenall Whitley's jokey beer mats. The inscription below – 'Smile please, you're in Greenall Whitley land'. You certainly ought to because you have no choice whatsoever. And this has to be wrong for the customer however good the pubs, and one or two round here are quite good.

The Cat and Lion **3** is only a short distance from the junction. It too has a little quote for us on a lovely oval painting on the outside wall of the pub: 'The lion is strong, the cat is vicious, my ale is good and so are my liquors.' On a foggy Sunday midday I tried to make it rhyme and almost made it. Nice old-fashioned pub inside. Food at lunchtimes. Quite a long way down the A49 towards Whitchurch is *The Chetwode Arms* **8**. It used to be *The Cock O'Whitley* but the Chetwode family buying the area left their mark. Lt Col Sir Somebody Chetwode sold it to Sir Gilbert Greenall in the forties. It, too, is an old-fashioned pub – one of its small rooms has only one table. A rather dour landlord.

The Thorn **7** allows you to drink between 3 and 3.30 pm on Monday, Wednesday and Friday if, that is, you are attending the Appleton potato exchange. I didn't bother to enquire since I found that the price of a half pint, if doubled, was 2p more than a pint.

The Birch and Bottle **5**, *The Wheatsheaf* **6** and *The London Bridge* **9** also have food. So do all three hotels. *The Hill Cliffe Hydro* **13** is the most expensive in terms of food and board, but only just. *The Birchdale* **14** is quite a lot cheaper for board but *The Old Vicarage* **12** is by far the most convenient.

Strange to say that a garage is friendly – haven't found too many of those. But the Northcott Brook **1** was. Their prices weren't too bad and they hope they are coming down.

1 Northcott Brook Garage. Hours: 8 am – 7 pm (10 am – 6 pm Sun). Workshop and breakdown in working hours (Norcott Brook 264)

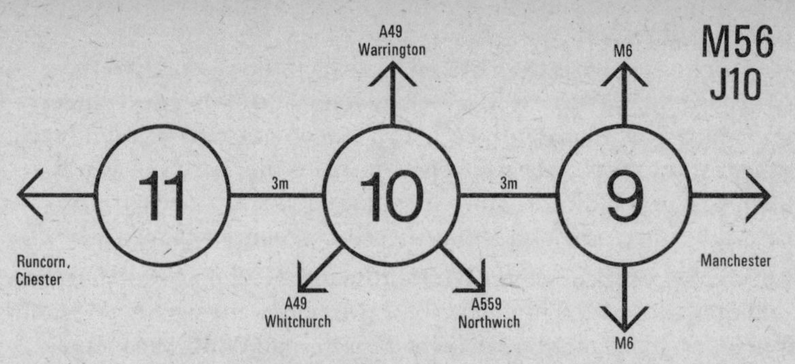

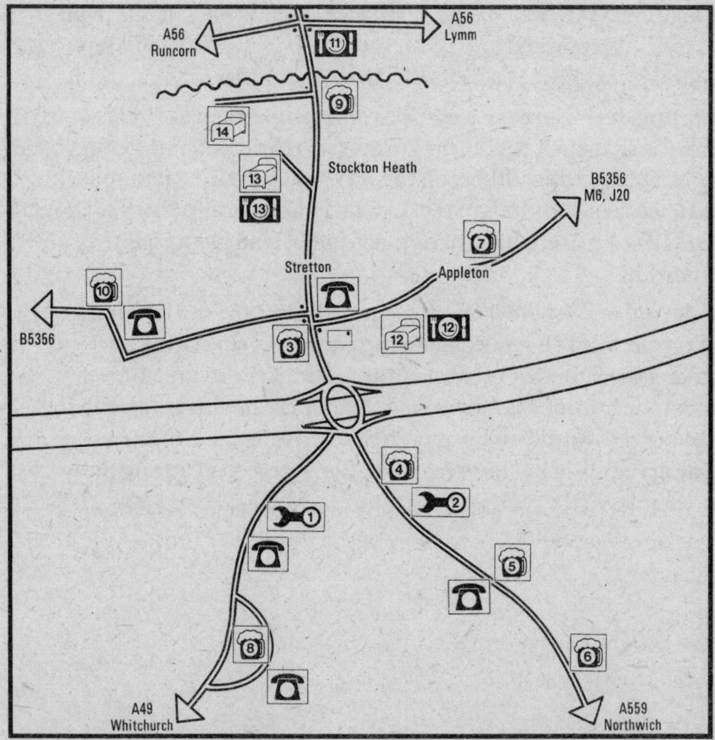

2 Ring O'Bells Service Station. Breakdown (Norcott Brook 551)
3 *The Cat and Lion,* Greenall Whitley
4 *The Ring O'Bells,* Greenall Whitley
5 *The Birch and Bottle,* Greenall Whitley
6 *The Wheatsheaf,* Greenall Whitley
7 *The Thorn,* Greenall Whitley
8 *The Chetwode Arms,* Greenall Whitley
9 *The London Bridge,* Greenall Whitley
10 *The Hatton Arms,* Greenall Whitley
11 *La Caradella Restaurant* (Warrington 68557)
12 *The Old Vicarage Hotel* (Norcott Brook 238)
13 *The Hill Cliffe Hydro Hotel and Restaurant* (Warrington 63638)
14 *The Birchdale Hotel* (Warrington 63662)

petrol/pubs/food

Runcorn new town is close by and if you have time to spare you could easily lose yourself there. More roundabouts than you've ever met, and roads which constantly seem to be decorously circling round each other. Many parts of the new town are interesting but if you want an awful vision of the future go to Shopping City. Warm and covered certainly, but plastic and boring as well. No room for change there.

On your way pick up petrol at by far the cheapest filling station on the junction, the Heath Filling Station **1**. Just follow the signs for Weston Village. While there you can break the Greenall Whitley monopoly by visiting *The Royal Oak* **4**, a plain local pub. Weston is one of the villages incorporated into the new town. For a view of the Mersey and its mud banks go to *The Prospect* **5** in name and deed.

This area seems to have a number of semi-spectacular bridges. Apart from the smashing Runcorn–Widnes road bridge and the crenellated rail bridge there are others on the way to Frodsham. Here you will find a tea room, an Indian restaurant **11** and many pubs. *The Old Hall Hotel* **12** is a reasonably priced place to stay and has a good restaurant.

Of the pubs, *The Golden Lion* **6** seems to be the nicest. It's largely got its old layout inside but needs some money to get rid of the part conversion of the last hundred years. Across the road is the red sandstone hulk of *The Bears Paw* **7**, a far more popular pub with the younger set and, given the most attractive collection of barpeople I've come across, I'm not too surprised. Both serve food during the week. Further down the road is the genuine local, *The Cheshire Cheese* **8**.

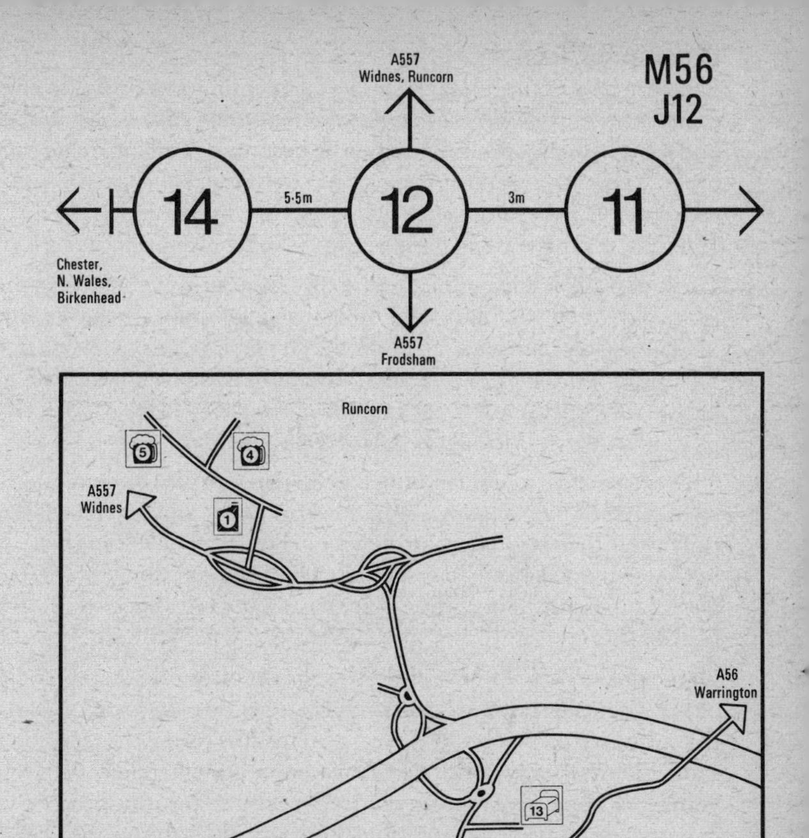

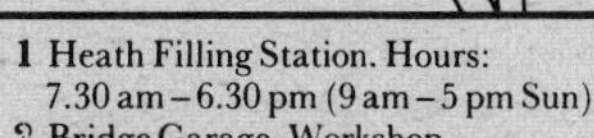

1 Heath Filling Station. Hours: 7.30 am – 6.30 pm (9 am – 5 pm Sun)
2 Bridge Garage. Workshop (Frodsham 31239)
3 Sutton Weaver Filling Station
4 *The Royal Oak*, Marston
5 *The Prospect*, Greenall Whitley
6 *The Golden Lion*, Samuel Smith
7 *The Bears Paw*, Greenall Whitley
8 *The Cheshire Cheese*, Greenall Whitley
9 *The Bridge Inn*, Greenall Whitley
10 *The Aston Arms*, Greenall Whitley
11 *The Garden of India Restaurant*
12 *The Old Hall Hotel and Restaurant* (Frodsham 32052)
13 *Runcorn Crest Hotel* (Runcorn 63444)

M61

Certain junctions are not included: they are either intersections with other motorways, don't exist, or offer no real alternative services. They are listed below.

J1

J2

J3

J4

J7

accommodation/petrol

Apart from *The White Swan* **3** this junction is not very interesting. The Beaumont Service Station **1** is useful and cheap – there is an attendant on duty all night. All three hotels have restaurants attached and have been graded by their price. *The Travellers Rest* **10** is small and cheap and seems to be undergoing changes. Fish and chips served to keep prices down and closed on Sundays. *The Mercury* **11** is a motel for commercial travellers and is a reasonable price. Its restaurant is closed Saturday lunchtime. *The Bolton Crest* **12** is like most others in the group. A single night will cost about £12 and the restaurant is open at all normal times.

The White Swan is a tiled Victorian drinking establishment. Some would even call it a watering hole – they even claim that the brews of Dr Holt have a medicinal property. On the evidence I saw I wouldn't call the property medicinal. But it is a loud, friendly pub with cheap beer. The landlord clearly has problems with a shrinking suit and one of the warders, waiters I mean, seems to have lost all his teeth. This pub is in strong contrast to *The Red Lion* **9** – which has a good-looking stone interior. But once inside there are acres of empty space. Why old pubs knock all their rooms into one is beyond my understanding. The result is uniformly ugly. Of the other pubs *The Three Pigeons* **4** serves food and *The Kings Arms* **5** has a good location. It's an old pub with room outside for the good days.

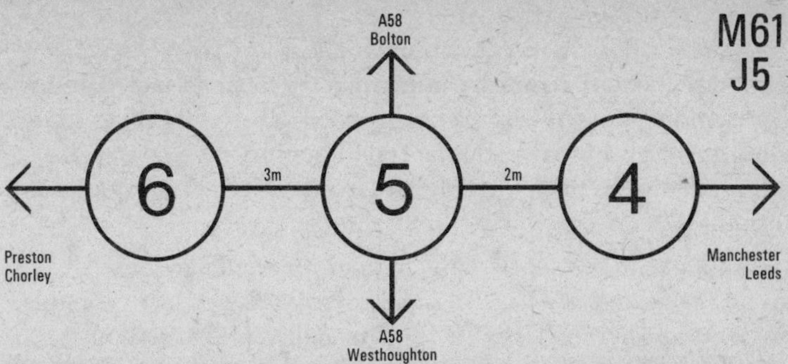

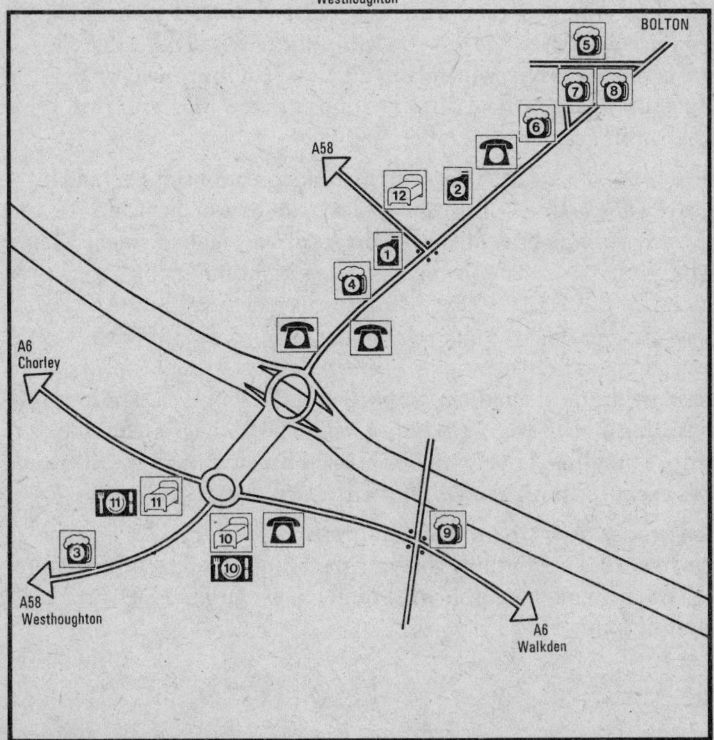

1 Beaumont Service Station. 24-hr petrol
2 Fernhill Service Station. Hours: 8 am – 9 pm. Workshop
3 *The White Swan*, Holts
4 *The Three Pigeons*, Tetley
5 *The Kings Arms*, Tetley
6 *The Rumworth*, Greenall Whitley
7 *The Queen Anne*, Watney
8 *The Stags Head Hotel*, Burtonwood
9 *The Red Lion*, Tetley
10 *The Travellers Rest Hotel and Restaurant* (Westhoughton 811446)
11 *The Mercury Motel and Restaurant* (Westhoughton 813270)
12 *Bolton Crest Motel* (Bolton 651511)

petrol
The petrol on this junction is extremely cheap and is likely to remain so because the stations are in competition. So cheap, in fact, that the nearest motorway service area has dropped its prices by about 10p a gallon and even advertises this fact on the motorway. You can take your pick between them but only the Greenwood **3** offers any kind of mechanical services.

If you wanted to keep up with the Joneses you would undoubtedly stay at *The Swallowfield Hotel* **13** run by Mrs Jones with many capable assistants and her son David, a TV personality. He has recently undergone a number of courses to refine his character all of which, on film, have been shown to viewers in the north west. To say that the hotel is run with style, wit and imagination would open one to the accusation of favouritism since I happen to know Master David. It is comfortable and the price is reasonable.

The pubs in the area are very much drinking establishments and if you are unlucky (or foolish) enough to go to some of them on a Saturday you will be deafened by the strains of amateur singers. The locals, perhaps deafened by years of work in the mills, don't seem to notice. *The Colliers Arms* **10** is an interesting old building and *The Queens Head* **7** serves decent beer but the Regency plush of its conversion has been overdone. *The Gerrard Arms* **8** should only be visited by the most fanatical supporters of Boddingtons. The most interesting of the pubs is *The Wagon and Horses* **6** which is a fine late twenties building. Lovely stained glass and a lot of brass. Food at all times except Saturday lunch, and a dining room for children.

For a proper sit-down meal of well-prepared food go to *The Georgian Restaurant* **12**. For anything else you may want – the Tesco Superstore **11** – which seems to inhabit an aircraft hanger large enough for a couple of Jumbos.

M61 J6

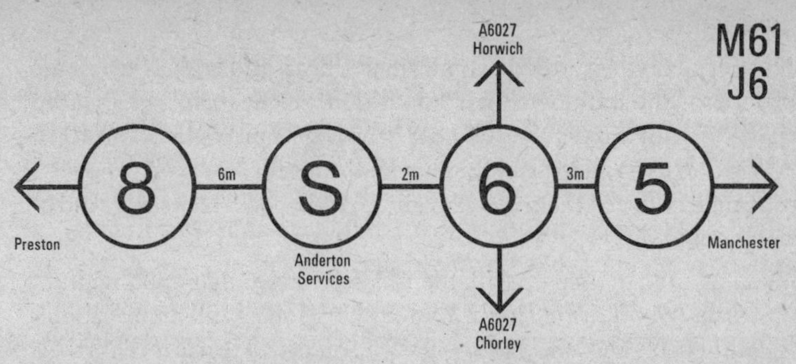

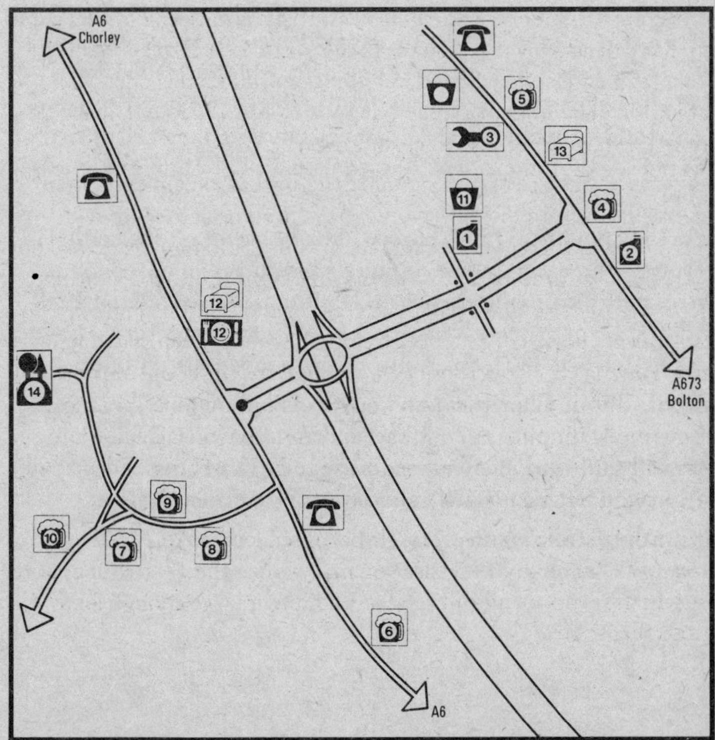

1 Tesco Superstore Self Service. Hours: 7 am – 9 pm (shorter at weekends)
2 Beehive Garage. Hours: 7 am – 9.30 pm (closes 8.30 at weekends)
3 Greenwood Garage. Hours: 7 am – 10 pm (9 am – 9 pm Sun)
4 *The Beehive*, Tetley. Cavalier Steak Bar
5 *The Greenwood*, Greenall Whitley
6 *The Wagon and Horses*, Burtonwood
7 *The Queens Head*, Tetley
8 *The Gerrard Arms*, Boddingtons
9 *The Coach and Horses*, Greenall Whitley
10 *The Colliers Arms*, Burtonwood
11 Tesco Superstore
12 *The Georgian House Hotel and Restaurant* (Westhoughton 814598)
13 *The Swallowfield Hotel* (Bolton 67914)
14 Haigh Hall Country Park

visits/petrol

There are many lovely places to visit on this junction and most will be there for a long time to come. But two of them have a sentence of death hanging over their heads. They are both pubs and are both owned by Matthew Brown. They intend to close *The Dressers* **4** or possibly to sell if off. It has the oldest licence in the area – and it looks it. Dark, thick-walled and very old-fashioned, with slatted wooden seats. It sells draught bitter and is liked by the locals.

The plans for *The Red Cat Inn* **3** suggest that its four tiny rooms are going to be knocked together. This would be an act of vandalism. So try and see this small country pub which serves good beer and decent food before it gets the 'treatment'. As evidence of what might happen visit *The Top Lock* **5**. Once it was a nice canal-side pub called *The Anchor*; then it had the 'treatment'. Full of Regency plush with a few nautical oddments for effect. All rather nasty with the smell of fried food spoiling the atmosphere. But it does have some interesting posters on the wall.

The cricket pitch at White Coppice **11** has to be the most beautiful in the world. Three white stone cottages, three heavy stone rollers; an oak tree with a crumbling bench and bracken-covered hills on three sides. And in those hills a Victorian piece of water engineering – now crumbling. Ducts and locks, slipways and ponds. All very interesting.

Astley Hall **10** in Chorley is also worth a visit. Reputedly it has the finest carved oak four-poster in the land and a pair of Oliver Cromwell's fur-lined boots. Some of the ceilings are so ornate that a DIY fan would hang himself from the nearest angel in despair.

Finally, the petrol at both petrol stations is cheap and the Jubilee **1** has a workshop on a 5½-day week.

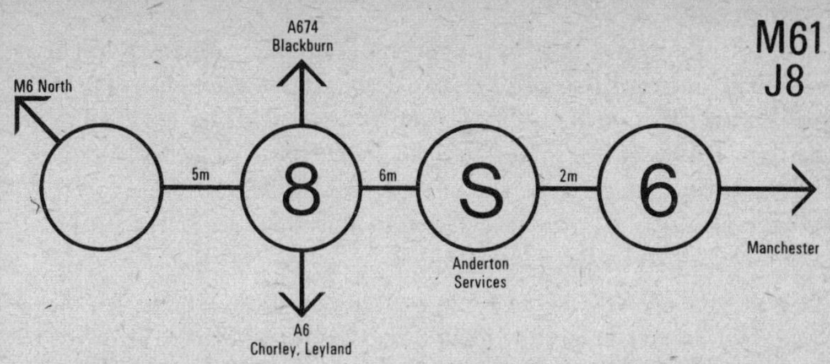

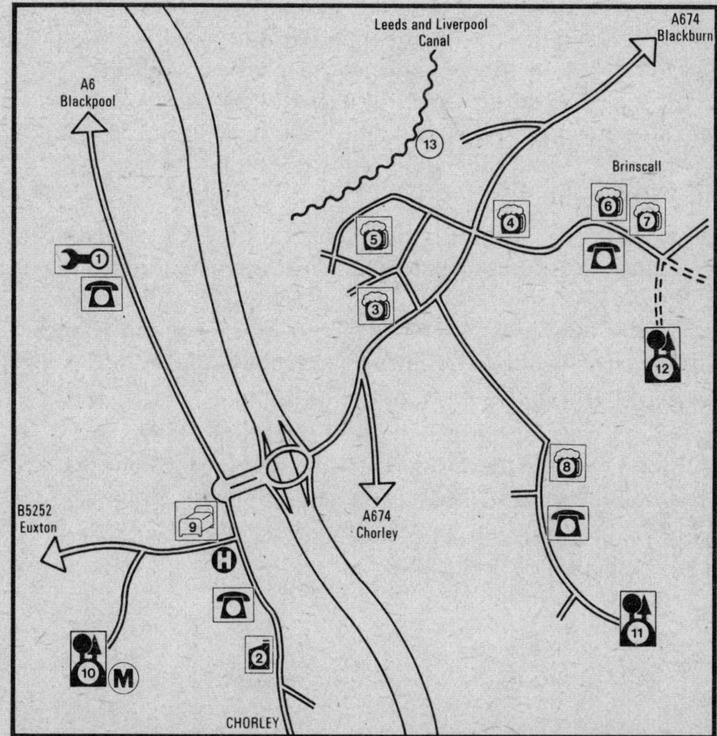

1 Jubilee Service Station. Hours: 7.45 am – 9 pm (shorter at weekends). 5½-day workshop
2 Telegraph Service Station. Hours: 7 am – 11 pm (opens 8 am Sat, 9 am Sun)
3 *The Red Cat Inn,* Matthew Brown
4 *The Dressers,* Matthew Brown
5 *The Top Lock,* Matthew Brown
6 *The Cricketers,* Matthew Brown
7 *The Bulls Head,* Matthew Brown
8 *The Railway Hotel,* Matthew Brown
9 *Hartwood Hall Hotel* (Chorley 70066)
10 Astley Hall
11 White Coppice Cricket Pitch
12 Brinscall Woods
13 Leeds and Liverpool Canal

M62

Certain junctions are not included: they are either intersections with other motorways, don't exist, or offer no real alternative services. They are listed below.

J1

J2

J3

J4

J5

J8

J10

J11

J12

J14

J15

J16

J20

J26

J27

J29

J33

J35

On the A5080 into Huyton and Liverpool there are three garages, one of them being almost on the roundabout. All are expensive. The cheapest, by a fine margin, is listed – The Hare and Hounds Garage **2**. To save at least another 5p a gallon you have to go to the Woodland Filling Station **1**. Take the first left, Whitefield Lane, off the A5080 towards Huyton – just before you reach *The Hare and Hounds* pub **5**. Then take the left turning at the T-junction.

None of the pubs are very special. *The Hare and Hounds* serves food. But *The Rose and Crown* **6** must have been a fine establishment in its day – even grand. Comfortable seating round the walls, bells everywhere, and brass moulds for stubbing out cigarettes. But it's fallen on harder times and has been tampered with – even to the extent of plastic padding at knee level on the bar. *The Brickwall* **4** is a large plain pub with an enormous car park which must be some kind of tribute to its pulling power – and to its distance from habitation.

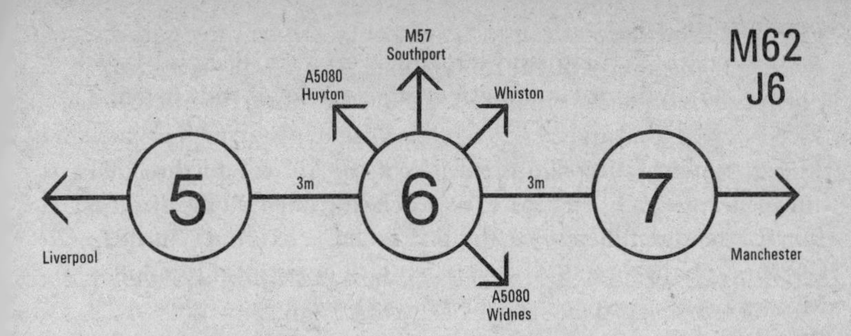

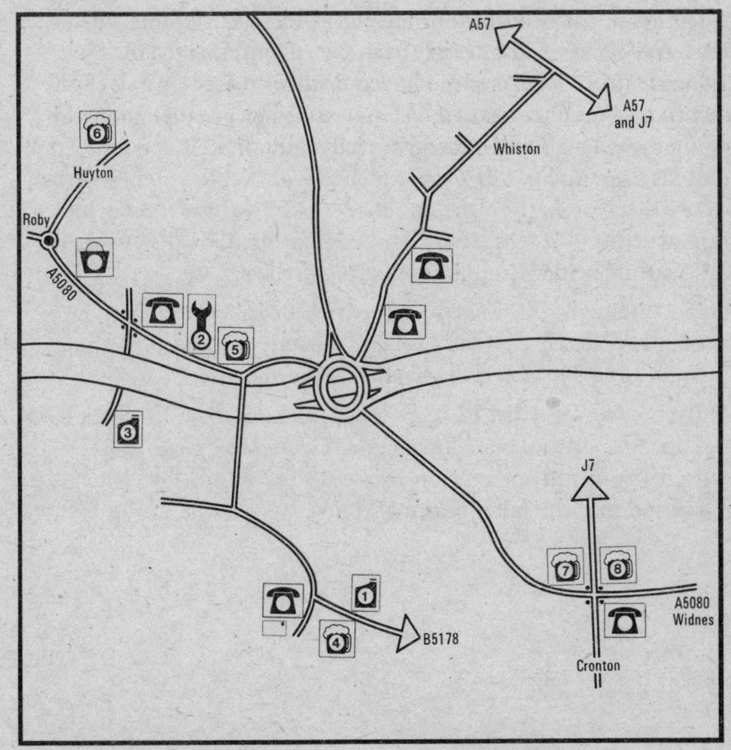

1 Woodland Filling Station. Hours: 6.30 am – 9 pm (opens 8 am Sun)
2 Hare and Hounds Garage
3 Wheatlands Service Station
4 *The Brickwall Inn*, Burtonwood
5 *The Hare and Hounds*, Greenall Whitley
6 *The Rose and Crown*, Tetley
7 *The Unicorn Inn*, Greenall Whitley
8 *The Black Horse*, Greenall Whitley

petrol/pubs/food

To the north of the motorway it is largely urban, to the south largely rural. Visually almost nothing. Yet quite a good junction in many ways.

There are petrol stations and garages on the A57 in both directions, only some of which, the closer, have been included. In the direction of Prescot the Rainhill Service Station **2** is cheap, as is the Whittle Inn Garage **3**, in the direction of Warrington. The petrol at Rainhill Motors **1** is more expensive, but it runs a breakdown service.

There are many useful pubs on this junction. For beer drinkers especially, but also for those interested in Victorian Gothic, *The Plough Hotel* **8** is worth a visit. It hasn't been too damaged by the passage of time – there is a smoke room and a news room as well as other bars. There are also a lot of interesting news items on the wall. Just up the way is *The Hare and Hounds* **9** – a small, well-decorated pub that sells draught beer. It's very much a local. Neither of these pubs serves food. Nor, in the other direction, does *The Broad Oak* **6** which is, again, worth a visit. One small bar with four small rooms attached. Wall seating, leaded fireplaces and draught beer.

For food at lunchtime, *The Griffin* **5**, which also allows children into one of its rooms. *The Ship Inn* **7**, a large modern pub, has buffet food. *The Black Horse* **11** has a grill attached to the main pub.

The Whittle Inn Restaurant **12** keeps long hours, 12 – 3 for lunch and 7 – 11 for supper, and has a long menu. *The Rockland Hotel* **13** has a licensed restaurant open to non-residents. Its charges for accommodation are fairly reasonable.

M62 J7

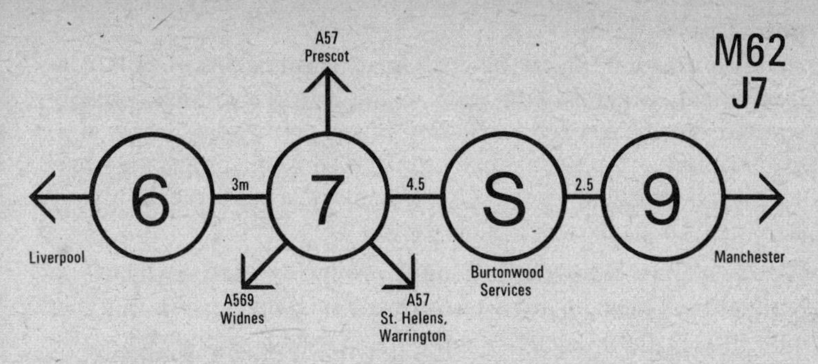

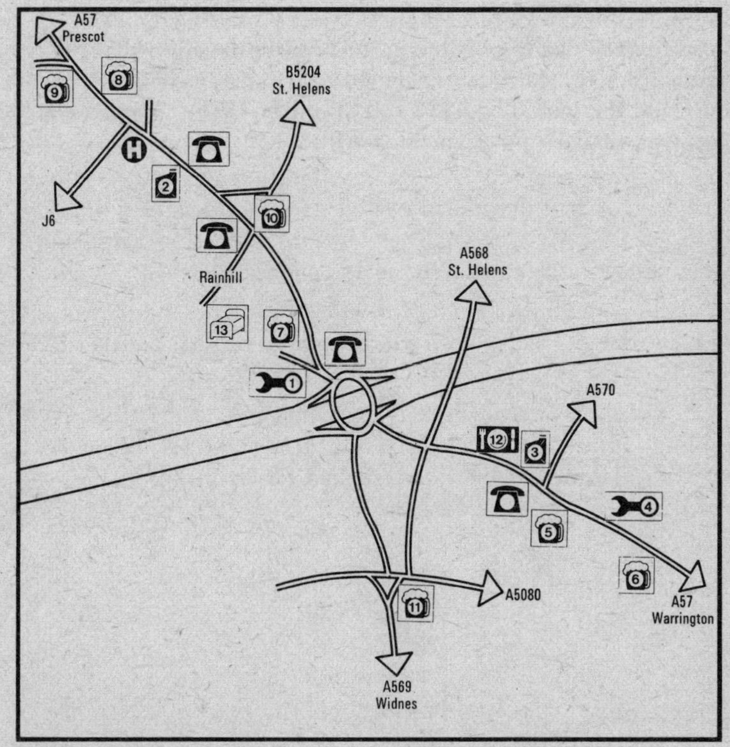

1 Rainhill Motors. 24-hr breakdown (051 426 4199)
2 Rainhill Service Station. Hours: 7 am – 10 pm (opens 8 am Sat, Sun)
3 Whittle Inn Garage. Hours: 7 am – 10.30 pm (8 am – 10 pm Sat, Sun)
4 Ace of Hearts Garage
5 *The Griffin*, Greenall Whitley
6 *The Broad Oak*, Greenall Whitley
7 *The Ship Inn*, Higsons
8 *The Plough Hotel*, Greenall Whitley
9 *The Hare and Hounds*, Higsons
10 *The Victoria Hotel*, Greenall Whitley
11 *The Black Horse*, Stables Grill. Greenall Whitley
12 *The Whittle Inn Restaurant*. Closed Sun evening (051 424 2259)
13 *The Rockland Hotel* (051 426 4603)

petrol

If it were not for the availability of cheap petrol right round the clock this junction would join the many on this motorway which should be ignored. The Heron Service Station **1** has a permanent cashier so you can buy as much petrol as you need. Don't misunderstand me – I am simply comparing the presence of a cashier to a petrol machine which slowly eats 50p pieces or £1 notes, if you have them.

The Swan **2** has recently been done up in a Jacobean style which is not really to my liking, having seen too many such conversions. But they have just started a lunchtime menu and it would certainly be worthwhile giving it a try.

If you are planning to join the M6 and head northwards you can save quite a distance by using this junction and crossing to **J22** on the M6. You could also look at both **J22** and **J23** on the M6 for the other places listed – particularly pubs which serve food.

M62 J9

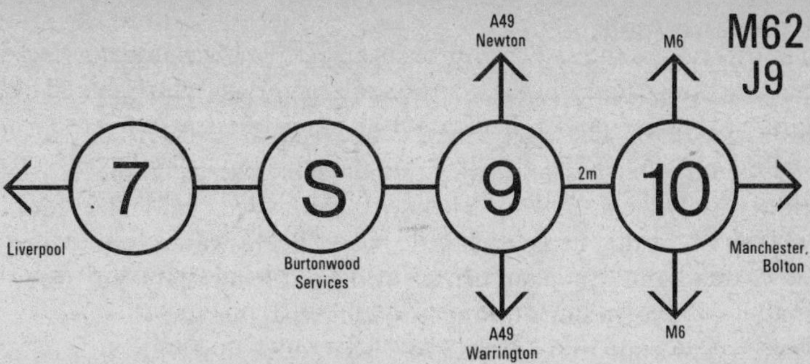

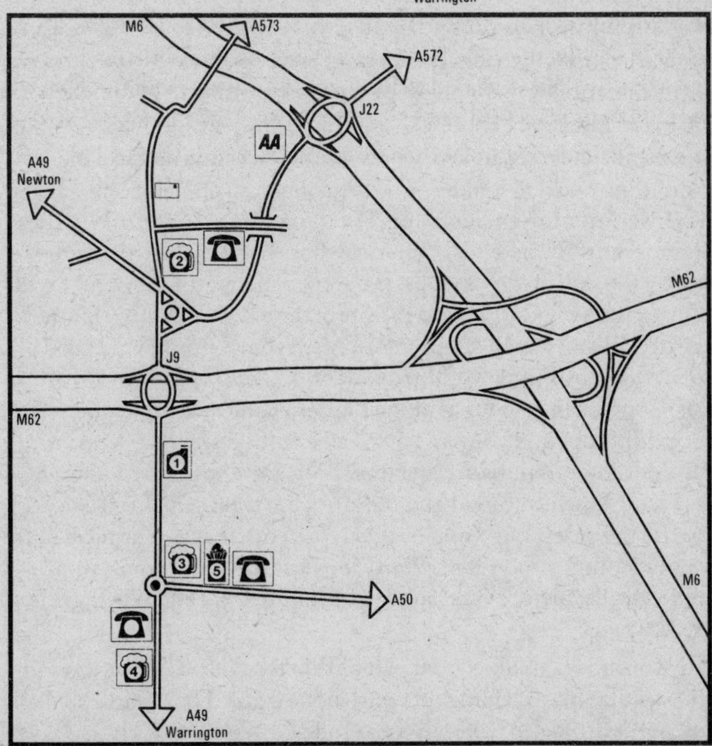

1 Heron Service Station. 24-hr petrol
2 *The Swan,* Wilsons
3 *The Longford,* Greenall Whitley
4 *The Horse and Jockey,* Greenall Whitley
5 *Mathews Fish and Chips*. Lunch Mon – Sat; Dinner, Mon, Tue, Thur, Fri

visits/petrol/pubs

Worsley is almost completely surrounded by a variety of motorways – surprising that it survived so well, because it is a beautiful and interesting place. The lovely houses, the green, the woods thick with rhododendron bushes, and, above all, the shiny red waters of the Bridgewater Canal. You don't believe the shiny red bit? Well, go and see. It was here that Francis, Third Duke of Bridgewater, started the commercial canal system in Britain by digging a 'navigable cut' from Worsley to Manchester. It was used to ship coal from the Worsley mines and was opened in about 1762. To build it, the Duke mortgaged most of his property and reduced his personal expenditure to £400 a year. By the end of that century his income from this enterprise (by then extended to Runcorn, the Mersey and therefore Liverpool) was £80,000 a year.

The Edwardian green in Worsley is unusual when so much of the surrounding housing is older. The dead fountain on the green with its Latin inscription gives some clue. For those who aren't scholars, the first line reads: 'I was a lofty column, whose panting nostrils were made by the skill of the Cyclops, the glory of the smith, The Duke was the instigator . . .' The green is the site of the old workshops' chimney and warehouses. Much of this information comes from a very good guide written by Frank Mullineux called *The Duke of Bridgewater's Canal*. Copies can be bought at the Lantern Gallery **9** where there are often exhibitions and you can have coffee or tea during the week. The three Boddingtons pubs are all large. Both *The Bridgewater* **3** and *The Cock* **4** have lunchtime food and the latter has a garden. *The White Horse* **5** is the oldest but could be much better than it is. The nicest and most interesting pub by far is *The White Swan* **6**. Many rooms, wood-panelled walls, pictures and solid food. The petrol at both garages is very cheap.

A late workman explained to the duke that the reason he was late for work was that his wife had had twins in the night. The duke said: 'Aye, well, we have to have what the good lord sends us.' The workman replied: 'Ah, notice he sends all t'babies to our house and all t'brass to yores.' The duke gave him a guinea. The man's wages at that time would have been a shilling a day.

M62 J13

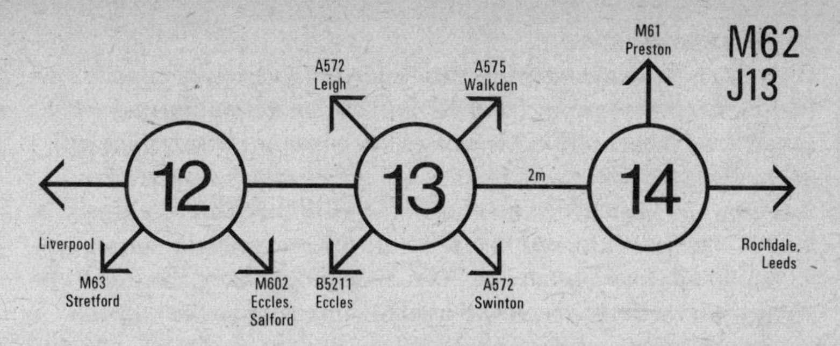

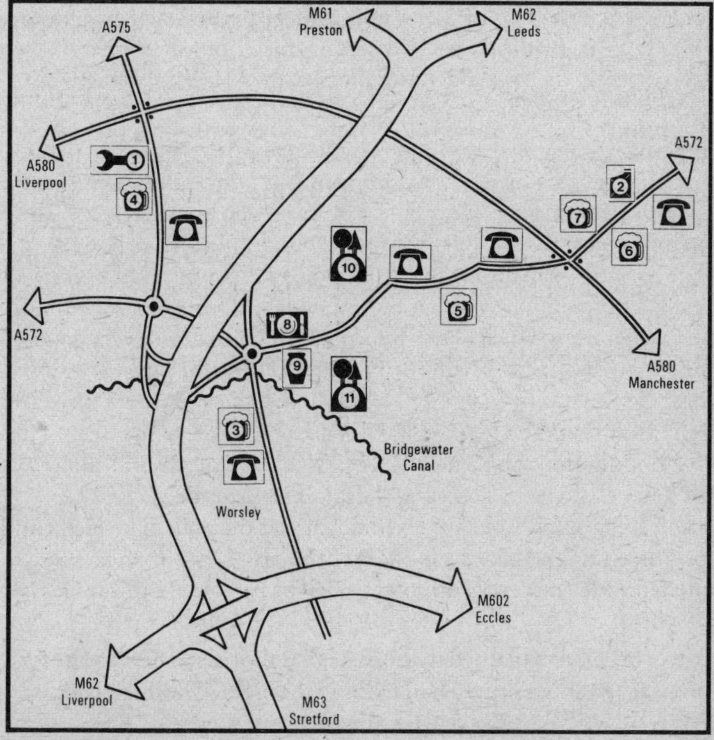

1 Walkden Road Service Station. Hours: 8 am – 9 pm (shorter at weekend). Workshop in working week; tyres, exhausts.
2 Swinton Service Station. Hours: 7.30 am – 10.30 pm (opens 9 am Sun)
3 *The Bridgewater Hotel,* Boddingtons
4 *The Cock Hotel,* Boddingtons
5 *The White Horse,* Boddingtons
6 *The White Swan Hotel,* Holts
7 *The Staff of Life,* Tetley
8 *The Casserole Restaurant.* Closed Sun, Mon (061 794 2660)
9 Lantern Gallery. Closed Mon, Sat, Sun am
10 Worsley Wood
11 Bridgewater Canal

petrol/repairs

Petrol is cheap, convenient and 24-hour on this junction at the Paddock Service Station **1**. All the five listed petrol stations are very cheap – the cheapest being Kirkham's **5**, but we are now talking about fractions of a penny. Quite a few of the garages have workshop facilities, the one with the longest hours being Dale's **4** which is attached to the Whitfield Garage **3**. Dale's works a six-day week and has a 24-hour recovery service. The number listed is the daytime phone – for nights you have to make contact via the police.

Heaton Park **16** covers a very large area, but the part closest to the junction is the least interesting. There is a lake within half a mile of the car park marked.

The whole junction is urban and the pubs are what you expect to find in that kind of area. The two Holts pubs closest to the junction, like so many of their pubs, are interesting architectural specimens from the turn of the century. *The New Grove Inn* **10** is friendly and darts-mad. *The Church Inn* **11** is smaller with nice glass. *The White Horse* **6** has old ladies nodding into glasses of Guinness – for medicinal purposes only, of course, and *The Grapes* **7** attracts the youth to play pool. All these pubs are really drinking establishments.

For food it's either *The Masons Arms* **13** which has a restaurant attached or *The Turn of the Century Restaurant* **14** – but did restaurants at that time have plastic table tops? – or *Lee's Chinese Restaurant* **15**. I would tend to wait for **J7** or **J21** – not that the M62 provides very much.

1 Paddock Service Station. 24-hr self-service petrol
2 Grimshaw's. Hours: 7 am – 11 pm (opens 8 am Sun). Workshop. Vauxhall dealers
3 Whitfield Garage. Hours: 8 am – 9 pm (opens 9 am Sat, 10 am Sun). Workshop on 6-day week
4 Dale's Garage. 24-hr breakdown (061 766 2412; or phone police)
5 Kirkham's Garage. Hours: 7.30 am – 10.30 pm (opens 9 am Sun). Tyres
6 *The White Horse*, Tetley
7 *The Grapes*, Greenall Whitley
8 *The Commercial Inn*, Tetley

M62
J17

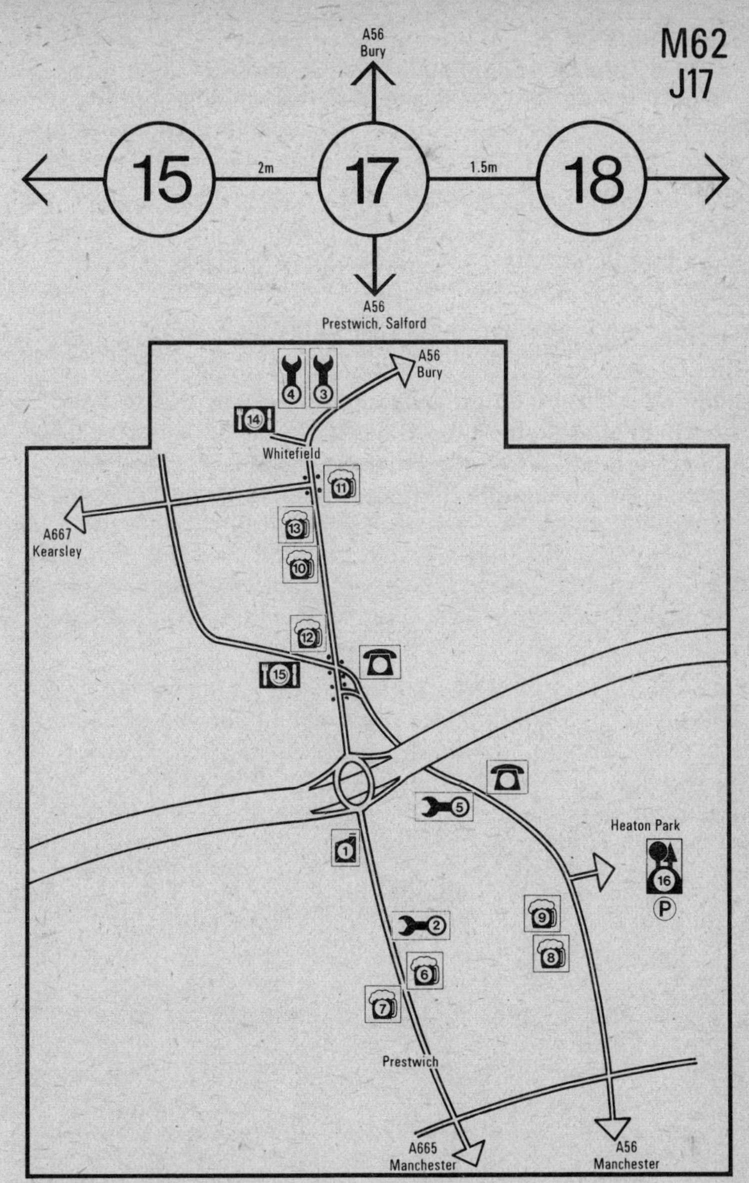

9 *The Parkside Hotel*, Boddingtons
10 *The New Grove Inn*, Holts
11 *The Church Inn*, Holts
12 *The Junction*, Whitbread
13 *The Masons Arms*, Whitbread
14 *The Turn of the Century Restaurant*
15 *Lee's Chinese Restaurant*
16 Heaton Park

petrol/pub food

The M66 in the direction of Manchester is only really a spur road one mile long. If you turn right off the roundabout you will find immediately on your right a very cheap garage and a pub. There is a break in the dual carriageway to allow you to cross.

The petrol at the Three Arrows Garage **1** is as cheap as any in the area and it will handle breakdowns and repairs during a normal 5½-day week (061 643 2791). But its hours are shorter than Heaton Park Motors **2**.

For lunchtime food *Ye Olde Three Arrows* **4**. A variety of ploughmans with cheese or meats. It has undergone surgery to give it a comfortable but not very attractive decor. Cocktails are also served. Apart from being the most convenient it is by far the best pub in the area. If you need a breath of fresh air, the enormous Heaton Park is available. For parking take the A6044 towards Swinton.

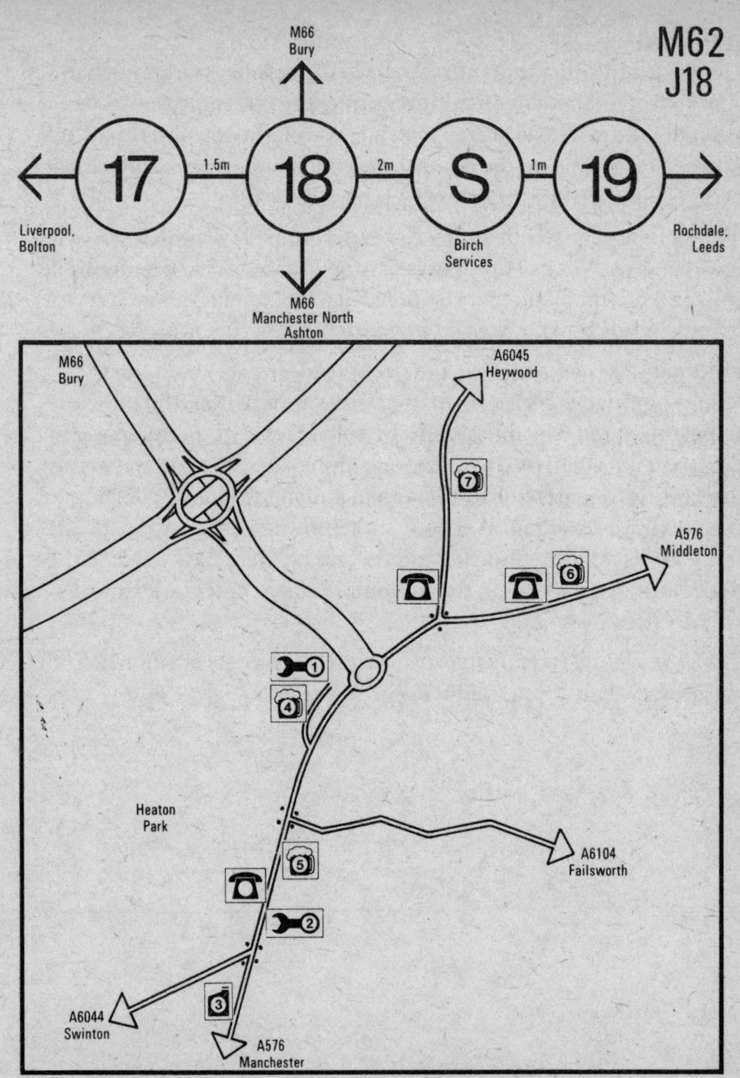

1 Three Arrows Garage. Hours: 7.30 am – 8 pm (opens 9 am Sun). Workshop
2 Heaton Park Motors. Hours: 8 am – 11 pm (opens 9 am Sun). Opel dealers
3 Crumsall Filling Station. Hours: 7 am – 10.30 pm (9 am – 10 pm Sun)
4 *Ye Olde Three Arrows*, Boddingtons
5 *The Heaton Park Hotel*, Whitbread
6 *The Carters Arms*, Lees
7 *The Jolly Butchers*, Bass Charrington

pub food

Like so many other junctions on the M62 this one is largely urban. The petrol is fairly cheap in either direction, but only a few p cheaper than the nearest service area which has brought down its prices and advertises the fact on the motorway. For cheapness and convenience the 24-hour petrol station on **J17** is hard to beat.

The pubs are largely drinking establishments. *Ye Olde Boars Head* **5** is worth a visit. None of the beer is very special but it is a genuinely old pub and has many pictures on the wall to document this fact. A leaning white and black front and a lot of small rooms inside.

For food *The Gardeners Arms* **7** and *The White Hart* **8** – both Bass Charrington and both a bit distant from the junction. But one can make the round trip and pick up petrol at Hebers **1** on the way. *The Gardeners* is a small pub with enough knick-knacks to make it almost interesting. Seems to be full of young, and not so young, courting couples in the evening. Weekday lunchtime food and a garden. *The White Hart* is slightly smarter and the size of its car park bears witness to the lack of competition thereabouts. Food at lunchtimes and a restaurant.

The Birch Hotel **9** is really for businessmen. Given its position in front of the motorway it appears a bit expensive.

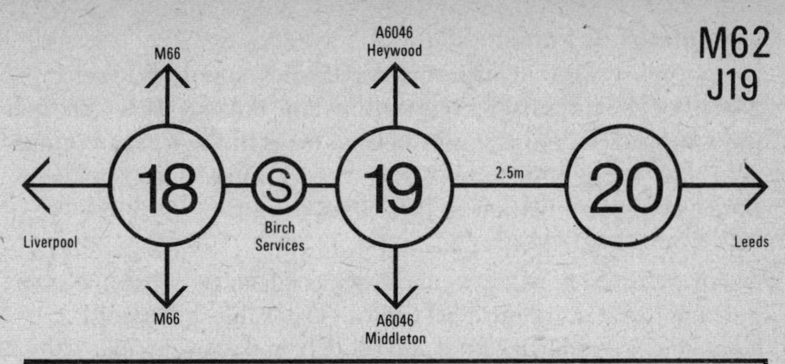

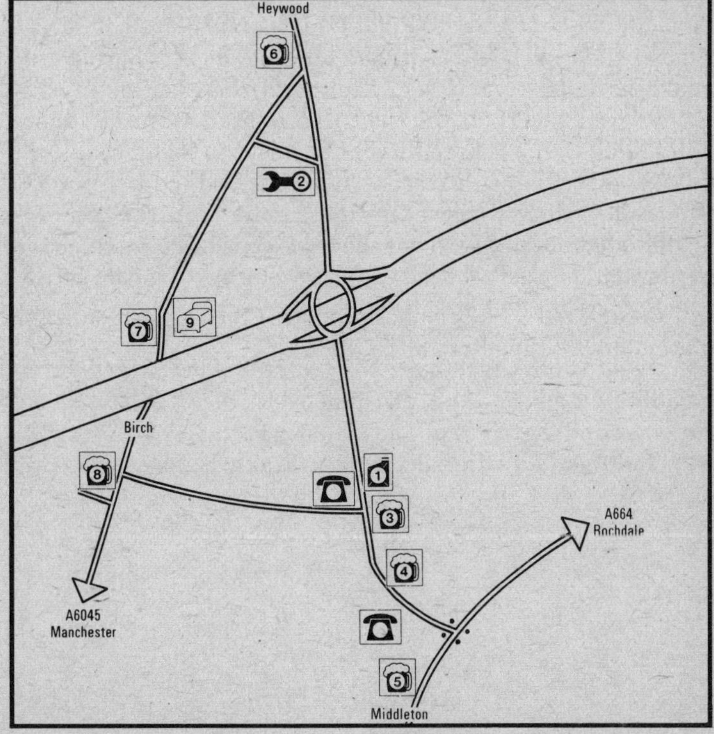

1 Hebers Service Station. Hours: 7.30 am – 9.30 pm
2 Coronation Service Station. Hours: 7 am – 10 pm (9 am – 9 pm Sun). Workshop
3 *The Gardeners Arms,* Whitbread
4 *The Red Lion Hotel,* Boddingtons
5 *Ye Olde Boars Head,* Free house
6 *The Black Swan,* Thwaites
7 *The Gardeners Arms,* Bass Charrington
8 *The White Hart,* Bass Charrington
9 *The Birch Hotel* (Heywood 60965)

restaurant/pubs/pub food

Apart from the lack of cheap or even convenient petrol this is a very good junction. Three of the restaurants, *The Moorcock* **12**, *La Pergola* **13** and *The Alpine* **14**, are virtually midway between **J21** and **J22** and will be described on the latter. Clearly one would leave by one junction and return on the other. They have assorted times of opening, and it would be wise to book.

Hollingworth Lake is well worth a visit, particularly in good weather. A little bit awkward to get to. Take the A640 in the direction of Milnrow and Rochdale. Then second right and with luck follow the signs and the B6225 for Littleborough. At *The Gallows* **5** you take a sharp left and right at the T-junction after about a mile. A large lake, a country park **15** at the far end, and a couple of pubs. *The Fisherman's* **7** puts a lot of tables outside in summer, has quite a good menu and is duly popular. Last year it had chic kebab (sic) on the menu – it remains to be seen whether they continue with this smooth dish. *The Beach* **6**, a large, modernized pub, also does food and has a garden.

On the other side of the junction Piethorn and Ogden Reservoirs are a good place to walk. Parking is very easy. Nearby is *The Bulls Head* **8** which seems to serve normal pub grub at all times. There's a cluster of nice pubs close to the junction in Milnrow. *The Free Trade Tavern* **9** has two small and one larger room. The beer is usually good and there is a friendly atmosphere; a kids' playground behind. *The Slip Inn* **3** is old-fashioned and slightly tatty, and I don't mean that rudely. It's a lively pub. *The Wagon* **4** is a bit difficult to find. An old building with a plain interior.

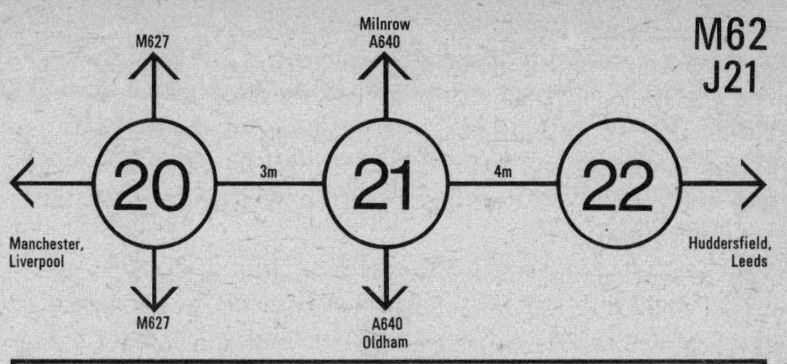

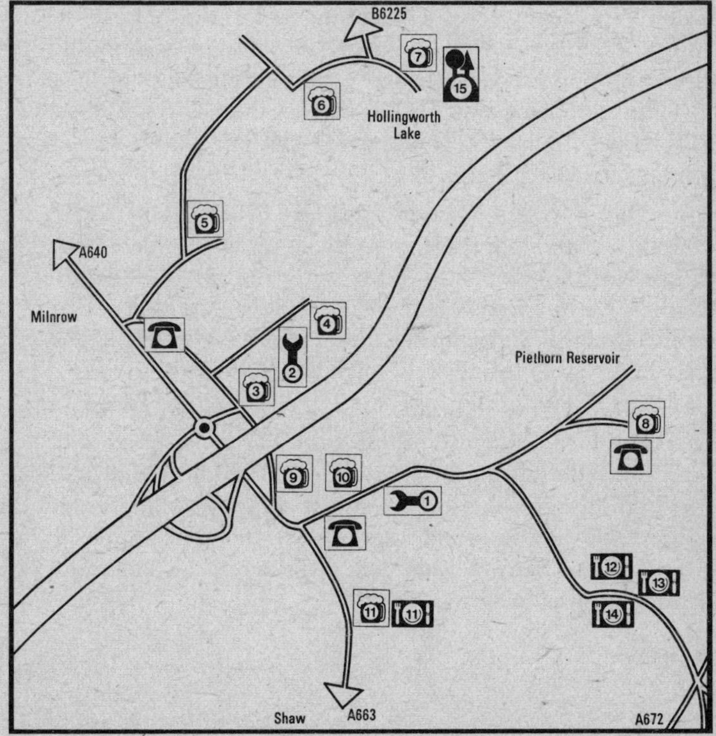

1 Newby Garage
2 Wagon Garage. Breakdown (Rochdale 33342)
3 *The Slip Inn,* Samuel Smith
4 *The Wagon Inn,* Burtonwood
5 *The Gallows,* Bass Charrington
6 *The Beach,* Watney
7 *The Fisherman's Arms,* Websters
8 *The Bull's Head,* Bass Charrington
9 *The Free Trade Tavern,* Lees
10 *The Bird In Hand,* Samuel Smith
11 *The Jubilee Inn and Restaurant* (Shaw 47450)
12 *The Moorcock Inn Restaurant* (Saddleworth 2659)
13 *La Pergola Ristorante* (Saddleworth 4392)
14 *The Alpine Restaurant* (Saddleworth 4245)
15 Hollingworth Lake Country Park

restaurants/pubs/walks

There is no petrol available on this junction. In fact there is nothing within two miles of the junction except a walk along part of the Pennine Way **13**. Parking is not easy but it is worth making the attempt in order to look down on the motorway from the spectacular footbridge. This is wild moorland country and seems to capture the winds, mists and fogs.

Three restaurants are included which are midway between this junction and **J21** – they are actually on the A640 back to Milnrow. The opening times of *The Alpine* **9**, a Swiss restaurant, are most peculiar. A popular place; it will cost about £4 a head for large helpings. *The Moorcock* **10** is a smart, discreet restaurant so you'll need to dress appropriately – much more the kind of place for a night out than for just dropping into. *The Pergola* **8** has the most regular hours; fairly ordinary Italian food, but generous portions – this might be the kind of place you *would* drop into.

On the other side of the junction *The Derby* **6**, which is a bit like an undertakers' parlour during the day but livens up considerably in the evenings with the loss of the lovely view and the start of the disco. Above it is *The Rishworth Lodge* **7** which has a reputation for decent food. You will realize that all these restaurants rely on people who come a long way for their wares – all therefore are slightly pricey.

Beer drinkers also travel considerable distances to visit *The Rams Head* **1** – and rightly so. Draught Theakstons beer and four very cosy rooms. Down the hill into Denshaw, *The Printers Arms* **4**, with draught Tetley and Thwaites, is also a very nice friendly pub which serves food at most decent times and others as well. Draught beer, too, at *The Junction* **2**. I don't like wood and stone conversion at all. Food at lunchtimes and a dining area for kids.

M62 J22

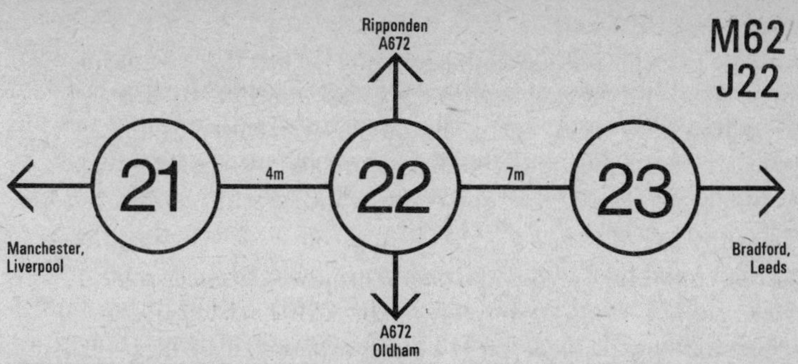

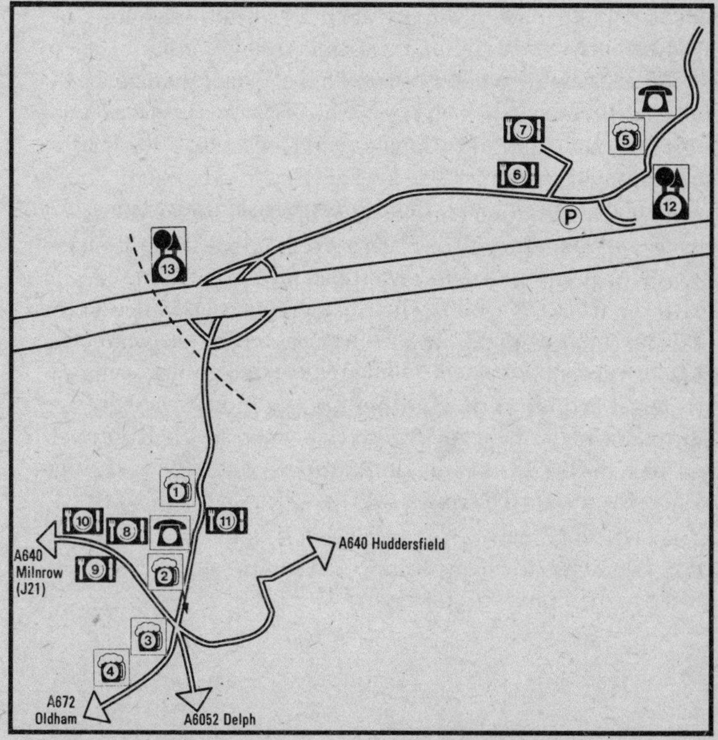

1 *The Rams Head*. Closed weekday lunch. Free house
2 *The Junction Inn*, Lees
3 *The Black Horse*, Bass Charrington
4 *The Printers Arms*, Free house
5 *The Cunning Corner*. Closed all Mon and weekday lunch. Free house
6 *The Derby Restaurant and Disco*
7 *The Rishworth Lodge Restaurant*. Open evening and Sun lunch (Ripponden 2263)
8 *La Pergola Ristorante*. Closed Sat lunch (Saddleworth 4392)
9 *The Alpine Restaurant*. Closed Mon, Tue, Thur lunch, Sun evening (Saddleworth 4245)
10 *The Moorcock Inn Restaurant*. Closed Sun, Mon; Sat lunch (Saddleworth 2659)
11 *The Moorlands Hotel*
12 Boothwood Reservoir Dam
13 Pennine Way Bridge

petrol/pub food/pubs

It is only possible to leave **J23** heading in the direction of Leeds; and it is only possible to join the motorway heading in the direction of Manchester. But since the two junctions are so close together and since the connecting road, the A643, is so obvious, the two are put together.

The petrol at the Mount **1** is the cheapest. Gee's **2** is slightly more expensive and the Birchcliffe **3** more expensive again. But the latter expects to cut its prices when it goes self-service. If you are heading west you should buy petrol on these junctions since there is none for the next three junctions – **J17** is, in fact, the cheapest and most convenient.

The Swan Inn **7** seems to function more like a restaurant than a pub. Steaks; barbecue sausage, black pudding, egg and chips for 70p; homemade pâté; soup and sandwiches. There is also a dining area where children can sit. *The New Inn* **4** also has food or snacks (basket meals) at most times. A well-built stone extension, fairy lights, boring furniture and friendly staff. The dogs however don't seem so friendly.

Between the two junctions lies *The Wappy Spring Inn* **8**. Its name, rather than the interior, recommends it – but if you were in a hurry for cheap petrol and a quick half this would be the place. The most interesting pub is the very small *Dog and Partridge* **5**. Very good hand-pumped Youngers, but quite a way to go. For *The Dog* and *New Inn* head towards Rochdale on the A640; bear right opposite *The Wagon and Horses* **6** on the B6112 to Stainsland; turn left off this road very soon – just before a bend to the right.

M62 J23/24

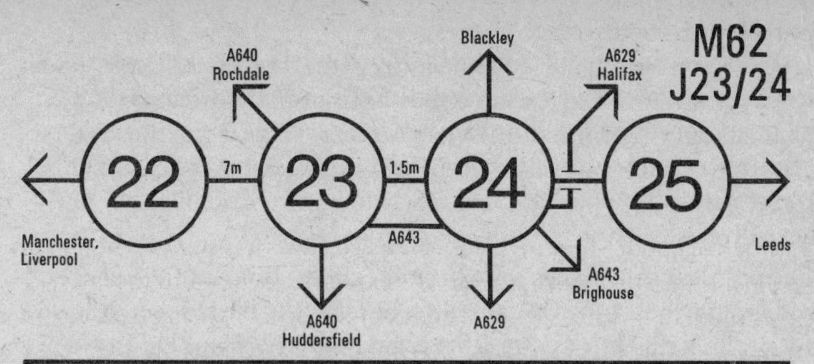

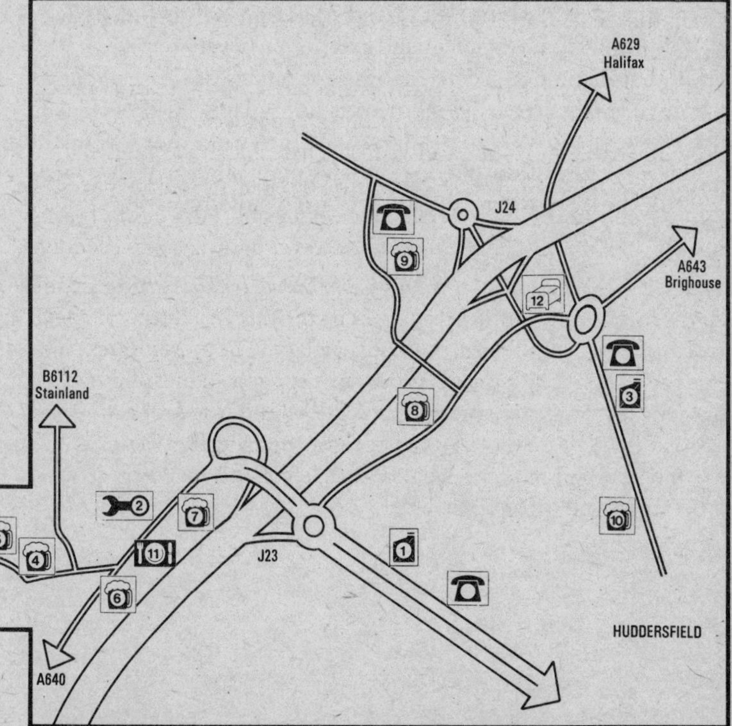

1 Mount Garage. Hours: 7.30 am – 10 pm (opens 9 am Sun)
2 Gee's Garage. Hours: 7 am – 6 pm
3 Birchcliffe Service Station. Hours: 8.30 am – 8 pm (opens 9 am Sat, 10 am – 6 pm Sun)
4 *The New Inn,* Free house
5 *The Dog and Partridge,* Free house
6 *The Wagon and Horses,* Bass Charrington
7 *The Swan Inn,* Bass Charrington
8 *The Wappy Spring Inn,* Websters
9 *The Golden Fleece,* Websters
10 *The Cavalry Arms,* Tetley
11 *The Clipjoint Café*
12 *The Pennine President Hotel*

petrol

There is very little of interest on this junction. In fact, this central section of the motorway is fairly dull. What makes it worse is that there are some breathtaking views, but most of the landscape has been destroyed by the works of man. Many of the towns seem grubby and squalid although, again, once when they were smaller they must have been very attractive villages.

The petrol at Brockholes **3** is extremely cheap. But for convenience and for long hours the Bradley Garage **2** is really the best bet. Next door (almost), *The White Cross* **9** has food and a beer garden. In a different direction *The Wise Owl* **11** and *The Armytage Arms* **6** also offer food. The latter has a very nice solid exterior but a very boring interior. The nicest pub seemed to be the one that was closest to the junction – *The Black Horse* **5**, in the expanding village of Clifton. Take the first right off the A644 to Brighouse and then wind your way up the hill. The pub a nice atmosphere – anarchic might almost be the word to describe the place when I was there. An old building with comfortable seating.

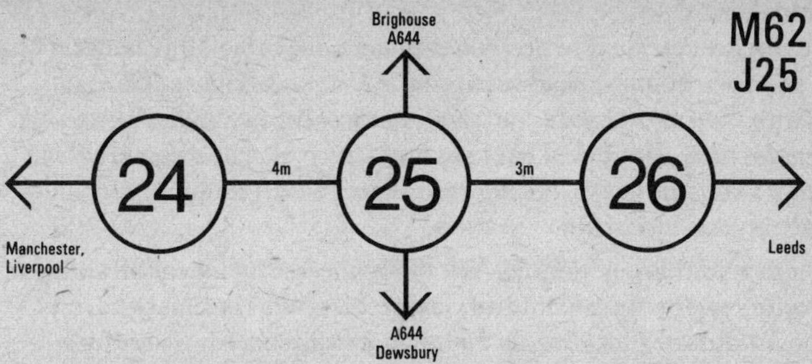

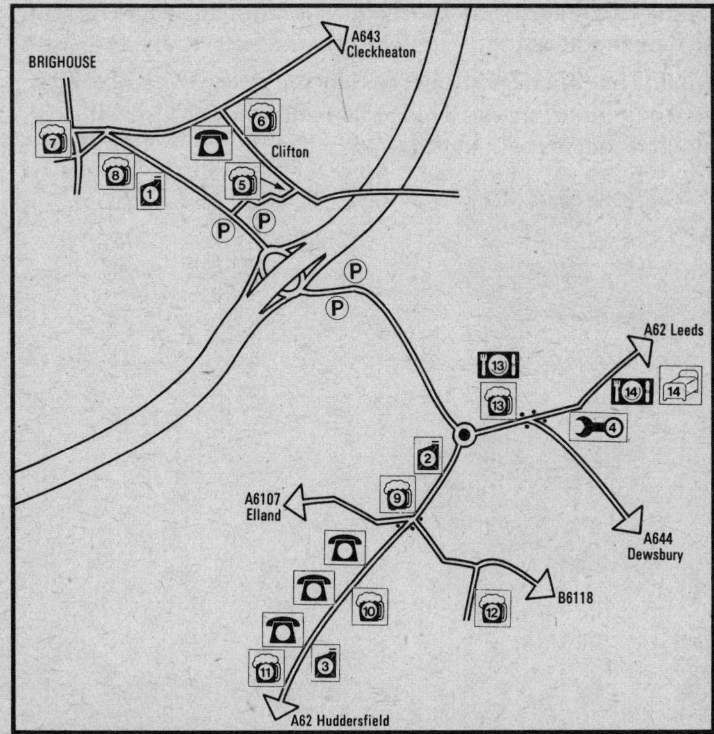

1 Service Garage. Hours: 8 am – 7 pm (8 am – 2 pm Sat, closed Sun)
2 Bradley Garage. Hours: 7.30 am – 9.30 pm (10 am – 9 pm Sun)
3 Brockholes Garage. Hours: 7 am – 10 pm (9 am – 6 pm Sat, Sun)
4 Three Nuns Garage. 24-hr breakdown (Mirfield 492391)
5 *The Black Hourse,* Whitbread
6 *The Armytage Arms,* Whitbread
7 *The Round House Inn,* Whitbread
8 *The Robin Hood,* Websters
9 *The White Cross,* Whitbread
10 *The Woodman Inn,* Whitbread
11 *The Wise Owl,* Bass Charrington
12 *Tavern Two,* Free house
13 *The Three Nuns.* Cavalier Steak Bar
14 *Little Chef and Motel* (Mirfield 495235)

petrol/food

Not an interesting junction. Cheap petrol at Murco **1** and Glovers **2**. If you were going to head south on the M1 you would use Glovers, within their short hours, and then continue on the A650 until you hit that motorway at **J41**. That junction is not particularly good either but it would be worth looking at since there are a couple of good pubs, one serving decent lunchtime food.

For food at this junction *The New White Bear* **7**, a Schooner Steak House, is very convenient and very predictable. It seems to have a good reputation locally. *The Fastnet Fish Restaurant* **9** has very long hours. A large modern establishment, it also has a take-away service with the same hours.

The Bulls Head **3**, a modern pub, has lunchtime food. The other *Bulls Head* **4** has limited snacks. The landlord there prefers his local customers, but the beer is good.

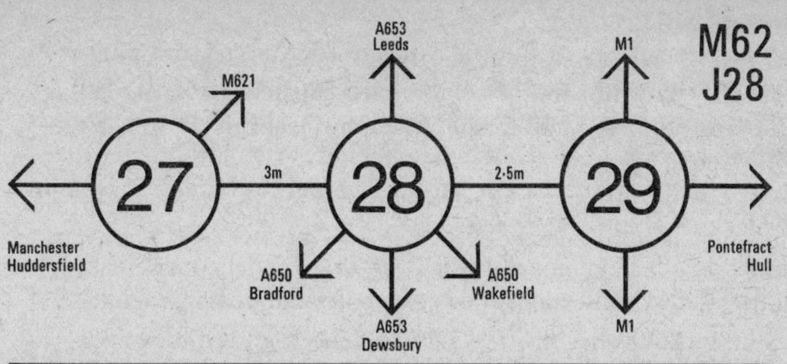

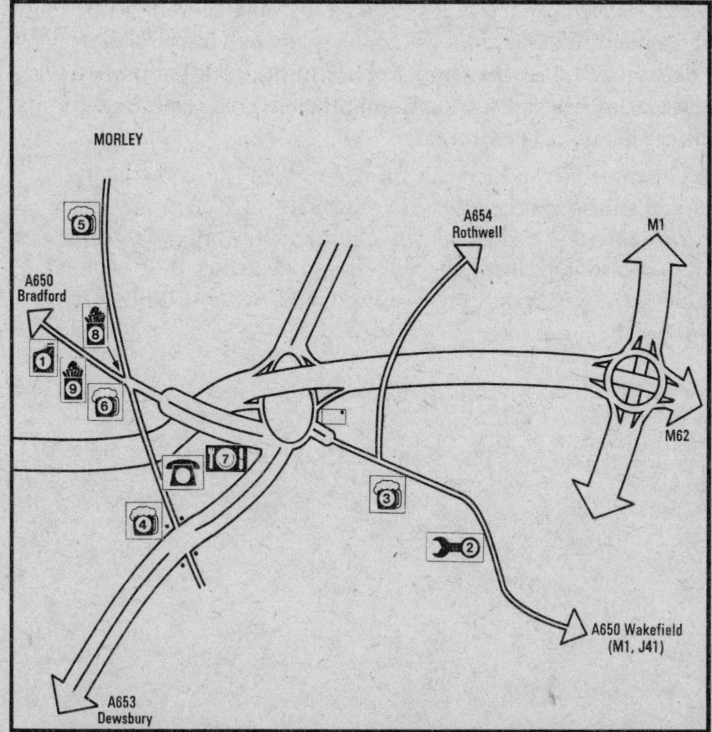

1 Murco Service Station. Hours: 7 am – 10 pm (opens 8 am Sat, Sun). Workshop, 5½-day week. Tyres, exhausts
2 Glovers Garage. Hours: 8 am – 7.30 pm (closes 6 pm Sat, 9 am – 1 pm Sun). Repairs in same hours
3 *The Bulls Head,* Tetley
4 *The Bulls Head,* Samuel Smith
5 *The Albion,* Tetley
6 *The Cross Keyes,* John Smith
7 *The New White Bear.* Schooner Steak Bar
8 *Tingley Bar Fisheries*
9 *The Fastnet Fish Restaurant.* 12 noon – 11.30 pm, till 11 pm Thur – Sun

petrol/pubs

Still in the area of mines and slag heaps; otherwise there would probably be quite a few places to walk or picnic. As it is, the only stopping point is alongside the motorway just off the B6135, in the direction of Methley.

The cheapest petrol is at the Rosemount **2**, but the difference in price isn't sufficient to make the extra distance worthwhile – unless you were going to *The Graziers* **7**. This is a pleasant. four-roomed pub, with quite a few plates decorating the walls; they also serve draught Camerons. A pub with an even better collection of china is *The Thatched Cottage* **13** – it is really rather a special place. Slightly frilly on the outside – white-louvred windows but no thatch. Fairly plain inside, apart from all the china. Some snacks and draught beer. To find two such basically unspoilt and pleasant Bass Charrington pubs on one junction is a rare pleasure.

The Cinema Garage **1** is easily the closest to the junction but its hours are quite short. Another pleasant pub on this side of the junction is *The Rising Sun* **5** – you head down to Bottom Boat opposite *The Railway* **6** – a single-roomed local. From there you can watch the perpetual motion of the trucks dumping slag and think of the view of the River Calder which must have once existed.

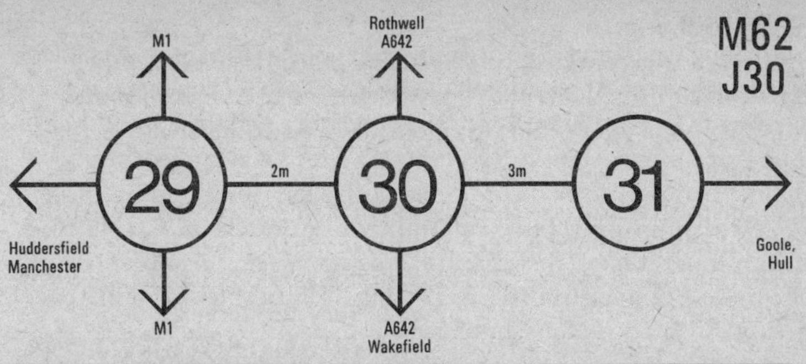

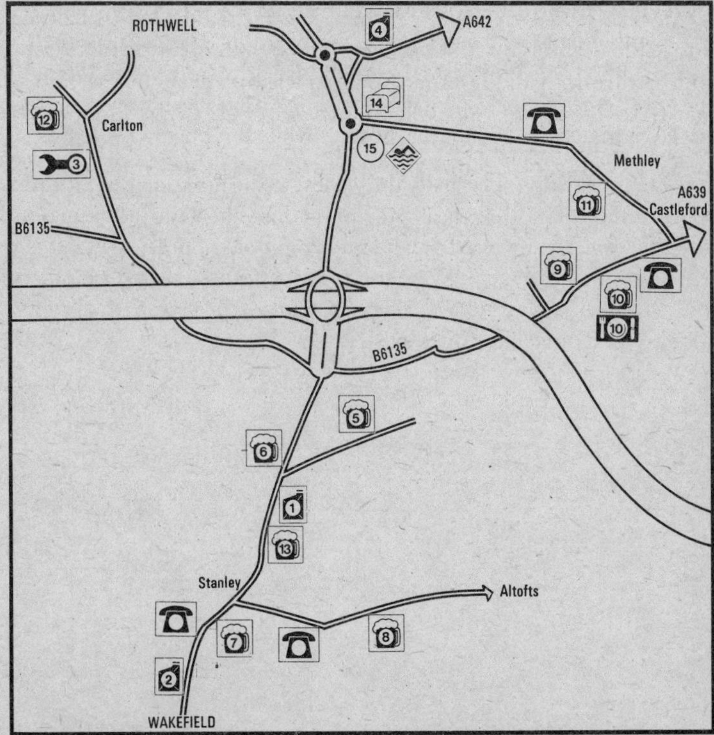

1 Cinema Garage. Hours: 8 am – 6 pm (to 5 pm Sat, 10 am – 4 pm Sun)
2 Rosemount Service Station. Hours: 7.30 am – 10 pm (9 am – 9 pm Sun)
3 Kenning Tyres
4 Regency Service Station. Hours: 8 am – 10 pm (8 am – 8 pm Sat, 9 am – 8 pm Sun)
5 *The Rising Sun*, John Smith
6 *The Railway*, Watney
7 *The Graziers*, Bass Charrington
8 *The Ship*, Watney
9 *The Mexboro Arms*, Free house
10 *The Viking Lounge Bar and Restaurant*
11 *The Rose and Crown*, John Smith
12 *The Queen*, Tetley
13 *The Thatched House*, Bass Charrington
14 *Crest Motel* (Leeds 826201)
15 Rothwell Sports Centre

petrol/pub

To glean, garner or use the little this junction has to offer, just head for Castleford on the A655. After half a mile you can fill your car with petrol at Tyke Petroleum **1** at a very good price and then, if the time is right, retrace your steps to *The Rising Sun* **3** for a good pint of beer, or whatever, and some food. *The Rising Sun* is a long low building, quite large, with uninspired but comfortable furniture and a nice collection of Toby mugs. One of those rare places which seems to have solved the problem of smell from deep-fried food. Half a chicken for just over a pound, liver and onions, burgers etc.

Only if you were heading towards Manchester would it really be worth your while to visit any of the pubs in Altofts. It is possible to rejoin at **J30** by continuing on that road through Stanley (see **J30** map). *The Lee Brigg Hotel* **7** will have finished its modernization by then. It seemed to be a place for those who like their beer. *The Robin Hood* **6** is a comfortable pub which serves normal pub food.

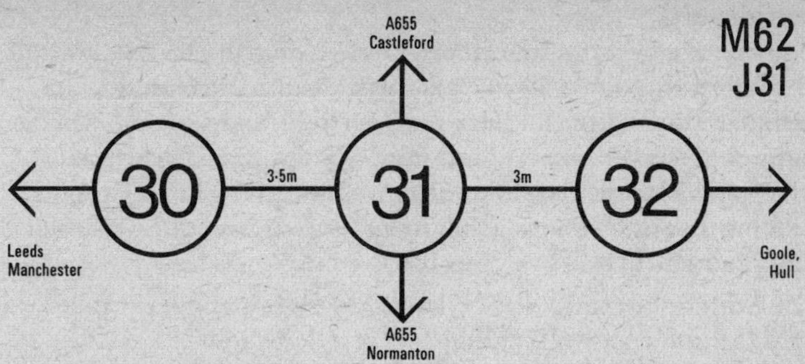

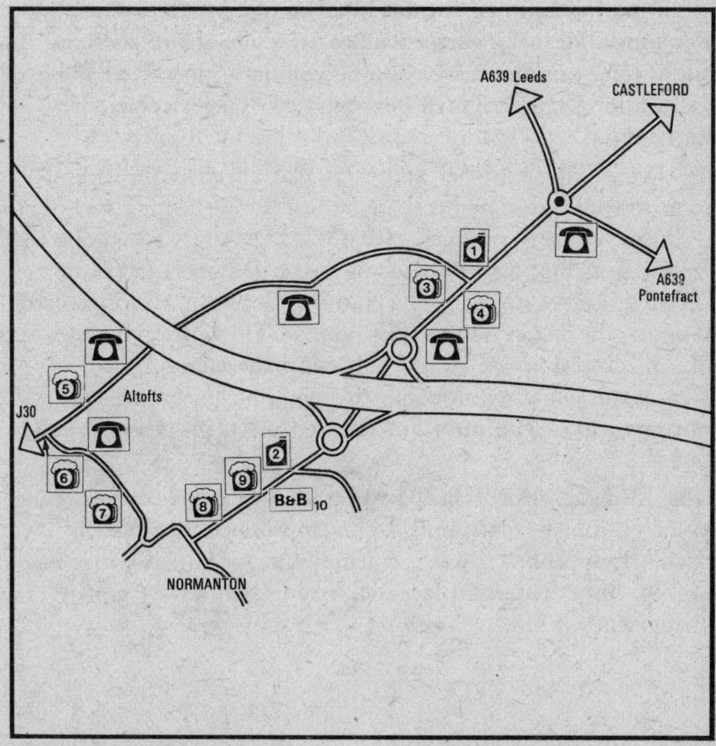

1 Tyke Petroleum. Hours: 7 am – 9 pm (9 am – 7 pm Sun). Workshop, 5½-day week
2 Willowbridge Motors. Hours: 7.30 am – 7 pm (8 am – 6 pm Sat, 9 am – 4 pm Sun)
3 *The Rising Sun*, Tetley
4 *The Mexboro Arms*, Whitbread
5 *The Horse and Jockey*, Watney
6 *The Robin Hood*, Tetley
7 *The Lee Brigg Hotel*, Darley
8 *The Black Swan*, Tetley
9 *The White Swan*, Watney
10 *The Sandpiper*. B&B

petrol/visits

Whether Pontefract is a useful place to include in this book is debatable. Famous for its cakes and castle and, more recently, architect Poulson, the town has not been well treated by time. Maybe they could revive tourism by reintroducing the practice of wife sales which took place in the market place well into the nineteenth century. Bidding usually started at a shilling and once, it is reported, reached the grand sum of 11/–.

The Gothic pile known as *The Queens Hotel* **4** is bringing some style back to the town. Or rather a mixture of styles – Gothic exterior, Regency plush interior, and a touch of the Wild West in the form of a honky-tonk piano player at most times. It is being refurbished and should, by the summer, have a number of rooms to let at reasonable rates. The food in the bar area looks good and there is a place for children to eat.

To get to the castle **5** turn left at the *Queens* and head for the highest place in town. It is just higher than the nearest slag heap. The castle and church **6** were victims of the Civil War. The church was going to be rebuilt from the proceeds of selling the castle stone. £1500 was collected and entrusted to one Dr Nathaniel Johnson. History records that he and the money departed for London. The church possesses a double blocked staircase – one of only two in the country. Two staircases spiral upwards round each other. But you will need to get a key to have a look. The interior of what remains of the church is quite pleasant.

All the listed garages sell cheap petrol and you will have to make your own choice from the many pubs around town since none looked particularly appealing to me. Incidentally, all the liquorice used in the cakes is imported from places like Spain, Greece and China. It died out locally in 1944.

M62 J32

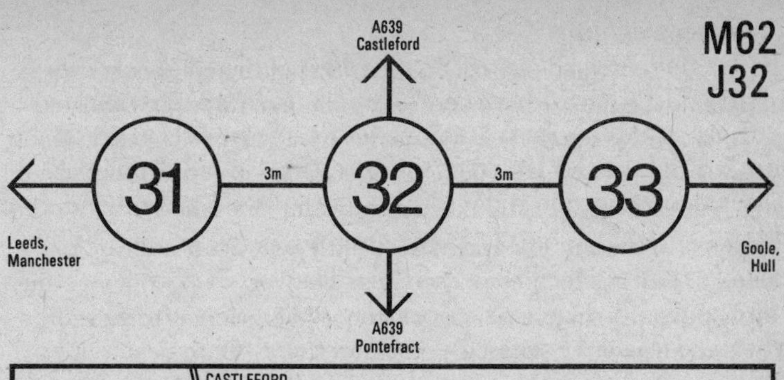

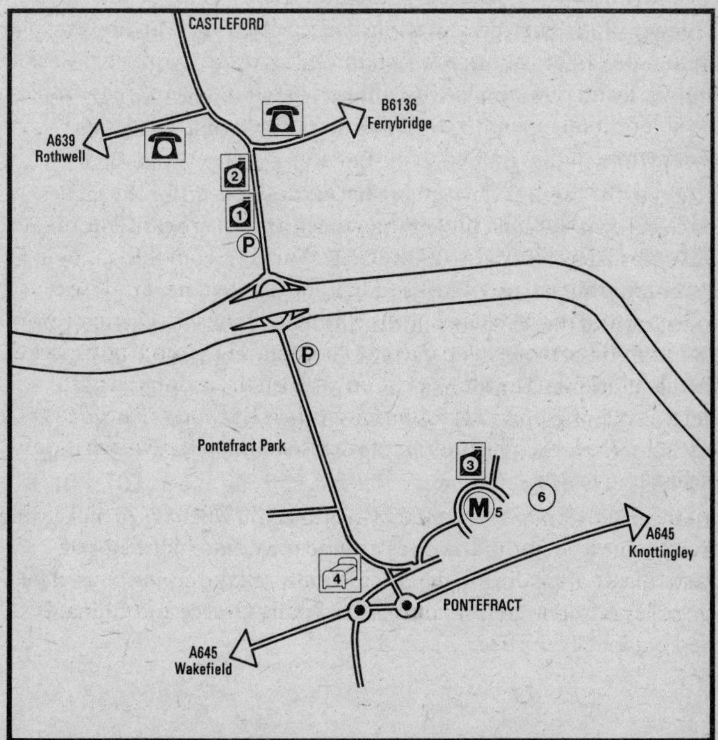

1 Burdins. Hours: 8 am – 7 pm (to 5 pm Sat, 10 am – 5 pm Sun)

2 Simpson's. Hours: 8 am – 8 pm (from 9.30 am Sun). 24-hr petrol machine (£1 notes only)

3 Azda Service Station

4 *The Queens Hotel* (Pontefract 702228)

5 Castle

6 Church

petrol/repairs/pubs

The flat, dull, drained plain of South Yorkshire, hereinafter known as Humberside, stretches from here to the sea. Yet it is packed with old settlements and churches. This junction has the lovely isolated church of St Edmund **10** and later works of man to admire: the Aire and Calder Navigation and the Eggborough Power Station.

The petrol at the Union **2** and at the Whitley Garage **3** is cheap, but Carroll's seem to offer all other services. The workshop is open during pump hours, a breakdown service at any other hour, warm milk for babies and tea for the stressed – or so they say.

Some of the pubs are quite interesting. *The George and Dragon* **4** was completed in 1939. Its interior design – the shapes, woodwork, metalwork and tiles – make it an almost perfect thirties pub. It does need some money spending on it and an uncluttering – the nuts dangling from ladies pinned to the bar arch – and it would then become rather special. A large garden at the back, equipped with swings and goat and the simplest of food. I wonder what beer John Smiths served here thirty-nine years ago?

The Bay Horse **8** is a very small pub in the village of Great Heck – take the first sign off the A645 to Snaith and Goole. One room covered with beer trays and draught beer. *The Red Lion* **7** is an extremely well-kept pub in Kellington. The lounge has an open range, the public bar a collection of horse-bits. *The Jolly Miller* **5** serves draught beer but needs something doing to it. *The Maine Motor Inn* **9** is an unattractive building and has fifteen rooms for letting, starting at over £9 for B&B.

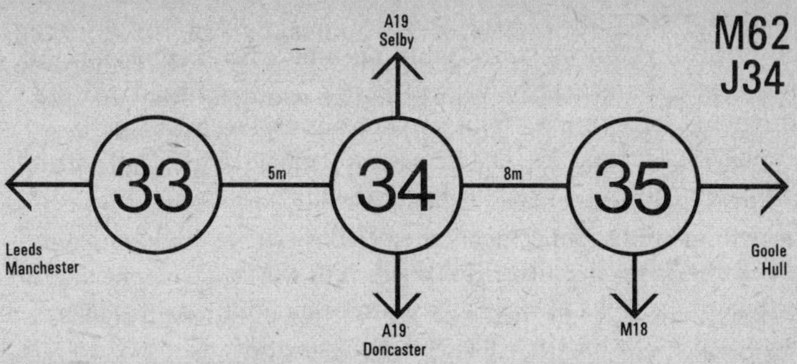

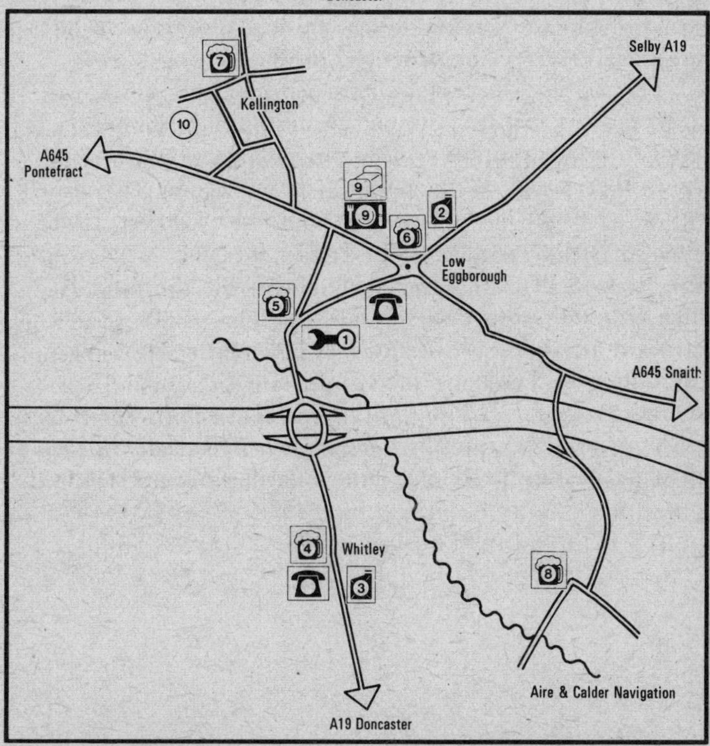

1 Carroll's. Hours: 6 am – 7 pm (9 am – 2 pm Sun). 24-hr breakdown (Whitley Bridge, day 661256, night 661668)
2 Union Garage. Hours: 8 am – 7 pm (10 am – 4 pm Sun)
3 Whitley Garage. Hours: 8 am – 8 pm (opens 9 am Sun)
4 *The George and Dragon*, John Smith
5 *The Jolly Miller*, North Yorkshire
6 *The Horse and Jockey*, Bass Charrington
7 *The Red Lion*, John Smith
8 *The Bay Horse*, Tetley
9 *The Maine Motor Inn and Restaurant* (Whitley Bridge 661395)
10 St Edmund's Church

Little reason to stop off at this junction unless you want to suffer some of the joys and hardships of Goole, a minor port set in a flat landscape – heavy lorries, hard drinking pubs and cafés, among other things. It's a good walk along the banks of the River Ouse from *The Victoria* **7** towards Hook. A quieter walk is along the River Aire **14** which joins the Ouse close to Boothferry Bridge. Both *The Victoria* and *The Percy* **3** are ordinary pubs, but rather nice when compared with some of the other pubs on the junction. Both serve sandwiches.

There is no really cheap petrol on this junction, but Kennings **1** is considerably cheaper than Glews **2**. Between them these two garages seem to provide most services – workshop, breakdown and car hire. There are, of course, other garages in Goole.

When is a Free house a Free house? Not when it supplies pressure beers by Bass Charrington or Youngers I would have thought. I am constantly disappointed by Free houses not living up to their name. *The Blacksmiths* **8** and *The Chequers* **10** are two such pubs. They may once, too, have been nice pubs. But they have been converted to look like any smart pub in Anytown – or, at least, the image of such a pub. Both serve food, that at *The Blacksmiths,* with its blood-red plastic seating, being of the steak and rainbow trout variety – and suitably priced. The food at *The Chequers* was much cheaper – more snacks, really, but their beer was overpriced.

The three nicest places on the junction are saved for last. *The Woodside Café* **13** has reasonably priced food, some of it homemade. *The Railway* **5** is a plain attractive pub in the centre of Goole, front and back bar serving draught bitter. Good beer too at *The Royal Oak* **12**, the locals' pub off the main road in Rawcliffe.

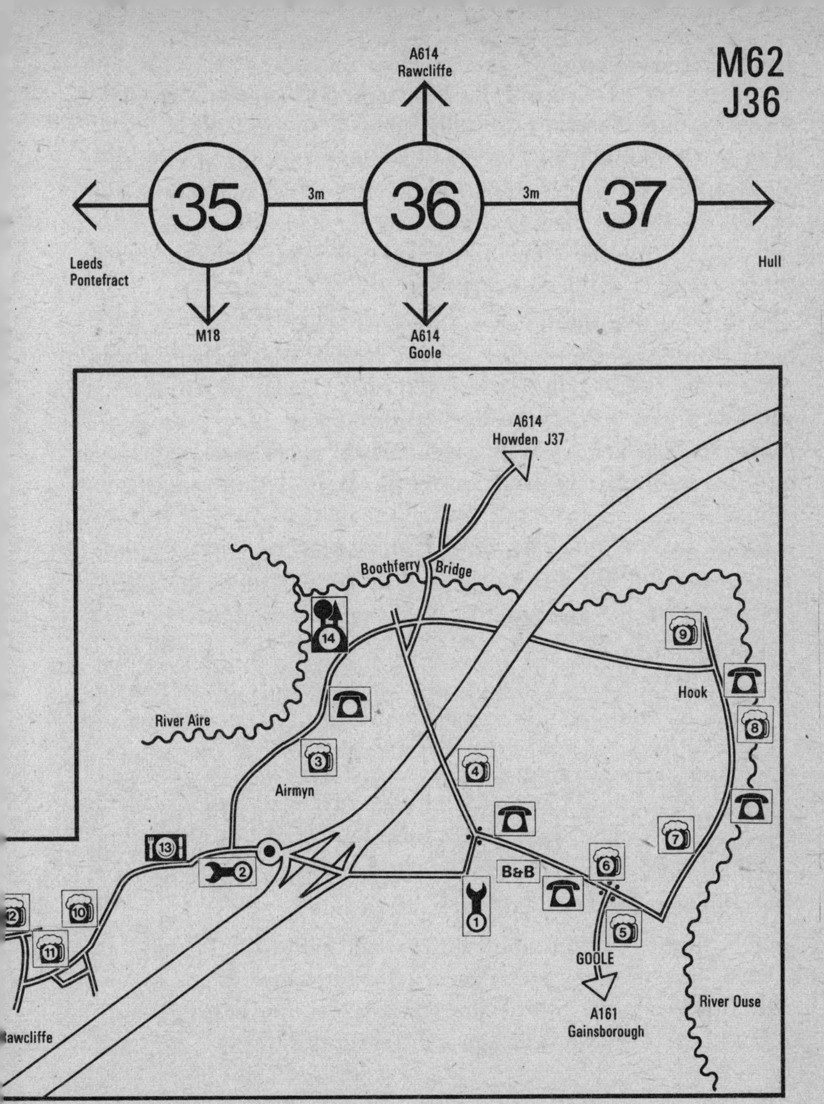

1 Kennings. Hours: 8 am – 8 pm (closes 6.30 pm Sun). Car hire and workshop on 5½-day week (Goole 3444). Leyland agent
2 Glews. Hours: 8 am – 9 pm. 24-hr petrol machine (50p pieces). 24-hr breakdown (Goole, day 2357, night 3570)
3 *The Percy Arms*, John Smith
4 *The Vikings Hotel*, Bass Charrington
5 *The Railway*, Tetley
6 *The Station Hotel*, Tetley
7 *The Victoria*, Bass Charrington
8 *The Blacksmiths Arms*, Free house (Bass Charrington)
9 *The Sotheron Arms*, Free house
10 *The Chequers Arms*, Free house
11 *The Neptune*, North Country
12 *The Royal Oak*, North Country
13 *The Woodside Transport Café*. 6.30 am – 6 pm Mon – Fri
14 River Aire walk

food/accommodation

The Minster Church of St Peter **12** in Howden has been falling down for a long time. The roof of the old choir collapsed in 1696 in a thunderstorm. But it's a lovely building to see, and much remains in good repair. The Saltmarshe family have their own burial area, one carved tomb dating back to 1338. Or rather, had, since the last of the line died recently; he left his money to a cats' home rather than to the preservation of, at least, his ancestors.

The petrol in this country area is none too cheap. The garages are listed by their cheapness. But, by good economic laws (Sod's law to others), the closest to the junction is the most expensive. However, if you were travelling to the west it would not really increase the journey to skirt Goole and buy petrol at Kennings **1** (some details of this town on **J36**). Although if you wait for **J34** there is cheap and convenient petrol.

Another easy route from **J37** to **J36** is through the small village of Airmyn on the River Aire **13**. There is a good walk along the river to Boothferry Bridge. The pub, *The Percy Arms* **5**, has sandwiches.

For accommodation you can choose between *The Wellington* **8** and *Bowmans* **9**. Whether *The Wellington* is half as comfortable for half the price I don't know but that's roughly the order. For lunchtime snacks the food at *Bowmans*, for nearly twice the price, looked twice as nice. If you see what I mean. Sweet and sour pork, or lemon sole, or cheese and tomato croquettes – all with veg – for a pound. At *The Wellington* it was varieties of chips. Howden is also the proud possessor of the only tied house belonging to the Selby Brewery – *The Board* **6**. None too special, but decent beer and a pinball machine.

Charles Dickens, in describing the Howden Fair, wrote of 'the English horsedealers . . . whose shrewd countenances bear some marks of the potations of beer and spirits which appear to be an essential part of all who manage or deal in horses'.

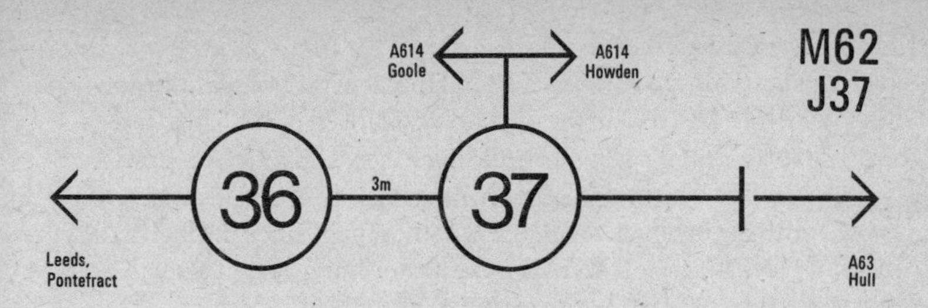

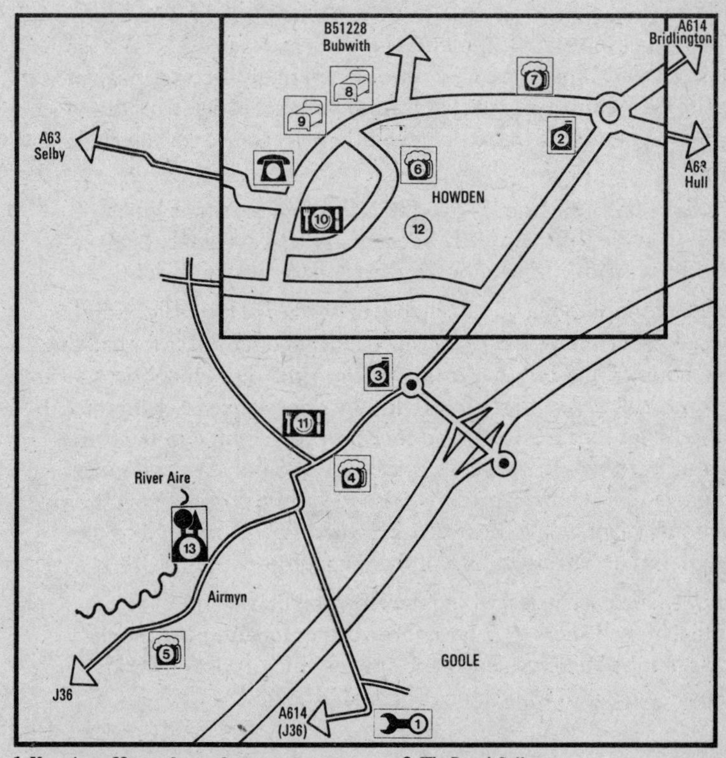

1 Kennings. Hours: 8 am – 8 pm (8 am – 6.30 pm Sun). Workshop and car hire on 5½-day week (Goole 3444)

2 Long's. Hours: 7 am – 8.30 pm (opens 8 am Sat, 8 am – 6 pm Sun)

3 Wardle's. Hours: 8 am – 5.45 pm (closed Sun)

4 *The Ferryboat Inn,* Free house

5 *The Percy Arms,* John Smith

6 *The Board,* Selby

7 *The Cross Keyes,* Tetley

8 *The Wellington Hotel* (Howden 30258)

9 *Bowman's Hotel* (Howden 30805)

10 *Paula's Pantry.* Café

11 *Transport Café*

12 The Minster Church

13 River Aire

M69

J2 on this motorway is not included as it is an exit only for Hinckley travelling in the direction of Coventry, and an entry only in the direction of Leicester.

food/petrol

Not an interesting or useful junction. The only really convenient place is *The Aviary Island Restaurant* **10** – an up-market transport café. Comfortable and slightly more expensive than such places usually are.

For cheap petrol you have to drive a couple of miles on the fast A5 towards Nuneaton. The furthest garage, but only by a short head, Dodwells **2** is the cheapest. The Burmah Autopoint **1** has longer hours. On the way to get your cheap petrol you cross over the Ashby-de-la-Zouch Canal. Right there you find *The Lime Kilns* **3**. A good old-fashioned pub with hard-backed wooden seating and draught beer. Little parking space but a lot of grass by the edge of the canal for the summer. *The Three Pots* **4** is much closer to the junction. It is a large roadhouse with large rooms and a large garden, but little character.

Lots of eating establishments on this road from which you will have to take your pick. The *Little Chef* **13** as usual and a couple of restaurants, *The Hinckley Knight* **11** and *The Windmill* **12**.

Hinckley is to be avoided as it is a confusing town with too few indications of how to escape. The strung-out village of Burbage is simpler, and, like Hinckley, contains a large number of Marston's pubs. I liked *The Cross Keyes Inn* **9** one of those pubs with a number of small rooms dotted round a central bar. Snacks seem to be available at most times.

In the village of Wolvey a secret Watney's pub, *The Blue Pig* **7**, is rather nice and has a bar billiards table. The village seems to be full of garages but the petrol is expensive.

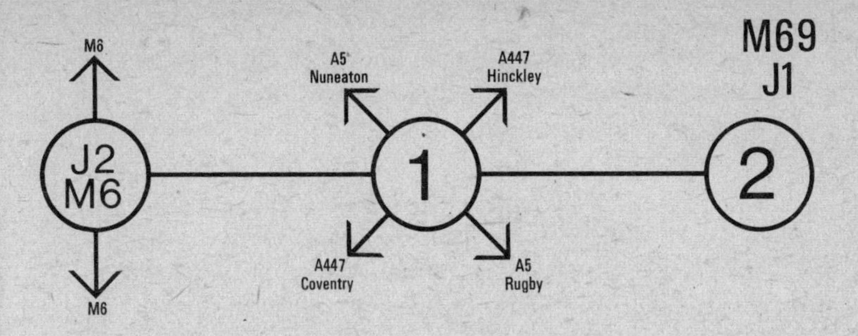

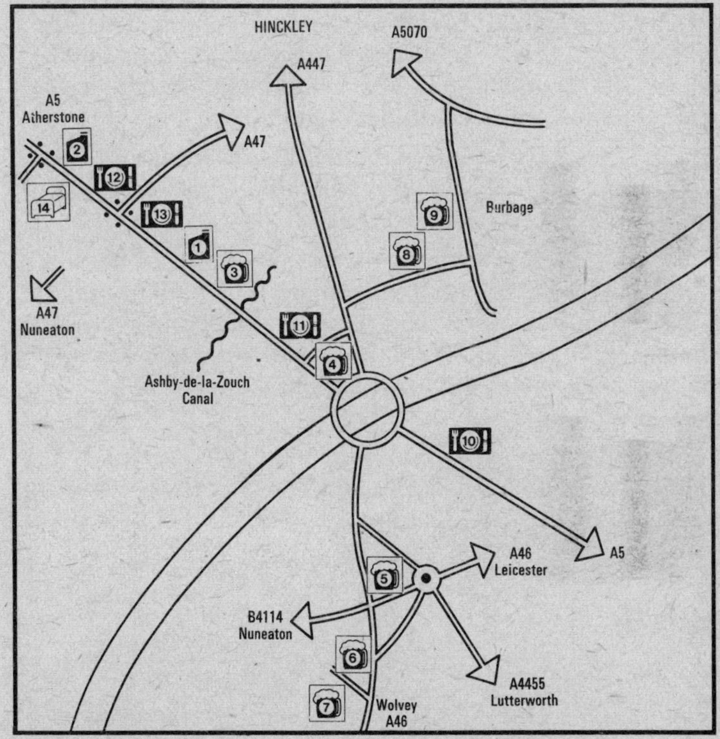

1 Burmah Autopoint. Hours: 6.30 am – 10 pm (from 8 am Sun)
2 Dodwells Garage. Hours: 8 am – 8 pm (from 10 am Sun)
3 *The Lime Kilns Inn*, Marston
4 *The Three Pots*, Mitchells and Butlers
5 *The Axe and Compasses*, Mitchells and Butlers
6 *The Bulls Head*, Marston
7 *The Blue Pig*, Watney
8 *The Sycamores Inn*, Marston
9 *The Cross Keyes Inn*, Marston
10 *The Aviary Island Restaurant*
11 *The Hinckley Knight Restaurant*
12 *The Windmill Restaurant*
13 *Little Chef*
14 *Nuneaton Crest Motel* (Nuneaton 329711)

comments/suggestions